Sweet Sleep

la leche league international

Sweet Sleep

nighttime and naptime strategies for the breastfeeding family

diane wiessinger, diana west,
linda j. smith, and teresa pitman

pinter & martin

No book can replace the diagnostic expertise and medical advice of a trusted doctor. Please be certain to consult with your doctor before making any decisions that affect your or your baby's health, particularly if you suffer from any medical condition or have any symptom that may require treatment.

Sweet sleep: nighttime and naptime strategies for the breastfeeding family

Published 2014 in the UK by Pinter & Martin Ltd.
reprinted 2017, 2020

ISBN 978-1-78066-155-1
also available as ebook

British Library Cataloguing-in-Publication Data
A catalogue record for this book is available from the British Library.

Book design by Elizabeth A. D. Eno

Printed and bound in the UK by Ashford Colour Press Ltd, Gosport, Hampshire

For bulk sales, contact info@pinterandmartin.com

Pinter & Martin Ltd
6 Effra Parade
London SW2 1PS
www.pinterandmartin.com

To you. Listen to your heart. Rest on the research.
Sweet sleep to you and your little ones!

contents

foreword

What if?

What if everything we did as mothers wasn't under constant scrutiny? What if every natural decision our bodies and our hearts led us to wasn't cause for a Facebook frenzy? What if every time we took our breastfeeding babies to bed with us it wasn't seen as irresponsible parenting? What if we didn't have to follow someone else's notions about sexuality, nurturing, and where our babies should sleep?

What if we could parent organically, without criticism, following our biologically programmed instincts, honouring the hormones that hundreds of thousands of years of mammalian parenting have placed in our bodies, brains, and, yes, breasts?

What if you had the education, resources, and support to make your nighttime choices with confidence, not fear?

I know how it could start: with the courage and devotion of a group of well-informed researchers and writers who speak up on behalf of safe bedsharing for breastfeeding families. It would take a book rooted in science, born out of love, and driven by a passion for helping mothers care for their breastfeeding children at night. That's the book you hold in your hands.

Sweet Sleep is all about understanding and responding to your baby's nighttime needs, understanding the challenges of the sleep decisions you make, and learning to parent safely and securely so that you all sleep better and grow stronger: baby, mother, family, and community.

Mayim Bialik, PhD,
Certified Lactation Education Counsellor

preface

Sleep (or the lack of it) looms large for parents-in-waiting—and it is pointless to pretend that your sleep will not be disrupted by your new bundle of joy. His stomach is tiny, and he will need frequent feeds all around the clock—he cannot wait eight hours through the night to be fed just because you need to sleep. He doesn't know that you will come back once you leave his sight. If he feels abandoned, he will cry frantically—it's his only method to attract attention and bring himself to safety. If he cries frantically, it will take a long time for him to calm down and you will have to help him.

The experience of sleep, and of being left alone for sleep, is very different for babies than it is for adults. The quicker you can understand your baby's needs—for comfort, food, reassurance, contact, love—the less disruptive nighttime baby care will become, and the less anxious you will feel. Rigid guidance that insists the only place your baby should sleep is flat on his back in a cot with a firm mattress ignores the reality that most babies do not die unexpectedly during the night but that all babies need frequent feeding, tending, comforting, cuddling, and loving. How to strike a balance between risk avoidance and need fulfilment?

Baby care is about trade-offs—balancing your baby's needs with your own needs, and adapting "official" recommendations to your own situation rather than following every guideline at all costs. This book takes issue with some of the sleep guidance currently given to parents by official organizations and "experts". It explains why, whom that guidance is meant to influence, and what it is intended to accomplish. If you are not the mother and baby the guidance is directed towards, if compliance would carry a greater risk in another aspect of baby care than non-compliance, you should make your own informed choice about which guidance to follow. This book gives you the tools to do so.

The dramatic departure that this book offers is to approach sleep safety via the management of risks to infants in different sleep scenarios. It offers a packaged method (called the Safe Sleep Seven) to help parents identify risks they should avoid, and to reassure those parents whose babies fall into the "minuscule risk" category. And as one would expect from La Leche League, this book takes breastfeeding and safe sleep sharing as normal facets of baby care.

It makes no guarantees: it doesn't guarantee that your baby will be a good sleeper (be wary of books that do) or that your baby will be absolutely safe. There are no guarantees in life, and tragic events sometimes happen even in the absence of observable risks. The authors do a great job of explaining the magnitude of different risks—those you take every day without thinking and those you agonize over unnecessarily. They also point out those instances where parents sometimes unwittingly increase their babies' risk because the reasons behind key guidelines are not properly explained—and parents take a greater risk in trying to eliminate a lesser one!

This book is like having a wise grandmother in your pocket. It's an antidote to new-parent sleep anxiety and the scary tales that you may have been told. It carefully guides you through your options; it unpacks the sensationalist headlines about SIDS and the old wives' tales about spoiling. It puts you in control and encourages you to make decisions that suit your family after carefully considering your situation, your baby, and your needs. It gives you permission to trust your instincts (although the only permission you need is your own).

It debunks many myths—some of which are held sacred in certain quarters. I have no doubt this book will cause controversy, and

I know that its authors have therefore done their homework very carefully. They have consulted with numerous specialist researchers and read hundreds of research papers. The questions they have asked and the evidence they have amassed have caused them not only to challenge the one-size-fits-all approach to infant sleep safety recommendations but also to challenge the dominant cultural viewpoint about "normal infant care" in modern society. After many months of reading and discussing the issues with them, I feel a warm sense of satisfaction that they have reached conclusions very similar to my own, which are based on my training as an anthropologist, 18 years of first-hand research in this field, and my experience as a mother.

The fundamental fact embedded in this book is that breastfeeding mothers and babies bedshare, and do so whether they are advised against it or not. It is a baby care strategy that makes sense to breastfeeding mothers, and it works for reducing the disruption of frequent night feeds, maintaining breastfeeding, and meeting their babies' emotional needs and their own sleep needs simultaneously. It's what women and babies have done for millennia, though we now do it in sleep environments very different from those of our predecessors. This book gives guidance not only on whether to bedshare but also how to bedshare as safely as possible. It firmly brings discussion about bedsharing into the open and provides an important resource for breastfeeding mothers in the 21st century. I could not be more pleased to introduce it.

Professor Helen Ball, BSc, MA, PhD

introduction

New-baby greeting cards joke about the 2.00 a.m. feed, but at 2.00 a.m., it's no joke. Too many of today's new mothers feel like zombies during the day, desperate for sleep that their night didn't provide. Their babies wail, their partners complain or take turns walking the floor. Every feed means time out of bed. Sleep training takes nerves of steel, but it's starting to look appealing. And everyone asks, "Is he sleeping through the night yet?"

Breastfeeding mothers can have even more concerns: "How and where do I breastfeed at night, and what if I fall asleep? How and where do I breastfeed lying down, and what if I fall asleep? Should I breastfeed my baby to sleep, and what if *I* fall asleep? Would it be easier just to express and have my partner bottle-feed at night? Would formula or solids make him sleep better? How do I switch sides lying down? Are we safer on the sofa? If I let this baby into my bed, will she ever leave?"

And maybe the most pressing question of all: *"If breastfeeding works best when I keep my baby close and breastfeed frequently, but everyone tells me it's not safe to be next to my baby for one-third of every day, then how on earth can I keep breastfeeding and keep my sanity?"*

Breastfeeding ≠ Bottle-Feeding

Sweet Sleep starts with a few reality checks. Breastfeeding isn't just bottle-feeding with a better-looking container. In fact, a breastfeeding mother and her baby are often viewed by researchers as a single unit—a "breastfeeding dyad"—with hormones, instincts, and reflexes that promote safe and nurturing interactions. It's an age-old recipe for mothering that research is just beginning to rediscover.

We're rediscovering, for instance, that the mothers who get the most sleep of all new mothers are—surprise!—the ones who sleep right beside their exclusively breastfed babies, just as mothers always did before they were told not to. But today's breastfeeding mothers are warned that this simple solution isn't safe. Since other arrangements mean less sleep, they'll try *anything* to get more rest. It might be a cot, a sleep-training method, nighttime bottles of formula, or a sofa, any of which can actually *increase* risk. There's a limit to how far a culture can bend normal, healthy biology before something has to give. This book's purpose is to help you use built-in instincts and research-based information to choose a healthy, *responsible* path that meets your family's, your baby's, and your own needs.

There's Risk—and There's Risk

Nighttime has always had risks. A mostly unconscious baby in the care of a mostly unconscious mother? Not ideal. But it's also not humanly possible to stay awake 24/7. So what's a mother to do?

After analysing the research and talking with researchers, we've developed the *Safe Sleep Seven:* seven very clear criteria that address the risks of Sudden Infant Death Syndrome (SIDS, or cot death) and suffocation. Meeting *all seven* means that your baby's risk of SIDS when he's sleeping next to you in your bed is no greater than when he's alone in a cot. And following this book's Safe Surface guidelines *hugely* reduces any breathing risks no matter where your baby sleeps.

In fact, we're recommending that all breastfeeding mothers prepare for bedsharing whether or not they ever intend to do it, since research finds that most breastfeeding mothers *do* sleep with their babies at some point and *preparing for bedsharing is safer than accidentally falling asleep together.* And even those researchers who are concerned about bedsharing agree that by four months, it's a non-issue.

These ideas may not be what you'll hear from your family, friends, or health care providers, so we'll back them up with research every step of the way. It's research that you haven't seen in sleep books before—research that we're realizing barely scratches the surface. Carefully designed research that begins with certain assumptions:

Breastfeeding is our biological norm. Much of today's sleep research uses the formula-fed baby—a *cultural* norm—as its starting point. This means we're likely to read that "breastfed babies eat more often and sleep less than normal." But when research starts with the *biological* norm of breastfeeding, as good science requires, it finds that formula-fed babies eat less often and sleep longer than normal. And that puts a whole new face on things.[1]

Definitions matter. This book is very careful with its definitions, because muddled terms have created serious misconceptions. "Co-sleeping", for instance, can mean sharing a room with your baby, or sharing a bed, or sharing a sofa or reclining chair. The term is meaningless when it can mean so many different things, so we won't be using it at all. "Bedsharing" is also a confusing term. To some researchers, "bedsharing" includes "sofa-sharing" and "recliner-sharing." Mixing beds and sofas and reclining chairs in one term could make mothers think they are all equally safe. They aren't. So in this book, we'll be using the term "bedsharing" to mean *exactly and only* sharing a bed. And we'll explain why some other settings can be risky.

Clarity is crucial. Some researchers and policy statements now combine SIDS with smothering and other completely different risks. We'll define the various terms and keep them separate so that you have a clear understanding of which situations involve which risks, how great the risks are, and what you can do to reduce them.

You'll learn about the "triple risk" theory that helps clarify which babies are vulnerable to SIDS, along with some ways to help protect them. And you'll learn some of the flaws in the research and policies that have made so many mothers afraid to follow their instincts and their hearts about how they spend their nights.

Bottom line: If you fit the Safe Sleep Seven criteria, careful research says you're not the mother the bedsharing warnings are intended for. But you *are* the mother this book is intended for.

What's in It for You?

This book is for all women who were, are, or plan to be breastfeeding mothers. Do you combine breastfeeding and bottle-feeding? Are you back at work? An adoptive mother? Do you have multiples? You'll find yourself in this book.

Part I, "Sleeping Better", gives you a ten-minute (or less) way to make your bed safe for "emergency bedsharing" on a night when you're just too tired to get out of bed one more time. It introduces you to the Safe Sleep Seven criteria and how to meet them. Part II, "Mothers and Babies Together", is about how breastfeeding mothers and babies are attuned to each other and what normal sleep patterns look like for each of them. Part III, "Sleep and Bedsharing Practicalities", is all about naps, nights, the personalities you spend the night with, and ways for you and your child to get more sleep. You'll learn about "front-loading," an effective way of structuring your days to make your nights easier.

In Part IV, "Sleep Ages and Stages", we'll cover the typical naps and nights for your baby, toddler, and preschooler. Part V, "Safe-Sleep Science," tackles the tough stuff—sleep training, suffocation, SIDS, and the flaws in the research that have made bedsharing so controversial. Part VI, "Help", answers some common questions, from pets on the bed to sleepovers at Grandma's. And finally, there's information on how to find help as well as how to give help to other mothers using the wisdom you've learned through your own family's sleep journey.

Sometimes it helps to keep information right at hand. The Tearsheet Toolkit at the back of the book has pages that you can tear out and post for yourself, share with your care provider, and even mail to your close-but-far-away friends and family. You'll also find electronic formats that you can email or text on the La Leche League International website at llli.org/sweetsleepbook.

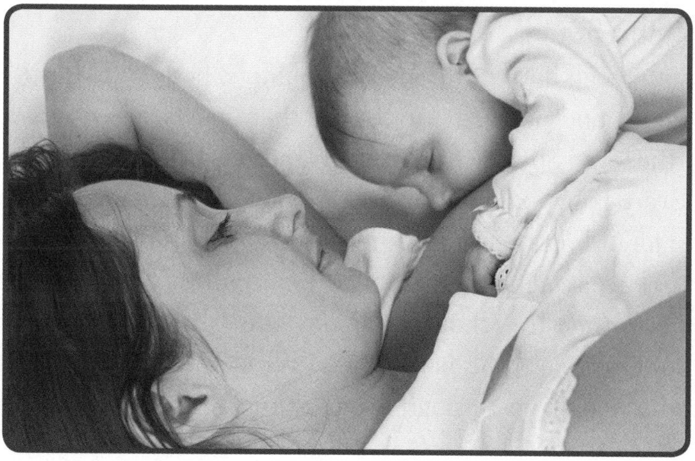

The Importance of Mother-Wisdom

Whether we realize it or not, we mothers are very good at what we do. Research from many fields confirms it: mothers' instincts are worth listening to. Those instincts have allowed us to give birth, sleep, breastfeed, and wean for generation after generation, with no expert advice at all.

In fact, mother-to-mother sharing is the reason behind La Leche League International's half-century-and-counting success. Since 1956, when seven mothers realized that breastfeeding their babies was much easier when they knew other breastfeeding mothers, La Leche League has been built on mother-to-mother sharing. At La Leche League meetings around the world, breastfeeding mothers gather to share stories, ideas, woes, and joys.

An important part of *Sweet Sleep* is this practical mother-wisdom in book form, a distillation from hundreds of thousands of mothers over the years. Ten per cent of the text is devoted to their stories in their own words. Many of those stories are supported by fascinating research on the science of maternal and infant sleep. It's been wonderful for us to confirm, over and over, that research supports our built-in baby care wisdom.

All Mothers Aren't the Same and All Babies Aren't the Same

We mothers all have different personalities, body shapes, interests and needs, and daily rhythms. And then maybe we change jobs, or partners, or homes. Or we add children or other responsibilities. Every baby is unique too. Some need a lot of holding. Some need a lot of breastfeeding. Some need a lot of sleep. A few babies seem to have read all the parenting books; most of them threw the books over their tiny shoulder on day one. All different, all changing. But eventually, the baby who never sleeps becomes the teenager who can sleep through an earthquake, with many stages in between.

At each stage and in many different ways, mothers look for the arrangement that will give the most members of the family the most sleep . . . tonight. Since research can't cover every scenario, you'll need to rely on common sense and your understanding of your family's particular needs. This is where *your* mother-wisdom comes in. As Dr. Benjamin Spock said more than two generations ago, "You know more than you think you do." While there may not be research-based answers for every sleep question, your overall instincts to respond to your baby and keep him close at night *are* thoroughly supported by the latest research. *Sweet Sleep* is tools, not rules, so you can adapt current, research-based information to your own life in your own way.

Four Writers, One Goal

Cot, bedsharing, bedside cot, separate rooms, other children, partner, no partner, too much milk, too little milk—we authors have had personal experience with more arrangements than we can count.

We've had babies who woke up smiling and babies who woke up crying. Babies who fell back to sleep easily and babies who fought sleep. A baby who avoided touch and one who couldn't get enough touching. We've slept in all kinds of beds, breastfed in all kinds of positions. Among us, we've talked with thousands of breastfeeding mothers. And we've been studying sleep issues with a growing interest over the last few years, meeting and corresponding with researchers around the world.

Diane Wiessinger, a La Leche League Leader since the 1980s and an International Board Certified Lactation Consultant (IBCLC), is the mother of two and grandmother of four. Along with Diana West and Teresa Pitman, she co-authored the eighth edition of La Leche League International's *The Womanly Art of Breastfeeding.* Diane has contributed to breastfeeding textbooks and written numerous articles and handouts on breastfeeding. She lectures across the United States and elsewhere on breastfeeding, birth, and sleep issues.

Diana West has been a La Leche League Leader and IBCLC since the turn of the millennium, and has three teenage boys. In addition to being a co-author of *The Womanly Art of Breastfeeding,* eighth edition, Diana has written several books and numerous magazine articles about breastfeeding. She co-owns a large private lactation consultation practice and speaks at conferences worldwide.

Linda Smith became a La Leche League Leader in 1974 and has been an IBCLC since the credential was established in 1985. She is actively involved in public health, childbirth, and breastfeeding organizations at the community, state, national, and international levels. Linda has written four textbooks for professionals. She presents lectures and courses on birth, breastfeeding, and sleep around the world. Her three children are grown and gone from the family bed. Four children now call her Grandma.

Teresa Pitman, our Canadian co-author for *The Womanly Art of Breastfeeding,* has 35 years of experience as a La Leche League Leader. She has written hundreds (that's right) of magazine articles, four books on breastfeeding, and another dozen on parenting topics, and she is a frequent and well-travelled speaker. She is the mother of four children, all breastfed, and has six breastfed grandchildren.

We are four very different mothers who followed very different routes with very different children, but each of us learned that our baby's needs didn't switch off when the sun went down. That reality—that babies' and mothers' and families' needs exist 24 hours every day—is at the heart of this book.

It's Not the Book We Planned

This introduction was the first thing we wrote. And it was the last thing we finished, because our thinking changed so dramatically during the writing. We had planned a book for all sorts of sleeping arrangements, including the cot down the hall. Then we read the research.

When a mother and baby don't spend the night together, stress hormones rise, vital signs change, sleep patterns are disrupted, neural pathways go off course, and trust can be tarnished. None of this shows on the surface, which is why sleep training can look so tempting. But "what lies beneath" was mind-bending for us. The more we learned, the more compelling bedsharing became. In light of the research we just couldn't write this book any other way.

However, we recognize that bedsharing isn't the most appropriate choice for every baby and every family. You may have risk factors that can't be changed or other reasons for needing a different approach. We cover some of these options in Chapter 9 and throughout the book.

Something to Sleep On

Being a mother isn't easy. But we're *hardwired* to mother our babies safely and well, without rules and instructions, day and night. And our babies are *hardwired* to be enjoyed, not just tolerated. Even with a baby in the house, sleep used to be a relaxed and straightforward part of every day, not a problem to be solved. Maybe it can be again.

Join us in exploring the biology, research, and mother-wisdom of sleep. Do with the information what mothers at La Leche League meetings are always encouraged to do: "just take what you like and leave the rest". We hope the knowledge and stories in these pages will add to your confidence in making responsible, information-based choices for you and for your breastfed baby.

part one

Sleeping Better

chapter 1

Quick Start:
Ten Minutes to Better Sleep *Tonight*

Desperate for sleep? Tired of getting up? Your baby can't sleep alone? If you can check off each item under the "Safe Sleep Seven" below, then you can *make your bed as SIDS-safe as a cot and greatly reduce other risks in just a few steps*. Follow these steps for "emergency bedsharing" and sleep better tonight (unless you want to do it again tomorrow).

The Safe Sleep Seven

You need to be:

- ☐ 1. A non-smoker
- ☐ 2. Sober (no drugs, alcohol, or medications that make you drowsy)
- ☐ 3. Breastfeeding

Your baby needs to be:

- ☐ 4. Full-term and healthy
- ☐ 5. Kept on his back when he's not breastfeeding
- ☐ 6. Unswaddled, in a sleepsuit or light pyjamas

And you both need to be:

- ☐ 7. On a safe surface

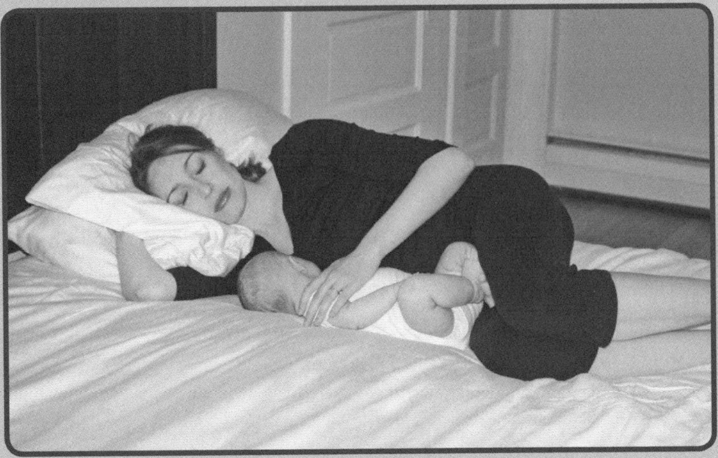

Here's how to make your bed a safe surface:

1. Have your partner, other children, and pets sleep somewhere else. Or you and the baby do.
   Just for tonight.
2. Strip the bed. Take everything off but a thin mattress topper (if you use one) and bottom sheet. Everything.
3. Put back your own pillow(s), top sheet, and lightweight blanket or duvet. No heavy covers or quilts.
4. Put your baby on his back in the middle of the bed. Lie down next to him, on your side and facing him, with his face at about the level of your breast. If your bed is near a wall, put yourself between him and the wall.
5. Breastfeed your baby and get some sleep.

There. A simple, quick, and research-supported bedsharing arrangement. Just for tonight. You'll find the details and research in Chapter 2. Sleep sweet!

Not sure you fit the Safe Sleep Seven? See Chapter 2.

chapter 2

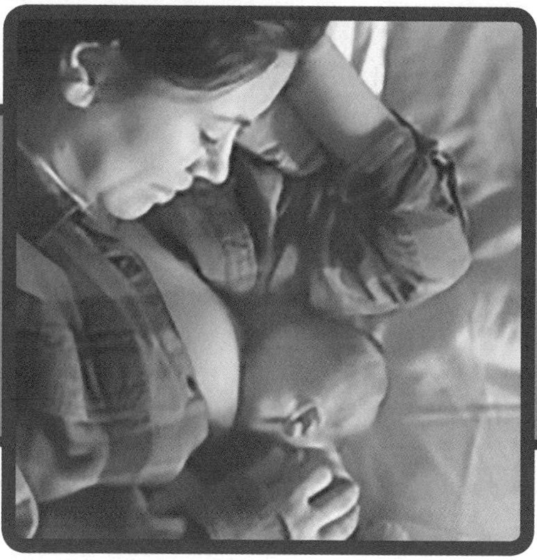

The Safe Sleep Seven

Wah! Wah! Wah! Drag yourself out of your nice cosy bed, pick up your screaming baby, sit down to breastfeed, try to stay awake, put him back in the cot, stagger back to bed, and hope, hope, hope he stays asleep for at least two hours. I had no idea I could feel that exhausted. I could *not* understand how other mothers survived this, because I didn't think *I* was going to.

My friend who's a La Leche League Leader came over and saw how worn down and bleary-eyed my husband and I looked. She asked if we'd thought about bedsharing to get more sleep. No. Not for us. Never. But she laid out seven things that make it safer. That night, out of pure desperation and sleep deprivation, I brought my son into my bed for part of the night . . . and I started the next day a bit brighter. He spent more and more time in my bed at night, and lo and behold, we both got more and more sleep.

—Monica

Today's culture says you should keep the baby in your room . . . but not in your bed. Feed him in bed and get really drowsy . . . but then get out of bed again. Two trips out of bed for every feed. By about six weeks, *something* has to give.[1] Weaning? Leads to short-term and long-term problems.[2] Night weaning? Not healthy for you, your baby, or your milk supply at this age.[3] Supplementing? Ditto.[4] Get out the sleep-training book that your friend gave you? Not as harmless as it seems (see Chapter 18).

A mother's first step is usually to find a place where she can relax for night feed. The NICE Guidelines, currently under review, quote DoH guidance which states "The safest place for your baby to sleep is in a cot in your room for the first six months. While it's lovely to have your baby with you for a cuddle or a feed, it's safest to put your baby back in their cot before you go to sleep".[5] Easy to say. When most of us are "ready to return to sleep", steeped in hormones that make us sleepy, the last thing we want is to get up again. If a mother's afraid to breastfeed in her own bed, her most likely options are a sofa, reclining chair, or armchair—all riskier places to sleep with a baby. One study found that 44 per cent of mothers who breastfeed in those places at night fell asleep there at least once.[6]

> My baby wouldn't sleep in her cradle. One night, after hours of walking and singing to stop her crying, I fell asleep in the reclining chair in the living room, waking just as my three-week-old slipped from my grasp. She only fell into my lap, but I was so frightened that, in desperation, I placed her against the back of the sofa, facing me, and stretched out on the narrow edge beside her. I fell asleep immediately, sure that her cries would awaken me within minutes. Three hours later, I awoke refreshed and was surprised to see Grace still asleep beside me.
>
> Finally, an experienced friend said, "Just put her in bed with you." I was afraid, but my need for sleep outweighed my fear. That night, we tried it and enjoyed hours of uninterrupted sleep. I was amazed.
>
> Today Grace is a delightful eight-month-old, and we are a bed-sharing, breastfeeding family.
>
> —Ann

Ann finally found a low-risk, long-term solution for sleep deprivation and an unhappy baby. More and more mothers are finding the same solution.[7] But, like Ann, they often go through several high-risk arrangements along the way.

The Definitions We're Using in This Book

Breastfeeding: *Mother and baby see the breast as the go-to source of food and comfort.*

Solitary sleeping: *The baby sleeps alone, out of direct sight and hearing of a responsible adult.*

Room-sharing: *The baby sleeps in the same room as, but on a separate surface from, a responsible adult who is awake or asleep.*

Sharing sleep: *The baby and someone else share a sleep surface.*

Bedsharing: *The baby sleeps with his mother on a flat, bed-like surface when she's awake or asleep. We're not using "co-sleeping" because it means different things to different people—a real problem in sleep research.*

Vulnerable baby: *A baby who already has a condition affecting the brain's arousal, breathing, or sleep centre—a result of smoking, prenatal drinking, or certain medications or drugs, certain cases of prematurity or other significant health issues (further explanations below). "Vulnerable" refers to a small group of babies, not all babies.*

Bedside cot: *A cot which is attached to or right up against an adult bed forming either a continuous surface or a separate surface below the adult mattress.*

Even though most new breastfeeding mothers today don't plan to bedshare, studies show that eventually 60 to 75 per cent of them will, at least some of the time.[8] Why? Probably because most breastfeeding mothers get more sleep when they bedshare.[9] In fact, a lot of mothers who say they *don't* bedshare actually *do.* If the baby starts the night in the cot, if the baby started the night in the cot last night, if the baby usually comes into his mother's bed at the first waking, even if a family simply owns a cot . . . any of those can lead a mother to say—and believe—that she doesn't bedshare when she actually does.[10]

The Key Points for Safe Sleep for All Babies

Stay smoke-free. Stay sober. Stay off sofas, armchairs, and reclining chairs for sleep. Keep your healthy baby lightly dressed, on his back, and near you for sleep. And, of course, keep breastfeeding.

But what about all the warnings against bedsharing? If you meet the criteria outlined in the Safe Sleep Seven, *then you're not the mother the warnings are for*! Only a small subset of babies with certain pre-existing vulnerabilities is at risk for SIDS. The risk for SIDS or suffocation is *far, far, far* greater in a household where the mother smokes, where alcohol or drugs are involved, where the baby is formula-fed, or in truly chaotic settings where the baby sleeps who knows where or with who knows whom (see Chapter 19). In an attempt to reach *certain* mothers and protect *certain* babies, the warnings have been made very clear, very strong, and very simple. The answers for *you* are just as simple.

All those scary warnings are about only the first four months. Beyond that? Even the researchers behind the bedsharing cautions agree that by about four months bedsharing by any responsible, non-smoking adult is as safe as having your baby sleep separately in a Moses basket or cot.[11]

If you and your baby fit the Safe Sleep Seven criteria, your baby's risk of SIDS is what one sleep researcher calls *vanishingly small.* And you'll virtually eliminate overlying and other suffocation risks. Let's walk through how the Safe Sleep Seven work and look at the research and common sense behind them.

The Safe Sleep Seven

First the gist of them, then we'll go over what each one means.

If you are:

- ☐ 1. A non-smoker
- ☐ 2. Sober and unimpaired
- ☐ 3. A breastfeeding mother

and your baby is:

- ☐ 4. Healthy and full-term
- ☐ 5. On his back
- ☐ 6. Lightly dressed

and you both are:

- ☐ 7. On a safe surface

Then your baby in bed with you is at *no greater risk for SIDS* than if he's nearby in a cot. The Safe Surface checklist explains number 7 and practically eliminates breathing risks no matter where he sleeps. Rolling over on your baby is *virtually impossible* because you have the cuddle curl (see below) and responsiveness of a breastfeeding mother. By the time the baby is about four months old, research indicates that bedsharing with a healthy baby by any responsible non-smoking adult on a safe surface is as safe as any other sleep arrangement.

The Nitty-Gritty of the Safe Sleep Seven

Sudden infant death syndrome (SIDS) is a potential problem for only a small subset of vulnerable babies, and mainly in the first four months (see the definition in the sidebar). For the vast majority of breastfed babies, breathing risks

> **The Key Points for *Applying* the Key Points**
>
> Every situation is different. Life is never 100 per cent safe. And everyone balances risks and benefits differently. Take the information we present and use your mother-wisdom to decide what's best for you, your baby, and your family.

are more of an issue, and the Safe Sleep Seven addresses them too. There's much more information on SIDS and suffocation in Chapter 19, but here's what we mean for each of the seven criteria.

> ### What if You Don't Fit the Safe Sleep Seven?
>
> Even if you don't meet all the Safe Sleep Seven criteria, you can cut your breastfed baby's overall risk dramatically—*hugely*—by following as many of them as you can. There are risks for your baby with nighttime separation, and sometimes there are risks for him with bedsharing. This book can give you information, but follow your head and your heart on what to do with it. And make sure that *you're* okay with how and where your baby spends his nights.

1. A Non-smoker

A *non-smoker* means that you don't smoke at all now. If you smoked during pregnancy, your baby was born with a higher risk of SIDS, and that's going to be true no matter where he sleeps.[12] But if you continue to smoke, the research is very clear that bedsharing substantially increases your baby's SIDS risk.[13] The amount of risk depends on how much smoke your baby is exposed to.[14] The more people who smoke at home, the greater the risk. The more your baby is exposed to smoke outside your home, the greater the risk. So you can reduce the risk by cutting back on your own smoking and keeping your baby away from others' smoke.

Even if you or your partner smokes, most research and health organizations still suggest keeping your baby in your room at night for at least the first half-year.[15] But you can minimize your baby's nighttime exposure to smoke by keeping his bed away from yours, by bringing him into your bed only for feeds, and by staying between him and a partner who smokes. Continuing to breastfeed helps reduce the SIDS risk, because formula adds another risk on top of the risk from smoke exposure.[16]

What about chewing tobacco, pipes, cigars, herbal cigarettes, clove cigarettes (kretek), or anything else smokable? The extent of the risk isn't yet known. Until we know more, your guidelines are the same as those for cigarette smokers. As for electronic cigarettes (or e-cigarettes), they're more than just water vapour, so it comes down to the chemicals that are used. We simply don't know enough about them yet.

Marijuana is risky for bedsharing, whether it's smoked, drunk, or eaten. Small studies have raised concerns—milk supply issues, SIDS risks even if only a partner smokes, higher levels of THC (marijuana's main psychoactive substance) in milk than in the mother's blood, and the presence of THC in the baby's urine.[17] There's also the chance of overlying because of impaired awareness.

What about smoke from fireplaces and wood stoves, especially in the sleeping area? They may pose a health risk, but we know of no research that has looked at it in relation to infant safety and sleeping arrangements.

2. Sober and Unimpaired

Sober and unimpaired means that you stayed sober and free of recreational drugs during pregnancy. It means that you aren't under the influence of any substance, legal or illegal, that significantly alters your alertness, co-ordination, or ability to think and react.

The most common impairment is alcohol, which can blunt your awareness of everything and dramatically affect your judgment. The risk with alcohol and bedsharing is that you'll sleep so deeply that you won't be aware of your baby and could risk rolling over on him, or throwing an arm or leg over him. In several large research studies, nearly all of the infant deaths from smothering or overlying were related to alcohol use, sofa sleeping, or both.[18] The risk of an alcohol- or drug-related rollover is especially high if the adult and baby share an already risky surface, such as a sofa or reclining chair, especially if the adult isn't one of the parents.[19]

The reality, though, is that breastfeeding mothers have had alcohol since time began, and it's generally safe in moderation. But what's moderation when it comes to bedsharing? We don't know. It takes about two hours per drink (one glass of beer or wine, or one mixed drink) to metabolize alcohol completely.[20] The two hours isn't a hard-and-fast rule, of course. There's body size, foods, and tolerance as well. According to "Medications and Mothers' Milk", a prominent pharmacology reference, "mothers who ingest alcohol in moderate amounts can generally return to breastfeeding as soon as they feel neurologically normal".[21] But that's breastfeeding. For bedsharing, it's up to you to make the call.

What about "pumping and dumping"? The only reason for it would be to support your milk production if there's a long time between drinking and breastfeeding. Alcohol passes both into and out of your milk through your bloodstream. As your blood alcohol level rises with a drink, the level in your milk rises by exactly the same amount, and as your blood level falls over time, your milk level drops to match it.[22] So it won't work to "pump the alcohol out".

In some cultures, mothers are encouraged to breastfeed their babies after they've had a drink to help the babies sleep better. A baby who drinks milk containing alcohol may indeed fall asleep faster, but the alcohol changes his sleep-wake patterns and he's actually likely to sleep less.[23] Alcohol also temporarily affects your milk release[24] and milk production.[25]

There are milk testing kits that allow you to check your milk for alcohol content. But small amounts of alcohol in your blood are not a problem, and the kit can't tell you for certain when it's safe to sleep with your baby.

So alcohol and bedsharing is a judgment issue. And, of course, the more you've had to drink, the poorer your judgment.

Being sober also means you're not taking any medications or drugs that can cause drowsiness, either intentionally (as in a sleep aid) or as a side effect. If you're taking a narcotic for postnatal pain, the drug should wear off completely before you bedshare. Over-the-counter non-narcotic painkillers are generally fine. Recreational drugs, including marijuana, generally are not. Check lactmed .nlm.nih.gov for information on specific medications or drugs and breastfeeding.

Being sober isn't just about alcohol or medications. *Anything* that gets in the way of normal "wake-ability" makes bedsharing less safe. If you haven't had a total of at least four hours' sleep in the last 24 hours, it can be like being intoxicated.[26] The trouble is that if you're getting that little sleep, bedsharing is the fastest way to get more sleep. It's a real Catch-22. Until you've caught up a bit, this can be where a bedside cot can be helpful. Sliding your baby into a bedside cot after breastfeeding would almost certainly get you more sleep than getting up to put her in a cot would.

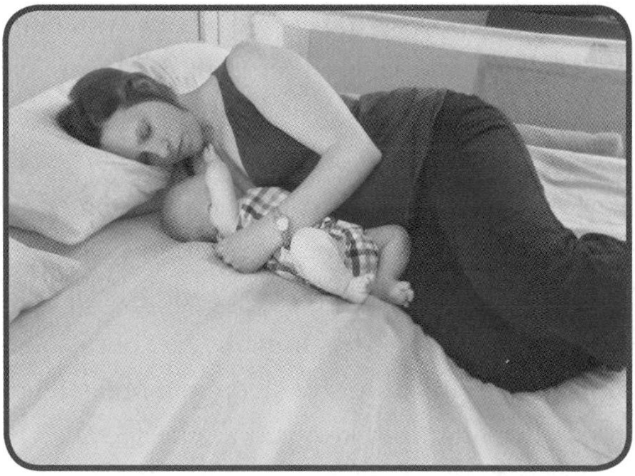

Cuddle curl

3. A Breastfeeding Mother

The Safe Sleep Seven definition of *breastfeeding* means that both you and your baby are totally breast-focused. During sleep, you'll automatically go into the same position as breastfeeding mothers all over the world and throughout time. It's called a *cuddle curl,* and it's nature's way of protecting a baby during sleep. Your knees come up and your arm tucks under your head or pillow, or curls around your baby, creating a protected space. There's no way for you to roll towards your baby because your bent legs won't let you. And no one else can roll into the space because your knees and elbows are in the way.[27] Very cool! (If you're worried about your partner, just sleep between your partner and the baby.)

Even during sleep a breastfed baby will instinctively stay with his face near the breast, because that's the centre of his universe (and his kitchen).[28] If your baby homes in on your breast, he's not going to wander up into the pillows or down under the covers (and your arm and legs won't let him).

There's another layer of protection too: normally, we're aware of the edges of our bed and the bodies of our pets, even when we're sound asleep. We don't roll over on a baby any more than we roll off the side of the bed or roll over on the cat. And of course both the cat and the baby would react if you tried.

A mother who has never breastfed loses some of these protections. She tends to move her baby closer to her own face, where those puffy, smothery pillows are.[29] And a baby who doesn't breastfeed is more likely to wander up there himself, even if the bottles are filled with his mother's milk.

What if you're still working out the kinks, maybe expressing for a baby who isn't breastfeeding yet? A newborn will automatically seek his mother's breast. If you've been focused on helping him breastfeed, you'll probably find yourself doing a cuddle curl, at least at first.

If you breastfeed most of the time but give occasional bottles of expressed milk, you'll probably still sleep in a breastfeeding cuddle curl, and your baby will most likely stay at chest level.[30] But if either of you sees a bottle as the more important food source, you and your baby may not automatically "think breast," and your bedsharing risk may increase.[31] If you're just not sure, think carefully about how you cradle your baby when you lie down, and maybe have your partner watch how you interact before you decide for or against bedsharing.

What if your baby gets formula sometimes? Exclusive formula-feeding increases the risk of SIDS (see Chapter 19); partial formula-feeding is a smaller SIDS risk.

By about four months, any responsible adult can bedshare as safely as a responsible breastfeeding mother.[32]

4. Healthy and Full-Term

Healthy and full-term means that your baby doesn't have serious health problems and was born at term, usually defined as 37 weeks or more. Research indicates that certain already-vulnerable babies, including some premature babies[33] and some babies with arousal, cardiorespiratory, or brainstem problems, are at risk for SIDS and suffocation. So are some babies who were sick enough with a respiratory infection to be hospitalized.[34] If your baby has been shown to have one of these challenges, then you know you have a vulnerable baby. Sometimes we just don't know. But remember that a category like "some premature babies" is a small subset of a small subset.

If your baby isn't already vulnerable, minor problems like colds or covers-lightly-over-the-head aren't known to increase risk. That's a big part of why safe-surface bedsharing usually works fine.

For an already-vulnerable baby, such as one who is premature, Kangaroo Mother Care, rather than casual bedsharing, may be an alternative (see Chapter 9). No one knows all your little one's quirks and competencies better than you, so listen, read, ask, and make sure you feel comfortable with where and how your baby sleeps.

5. On His Back

On his back means exactly that; the "Back to Sleep" campaigns are probably the major reason that SIDS rates fell so much in the early 1990s.[35] Unless he's on an adult's sloping chest, sleeping tummy-down is a SIDS risk for a *vulnerable* baby.

In the past, mothers were advised to put their babies in the cot on their stomachs in the widespread belief that babies would sleep better that way. And babies usually did—at least in the sense that they didn't wake up as much. The problem was that sometimes they didn't wake up at all, possibly because they slept *too* deeply or couldn't lift their face free from soft bedding. Now we know better.[36]

The big exception to putting a baby on his back is if the baby sleeps on an adult's chest with his head higher than his bottom. That position gives him the stability he craves and the adult's breathing and movement stimulate the baby's own breathing, even if they're both asleep. Being tummy-down on an adult chest has no documented risks, only documented benefits.[37] It can even be life-saving for premature babies.[38] A baby asleep on his tummy on an adult is in a normal position. A *vulnerable* baby *alone* is safer sleeping on his back.

The baby who *isn't* vulnerable who's put on his stomach? No research. Until we know more, it makes sense to put your baby on his back when he's alone. It happens almost automatically with bedsharing—your baby comes off your breast and rolls completely or mostly onto his back. A baby who breastfeeds on his side is fine, so long as he rolls over onto his back eventually.[39] And he almost always does if he's bedsharing. A baby old enough to roll over and back by himself is considered fine in any position.[40]

6. Lightly Dressed

Lightly dressed means the baby has about as many layers of clothing and covers as you have. Overheating during sleep seems to be a SIDS risk for vulnerable babies,[41] and it's not that comfortable for *any* baby. But during bedsharing, your baby is next to you, a toasty heat source. A light blanket and daytime-weight clothes are probably all your baby needs in most settings. Save the hats and mittens for chilly days outside. You'll find more about "dressing for bed" in Chapter 6.

A swaddled baby can't regulate his temperature as easily. He's also helpless, no matter where you put him, but in your bed he can't move towards or away from you. He can't push the covers away or shift his body away from a problem spot.[42] So being swaddled packs a double whammy for a bedsharing baby. For more on swaddling, see Chapters 12 and 19.

7. On a Safe Surface

Even though a safe surface is the last point in the Safe Sleep Seven bedsharing requirements, it's the most important one of all for Safe Sleep Seven mothers, and it deserves its own section in this chapter. SIDS is an issue only for vulnerable babies. Suffocation is an issue for *all* babies. But it's a very straightforward issue to deal with.

Making a Safe Surface

Although there is research on obviously risky sleep surfaces, we can't describe every dangerous bed surface. And we don't need to. Once you know what to look for, you'll spot any potential problems with your bed very quickly. Let's start with the checklist. Then we'll go over it in detail.

The Safe Surface Checklist

Avoid these possible smothering risks:

- ☐ Sofas and reclining chairs
- ☐ Softness or sagging that rolls your baby against you or keeps him from lifting his head free
- ☐ Spaces between mattress and headboard, side rails, or wall where a baby could get stuck
- ☐ Pets that could interfere

Clear your bed of:

- ☐ Unused pillows
- ☐ Stuffed toys
- ☐ Heavy covers and comforters
- ☐ Anything nearby that dangles or tangles (such as cords, strings, scarves, ribbons, elastics)

Check your bed for possible hazards:

- ☐ Distance to floor
- ☐ Landing surface
- ☐ Sharp, poking, or pinching places

Softness or Sagging

If your baby manages to roll to a tummy-down position (which is always possible, even with a newborn), will he be able to lift his face clear? Is your mattress firm enough that he can't get trapped in the valley your body makes? Can he roll away and onto his back? We can't say that pillow-top mattresses are risky, that memory foam is risky, or even that waterbeds are risky, because there's so much variation. See the sidebar on page 18 for a website that offers an easy test. Beyond that, you'll need to check out your own

The Safe Sleep Seven Bedsharing Song

(to the tune of "Row, Row, Row Your Boat")

No smoke, sober mum
Baby at your breast
Healthy baby on his back
Keep him lightly dressed.

Not too soft a bed
Watch the cords and gaps
Keep the covers off his head
For your nights and naps.

mattress to your own satisfaction. Experiment to see how much your baby compresses your mattress and how your two bodies interact in different positions.

> ### Testing Your Mattress Softness
>
> You'll find a clever way backed by research at goo.gl/k5u6DK.[43] Ignore the ads—the products advertised aren't necessarily safe for babies.

Want to make your mattress less squishy? A board under your mattress can help, or maybe there's a firmer bed you could use. Another possible solution is to put a firmer surface, like a yoga mat, under the bottom sheet. Choose one big enough for you and your baby to share, so that your firmer surface is continuous and the baby can't roll off it.

Spaces Where a Baby Could Get Stuck

Even young babies are mobile enough to end up "in a pinch", but they may not be mobile enough to get out of one. The cracks and crevices in sofas and reclining chairs are notorious baby traps. Cracks and gaps in beds can easily be dealt with.

Here's one that you may have wondered about: Why do cot slats have to be so close together? After all, there's no way a baby's head could fit through a gap even twice that size! It turns out that most

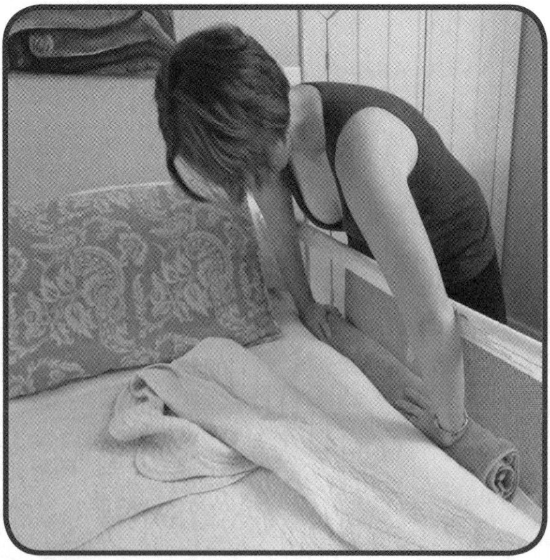

Filling the gap between a side rail and mattress

of us have our mental image backwards. The danger isn't the baby's *head* going through and getting caught, it's the baby's *body* going through and his head being too big to follow. A horrible image, but it may help you see similar gaps that are easy to eliminate.

Closing the Gaps

Some parents reduce risks by "filling in the gaps" around their bed. If there are spaces between your headboard and the mattress, along the bed rails, or between a mesh side rail and the mattress, fill them up. Beach towels, firm pillows, or quilts often work well, with smaller packing for smaller spaces. It's important to really *wedge* the stuffing in so it's totally firm and solid, with no puffiness and no gaps.

If the side of the bed is against the wall, push the mattress over

Filling in the gap between a bedside cot and an adult mattress

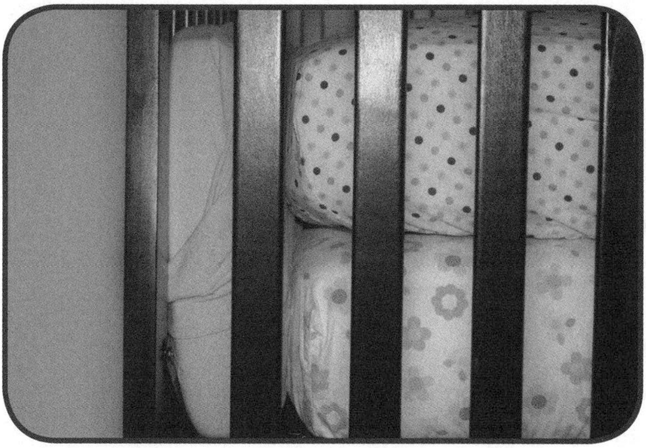

to close any gap, or fill the gap with suitable padding (making sure the bed doesn't creep away from the wall). Some parents just sleep on that side of the bed. If you're using a bedside cot, some parents find it works better to slide the cot mattress over so it's tight against their own bed and then fill the gap on the far side of the cot with towels or even a piece of fabric-covered foam. A product that may help is a thin foam strip called a "bed connector" that fills the gap between beds to create a seamless, continuous surface.

Making the Gaps Wider

Sometimes it's easier to get rid of a gap by widening it. Pull your bed away from the wall so that the baby who somehow manages to go in that direction can at least drop to something soft on the floor instead of getting wedged (see our thoughts below).

Speaking of wedging, all those sleep positioners and box-like devices that are supposed to protect your baby in your bed are sleep hazards, not sleep protectors, as we explain in Chapter 12. They're a suffocation or wedging risk, no matter where or how they're used.

Bed Partner, Other Children, and Pets

Maybe your bed partner is a thrasher or heavy sleeper, or isn't terribly "baby-sensitive". To solve the problem easily, just sleep between your baby and your bed partner. Or your partner can move to another place to sleep for a little while. (We discuss sleep temperaments and bed configurations in Chapter 7.)

Having children share a bed of their own can work great when they're older. But an older child sleeping next to a baby doesn't have an adult's awareness. You could sleep in between them, or have a separate sleeping space for the older child. Sometimes a toddler is happy to sleep on a mattress on the floor beside your bed.

There's no research to say that pets are a bedsharing risk. You know your pets—their size and temperament, where they sleep, any jealousy towards the baby—so you're the best judge of how safe it might be to have your pet in bed with you and a new baby. We have more thoughts about pets in Chapter 22, but the bottom line is that your baby takes precedence over your pet, even if that pet has been your baby for years.

Pillows, Toys, Heavy Covers, and Other Hazardous Objects

Babies can be pretty skilled at turning anything puffy or squishy into a pillow over their face, even if they start out on their backs. The pillow or pillows under your head don't count as a hazard, because as a breastfeeding mother, you automatically move your baby into the protective side-lying cove between your arm and your thigh.

With a sheet and a couple of light blankets, your body "tents" the covers in a way that lets in enough air even if they flip over your baby's head now and then.[44] Healthy, full-term babies are good at batting covers off their heads, but they can't handle heavy bedding. What babies *can* do is tangle themselves in anything nearby, including cot bumper ties, curtain cords, and dummy chains. Anything small enough to fit in a baby's mouth, other than his fist, fingers, toes, and your nipples, is a choking hazard, so do a visual sweep before bed, keeping in mind that babies can move pretty fast when no one's looking.

Distance to Floor, Landing Surface

This is usually a much bigger issue with older babies who roll and crawl, but even small babies can fall off a bed that isn't set up well. First step: prevention. If the baby is between you and your partner, you're all set. If you'd rather (or need to) be between your baby and your partner, you have an edge to contend with. Can you move over to give your baby more room? If not, a bedside cot not only gives you more room in the bed, it also gives you built-in rails to prevent falls.

Many mothers have found that a mesh side rail designed for toddler beds works just as well on adult beds. Don't forget to fill in the gaps. (There's more info about side rails in Chapter 12.)

Some mothers use a hard foam pool flotation toy ("noodle") under the bottom sheet as an edge reminder for older babies. If your baby is a pole-vaulter who might go over any edge (and even if he's not), it's worth softening the potential landing area with a folded blanket or a cot mattress. Nothing that's softer or poufier than a cot mattress, though.

Or put your own mattress on the floor! Families who have taken the bed apart and put the mattress on the floor (with all the gaps widened or filled for little ones) often find it gives them months or years of worry-free sleeping space.

If you want your mattress a little lower but don't want it on the floor, you can skip the divan when you buy a new mattress, and just cut boards to fit the bed frame. There's no difference in comfort.

Sharp, Poking, or Pinching Places

This one's not likely to be an issue because you've probably already removed anything like that for your *own* safety. But think about your bed from your baby's perspective. Is there *any*place a little wiggler could catch a finger? Any sharp or rough edges?

Life always has risks. But now you've taken care of the *exact same issues* that baby furniture makers try to take care of, with a huge layer of protection that they can't offer: *you're* there. And the checklists eliminate the biggest risks of all for your baby, whether your baby sleeps alone in a cot or with you in your own bed.

A Safe Surface Is Mostly Common Sense

There's no way to come up with a safety rule for every single bed-sharing situation. Our checklists give you broad guidelines and some "hot spots" to look for. From there on, it's your own common sense.

But can you *trust* your own common sense? Look at it this way: the bottom line for baby furniture companies isn't your baby, it's (1) profit and (2) avoiding lawsuits from manufacturing errors and corner cutting. And the CEO has never met your baby.

You, on the other hand, care passionately about your baby. You're already using common sense with just about every mothering move you make. You shift his position to make him more comfortable. You test his temperature with your lips. Try *that,* major industries! You have it all over any cot guidelines when it comes to the moment-by-moment commonsense monitoring of your baby's safety and well-being. Especially when he's right beside you.

So take the basics—the Safe Sleep Seven—from this chapter,

and then it's just like any other baby safety issue: adapt the information to your own circumstances. Love and common sense are a highly protective combination!

What if You're Not Planning on Bedsharing?

Maybe you have concerns about bedsharing that you just can't get past. Let's go through some of them and see if we can put your mind at ease.

"I'm Afraid of Rolling Over on Him"

Mothers have been warned against overlying since time began because it can happen—in certain circumstances. *But overlying deaths are wildly unlikely among Safe Sleep Seven mothers.*

In the past, spacious, flat, firm beds didn't exist. Babies suffocated in hammocks, in rope beds, in crowded beds, and on straw mattresses. Some were smothered deliberately by desperate or desperately poor mothers or families. Tobacco has been in use for centuries. Alcohol has been around even longer, especially in places where the water wasn't safe to drink.

Things are different when you're sober. When was the last time you fell out of bed or rolled over on the cat? Whether you're in light sleep or deep sleep, some part of you always knows where you are. Add the breastfeeding mother's radar, add the cuddle curl—and the "melon effect" (see the sidebar)—and you get a sense of how incredibly unlikely overlying is. If you're worried about your partner rolling over on the baby, just sleep between your partner and the baby.

"I Just Don't Believe It's Safe"

Some child care "experts" today believe that a mother is an inherent risk to her baby—that sleeping babies are safe only when they're not with their mothers. But a non-smoking, sober, breastfeeding mother is not a risk to her baby. Her *furniture* may be, but *furniture* problems can be fixed, as this chapter has already discussed.

You Won't Squish the Melon

Try this: Put a melon in your bed and lie down next to it in any position you want. Now roll over onto it. You're going to run into two problems. First, you have to roll uphill to do it. And second, it's really uncomfortable once you get there.

Now imagine it's a melon with attitude. Healthy babies are fully capable of kicking, hitting, wiggling, and squawking. They've been doing it for millennia, anytime an arm or leg or torso goes where they don't want it.

So no, you're not going to squish the melon. It's too hard to do. And the melon won't let you.

Chapters 19 and 20 take a close look at the risks of SIDS and suffocation, as well as at the controversies that surround public policy campaigns against bedsharing. The bottom line is that thorough scrutiny of the research shows that sharing sleep is healthy and your baby's risk of SIDS or suffocation while bedsharing is minuscule if you follow the Safe Sleep Seven.

"I'm Already Using a Bedside Cot"

Have you ever breastfed lying down in bed? Has breastfeeding ever made you sleepy? That's why you need the Safe Sleep Seven. Yes, the bedside cot is a good idea, but those breastfeeding hormones can make you nod off as soon as your baby settles in to breastfeed. That's what they're designed to do. If you've planned ahead, you can scoop your baby from that very safe bedside cot into your very safe bed at the first peep, and you won't have to worry if you somehow don't manage to slide him back.

"Bedsharing's Just Not Going to Happen—Full Stop"

Car accidents aren't going to happen either. But they do. That's why we wear seat belts. It's not that we're *planning* to have an accident; it's that accidents are never planned. So we plan ahead, and we don't give it another thought. Simple and safe—or as safe as being in a car can get.

A planned-ahead bed is just a seat belt. Then at 3.00 a.m. when your baby just can't sleep alone even though you've tried everything up, down, and sideways, you can collapse in bed with your baby and stay there snugly until morning. Tomorrow morning you can decide what you want to do tomorrow night.

Life is risky, no matter how you live it. A safe bed, like a seat belt, can greatly reduce that risk.

> I started out thinking I was not going to bedshare. Ever. The reality turned out to be much different. I ended up bedsharing in the hospital just so I could sleep (my son cried when he was away from me). The first night home, I tried to put him to sleep in his cot. It lasted all of an hour. When he woke up and realized he wasn't in my (or someone's) arms, he wailed! I sat up, breastfed him back to sleep, then laid him down between me and my husband. We all slept for a few hours after that.
>
> —Jolie

"Putting the Baby in My Bed Could Mean He'll Never Leave"

Those who've bedshared can reassure you that he'll *definitely* move into his own bed eventually. Children are hardwired to grow up and take care of themselves. From the time they can crawl, they're actively moving away from you—but at their own pace, which varies hugely. Yes, they'll leave your bed. The only question is when, and that's something you and your child will work out together. Since the "working out" varies with age, we'll talk about the specifics in Chapter 11 and in Part IV, "Sleep Ages and Stages". It's not something you need to worry about this week.

"If the Baby's in Bed with Us, We Can't Have Sex"

Of course you can! Sleeping babies don't care what you and your partner are doing in another part of the bed or bedroom. An infant seat isn't an all-night sleep space, but it's fine for the length of a "romantic interlude". So is a bedside cot. And, of course, the bedroom isn't the only place for romance. We'll talk about it more in Part IV.

No Need to Memorize

All these lists and numbers and explanations aren't anything you need to remember. The Safe Sleep Seven checklist describes things you either are or aren't and do or don't do. Don't smoke? You're not going to start without realizing it. Always put your baby on his back? You're not going to forget to do it. And you're quickly becoming an expert on babyproofing your surroundings. You can always take the handout from the Tearsheet Toolkit at the back of the book to your in-laws' or doctor's appointment. So take care of anything you can that you haven't been doing, consult Chapter 9 if you don't fit the Safe Sleep Seven, and you never have to come back to this chapter again . . . unless you like to sing the song.

Something to Sleep On

Research on infant sleep risks, which we go over in depth in Chapter 19, shows again and again that the big risks of shared sleep are a mix of SIDS risks that affect vulnerable babies and breathing hazards that affect *all* babies: smoking, alcohol or drugs, risky surfaces like sofas, baby on his front (unless he's on an adult's chest), and formula-feeding. Combine two or more of those, and the risk can skyrocket.

If you and your baby meet the requirements in the Safe Sleep Seven checklist, you've already eliminated all the biggest SIDS risks. And if you prepare your bed, then your baby's overall night-time risk becomes vanishingly small. It's like putting your seat belt on and then driving slowly on a deserted (and lovely!) country road. Enjoy having your baby beside you for the journey.

part two

Mothers and Babies Together

chapter 3

Attached and Attuned

> In her book *I Know Why the Caged Bird Sings*, Maya Angelou writes about how her mother encouraged her to bring her infant son into her bed. When Maya realizes she hasn't crushed her son, as she had feared she would, she hears her mother whisper, "See, you don't have to think about doing the right thing. If you're for the right thing, then you do it without thinking."[1]
>
> —James McKenna, *In Defense of Maya's Mother*

Many of us start out breastfeeding because we know we're supposed to, and because we've heard about the health "benefits". The health differences are real, but breastfeeding is so much more. It's the first human relationship our babies will experience—the one that starts them on the path towards all their future relationships.

Your breastfeeding relationship is communication, long before your baby can talk. It's sending her off to sleep, long before she can understand bedtime stories. It's even being silly together, long before she can deliver a punch line. Breastfeeding is an intense relationship with great food on the side, not a perfect infant food that may include a relationship.

> I started breastfeeding thinking it was food. Very good food, but just food. As the days and months went on, it became clear that breastfeeding was a relationship and a way of mothering, and not simply a food delivery system. It was the first and (later on) best way I communicated with my baby. It fixed all the hurts, made the naps happen, soothed both of our anxieties. . . . In fact, when he weaned at two and a half, I felt lost at first. I didn't know quite how to mother without breastfeeding.
>
> —Sherrie

All the feel-good things we adults enjoy—a hug, a morning cup of tea, a favourite T-shirt—we get to choose for ourselves. Breastfeeding and being held are the only comforts a baby has in this strange new world, but he can't get them on his own. How cool that when we use breastfeeding to meet our baby's *comfort* needs, it automatically provides all the *food* he needs too.

In a novel about a fictional talking gorilla, the gorilla says this about how his family eats:

> *Wherever one turns, there is something wonderful to eat. One never thinks, "Oh, I'd better look for some food." Food is everywhere, and one picks it up almost absentmindedly, as one takes a breath of air. In fact, one does not think of feeding as a distinct activity at all. Rather, it's like a delicious music that plays in the background of all activities throughout the day.*
>
> —*Ishmael* by Daniel Quinn

What a graceful introduction to life we can offer our babies. And how important it is to provide it! Our milk production is usually driven not by how much milk we can make but by how much milk our babies take. A baby who breastfeeds poorly or who has to breastfeed according to his mother's schedule may not take all the milk he needs, and that means her breasts automatically begin to make less. If we breastfeed more often on a day when he's especially hungry, he increases our milk production. He can fine-tune the system to meet his needs exactly, as long as we're the delicious music described above. *We* don't need to figure and measure. Our babies do it all themselves. Babies are just as skilled at getting their emotional needs met if we let them. (If this freewheeling system isn't working for you and your baby, check Chapter 23 for resources. You and your baby deserve to enjoy breastfeeding!)

Little Body, Big Brain

We humans have a really big brain for our size. We also walk upright, which means that our legs are directly under us, attached to a narrow pelvis that our large-headed babies have to fit through. The solution: our babies are born while their heads are still small.

Our newborns' brains are only a quarter of their adult size; a chimpanzee newborn's brain is nearly half the size of his mother's.[2] That means human babies are not very competent compared to other primate babies. The baby chimp can cling to its mother's body as she moves around. Our babies need us to hold them.

> The mere presence of the mother not only ensures the infant's well-being, but also creates a kind of invisible hothouse in which the infant's development can unfold. This is a private realm of sensory stimulation constructed by the mother and infant from numberless exchanges of subtle cues. For a baby, the environment is the mother.[3]—Myron Hofer, MD, founding director, Sackler Institute for Developmental Psychobiology, Columbia University

Life on the Outside

Being born just puts your baby on the other side of your skin. Your body is still essential to her well-being. She draws her security and stability from your smell, your feel, your voice, the rise and fall of your chest, and your heartbeat. Without you, her own breathing and heart rate are less stable and her stress level rises.[4]

The two of you share an immune system, hormonal patterns, and daily rhythms. You respond to the distress in her cry with distress of your own and a powerful urge to tend to her. When she breastfeeds, she feels relief from hunger or discomfort, and you feel relaxation and relief from the fullness in your breasts. A win-win.

Hardwired for Each Other

Your baby's nervous system—her wiring—isn't well developed at birth, and her nerves are literally raw, without their final, lifelong protective coating. She's going to spend the next three years growing and modifying her brain cells to create all the connections that she'll use from that point on. We'll revisit this later in the chapter.

Her wiring may not be complete at first, but she *does* come hardwired to make you fall in love with her. Which makes sense: if you love her, you'll be more likely to respond to her needs, protect her day and night, keep her with you virtually 24/7, and help her finish connecting all her wiring—physical and emotional—appropriately.

> There is no such thing as a baby, there is only a baby and someone.—Donald Winnicott, MD[5]

Right after birth, your baby's first gaze draws you in. Your hormones respond and you *drink* her in. There's a "hormonal cascade",one hormonal response triggering another, that normally leads us through birth right into bonding and breastfeeding. It's an immediate high that is blunted because of the way modern birth is often managed. But our baby's need for us and our need for our baby are so powerful and interwoven that we can overcome almost any rough start. In fact, the oxytocin we release when she starts to breastfeed is "the triggering hormone for maternal behaviour".[6] So your baby's breastfeeding behaviour helps you fall in love with her. (The artificial oxytocin called Pitocin or Syntocinon, used during labour, doesn't have that effect and actually can reduce your natural oxytocin temporarily.)[7]

Because you come hardwired to respond to her, the sound of her crying cuts to your core. When you respond by breastfeeding, the hormones in your milk help her digest her food . . . and they make her sleepy. The hormones you release when you breastfeed help you relax . . . and they make you sleepy. It's another hormonal synchrony between the two of you that encourages rest and relaxation. Those who advise "Don't let the baby fall asleep at your breast" are fighting nature on both ends—your baby's and yours—with no research at all to support them.

> The mother's body is the baby's natural habitat.—Nils Bergman, MBChB, DCH, MPH, MD

Magnetic Mothering

Picture a mother and a baby as two magnets. If you hold them far apart, there's no tension between them. When food comes from a bottle that anyone can give, the mother could be in Tuscany and her baby in Taiwan at feeding time, and there's isn't a physical or hormonal connection pulling them towards each other.

Snap the magnets together and there's no tension between them either. That's the pattern of the breastfeeding mother and baby as it has happened for aeons. The baby is in his happiest place—on his mother's body, or in her arms, or by her side. Breastfeeding happens on a whim—hers or his. Their hormones rise and fall in synchrony, the milk constantly adjusts to the baby's needs, and she always knows how her baby is doing because he's right there. Usually he's doing well . . . because *she's* right there.

Now hold the magnets close together but don't let them touch, and you'll feel the tension of Western-style breastfeeding: "Breastfeed your baby . . . but not too often (you don't want your baby to use food for comfort or use you as a dummy)." "Hold your baby . . . but not too much (he needs to learn independence and you don't want to be manipulated by him)." "Keep your baby close at night . . . but not too close (you're a danger to him at night)." "Feed him until he's full . . . but take him off if he starts to fall asleep (he needs to learn to self-comfort)." *This is mothering at its very hardest.* It's adversarial and confusing to both of you. But it's where many of us begin when we're told that responsible parents have to fight their own and their child's instincts.

With that kind of tension, most mother-baby pairs eventually either fly together or fly apart. UNICEF reports that 90% of women who stop breastfeeding in the first six weeks did so before they had wanted to.[8] Why put up with such complicated parenting when formula is so available and so "normal"? Yet mothers who let the magnets snap together—who ignore the rules that someone else came up with and listen to their instincts—often see breastfeeding as one of the best parts of having young children. They no longer watch the clock, gauge the baby's hunger, follow someone else's rules, or feel the impossible tension of holding themselves at arm's length. Instead, they just start . . . breastfeeding.

> At a health fair, I tried to draw people to our breastfeeding table by asking, "Do you know anyone who's having a baby?" I got two main responses: Hands out in front as if pushing away, with something like, "No, thank goodness! I'm through with that!" Or a wistful face and voice: "Ooh, no, but I miss those days!" If only there were a way to let women know how much they lose by keeping their distance from their own baby.
>
> —Claudia

Melting into Motherhood

For many of us, there is a "melting into motherhood" that has to happen before we can tune out the cultural voices and tune in to our baby.

It's a lot like falling in love. You take a leap of faith towards that certain someone without knowing where you'll end up. Yes, the feeling of being out of control can be unsettling, even scary. But once you realize that you *can't* be in control and you don't *have* to be in control, you can just enjoy the deliciousness of love.

There's an old La Leche League story of two new mothers, one of whom says with a tired voice, "It's been way worse than I expected! If I'm not holding him or breastfeeding him, he's crying." The other says, "It's been so much easier than I expected! All I have to do is hold him and breastfeed him, and he's happy as a clam." Some babies are definitely a lot easier than others. In general, though, the more you carry your baby, hold your baby, and sleep with your baby, the less stress both of you will feel.

Babies know this, and they let you know. One study found that babies who were carried at least three to four hours a day cried and fussed about 40 per cent less at six weeks of age.[9] Let's turn that around, since carrying is just normal behaviour. The baby who is carried *for fewer* than three hours a day cries *more than one and a half times as much* as the baby who is carried at least three hours a day. The more you try to distance yourself from your baby, the more stress you'll both feel.

Breastfeeding and Carrying Are Just Normal

People may say that breastfed babies are "smarter", have "fewer illnesses", are "more likely to wake up at night". When they say it that way, they're using formula-feeding as the baseline, as if breastfeeding offers bonus points beyond what's normal.

In fact, formula-feeding is the awkward newcomer and breastfeeding has been around for as long as there have been babies. That means that breastfeeding behaviours are the baseline and formula-fed babies are at an IQ disadvantage, have more illnesses, and sleep more than they're meant to.

When a carried baby "cries less" than the baby away from his mother, what we're really saying is that babies who aren't carried are protesting about the lack of normal contact. Breastfeeding and mother-baby contact? They're just normal. You'll find that perspective throughout this book.

Living in Your Right Brain

Do you feel you lost your sense of reason as well as your sense of control after the birth? In a way, you have. New mothers "live" in their right brains at first—literally the right side of the brain. The left side of our brain is verbal, logical, in charge of "book learning". Our right brain is emotional, spontaneous, and the source of "body memories" such as practising an instrument. The right brain is ideal soil for growing a mother—and a baby and child; for about the first three years, our children are almost completely right-brained.[10] They operate in a world of instincts and emotions, and they look for stability and reliability from their mothers or the special someone who's constant in their lives, in order to feel secure now and in the future.[11] As child development specialist Dr. Uri Bronfenbrenner put it, a child needs consistent care from "someone who's crazy about him".[12] And being head over heels is a right-brained affair.

Wiring, magnets, softening, right brain—no matter how you come at it, breastfeeding works best, lasts longest, is enjoyed most, and reaps the greatest number of long-term emotional benefits when a mother understands it first as a relationship and secondarily as food. That's not being gushy. That's hard science.

Attachment

Attachment is a "stick-together" relationship—a strong desire to be with each other. The research evidence grows and grows—babies need a strong attachment to someone in order to reach their full potential. Loving reassurance from a distance isn't enough to build that attachment. The younger they are, the more it has to be touch and holding and interaction. Lots and lots of touch and holding and interaction. You can give an older child a torch and verbal reassurance. A younger child gets his reassurance from being with you. The youngest of all get their reassurance from lots of touch, not lullabies. And it happens automatically when a mother nurtures her baby at her breast.

> The newborn baby will have only three demands. They are warmth in the arms of its mother, food from her breasts, and security in the knowledge of her presence. Breastfeeding satisfies all three.—Grantly Dick-Read, MD

"Attachment parenting" gets a bad press in some parenting books. But in scientific circles (and in La Leche League philosophy), parenting to promote attachment has long been considered the basic building block of emotionally secure children and adults.[13] Study after study is finding that being attached to your baby is the most important thing you can do for his lifelong emotional health.[14] That close emotional connection tunes your right brain and your baby's right brain into each other in wordless synchrony.[15]

Attunement

Attunement is a "read-your-mind" relationship in which you and your baby move smoothly in step. You interact when he's feeling social, and you stop when he's had too much. You meet his needs without questioning his reasons. You respond quickly and with love: "I understand what you need and I'm here to help you with it."

Because your baby's brain isn't fully developed at first—because he uses only the emotion side of his brain—his actual *thinking* is very basic. Sophisticated ideas like "later" and "soon" are beyond him. His needs are immediate and intense. Once a need is met, whatever it is, it goes away, at least for a while, but an unmet need just keeps on needing, even growing over time. When you "read his mind", you take care of his needs until he can take care of his own.

A baby's thinking may not be well developed at first, but he's born with more brain cells and more potential nerve pathways than he'll ever use.[16] Within the first few years, he lays down emotion-related pathways that he'll rely on for life. It's a little like wearing down smooth paths in a field. The more those pathways are used, the easier they are to use. Some of the unused brain cells actually disappear, so there's a tendency for us to continue to use the well-established pathways from our earliest years. If we come from a stressful, uncertain background, we're more prone to stress as adults. A calm, confident adult is more likely to have had an attentive mother figure.[17]

Babies are no more manipulative in seeking warmth, breastfeeding, and emotional connection than an adult is in seeking a heat source, dinner, and friendship. Mothers are no more wishy-

Dr. Nils Bergman and his wife, Jill, have great resources to help parents and lactation professionals understand the neuroscience of newborn attachment and ways to help it happen more easily (you'll read more about their work in Chapter 18).

kangaroomothercare.com

goo.gl/wMKLE8

Grow Your Baby's Brain (DVD)

Hold Your Premie (book or DVD)

Other good references:

Gentle Birth, Gentle Mothering by Sarah Buckley

The Science of Parenting by Margot Sunderland

washy in "giving in" to a baby's needs than a friend is wishy-washy in giving you a hug when you're feeling down. Mother, friend—we're just responding in a normal way with ancient and effective interpersonal skills.

Bedsharing and attunement flow naturally together for a breastfeeding mother and baby. The mother who is in tune with her baby and feels as if he's an extension of herself is less likely to feel comfortable putting him aside just because it's night. She'll want him with her, maybe *especially* because it's night.

Imagine your first night living with your partner and saying, "Sweetie, you sleep in that bed over there and I'll sleep in this one over here. I can get out of bed sometimes and come to you, but we mustn't fall asleep touching. I'll just bite the inside of my cheek to keep myself awake while we're together." Unnatural, illogical, uncomfortable, and sleep-depriving. The synchrony that you and your baby have built up during the day gets pulled apart if you're kept apart during the night.[18]

Now look at how bedsharing works. Your baby starts to stir, which moves you to a slightly higher level of consciousness. When he starts wiggling and rooting for a snack, you're already on your way to responding. Or maybe *you* start to stir because your breasts are overfull, and bringing *him* towards your breast brings him to a little higher level of consciousness. Neither of you wakes up completely. You roll together, breastfeed, and the hormones you both release help ease you both back to sleep. You rouse a little later on, rub your lips on the top of his head, and adjust your covers and his.

He rouses a little, tips his head back to feel your breath, and settles down with a sigh. And so it goes through the night—a little unconscious dance that weaves through your shared sleep. In the morning, you can't count the number of feeds (neither can your partner) and you have no idea that you checked her temperature umpteen times. There's a lovely video clip of this mother-baby dance in another species at i.imgur.com/NzpcK.gif.

Bedsharing and attunement

That unconscious monitoring, all within your protective cuddle curl, is the reason Dr. James McKenna, an expert on mother-baby shared sleep, considers breastfeeding a prerequisite for bedsharing, and bedsharing a way to support breastfeeding.[19] You'll learn more about normal sleep, yours and your baby's, in the next chapter. But it's pretty obvious that responsible bedsharing reinforces all the good feelings and trust and synchrony that you two are developing.

Dr. McKenna has collected many stories from mothers whose baby's seizure disorder, apnoea, near-SIDS event, fever, or other nighttime problem was discovered through the "radar system" of attunement: mothers waking to silence or stillness or a slightly different breathing rhythm or temperature—things that they couldn't have noticed if their baby hadn't been right there.[20] We've heard many similar stories from mothers through the years.

Does Bedsharing Take Attunement Too Far?

Bedsharing is the norm in cultures as diverse as India, Japan, and Guatemala. In one study, Mayan mothers in Guatemala were shocked to learn that American babies and toddlers are expected to sleep alone. These bedsharing mothers reported no sleep problems in their children. They also said their own sleep wasn't interrupted because they breastfed without waking up.[21] In the United States, subcultures that tend to bedshare are less likely to report

Wrong Focus Leads to Wrong Results

Most of the infant sleep research is based on *abnormal* sleep because it looks at babies sleeping alone in cribs—babies whose breathing, heart rate, temperature, and sleep patterns are disrupted because they don't have their mothers nearby.[23]

sleep problems in their children.[22] And the mothers get more sleep too.

Here are the results of some studies that have looked at the long-term outcomes of "co-sleeping", which usually referred to bed-sharing. The studies were originally written as if separate sleep was the norm—bedsharing children had "higher self-esteem", for instance. We've reworded the results to reflect the normality of the original human sleeping arrangement:

- Children who never bedshared were harder to control, were less happy, had more tantrums, and didn't handle stress as well.[24]
- They had higher cortisol (stress hormone) levels at 12 months.[25]
- They were less self-reliant at tasks such as dressing themselves and had a harder time making friends on their own than children who had bedshared from an early age.[26]
- Children who were never allowed to bedshare were more fearful and less happy than children who always slept in their parents' bed.[27]
- The non-bedsharers had lower self-esteem.[28]
- Another study also found lower self-esteem in women who had never bedshared in childhood.[29]
- Children who slept alone tended to have lower cognitive competence scores at age six.[30]
- Children who had *not* bedshared were more likely to have needed counselling than those who had bedshared.[31]
- And here's a sad one: at five weeks, the baby who's been sleeping alone responds to a simple bath with greater stress than the one who's been bedsharing.[32]

These were all small studies. But they come from numerous countries and populations, and they found over and over that there's *no emotional or developmental downside to bedsharing*. That's true for older children, too! You'll find an equally amazing list at the beginning of Chapter 17. The take-home message? Do what feels right for you and your family.

Krystal (see below) went through the whole melting-into-motherhood process, starting from a disruptive birth and left-brained approach to breastfeeding and bedsharing, then falling fully and finally in love. Breastfeeding, attachment, bedsharing, attunement. Their story was unique to them, but some version of it plays out night after night, whenever those magnets snap together.

When I got pregnant unexpectedly, I went through lots of different emotions—anger, fear, joyfulness. I was an emotional mess. I never felt connected to my pregnancy. I approached pregnancy, motherhood, and parenting logically and not emotionally.

Everything about Eleazar's birth went wrong. When he was finally born, I extended my hands and whispered his name, but my hands were left holding nothing but air. A nurse had swooped him away. Nearly three hours later I finally held my son in my arms, only he wasn't mine, not in my heart. I looked at this alien creature bundled up in a blanket, ointment on his eyes, and a little blue striped hat on his head, and all I wanted to do was give him to someone else to hold.

At home, Eleazar slept in a Moses basket by my bedside. Like clockwork, I woke every two hours to breastfeed him, burp him, change a nappy, and put him back inside his basket. One night this creature wouldn't stop crying. Every time I put him down, he screamed. I didn't know what to do, so I brought him to bed; he latched on, and we fell into a deep sleep for five hours. When I woke up, he was completely safe and snuggled near my heart. After that, we slept cradled to each other, but this still didn't feel like my child. Then one morning in bed, he looked up at me with his big beautiful eyes and smiled. And I looked into his eyes and for the first time was able to tell my son, "I love you." I believe if I hadn't breast-

> fed him, if I had kept him at a distance at night, I would never have grown to love Eleazar the way I do now.
>
> —Krystal

If you haven't been living a life of pure and perfect attachment and attunement, have you failed your child? Of course not. We all do best with little stresses in our lives. Not big ones, just the day-to-day glitches and goofs that make us human. Research shows that our children are most resilient if we (1) love them to pieces in a way that shows in our behaviour,[33] and (2) aren't perfect.[34] Doing your best, and doing it with love made tangible, is exactly what we're built for, and it's not just good enough. It's exactly right.

Something to Sleep On

From their first moments, our babies help us fall in love with them, and breastfeeding can make it happen more easily. It helps ensure that we'll care for them and keep them with us where they are safest. Our responsiveness—our *attachment*—to them protects them and even helps them build and protect their own food supply. Our *attunement* to those needs—the way we sense them and respond to them day and night, especially to their signs of distress—guides their emotional development now and for the rest of their lives.

Our immature babies don't have much choice in how they behave. But we mothers, with our fully developed brains, can *choose* our behaviours. Our brilliant little still-developing babies, who are helpless without us, count on us to choose well. We're not just filling their stomachs; we're feeding their souls. And our own.

chapter 4

Normal Sleep

> A human infant is biologically designed to sleep next to its mother's body and to breastfeed intermittently throughout the night, at least for the first year of its life. . . . [N]othing a human neonate [newborn] can do or cannot do makes sense except in light of the mother's body.
>
> —James McKenna, PhD, director, Mother-Baby Behavioral Sleep Lab, University of Notre Dame, and Lee Gettler, BA[1]

Most babies don't "sleep like a baby", which is why some 30 to 60 per cent of new parents in North America seek help from their paediatricians in solving their baby's "sleep problems,"[2] even though it's usually normal behaviour. But when it comes to disrupted nights, normal can be a nightmare. Here's the science behind what's going on, which is a start towards finding a solution.

Why Do We Sleep?

Almost all animals, right down to insects, sleep. But sleeping seems to mean different things for different species. Some sea mammals and birds can sleep with only half of their brain so that the other half can keep watch for predators. Most mammals sleep more in childhood, but some, including certain whales and dolphins, don't sleep at all until they're older.[3]

We humans organize and cement our memories during sleep.[4] We heal better and faster during sleep,[5] it helps us fight off illnesses,[6] and it helps our babies' brains develop.[7] Without sleep, we quickly lose our ability to think clearly or rationally. We become irritable, more emotional, even depressed.[8] We can't remember things as well.[9] Our bodies ache, we have less energy, and our reflexes and reaction times are slowed. Weight gain and certain diseases are more likely when we don't get enough sleep.[10] So, yes, sleep is important, and we're not happy or even healthy when we don't get enough.

Normal Sleep for Adults

When people ask, "How is your baby sleeping?" they're really asking how *you're* doing. Normally, babies manage to get enough sleep one way or another. Because we mothers are usually the ones on both the day shift and the night shift, we're often the ones with the sleep issues. So, what's normal for us?

As adults, we seem to need somewhere between seven and nine hours of sleep, moving in and out of various stages throughout the night—awake, REM, and Stages 1–4. In Stage 1 (light sleep) our eyes open and close slowly and we gradually lose touch with reality. This is the stage where we may give a sudden jerk, as if we're about to fall off a cliff or step into a hole. We enter Stage 1 only on our way to and from full consciousness at either end of the night and any time that we waken fully during the night and fall back to sleep.

In Stage 2, we completely lose awareness. We spend roughly half our night's sleep in repeated short stretches of this dreamless, unaware state. We may snore, but we're reasonably alert if we're wakened.

In Stages 3 and 4 (deep sleep), we're susceptible to mindless actions like sleepwalking, bed-wetting, and night terrors (as opposed to nightmares, which happen in story form when we dream). Deep sleep is associated with memory consolidation, healing, and recovery from the day's activities. If we're wakened fully from the deep sleep of Stages 3 and 4, we're groggy, disoriented, and just not ourselves.

From that deepest sleep, we tend to rouse only enough to enter the rapid-eye-movement (REM) stage of sleep, which is just this side of waking up. Our eyes dart back and forth underneath our closed eyelids, as if we're watching a scene. Maybe we are. We dream during our REM stages, though researchers haven't yet figured out the reason for dreaming. Those dreams in which you try and try to run but you just can't? It may be because we really do lose our ability to control our movements during REM sleep. If you're sitting up, your head drops forwards or an arm slides from your lap. You go limp. We're more likely to move into this stage when and where we feel safe and comfortable.

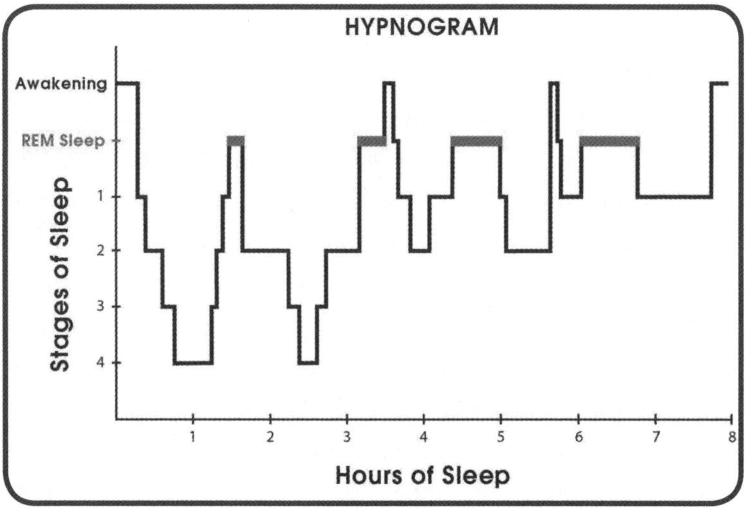

Normal adult sleep stages through the night

We dream for a while without necessarily rousing fully, then slide down again into sounder sleep. That first full cycle of sleep, from being awake into deep sleep and then through our first stretch of REM sleep, tends to last about an hour and a half. We cycle a few more times through the night, and wake up briefly at least a couple of times whether we remember it or not. Towards dawn we tend to have slightly longer cycle lengths and spend more time—a quarter of the night overall—in REM sleep. In the morning we may tell our partner, "I had the strangest dream last night," usually remembered from that last bit of REM just before we woke up.

Those periods of light sleep are when we're likely to rouse gently on our own. Alarm clocks don't respect our sleep cycles and can jangle us awake from the deepest of sleeps. Not fun. Not fun in the form of a crying baby either. Hang on to that thought.

Our levels of melatonin and our body temperature are linked to the rhythm of our days and nights.[11] Melatonin is a sleep-encouraging hormone that's low during the day, higher at night. One of melatonin's effects is to decrease body temperature,[12] and sure enough, our temperature drops through the night and is higher during the day. That change is evidence that we have our days and nights straightened out. Hang on to that thought too.

Now we're going to disrupt this scientific description of normal adult sleep, because the truth is, it's not normal.

Why "Normal" Isn't Normal

Western cultures probably haven't experienced normal sleep patterns for 200 years. That's because our natural sleep patterns developed when day and night shaded gradually into each other, long before the invention of bright gas and electric lights.

Darkness averages 12 hours a day over the course of the year everywhere on earth. So what did we do during those long, dark hours? Based on today's hunter-gatherer cultures and early European writings, we didn't just sleep. We began our long and leisurely night with what Charles Dickens and others called "first sleep," followed by a couple of hours during which we were awake—musing, talking quietly, making love, recording deep thoughts, even getting up and doing housework or taking a walk—and then slipping into a "second sleep" until dawn. The pattern was so well understood, so expected, that by the mid-1700s several devices had been

> Never was there a worse swindle perpetrated on humanity than that which asserts that when a man wakes from his first sleep he ought to get up [for the day].
> —Philadelphia *Record*, 1884

invented for writing in the dark so we wouldn't lose the calm, organized, fleeting thoughts that the interlude seems to have promoted.[13]

That's the kind of night our biology is still geared for. In a recent experiment that removed all artificial light, the participants slept "normally" at first. Over time they developed a pattern of two stretches of sleep each night, with a couple of hours of quiet awake time in the middle. And then they began to look forward to that private time.[14] As a *New York Times* writer recently pointed out, "Doctors who peddle sleep aid products and call for more sleep may unintentionally reinforce the idea that there is something wrong or off-kilter about interrupted sleep cycles."[15]

Those of us who have middle-of-the-night insomnia—or babies—can take enormous comfort from our two-sleep biology. Whether we're new mothers or great-grandmothers, we don't *need* to sleep in an unbroken eight-hour chunk. We just need to set aside enough time overall. (See Chapter 10 for ways to carve out extra time.)

Normal Sleep for Postpartum Breastfeeding Mothers

When you are breastfeeding, the quality of your sleep after your baby is born depends a lot on whether or not your baby sleeps next to you. Most people (who haven't slept with babies) assume that parents get more sleep with a baby tucked nicely into a cot across the room. It's true that when a breastfeeding mother sleeps with her baby she tends to wake up more often than she would otherwise. But she also spends more time in deep sleep—the kind of sleep that helps with memory and helps our brains recover from the day's activities.[16] It turns out that *the bedsharing, exclusively breastfeeding mother gets the most sleep of all new mothers.*[17] You'll read more below about why the new bedsharing mother, even though she may not be well rested, is actually in better shape than her next-door neighbour whose new baby is in a cot.

Normal Newborn Sleep: The Importance of Sleeping Together

Bedsharing continues a connection that the two of you have shared right from the start. Before your baby's brain started to develop, sleep wasn't an issue. As she grew, she began to spend most of her time in a sort of twilight state, neither awake nor asleep. During your third trimester, she began having REM and non-REM sleep. Not mature, but recognizable. And she varied those budding sleep states according to the time of day. Not because she was terribly good at it herself but because *you* were ever-present. Your heart rate, stress levels, body temperature cycles, and daily activities sent ongoing signals to her that helped her develop the beginnings of her own circadian (daily) rhythms.[18]

That intimate and automatic sleep connection ended with your baby's first breath. Now she's on her own, but she's still way too immature to structure her sleep without you. So she relies on you to be her "sleep architect". You help her build more mature sleep patterns by keeping her in touch, literally, with your own sleeping body.[19]

The World Health Organization and breastfeeding experts talk about the "mother-baby dyad". A mother and baby are two-people-but-one-person before the baby is born, and if they're breastfeeding they continue to be an "inseparable biological and social unit" after the cord is cut.[20] Your baby shares your immune system. Your milk production responds to his growth pattern and age. His heart rate, breathing, and temperature are steadied by direct contact with you.[21] When he lies against you, feeling your warmth and heartbeat, he sleeps more calmly.[22]

Most sleep researchers agree that mothers and babies should sleep "in sensory proximity"—within sight and sound of each other—through the early months, when SIDS risk is at its highest.[23] Many would say within arm's reach. If you're farther apart, you can't influence each other as well.[24] In fact, more than eight inches (20 cm) away and your baby doesn't get the bursts of carbon dioxide that your breathing provides that may help stimulate his own breathing.[25]

Dr. James McKenna and his colleagues recorded waking episodes for mothers and babies during both bedsharing and separate sleep. When you and your baby share a bed, you tend to rouse each other gently with your breathing and rustlings. You actually synchronize your wakings[26]—a big part of why waking to a bedsharing baby is so much gentler than waking to a crying baby in a cot. And your little movements and noises help keep him from dropping into a deeper sleep than his immature nervous system can lift him from reliably and safely.[27]

When your baby rouses, it isn't necessarily to full waking. On your chest or lying beside you, he might search for your nipple, breastfeed, and let go, all without opening his eyes. That means that once you have any breastfeeding bugs sorted out and have worked out how to breastfeed lying down, neither of you has to wake up all the way to breastfeed.

Will your bedsharing baby wake up more often than the baby alone in a cot? Almost certainly.[28] Is that a good thing? Absolutely. The bedsharing baby's sleep patterns are normal infant patterns. Nothing wrong with them at all!

These two charts show the heart and breathing rates of a premature baby alone and on his mother's chest. It works pretty much the same for full-term babies:

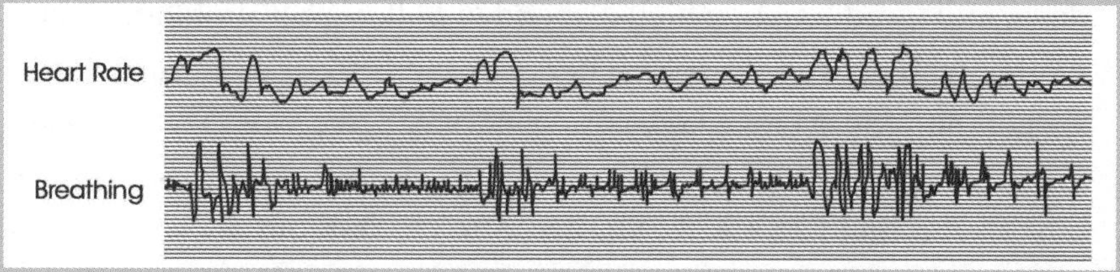

A premature baby alone in an incubator—note the ragged heart rate and breathing

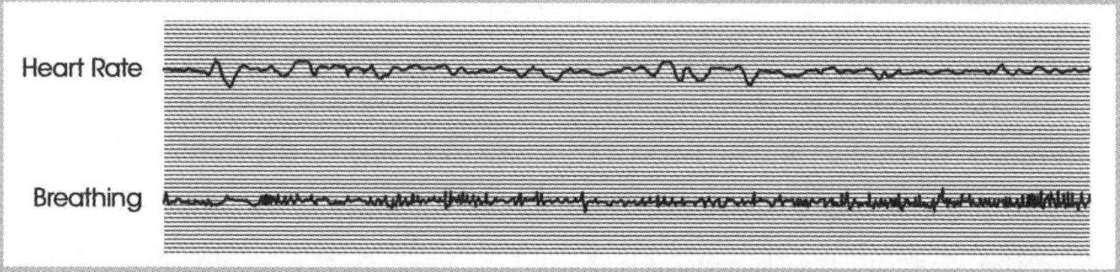

Here's the same premature baby on his mother's sloping chest, his skin against hers, while she leans comfortably back

It doesn't take a medical degree to see that a mother—no matter what her background or education or income is—does more for her baby just sitting still than the highest-tech, most expensive incubator can do.

> When my second son was a few months old, the health visitor asked me how often he woke up at night. I stared at her while I tried to figure it out. Finally I said, "I have no idea," and thought about how right that answer was. The health visitor must have thought so too, because she just smiled and moved on.
>
> —Linnea

A breastfeeding mother who sleeps *without* her baby doesn't wake up as often as a bedsharing mother does, because her baby doesn't breastfeed as often.[29] But she can't sense her baby's early hunger cues, so she may be forced out of deep sleep by his cries. It's like an alarm clock going off several times a night. She has to wake up more completely in order to get out of bed, go to the baby, calm him down (because he had to fuss or cry to get her attention), and go somewhere to breastfeed. That's a lot of middle-of-the-night disturbance, and it's likely to take her longer to fall asleep again. The longer intervals between feeds are a signal to her breasts to slow down milk production, which can end in milk supply problems. The mother who doesn't sleep with her baby tends to stop breastfeeding sooner than the average bedsharing mother.[30] She's also more prone to postnatal depression.[31] She may go to sleep faster at the beginning of the night and wake up less often.[32] But she doesn't get as much rest. And breastfeeding is less likely to go well.

Separate sleep, formula-feeding, and stomach-sleeping don't "help a baby sleep better". They all suppress his normal and healthy arousal pattern. One theory that's gaining some traction is that not being able to rouse normally may be one of the causes of SIDS.[33] You'll read more about the consequences of solitary sleep in Chapter 18.

Bedsharing mothers have it easier. There's no sense of anxiety about where the baby is or whether he's breathing. Your chick is in the nest. You're not being jarred awake. You don't have to be vigilant about *staying* awake, so you can drift off whenever you feel sleepy. Even if you have to sit up to breastfeed easily, your bare feet never have to hit the bare floor. The snuggly feeling of having your baby in your arms and nuzzling that wonderful fuzzy head is delicious. It's like having your own personal teddy bear.

One of the best parts of bedsharing is the ability to take care of your baby in your sleep (literally!). Without being fully conscious, you may adjust his covers, move him closer or further away or up or down, stroke his back, and put your lips on his head. You become attuned to his presence, tending him instinctively and well.

There's nothing like waking up to your baby's beautiful eyes looking at you as if you're the centre of the universe. It can melt your heart and reassure you that you're doing this "mothering thing" just fine. And, of course, as your baby's sleep pattern begins to mature,[34] your own sleep will become less fragmented, right in step with your baby's pattern.

If you find that you're so aware of your tiny baby next to you in bed that you can't relax enough to sleep well, give it a chance. That anxiety tends to fade after a week or two.

Sleep Positions

Like all baby mammals, human babies are most secure and competent when their chests are supported. Mothers instinctively bring a crying baby to their own chest in that chest-to-chest position, and babies are almost instantly at least a little calmer. And from that position, they can even push themselves over to their mother's breast. Chest-down on a sloping surface, with head higher than bottom, is a low-stress position for newborns. It's the position that many newborns sleep best in: on their mother's chest.

So why is it considered dangerous to lay a baby tummy-down in a cot for sleep? Look at the differences. The baby on his mother's chest is angled, head higher than bottom. Pressure on his chest is reduced, his airway is clear, and he gets constant stimulation from the rise and fall of her chest and the sound of her breathing.

Babies didn't sleep prone alone until adults started making them sleep alone. It's a very unnatural position for infants. They do wake less often and rouse less easily when they're chest-down alone, which is exactly why it was recommended years ago. But that also may be what makes the position risky for vulnerable babies. We just don't know.

Sorting Out Day and Night

Normal newborn sleep involves short cycles, day and night. And that's a good thing. She's about to grow faster than she ever will again. She's going to do it with the smallest stomach and shortest intestines she'll ever have (think about how gastric bypass surgery makes it harder to gain weight). And breastfeeding provides quickly digestible milk that requires frequent feed—lower in fat than the milk of most species, but very high in brain food.

All of this means that your newborn, who received food constantly and automatically before birth, needs to eat really often now. She's a fast-paced growth factory that has to keep the furnaces going 24/7 in order to run smoothly. She may need more *total* sleep than you do, but even if she's glued to your body, she can't afford long stretches of sleep. She literally doesn't have time for them. So she cycles, all day and all night. It's her full-time job, her lifeline, and she's going to need to refuel about every two hours at first.[35]

Some young babies spend as much as 19 hours asleep each day (in short segments), while others spend as little as 9 hours.[36] Sometimes they totally conk out and stay asleep for several hours. Sometimes they'll cluster their feeds—feed, quick break, feed, quick break, feed, longer sleep. It may be a normal pattern, but it's spread just about equally between day and night, and it's not predictable. At least not at first.

In the early weeks, your baby may have one (count 'em, one) "long" stretch, maybe even at night. If you get a long sleep stretch, expect feeds to bunch together at some other time of the day. In fact, expect more breastfeeding overall than you were probably told to expect—8 to 12 times a day is a *minimum,* not an average. When it comes to breastfeeding frequency, most baby care books are wishful thinking.

Your newborn's sleep cycles aren't just shorter than your own typical sleep cycles; they're just plain *different.* Your baby's body temperature doesn't fall at night the way yours does—part of the evidence that her 24/7 factory truly can't distinguish between day and night at first.[37] Her sleep stages are simpler. She spends more time in active sleep (light and REM-like) than you do. She also has periods of quiet sleep, especially when she's in physical contact with you, when a lot of vital brain development takes place.[38]

Every day your baby's breastfeeding efficiency improves, her stomach grows, and her intestines lengthen—developments that help her eat, store, and process food more efficiently. Sometime between about six weeks and three to four months, most babies begin the process of "sleep consolidation", running two or more sleep cycles together to give themselves (and you) a longer chunk of sleep.[39] Though, of course, the first longer stretches may occur during the day rather than at night. By the time babies begin to consolidate their sleep, their temperature has also begun to drop at night, a sign that their circadian rhythm is maturing.[40]

So babies don't "have their days and nights mixed up". They just can't sleep for long stretches, day or night. By three months, about 70 per cent of babies have begun to consolidate their nighttime sleep, though about half of those revert at some point—two steps forwards, one step back.[41]

The sorting-out process is a major neurological shift that continues for some months. There isn't much you can do to hurry or change this process. Sleep consolidation is all about a baby's unique developmental rhythm and timetable. Sleep training carries significant risk (see Chapter 18) and won't speed up the process, although it can make the baby stop signalling that he's awake. In fact, at a year, about half of all babies are still waking regularly at night.[42] What exactly does "sleeping through the night" mean? We asked some families:

- About eight-ish to five-ish.—Michelle, USA
- When my partner doesn't know the baby woke up. —Therese, Hong Kong
- My baby staying asleep when I want to be asleep. —Dawn, USA
- I suppose I don't really think too much about "sleeping through the night". As long as everybody gets the rest they need somehow, it doesn't matter to me when it happens. —Trevor, Canada
- I haven't slept through the night in years.—Ger, grandmother in Ireland

There's no standard definition for sleeping through the night. Most research studies consider it to be sleeping—brace yourself—from midnight to 5.00 a.m., or for a mere five-hour stretch at any time of night.[43] So you'll be telling the truth if you say your baby slept through the night. It was just a short night.

Sleep consolidation isn't a switch we can flip or a programme we can load, and some nights are better than others. An exciting day, new skill, growth spurt, or stuffy nose can make nights more wakeful and breastfeeding more frequent. If there wasn't much napping on Thursday, it's possible that there will be more sleep Thursday night. Longer naps Friday? Maybe less sleep Friday night. Illness? Probably some broken sleep for a while. Think stock market charts over the long haul: peaks and valleys with a generally upward trend (hopefully), and it's not always possible to figure out what caused a particular peak or valley. And then, of course, the clocks change or you go away for the weekend, and you and your still-adjusting baby have to readjust his adjustments. Sigh.

Normal Sleep in Childhood

Through the early years, it's still very normal for children to wake up and need their parents.

Some night waking is still the norm through the preschool years.[44] They might wake up, but they are better at settling themselves back to sleep without help from an adult. And so it goes. Night sleep gets longer, the number of naps drops to zero, and by the time your baby is a teenager, you'll probably have to drag him out of bed in the morning. It's a normal process, and anything normal goes in fits and starts.

But just because children sleep better with their parents doesn't mean parents don't have questions and concerns. Is sharing a bed with your child going to make him gay? Is it tempting incest? No. Our culture confuses sleep and sex. The separate issues of sexual identity, family dysfunction, and criminal activity have nothing to do with babies and children sleeping securely with their parents. Will it hurt your marriage or your sex life? As one mother put it, "Good sex is about more than beds." Will your child ever leave your bed? Of course, and that's guaranteed, whether you encourage it or

> Javier is eighteen months old and a "bad sleeper". Every night he calls to his mother, Maria, asking for a story, for a drink of water, anything, and it has become an ordeal for the whole family. They all say: "Just let him cry; there's nothing wrong with him."
>
> Today, Maria and Javier have gone to visit a remote village. [They] are the only people to get off the bus in the deserted bus station at one-thirty at night. Mother and child find themselves alone in the poorly lit waiting room. At about three o'clock, five leather-jacketed bikers appear. They begin drinking beer, shouting and fighting. This goes on for an hour and a half. Needless to say, Maria spends the long hours awake clinging to her son and their luggage. Javier, on the other hand, spends the whole time asleep in her arms. Which of them is the "bad sleeper" now? In his mother's arms, in a remote town surrounded by intimidating strangers, Javier feels safer than he does in his own house, in his own room, in his own cot. For a child of that age, mum is Supermum, the Invincible Protectress. Her lap is his home, his country, his Eden. —Carlos González, in *Kiss Me! How to Raise Your Children with Love*, Pinter & Martin

not. Chapter 21 will explain further and help you address criticisms you may get about these issues.

Something to Sleep On

The practice that comes naturally to both you and your child—sleeping together—doesn't just feel good. It's normal. And normal never has to defend itself. That means that anyone who insists that a mother and baby sleep apart needs to establish that separation is *better* than normal. Part V, "Sleep Science", goes over the lack of solid evidence for keeping mothers and babies apart. We hope you'll find it reassuring.

part three

Sleep and Bedsharing Practicalities

chapter 5

Naps

> It's easy to say, "Just put your napping baby in a sling and go about your day; nothing could be simpler!" But it was *not* that simple. My babies are big to begin with and get bigger fast. Elliott, my second baby, couldn't tolerate the sling any higher than his shoulders, I think because he needed to feel he could pull away easily if my milk came too fast. So I put the bottom three-quarters of his body in the sling and supported his shoulders with my hand. That meant I never had more than one hand free, though.
>
> As Elliott reached about six months, I was able to breastfeed him to sleep and creep away for periods. I couldn't nap with Elliott all the time the way I had with Graham. But now I get in a little bit of what I need (some exercise, a chance to prepare dinner) and Graham and I get to read or play. I think it doesn't work to treat all napping babies the same—age, personality, and other children are huge factors.
>
> —Laura

And here you thought naps would be simple. Maybe you expected that your baby would breastfeed, get a nappy change, and then sleep peacefully for a predictable couple of hours while you lived your adult life. That's what we see on TV, and maybe it *will* be that way at some point, but probably not at the beginning.

First, let's define "nap." At the start, you and your baby might have different definitions. Most people would say your baby's nap is any time he sleeps during the day. But what would your newborn's definition be?

Little Babies, Little Naps

"Naps, nights, what's the difference?" If your newborn could talk, that's what he'd have to say about sleep. As you read in Chapter 4, it's not that he has his days and nights mixed up; he just doesn't *have* any days or nights. He just sleeps when he sleeps, so you might as well roll with it.

The upside is that breastfeeding *helps* you do that, because of the calming, sleep-inducing breastfeeding hormones that kick in for both of you when you breastfeed (see Chapter 3). Feeds in the early days often lead to naps for him and either rest or sleep for you. In fact, breastfeeding's tendency to make your baby mellow and drowsy is likely to become one of your best mothering tools. Fussy baby? Try breastfeeding. Want to talk with friends or eat supper uninterrupted? Try breastfeeding. Want to put your feet up for a while? Try breastfeeding. Want to get your baby to sleep? Try breastfeeding. Want to take a nap yourself? Try breastfeeding! Breastfeeding and naps and your own rest are hardwired to go together, and they don't have to start with your baby being extra hungry. Freewheeling breastfeeding and the relaxation that follows are just the nature of things. The system has worked well for billions and billions of mothers and babies.

Of course, it's harder to roll with it if you're dealing with breastfeeding problems and maybe having to express or supplement or both. But with help and a good plan, feeding your baby gets easier. Most breastfeeding mothers find that breastfeeding—and nights, and mothering—go from survivable to doable to enjoyable. It just takes time. If you can accept the normality of your newborn's patterns, and if you can listen to your baby and not your clock or your older sister, motherhood almost always gets to be a whole lot more fun.

Just knowing "the wide range of normal" can help. With my first, everyone was telling me that it wasn't normal for him to not be able to nap alone. I was worried and felt like I was doing something "wrong". I stopped telling anyone how my baby napped, and I felt inadequate and odd for taking three naps a day with my baby when (I imagined) the other mothers were up and doing their nails! During our won't-nap-without-you days with baby number two, I knew that his brother had done exactly the same thing and that he *had* eventually napped on his own.

—Marian

Baby on Your Body

You know from Chapter 3 that your body is everything to your newborn. He may be *able* to sleep without you, but he'll be most stable and relaxed if he's in physical contact with you.

In these early days, the easiest way for both of you to get enough rest is to make sleep as simple as possible. Simple, to your baby, is in your arms. Or on your chest. Or in a carrier that you wear that keeps him snuggled against you. Touching you means total security and easier sleep. And when things go more easily for your baby, they go more easily for you.

Napping hands free and securely on a sofa

There's more. You've seen your newborn curl his legs up and bring his arms in. It's called a *fetal tuck,* and it's the natural position for newborns. Upright is natural too. So where is your baby most likely to be in his healthiest, calmest position? On your chest, held either by your hands or by a wearable wrap, sling or babycarrier. And when is he least able to get into that neurologically normal position? When he's swaddled.

Holding Your Newborn Through Naps

It's your right and privilege to hold your baby as much as you want, and it does only good things for both of you. Spoiling? Can't happen at this age, neurologically, biologically, or emotionally. So go ahead and enjoy your baby. You'll remember those quiet times together much more fondly than you'll remember how many emails and texts you answered.

In fact, part of "melting into motherhood" is just *watching* your baby. So try this: sit on the sofa with your baby asleep tummy-down on your chest, then move your bottom forwards so you're slouched back like you're watching television after a hard day. Your baby's weight is *solidly* on your chest. Because babies like to have their front supported, he'll probably sleep happily there, and you'll have at least one of your hands free to stroke his back and play with his feet (or use the remote). Shift his position or yours whenever you want to. He'll almost certainly stay asleep so long as you don't take him off your chest.

It can be delicious to watch your own baby sleep. His eyelids flicker now and then. Every so often he has a fleeting smile, maybe followed by a chuckle. Those "butterfly smiles" that flit gently across his face aren't gas. They mean he's at peace with the world, relaxed and certain of your presence. Smell the top of his head. It's your milk that makes him smell that way. Feel his hands (oh, if you could bottle that silkiness!) and play with his toes. Feel your own body relax, because you know *he's* content . . . and you get some time to rest and chill. Of course, getting *toooo* comfortable can make you dozy. We know. We've all been there.

If you're truly sleep-deprived, you're better off taking your baby to your Safe Sleep Seven bed for a shared nap. But when you're just feeling dozy, try leaning back a little more, so that gravity holds your baby firmly against your chest. For extra security, you can even use a wearable carrier. Or breastfeed first, with the carrier loose around you both. When she's finished breastfeeding and you're getting drowsy, ease her upright onto your chest and snug the carrier around you both.

What about the warning not to sleep with your baby on a sofa? When you and your baby are *both* upright and you're leaning back chest to chest, you have a "friction fit" that creates a pretty effective alarm system if he starts to slide. It's different when either you or your baby is lying down in a horizontal position. Even if *you're* upright, falling asleep with the baby lying horizontally on your lap (or on a breastfeeding pillow) can cause you to slump forward onto the baby, or he could roll off your lap to the floor or a crevice in the sofa. And lying down to sleep with him on a sofa may put you both on a squishy surface with gaps and crevices. But upright, leaning back, solid friction fit? It can be bliss.

> From very early on, our son has had every single nap on my chest or my partner's. I hated trying to put him down, sneaking away to practise my violin (I'm a musician), and then dashing upstairs to him when he cried. For now, I've given up practising violin, but I don't mind. It just wasn't the right thing to try to do around a young baby. I know I'll get back to it at some point. These days we write and read during his naps because we can do those things while we hold him. Our house isn't as clean as it was, but nobody cares. I believe it's important for a baby to know that someone is right there or very, very close when he or she wakes up.
>
> —Ian

Naps in Partners' and Grandparents' Arms

If you want a break, other willing, loving arms can be a cosy place for your drowsy and comfortably fed newborn. Most babies love the chest-to-sloping-chest position described above. And it's a triple-bonus position. The baby has a happy snooze with the body contact he craves; the adult, especially a doting partner or a devoted grandparent, will love the cuddle time, rubbing a face against that fuzzy head and fondling those tiny toes; and you get some both-arms-free time. Just make sure Grandma knows to lean back for a solid friction fit, and listen to your hormonal urging to touch base frequently. The other-arms arrangement is probably not going to last beyond the earliest days; willing arms eventually go home or back to work. That's often when mothers start using a babycarrier or sling.

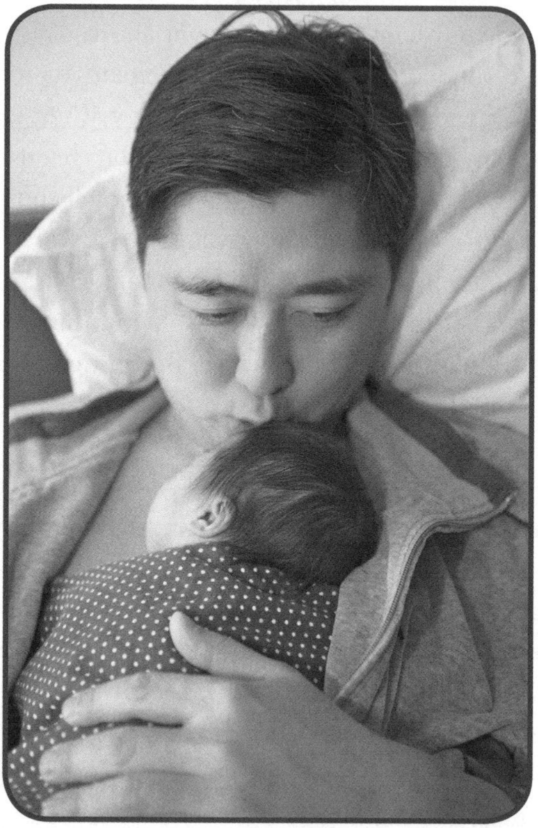

Baby held by a family member when Mama wants a break

Wearing Your Baby for Naps

Indoors or outdoors, when you really need or want to get something done during naps, a *babycarrier*—a sling, wrap, or buckle-on carrier—keeps your baby snuggled close and frees your hands. Many mothers find that babycarriers are so convenient and easy on their backs that they use them instead of the detachable car seat when they get out of the car to run errands. Doors and stairs? No problem. And if you wear the carrier (without the baby) while driving, it saves a step when you get where you're going.

Babycarrier Tips

In any type of carrier, your baby needs to have his head higher than his bottom and his back fairly straight. Carriers that hold your baby upright and chest to chest are probably the hardest to use wrong and tend to be the easiest on your back. A carrier that positions your baby horizontally or slumped sideways below your breasts can curl him so that it's harder for him to breathe, and you may not see or hear his distress. The UK Consortium of Sling Manufacturers and Retailers created an acronym called TICKS,[1] but we think babies are more like CHICKS:

Chin off chest
Held close
In sight
Comfortable
Kissable head height
Straight back

Once he's in place, start moving with the sway and jiggle and patting that come naturally to you. You've probably noticed that your baby's natural reaction to being carried is to relax and settle. A recent study found that when a baby under six months is carried, he reacts very much like a baby mouse being carried by his mother. He settles down. He stops wiggling, he fusses less, and even his heart rate decreases.[2] It makes sense: any mammal baby needs to respond quietly and calmly when his mother moves him around. She's moving her baby for a reason, and the reason may have to do with his survival. How wonderful to know that, as the study points out, "the infant calming response to maternal carrying is a coordinated set of central, motor, and cardiac regulations". In other words, our urge to carry our babies and their response to it are hardwired into us.

Carried babies are more likely to move seamlessly in and out of sleep, without the increasing fussiness they have to use to get our

attention when they're not with us.[3] When they feel you right there, there's one less reason to fuss.

Very young babies usually prefer to be upright in a babycarrier in a fetal tuck, their whole front in contact with the adult's chest. You can stabilize a small baby's head by pulling the sling up to about mid-ear (keeping his face clear). Older babies with total head control may want to ride on your hip or your back, or face the world by sitting cross-legged in a sling or wrap with their back to your front. If you spread the sling's fabric in a wide band across and part way down your shoulder, you'll find it a lot more comfortable. Check commercial carriers for age and weight ranges and positioning tips.

Cold weather? He'll be so toasty in there that just pulling your own coat around him is usually enough.

Are you frustrated that your baby doesn't like the babycarrier you chose? Where's that calming reflex? Give it a little time, try making the carrier a bit looser or a bit snugger, and play with different positions. If that doesn't work, there are tutorials about baby-wearing on YouTube. Be sure to pull the carrier snug enough so you feel completely comfortable going hands-free and moving around. Immediately start to walk, maybe with a gentle bounce, and gently rub or pat your baby's back to help him settle. If it's still not working, check with other mothers for more ideas, look for a Sling Meet in your local area or check out the advice on websites such as babywearing.co.uk, slingguide.co.uk or naturalmamas.co.uk.

If you have a baby with special needs, you may want to check with your doctor, but babywearing is almost always health-promoting and a very, very good idea. It gives your baby important stimulation and emotional closeness and helps him conserve calories. You may need to give extra attention to positioning to make sure your baby stays upright and his chin isn't tucked.

> Huck, who had reflux, took one look at the sling, considered being crunched up in the middle, and thought better of it. He slept for many, many naps in a figure-of-eight wrap, which held him in his "reboot" position—upright with his legs straight.
>
> —Jeanette

This Nap's for You

No matter how well your baby's birth goes, it knocks your body for six and you need time to recover. Most traditional cultures pamper the mother for a full month or more after birth. Our culture tends to step all over a new mother's sleep needs right from the start, with overnight visitors and drop-in visitors, all on top of having to learn how to take care of a baby, breastfeed, and grab the occasional shower. It can run you ragged pretty fast. The old saying "Sleep when the baby sleeps" isn't always a real-world option. But at the very least, in the early days your baby's downtime is your own chance to just plain *rest*.

It takes some headwork to accept that rest and sleep are much more important right now than talking, tweeting, texting, posting, writing thank-you notes, or catching up on house work. But as a new mother, you're fully entitled to say, any time you want, "I really need a nap," and take your baby off with you to a quiet place. So listen to your body, which is telling you to rest and focus on your baby.

For some mothers, naps are easy. Others find they've got out of the habit of napping. They haven't slept during the day for a very long time. Now, suddenly, as a new mother you're *allowed* to rest at odd times . . . and you've forgotten how. And how can you sleep when there is so much to do? Here are some ideas.

Getting Flat

Nothing feels as r-e-a-l-l-y g-o-o-d as getting yourself horizontal when you're exhausted. And the chance for you to do that should come along every couple of hours. When your baby breastfeeds and naps, you can too. Not that you'll always make use of those chances, but the hormones that make *you* sleepy when you breastfeed are very cleverly designed to ease you into resting at the same time and in the same place that your *baby* does. (One mother called these "mandatory naps—there was just nothing I could do about it except fall asleep.")

The simple solution for safe and solid daytime sleep is just to breastfeed in bed when you can. Get comfortable in your already-checked-out Safe Sleep Seven bed (see Chapter 2 for the safe bed-sharing checklists). Lean back against a pillow or curl up on your side, and fall asleep with your baby. Chapter 6 has an explanation of how to breastfeed lying down. If bedsharing is a riskier option for you, you can breastfeed the baby to sleep, oozing him onto a separate surface (see the section below), and lie down somewhere comfy.

Even if you don't fall totally asleep, just being horizontal can go a long way towards reducing sleep debt. So here's a good general rule for new motherhood: don't stand if you can sit, don't sit if you can lie down, and don't just lie down if you can sleep.

But wait! Are you hoping he'll go to sleep so you can get the dishes washed or the laundry folded? It might work better to get those things done while the baby's awake. Try a babycarrier. It isn't just for naps, although it might lead to one.

Oozing

If you want to get out of bed while your baby sleeps, you may want to learn to ooze—another valuable mothering tool for the next few years. It's what you're doing when you slide your please-don't-wake-up baby onto another surface, or when you slide away from him in bed. It's a slow process, but it'll probably save you from having to start all over again with a baby who wakes up crying, "Wait! What? Cool air? New surface? Nooooooo!"

After he's been asleep for a while, lift and gently drop his arm. If it's totally limp, he's probably in a deeper sleep from which he's not likely to waken as easily. If you're already in bed together, you can just ooze him right onto the bed next to you, where he'll feel your body and maybe sleep just as well as if you were holding him. And of course, when you get sleepy yourself you can just ooze right down next to him.

If you're sitting up somewhere and want to lay him down, you might want to start by breastfeeding him with a receiving blanket at his back. Then you ooze him *with* the blanket, so that he still feels that same warm surface against his back and isn't as likely to startle awake. You can ooze him down on the sofa beside you—the easiest option—if you're not at all sleepy and are going to keep sitting there or if you'll be staying very close by. Or you can ooze a young baby onto a blanket on the floor or into a Moses basket (described later in the chapter) and either lie down on the sofa alone or take the basket with you wherever you're headed.

If you want to ooze him from a babycarrier, try bending over a safe surface and slowly transferring his weight to it. Then loosen the fabric and slip him out of the carrier. If all goes well, the baby will stay asleep (with you nearby and with any loose fabric *well* away from his face and head).

Some babies are never fooled by oozing, while some do fine once they're solidly asleep. It's always worth a try! Mothers of toddlers ooze off the bed, one foot at a time like a ninja, and tiptoe from the room, holding their breath.

If you've oozed away from your non-rolling infant on your bed, make sure she's on her back and away from pillows, and stay in the room. Avoid fluffy bedding and make sure your bed is wiggle- and fall-safe. Your baby may be able to roll, slide, squirm, or wiggle to the edge and over it faster than you'd think.

Places to Sit

If you're not a bit sleepy, you're probably just looking for a comfortable place to sit. Something with high arms can be awkward, and a chair with no arms at all can be tiring. Low, padded arms let you position your own arms any way you like. A chair with cushioning behind your lower back, or a pillow strategically placed, will feel good after a long day of bending and lifting.

> I made up two napping spots for myself besides my bed—one in the kitchen and one in the living room. One was a futon mattress that I put on the floor. The other was just two folded blankets, to make a pad for me that wasn't too fluffy for Elisa. I could nap upstairs or downstairs. And when I napped downstairs I could slide away and work in the kitchen or living room and still have her there with me.
>
> —Eva

Separate but Not Solitary

There will come a day when your baby wants to sleep and you have things to do that can't be done even with a babycarrier. That's when having a safe napping spot prepared and ready to go will give you peace of mind while your baby is asleep.

Authorities agree that your baby is safest where you can see and hear her and she can hear you for about the first six months.[4] But does this mean your baby has to be in sight every second? That's where common sense comes in. Having your baby out of sight for just a few minutes is in the same league as being a passenger in a car and unbuckling your seat belt to get something from the backseat. No responsible person would recommend it (we certainly wouldn't). But that small window of time is *vastly* different from not wearing a seat belt at all. Your breastfed baby in a non-smoking household is already at very low risk if the sleeping spot itself is safe and your baby is on his back. Here are some ideas for separate, safe, planned-ahead napping spots.

Floor Naps

Many mothers just lay their napping baby on a blanket or playmat on the floor when they want to get something else done. It may be even easier to lie down on the floor with her, breastfeed her to sleep, and ooze away. The floor is a safe place, assuming there are no large and lumbering pets or young children or other hazards nearby. Just remember to stay in the area, and take your baby's "mobility ability" into account.

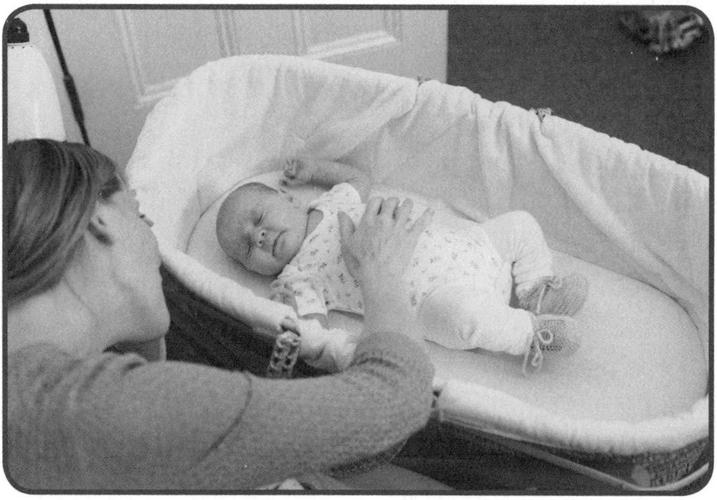

Baby sleeping in a Moses basket

Scoop-and-Go Beds

For the baby under 15 pounds [7 kilograms] or so who can't push himself up yet, consider a baby bed with low sides (no less than about 9 inches [23 cm]) that you set on the floor—never above the floor or inside a cot, playard, or other container. A sturdy handle is a plus. You can do whatever work you need to do, move wherever you need to, and still keep your baby in the room with you. Make sure to remove any soft toys or dangling objects. The single-layer liner in the photo is probably fine. Simpler is safer.

A laundry basket also works. It's airy, safe, and easy to carry from room to room. Fold up a lightweight blanket for a bit of padding on the bottom and voilà—instant baby bed!

Travel beds and travel cots are either soft-sided and folding or hard-sided with a handle, like a Moses basket. But the "travel" part doesn't necessarily mean "carry it with the baby in it", so don't assume that you can pick it up like a Moses basket until you've checked it out. It's still a good stationary bed for babies under about 15 pounds [7 kg] who aren't mobile enough to flip or roll out of it.

Even an empty drawer with a small folded blanket as a mattress works as a baby bed. It isn't easy to carry from room to room, but it's perfectly adequate, day or night, so long as the sides are high enough to keep an active newborn pole-vaulter from flopping over the edge. (Just don't put the drawer back with the baby in it!)

Standard Nap Furniture

Parents often use a playard, cot, Moses basket, or cradle as a napping spot as well as a night spot, and we cover them all in more detail in Chapter 12. Their only drawback for naps is that, with the exception of the Moses basket, you're not likely to move them from room to room. If your baby is under about six months old and you're going to be busy in that room or the next for the length of a nap, great. But if you're planning to vacuum the house, make sure you use a Moses basket.

> We couldn't sit at the dinner table for the first three to four months after our daughter was born. She wouldn't sit in her fancy reclining high chair and wasn't happy on the floor. So we put Hannah in her infant seat in the centre of (we know, we know) the dinner table. She made the most adorable centrepiece! She even napped there while we ate. We felt very civilized the first night we all ate at "the big table", and there was no way Hannah could fall off.
>
> —Maria

[*LLLI comment:* There are often real-world exceptions to general prohibitions. Hannah was surrounded by protective adults and wasn't going anywhere. An infant seat on the kitchen work surface while you put the shopping away? Not at all the same and not at all safe.]

What About Tummy Time?

"Tummy time"—a baby spending awake time on his tummy—gets a lot of press these days. You might hear that if your baby spends all his time on his back or in an infant seat or car seat, his muscles may not develop as well and his head can become misshapen. But wait a minute! If so many of our babies need tummy time and maybe even a helmet to achieve "normal", doesn't it mean that something about our current behaviour has somehow strayed from normal?

Let's think about what happened in the era BC: Before Carpeting. Tummy time would have involved packed earth, sand, long grass, or maybe sticks and leaves. Instead, babies were carried almost all the time, and not just by their mothers—they'd be passed along to older siblings, Dad, grandparents, or doting friends. The baby who's carried is constantly jostled and shifted, and does his own jostling and shifting in response, awake or asleep. Automatic exercise. And his head isn't pressed against something firm and immobile. Automatic normal growth.

Tummy time is an imperfect attempt to re-create what babies get from being carried around most of the time. Babies often fuss or cry when they're expected to do tummy time on the floor, but if they're on a parent's chest, they're happy. In fact, the baby who is carried far more usually cries far less.[5]

If you don't carry your baby much, tummy time may have its place. But remember, carrying your baby strengthens muscles, teaches balance and co-ordination, and involves your baby in a world of movement, changing images, and language—much more than a few minutes a day on the floor can. Consider shaking out that sling or wrap that you got as a baby gift and talking to some sling-wearing mothers about the how-tos. Or check out the sections on babycarriers above and in Chapter 12. You and your baby will probably both enjoy the ride.

Some babies seem to need motion in order to relax enough for sleep. Here are some ideas:

- Baby Kai often resists sleep. Now that he's six months old, he'll nurse to sleep maybe a third of the time. When he doesn't, we often gently bounce him to sleep on our yoga ball while singing one of his favourite lullabies, or walk him to sleep on our bodies in a carrier. —Therese
- For the first few months Max napped on me in a carrier. He needed movement to fall asleep, so we would go on big walks around our neighbourhood. He would fall asleep and stay asleep after we got home. I just couldn't sit down or that was the end of that. —Kathryn
- When I just couldn't take the weight on my back, we would get Julia to sleep in the sling, and then I would lie down with her in it, then ease it off. The sling became her blanket. —Eva
- Kate required constant motion during naps. So that I could do something—anything!—sitting down, we bought an inexpensive stand for a birth ball (looks like a ring the ball sits in). I could help her have a nap in the sling and sit and gently bounce her while eating a meal, watching TV, or working at the computer. —Tanya
- We pushed a lightweight buggy back and forth over our tiled floor. The bumpity-bump-bump, over and over, often soothed him to sleep. —Diane
- Oh, right! Motion babies! I had one of those! —Melissa

Napping at the Shops (Your Baby, Not You!)

Some babies naturally fall into predictable naptimes, but lots of them don't. Either way, babies are usually adaptable and can sleep anywhere their mothers are. If it's his typical naptime and you're still out and about, you may be able to stop long enough to breastfeed and just keep going. It's a rare baby who's well-fed and sleepy and in a babycarrier who doesn't find the shops a perfectly acceptable napping place. In fact, fussy babies often sleep better when out than at home. Maybe it's that notion babies seem to have that if their surroundings sound comfortably busy, they feel safe enough to sleep. When the going gets tough, sometimes the tough go shopping! (Even if it's just window shopping.)

A pushchair reclined to flat or nearly flat can also be a good public napping place, especially if you have a bad back or heavy baby. But most of the time, a babycarrier is easier and less of a hassle when there are doors and stairs and narrow shop aisles to navigate. Your baby is also a lot less likely to fuss in a babycarrier. There's a reason you see some mothers pushing an empty pram with one hand and carrying the baby with the other!

Breastfeeding in Public

You may also see some mothers on a bench at the shops, bottle in hand, baby still in the pram, feeding their baby with no body contact at all. Not very cosy, but . . . just how do you breastfeed discreetly in public? First of all, you don't have to hide. In the UK mothers who are breastfeeding a child of any age cannot be discriminated against under the terms of the Equality Act 2010. It is against the law, for example, for the manager of a café to ask you to stop breastfeeding or do it somewhere more private, or to leave because you're breastfeeding. In Australia the right to breastfeed in public is protected by the Sex Discrimination Act 1984. In New Zealand the same rights are protected by the Human Rights Act 1993. South Africa has no explicit legislation covering discrimination against breastfeeding but it is not illegal to breastfeed in public. There are very few places in the entire world where public breastfeeding is prohibited.

If you want to do it discreetly, one technique is to sit near a wall or other barrier, turn to face it while you get your baby attached, then settle your clothing and turn back towards the public again. Practise at home in front of a mirror, or have a friend critique your performance. What's to see? Maybe a few wrinkles on one side of your shirt; your baby's head and body cover everything else. Loose tops, pulled up from below, can work well. Breastfeeding tops work fine too. There are even breastfeeding "camis". Or try two camisole tops—one to pull up to open up the "restaurant" and one to pull down that keeps your tummy covered. A baby's floppy hat is a great shield. And an open shirt or jumper can cover your sides in any outfit.

The elaborate blankets, shawls, and wire hoop arrangements designed to camouflage what you're doing make the fact that you're breastfeeding *more* obvious, not less. They might as well be printed with "Look! I'm Breastfeeding!" And many babies hate having that fabric draped over them while they're eating.

Depending on your build and your baby, you may be able to breastfeed in a babycarrier. Or you can loosen the carrier, breast-feed the baby to sleep, and readjust it afterwards.

And if someone *does* guess that you're breastfeeding your baby? It's good for everyone, especially other women and their children, to see a baby getting his normal food in his normal way, no fuss. If people in this society don't *see* casual public breastfeeding, they're not going to *accept* casual public breastfeeding. Bottom line: your baby's needs are more important than someone else's opinion. Keep your cool, stay polite, and don't feel any need to apologize. *They're* the ones with a problem, not you.

Toddler Naps

Your baby keeps getting older, and naps keep changing. At some point, daytime sleep may actually become predictable (pretty much) and reliable (sort of), so you can get something done (sometimes). It's a brave new world.

But like almost everything else about bringing up a little person, naps are a progression, not a switch that gets flipped. Just when you think there's a pattern, the pattern changes, but with a general trend towards longer, more predictable naps. Then there's a gradual dwindling in the number of naps, until the days when you wish they'd nap and they don't, or they take one nap too many and aren't sleepy at bedtime. Gradually, naps fade from your vocabulary—except when you're talking about your own naps.

> We used to breastfeed with me sitting up on the sofa, which forced me to have downtime. My son would fall asleep breastfeeding, and I could read or go online. He would also sleep in the pram, and when we got back I could sit outside and read until he woke up. When he was about eight months old, he started napping in our bed. I could feed him, sneak out of bed, and turn on the baby monitor. Now, at three, he naps in his "big-boy" bed in his room.
>
> —Kathryn

This Nap's for You . . . Again!

As naps become more predictable, they become a quiet space in your day—a time to do things for yourself or a time to nap with the baby. Napping or "doing", you'll begin to have breathing space in your day that you didn't have at the beginning. Enjoy it! And when your children are older still, *you* may be the one taking naps.

If you're going back to work or college, in Chapter 8 you'll find strategies and ideas about naps when you're not together. The chapters in Part IV will give you a window on what you can expect at different ages, based on the experiences of other mothers.

> When my children were older, I realized that they were putting *me* down to nap! We went to bed, I fell asleep, and they left, closing the door to let their mum sleep. . . . At their ages, I knew I could close my eyes and they would survive.
>
> —Micaela

Something to Sleep On

When it comes to navigating the changing landscape of naps, you may find your road is smoothest if you:

- Keep your newborn on your body as much as you can.
- Keep your under-six-month-old on your body or within your vision and earshot.
- Savour naptime snuggles and books-instead-of-naps with your toddler.
- Expect some forward and backward "sleep consolidation" all along, and at each stage try to find both a chance to get things done and a chance for *you* to rest and recharge—you've earned it, every step of the way.

chapter 6

Nights

With my first baby, for weeks and weeks I felt profound relief every single time the sun came up. I hated and dreaded and feared the nights. I was having trouble with breastfeeding. I'd had a caesarean, and I couldn't breastfeed in bed. Because of those issues, every time my son woke, I got up, went into the living room, put on the light and sat on the sofa, latching and relatching and curling my toes at the pain. By the time we finally lay back down, I had only a short time to rest before he woke again. It got better, of course, but those early nights . . .

What a difference with my second. The days were hectic because my first-born was still adjusting to having a brother and I was learning to juggle two children. But the nights were mine and my newborn's. I gave birth at home and my body felt good. Breastfeeding was completely comfortable. We lay together on the open futon in the living room and breastfed and slept, and that was my time to stare at him and breathe his smell. I kind of hated to see each night end.

Even though those nights with my first newborn were incredibly hard and I dreaded them, I also loved them, and I love them still. That is when I became a mother.

—Laura

Nighttime is when the sleep issues really hit. You can get through the day, but you're used to a whole night of rest and restoration—and now your nights are a blur of waking, feeding, dozing, waking, crying, feeding. . . . It's dark. Your partner is snoring. So is your dog. It seems like everyone else in the world is getting a good night's sleep, and here you are, up again.

Unfortunately, some of that is just the way it is. If you've read the chapter on normal sleep, you know that it's normal for babies to wake at night and need to breastfeed. We can give you some suggestions about sleeping arrangements that might help you get through those interrupted nights and maximize your own rest. And we *can* promise you that it will change, although not always in a straight line—babies sleep more, then less, then more, but eventually they do sleep longer and need you less at night.

Where you, your partner, and your children sleep often follows an uneven path too. Most of us start out thinking very conventionally: baby in cot, maybe even baby in his own room. If we're lucky, we already know that it's safer—and better for breastfeeding—if the baby is in our room. We may investigate a bedside cot. At some point, many of us move on to an even closer arrangement at least part-time. We're going to follow that sequence in this chapter, from separate sleep to bedside cot to snuggling in bed together with a sigh of relief.

Preemies and Multiples

The thoughts in this chapter are the basics for healthy, full-term babies. Preemies (born before 37 weeks), twins and more, and not-yet-mobile babies with health issues have a few extra safety needs through the early months. Be sure to check Chapter 9 for ideas on keeping your little one (or ones) snug and safe at first.

Baby Sleep, in a Nutshell

Nights feel less like a battlefield if you keep in mind what's normal for your baby. In a nutshell:

- Babies need to be in their parents' room for about the first half year for safety and to establish a pattern of security and trust that will reduce their need to cry.
- Newborns *can't* sort out day from night, and can go no more than two or three hours between most feeds.
- Young babies are more stressed when they're not in physical contact with their mothers. Prolonged stress isn't healthy.
- For many months, babies average one-third of their food at night.
- A vulnerable baby's SIDS risk peaks between about one and four months.
- By about three months, most babies sleep longer at night at least some of the time. But it's two steps forward, one step back.
- By about four months, the Safe Sleep Seven opens up to include any responsible adult.
- Babies of any age can travel a surprising distance when no one's looking.
- Babies who are learning a new skill—sitting, crawling, walking, adding words—may return to shorter sleep cycles for a while.
- Towards the end of the first year, many (not all) babies can be nudged gently towards longer or more separate sleep (see Chapter 11).
- Most parents welcome small children into their beds at least now and then, for snuggles, or after nightmares, or on Saturday mornings. Children may remember those times fondly, but parents often forget; don't believe every "I never bedshared" story you hear!
- *All* children leave their parents' bed eventually, no matter what you do or don't do.

Breastfed Baby Bedtimes in the First Few Months

In the early weeks, your baby won't have much of a bedtime. She'll be up and down all day and all night. So you can just keep her nearby until you're ready to go to bed, then take her along to your room when you turn in. The chances are she'll spend her evenings in a series of naps and feeds anyway, so there's not much point in trying to "put her down for the night". Besides, of course, it's not a good idea to have her out of sight for more than a few minutes at a time.

Lots of young babies "cluster-feed" in the evening, breastfeeding really frequently for several hours.[1] It may be a response to built-up tension from a day in this unaccustomed new world or to a less forceful milk flow (even though there is still plenty of milk). Whatever the reason, lots of mothers see a stretch of breastfeeding-breastfeeding-breastfeeding through the evening.

This "frazzled time" is when all three of you are frazzled from a long day and the baby is fussy and you haven't eaten yet and bedtime is still hours away and you all wish there were grandmotherly arms to hold the baby for a while. It tends to get better by around three months. (Even when nothing seems to help the baby, a pre-dinner snack for the grown-ups can help.)

No need to tiptoe or whisper if your baby falls asleep before you go to bed. Most babies aren't disturbed by noise unless it's abrupt and unpredictable. In fact, babies often sleep more soundly with adult activity around them. Maybe routine background busyness reassures the baby that "life in the village" continues to be peaceful and safe. So keeping her near you—especially if you wear her—may actually give you *more* free time, not less.

How Your Days Affect Your Nights

Chapter 10 is all about tending to your own sleep needs in the midst of this very busy time. Some of it involves little daytime changes you can make—winding down earlier in the evening, for instance, and sleeping as late as you can in the morning. Even if you're awake, staying in bed will give you more rest than getting up will. Many babies love "snuggling in" towards morning, even if they spend most of the night in a cot, and do some of their best breastfeeding (and cutest moves) in bed with Mum before the sun is all the way up. And many mothers remember these morning snuggles as very happy, relaxed times—soaking him up; feeding him, body and soul; and getting a few more minutes of downtime all at the same time.

If you're returning to work or college, see Chapter 8 for strategies that take your working day away from your baby into account.

Nighttime Separate Sleep Options

When a baby sleeps alone, it's usually in a cradle, cot or Moses basket. Make sure yours meets current safety guidelines. No bumpers, dangling objects, soft toys, crevices, or gaps. And, of course, your baby is safest in your own room for at least the first half year.[2]

Babies outgrow cradles quickly. In fact, depending on the tippiness of the cradle and the liveliness of the baby, your lovely antique cradle may do best as a toy or laundry catch-all right from the start.

If you decide to use a cot, keep as short a route as possible from bed to cot and from cot to breastfeeding spot, so you can respond before your baby has to cry and get back to bed simply and quickly after breastfeeding. A quick nighttime response can help reduce daytime crying by showing him that you're responsive to his needs. (See Chapter 18 if you're worried about spoiling.)

Safe Sitting

You'll need somewhere to sit comfortably to breastfeed if you're not planning to breastfeed lying down. And it needs to be somewhere your baby will be safe if you fall asleep. But where, exactly, is that? The no-bedsharing organizations don't say. One no-bedsharing organization sums it up this way: your baby should not sleep in an adult bed, on a couch, or on a chair alone, with you, or with anyone else.[3] But standing up doesn't work. If you sit up unsupported, even on the edge of the bed, you risk slumping onto the baby or dropping him if you doze off. And nearly half of all breastfeeding mothers who sit up at night say they've fallen asleep that way at least once,[4] which makes sense because breastfeeding hormones make you even sleepier. Bring your baby into bed with you just for breastfeeding? If you're *likely* to fall asleep in a chair, you're *going* to fall asleep in the bed. So what's left?

A thinly padded upholstered chair with low arms is a real-world possibility. The low arms can both support your own relaxed arms and make it easier for you to arrange yourself and your baby. There also may be less chance of your baby slipping into a crevice if you fall asleep.

Planning on Separate Sleep? Prepare Your Own Bed Anyway!

The safest option of all may be to breastfeed lying down in your own prepared bed. At three in the morning, there's a very good chance that your firm resolve not to have the baby in your bed, ever ever, may be totally blindsided by just plain falling asleep. If you're feeling desperately sleepy and your baby needs to finish her meal, you may decide it's safer to move to your bed and lie down than risk falling asleep in the chair. So prepare for that possibility. See Chapter 1 for a quick way to prepare your bed for emergency bedsharing.

> **Thinking About Sleep Training?**
>
> Read Chapter 18 for an in-depth explanation of its short-term and long-term risks. And keep in mind that breastfeeding is likely to end sooner when parents sleep-train or hire a sleep nanny. The gentle nudging ideas in Chapter 11 may take some of the stress off if you choose not to sleep with your baby.

The Bedside Cot Compromise

Maybe you've already discovered that having a baby in your bed gives you a lot more time there yourself. But maybe you or your partner or both of you just can't get comfortable with the idea of bedsharing. Or you aren't sure you want it to be your routine. A bedside cot can be an excellent compromise. You can reach over, lift or move your baby into bed, breastfeed, and slide your baby back when he's finished. Or not, since your bed is ready either way. If the cot is level with your bed, it gives you a little more space to stretch your arm or leg.

A bedside cot tends to reduce nighttime excursions and sleep disturbance for both parents, which means you're more likely to have a willing partner in this. What happens from there—regular use of the cot or the occasional (or long-term) slide into bedsharing—is up to the three of you. (After moving the baby permanently into their bed, one father said, "The bedside cot is the most expensive laundry basket ever.")

ISIS have more information on bedside cots at isisonline.org and the NCT sell one in their shop. Durham University are currently undertaking research into the issue of their use in the home following on from previous research into their use in postnatal wards which found them to be no greater risk than traditional cots.[5]

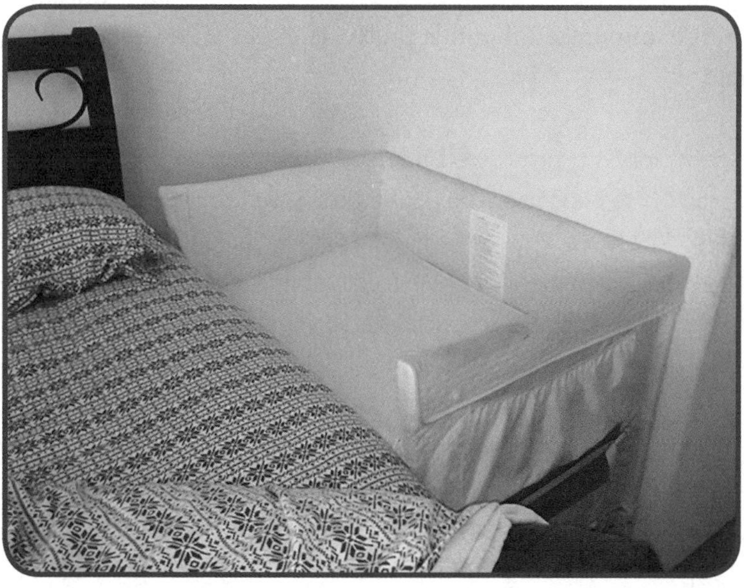

The bedside cot: a compromise between bedsharing and getting up

During my pregnancy, the cat really, really wanted to sleep in the bedside cot we'd acquired. After the birth, the baby really, really wanted to sleep with us. As for us, we just really, really wanted to sleep! After a few nights of unhappy baby, unhappy cat, and unhappy parents, the solution seemed obvious. Our friend pointed out, "You've never rolled off your bed, have you?" I had never rolled onto my cat either.

So we became human bed rails. Liliana was in bed with us, the cat got the bedside cot, and we all slept better. Yes, the first year was hard. But thanks to bedsharing, it wasn't harder than it needed to be.

—Elissa

Bedsharing Basics

Many parents who never saw themselves as snugglers have been amazed at how much they enjoy sleeping in the same bed with a baby. On top of that, sharing a planned bed with your baby is the most effective way to combine as much sleep as possible and as smooth a breastfeeding experience as possible—all with suffocation risks minimized. Sounds pretty delicious when you're short on sleep!

Rob pretty much followed my lead about our sleeping arrangements. We had Phoebe in our bed pretty early on—like maybe the first night home. And he is the one who encouraged me to breastfeed her when she was cluster-feeding and I was crying because it was not the two-hour schedule everyone had said would happen.

—Leigh Anne

Chapter 2 has lots of information on preparing your bed for permanent or part-time bedsharing. Mesh rails can keep people of any size from falling out of bed (see also Chapter 12). Be sure to fill any gaps first. If you sleep between your baby and the edge of the bed, you *are* the rail! Move your baby to the middle when you get up in the night to pee or if you get out of bed in the morning (or at naptime) before your baby is awake. Don't be lulled into thinking a pre-mobile baby can't move to the side of the bed. Even a newborn can move around, so stay nearby.

Some families put their mattress on the floor and end up keeping it there for years, maybe even adding a single bed mattress to extend the sleeping space as the family grows. Your own arrangements will probably change over the years. Whatever you start with may not be what you end up with.

> I can't believe we bedshared for so many years in a high, antique, smaller-than-double bed! Something silly in us said bedrooms should look a certain way. If I had it to do over, I'd absolutely get rid of the antique bed, invest in a bigger mattress, and put it on the floor. Nights would have been soooo much more comfortable! We sacrificed easier nighttime parenting for a room that nobody else ever saw anyway.
>
> —Diane

Breastfeeding Lying Down

No matter where your baby sleeps, you'll get more rest once you learn how to breastfeed lying down.

As with any other breastfeeding position, there are as many subtle variations as there are mothers. Your body shape, your breast shape and size, and your baby's preferences and size can all affect what works best for you. Here are three basic themes to start from. There are no rules for how you do it; whatever makes both of you comfortable and lets your baby breastfeed easily is right.

Lying Back on Pillows

Until they master the art of breastfeeding lying down, many mothers create a backrest out of pillows, and spend much of the night semireclined with their babies on their chests. In fact, lots of newborns sleep best on their mother's sloping chest. Make it a solid friction fit and make sure that there aren't crevices or pillows (including your own) in places that could cause a problem.

You might not even have to shift from this position to breastfeed; with gravity holding your baby against you, he'll probably be happy to take care of it himself with only a little support from you.

What about wearing a wrap or a Velcro-closure nap wrap for holding a sleeping baby on your chest at night? They can be great for naps, but use one with care at night, when a baby needs to be free to adjust to your shifts in position.

Sleeping with your baby on your chest

Starting on Your Side

Get comfortable on your side, facing your baby. If you lift your lower-side breast and put it back down on the bed, you'll get your breast fully out from under you and your nipple fully out from under your breast. Lie so that you don't have to use any energy to keep yourself on your side. You'll find that you automatically make a cuddle curl, the instinctive position described in Chapter 2. It's important for you to be comfortable since you'll be in this position for much of the night. Feel free to use a pillow behind your back or between your knees, and certainly one or two under your head.

Your lower-side arm might curl up under your pillow and keep your baby from inching up there. Or you may find that you want to curl your lower arm down around your baby. That's every bit as good, if your arm rotates comfortably to that position.

Once you're lying on your side, roll your baby onto her side, facing you. Then move her down so that her eye (yes, her eye!) is about level with your nipple, and put your hand in the middle of her back so that if you press, her back will arch slightly. Because her eye is near your nipple, she'll have to tip her head back a little to latch on, which means her chin will land on your breast—a powerful latching trigger—and her nose will lift away from your breast. You can use your upper hand on the small of her back to snuggle her in and get comfortable.

She'll use her feet to push herself higher up the bed. If she overshoots, you can pull her back down and let her try again. If you feel you need to give some extra help, you can switch hands and use your top hand to shape or move your breast. Be sure to keep the finger that's near her lower jaw *well* out of her way! Once she's latched on, you'll probably be the most relaxed with your bottom arm curled up under your pillow and your top-side arm gently supporting your baby's back.

If you breastfeed with your lower arm curled around your baby instead of up under your pillow, you may find that her head rests on that arm. That can work well if you have a larger breast that the baby can access easily from that cuddled position. You probably won't be fully on your side in that position, so you may find that a pillow behind your back makes you more comfortable.

Maybe it all worked great the first time you tried it, but you couldn't get your baby to latch on when you tried again at 2.00 a.m. It's a lot like learning to tie shoelaces or write your name—your first attempts are often awkward. It will get easier with practice. The best time to learn is during the day. Three in the morning is a terrible time to practise anything new. But day or night, if you fall asleep practising, you *know* you've got it right.

Still having trouble? Ask a friend or a mother-to-mother group. It's not uncommon to see a mother on the floor at a La Leche League meeting, demonstrating what works for her with her own baby.

Starting by Sitting Up

Some mothers who just can't manage latching lying down at first start by breastfeeding sitting up and then either slowly ease themselves and their baby into a lying-down position or have their partner help them. Remember that your bodies are parallel when you're lying down, so if you start by sitting up, try to angle your baby's feet down towards your legs rather than having him sideways across your chest.

If you plan to sit up all through the feed, a pillow in your lap isn't a good idea. It could be a suffocation hazard if you fall asleep. Better to lean back after your baby is latched on and let your baby be supported by your own body.

Switching Sides to Breastfeed

At first, rolling over to breastfeed on the other side means either switching the baby to the other part of the bed before you roll over or rolling over while you hold her on your chest. Of course, "rolling

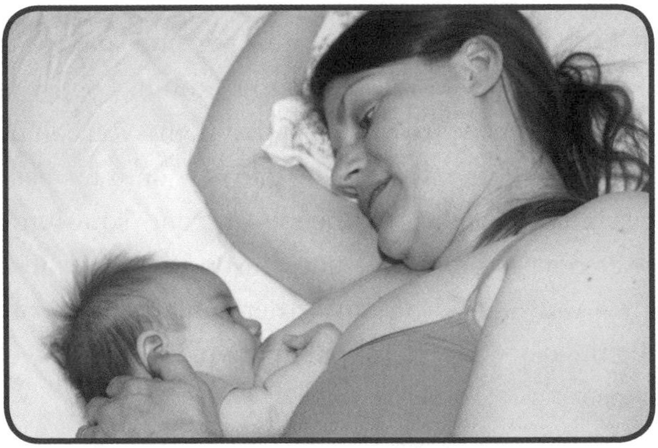

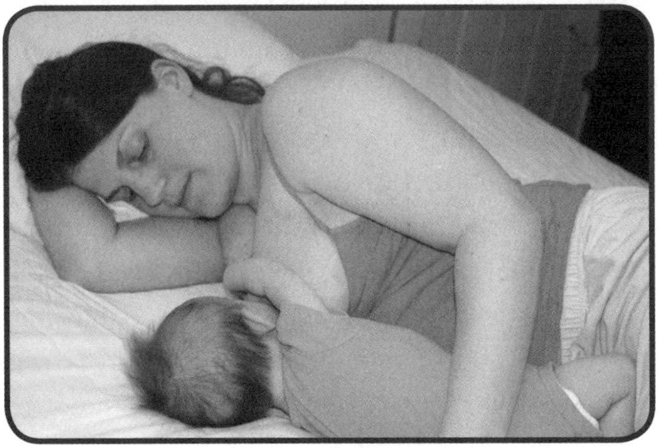

over" is a too-casual term for the wiggling, manoeuvring, and rearranging involved. Some mothers even leave the baby in place and get out of bed to move around to the other side.

After the first few weeks, it can be much easier just to lie on the same side for both breasts if yours are a size and shape that allow it. Breastfeed on the lower breast first, to soften it. For the rest of the feed, or the next time you breastfeed that night, you can use the top breast. Many mothers roll the baby partially onto his back and roll themselves a little more onto their own front, squishing that softened lower breast somewhat (one reason it's harder to do this in the first few weeks). As with any other lying-down variation, practise during the day when your brain, patience, and sense of humour are all in gear.

Breast Dressed

How you feed your baby changes everything from what you wear to bed to how you make your bed.

The Breast-Dressed Mother

You already know what clothes you like for bed, or whether you like clothes at all. Breastfeeding adds just two more considerations: easy breastfeeding and staying warm. In a way, easy access and staying warm are conflicting considerations. Breastfeeding means that (1) part of your front is going to be bare for part of the night, and (2) if you breastfeed lying down, your baby needs an air space—and just might hate being covered—so your bare top may be more bare than you'd like.

There's breastfeeding nightwear at many stores and online breastfeeding boutiques. But depending on your body type and breast shape, concealed openings that look good in the shop may turn out to be a total nuisance at night. Many mothers don't bother with special breastfeeding nightwear at all. A T-shirt, camisole, or tankini top usually works fine. So can a nightdress with buttons down to your rib cage, a jumper, or a sweatshirt cut down the front. You can even cut breast-size holes or big slits in a T-shirt or sweatshirt—warm shoulders and midriff, easy access. (Just don't answer the door that way!)

Many bedsharing mothers bring a blanket up over their shoulder and slant it down in front to create a warm, loose tent over their breast and baby, pulling the covers down enough to keep the baby's head clear.

Whether you sit up or lie down for night breastfeeding, skip the bra if at all possible, unless you really need one to hold pads at first. In that case, wear your very loosest bra, one that leaves no marks or dents on your skin. Your hardworking breasts deserve time "out of the corral". The old advice to wear a sleep bra for support is, well, unsupported. Many mothers just use a cloth nappy or a towel underneath to catch any drips, with spares at their bedside. Leaking at night is usually a temporary issue.

If you have long hair, you might want to consider plaiting it or tying it up at night for the baby's safety.

> I found some tank tops with built-in bras and an extra stretchy neck at a discount store. Not something I would ever wear during the day. But they were so perfect for the night. The "bra" had only enough support to hold the breast pads in place. And I loved the stretchiness of the top. I just pulled it down to breastfeed.
>
> —Eglantina

> I usually slept in a nightdress that buttoned down the front low enough that I could open it to breastfeed. I tend to be cold at night and hate having bare shoulders and arms, so that worked well. My children, on the other hand, tend to be warm at night, so they usually slept in just a nappy.
>
> —Caroline

The Breast-Dressed Baby

For you, nightclothes are probably about staying warm enough. For your baby, they're mostly about staying cool enough. Since overheating may be a risk factor for SIDS for vulnerable babies,[6] it's important not to dress your baby too warmly at night. Dress her only as warmly as you dress yourself when you're awake, and remember that a bedsharing baby is right up against a furnace (you). Is your room reasonably warm? A nappy or a nappy and sleepsuit is probably enough. Some mothers keep their baby outside the covers with heavier sleepsuit or a sleeping bag or in regular pyjamas with a small, light blanket.

If your house isn't well heated in winter, you may need to dress your baby more warmly. Again, the number of clothing layers *you* need to stay warm is a good guide: if you're sleeping in long johns under fleece pyjamas, give your baby extra layers too.

When you're bedsharing, or if your baby is in a bedside cot and comes into bed to breastfeed, swaddling may put your baby at risk. Imagine being bumped around casually by a crowd. No problem. Now imagine being in a straitjacket in that crowd. Can you see how unsafe ordinary living suddenly becomes if you can't move your arms and body? And since swaddling is meant as a substitute for being with Mum, there's no point to it anyway. *You're* there.

Nappy changes? Look for baby outfits that allow you to uncover her bottom without uncovering her top. Imagine how wide awake (and upset!) you'd be if someone hauled you out of bed, stripped all your clothes off, and wiped your whole backside with a wet cloth. But separates tend to be bulky and confining. A long-sleeved sleepsuit or sleeper with snaps at the bottom is probably going to be more comfortable for her. (And as far as comfort goes, poppers or buttons up the back could be uncomfortable for any back-sleeping baby.)

If your baby will be sleeping alone, take everything out of her bed. A small, light blanket, baby sleeping bag, or warm outfit with no covers should do. And, of course, lay her on her back.

If you're bedsharing, you'll automatically monitor your baby's temperature throughout the night, adjusting her covers when you adjust your own. A good sleeping temperature is harder to gauge if your baby sleeps alone; cool hands or feet don't necessarily mean she's too cold. But you'll develop a feel (literally!) for her everyday temperature. Aim for that same feel at night. If either of you uses clothes at night, it helps to keep spares of everything handy so you can change easily if either of you gets wet. If you can keep your bedroom warm enough that you can leave your baby in just a nappy and sleep naked yourself, you'll reduce the amount of extra washing you need to do.

Nappy overflows happen, and being in a wet bed isn't pleasant, especially in cool weather. What can you do? Use nappy doublers.

They look like sanitary pads and can be made of cloth or the same material as disposable nappies. Use one as a nappy liner with cloth or disposable nappies and there you go—drier nights! Do you have to change nappies at night? In the early weeks it's a good idea, to avoid nappy rash. At some point, your baby will stop pooing at night and you can experiment. No rash and no fussing? Then you're probably lucky enough to have one of the babies who doesn't mind being wet.

> It never ceased to amaze me how even when they were very young our children could successfully kick the covers off themselves and partially off their parents! I think part of the reason why some of them started sleeping in the H position (sideways) was to avoid having me keep pulling the covers back up over them. We live in northern Hokkaido, Japan, where winters are cold and long. So I was concerned that they would be cold. But they never were.
>
> —RuthAnna

> I live in the US. I'm continuously tucking the covers back up over my two and having them squirm and kick too. So funny how common our nighttime experiences are around the globe!
>
> —Jonna

The Breast-Dressed Bed

No matter where your baby usually sleeps, you'll probably use your bed as a changing table or breastfeeding spot at least some of the time. When you combine leaks, breastfeeding, nappies, and general baby care, we all end up dealing with various fluids day and night. Mothers use waterproof mattress pads under the bottom sheet to protect the mattress, but of course that doesn't protect the sheet itself. You can find wonderful cot-size flannelized plastic or rubber sheets—soft and fuzzy on each side but with a waterproof middle—at many baby product stores or online. If you can find some suitable fabric, you can easily cut your own. It can go on top of your bottom sheet and can be replaced in a flash as needed. Bath towels work too, but they're more likely to bunch under you and can soak through to the sheet below. Bedsharing mothers also sometimes use a cloth nappy or muslin cloth under the baby's head to catch some of the almost inevitable dribbles after nighttime feeds. Sheepskins are too smothery to use with babies, but a thin woven wool pad can work.

> Huck was an epic spitter-upper. Probably the best baby product we owned was a thin wool pad (not a sheepskin) that he slept on that sucked up all of the spit-up, leaky nappies, and other sheet-soakers.
>
> —Jeanette

The Breast-Dressed Room

No, we're not talking about matching curtains and wallpaper. The ideas below come from breastfeeding mothers who, like you, were looking for any ideas that could give them a few extra minutes of sleep.

- A nightlight in your room is a big help during the early weeks and maybe even long term. It's dim enough for sleep but gives enough light for breastfeeding or changing a nappy. And it is certainly better than turning on a bright light several times a night.
- A water bottle and a small stash of durable foods like sports bars can let you stay in bed even when you're thirsty or hungry in the night. Loosen the lid or open the wrapper before you go to bed, so you don't have to wake up as completely.
- Is your changing table in a different room? Keep at your bedside a few nappies, a box of wipes, and something to toss them into, so you won't have to make the trek in the middle of the night.
- Get out spares of whatever you and your baby wear to bed at night. Some of us have changed tops several times at night during the early—and often very leaky—weeks.
- If you're sensitive to light when you sleep, consider adding blackout curtains or blinds or thermal curtains to your windows so that dawn's early light isn't a problem. Thermal

curtains might also help reduce outside noise if you live in a busy city or have loud morning birds. Light and noise are usually more disturbing to adults than to babies, so your baby will probably be fine with whatever suits you.

Complaints Department

Bedsharing isn't always a bed of roses. So what are some of the common complaints?

- *I tend to stay in that cuddle curl all night, and my hip/knees/ shoulder/lower arm (choose one or more) gets sore.* If you have a hard mattress, you might want to consider a somewhat softer one if it's within your budget. You may be sharing it, at least some of the time, for years to come. (This could be your chance to get a bigger, more family-friendly size too!) Your partner may even find that subtle aches and pains clear up when you give up that slab of marble you've been using. If a new mattress isn't on the cards, some thin padding on your part of the bed may make a world of difference. Just don't get something so squishy that you have concerns about your baby. Other ideas: see if your baby will let you roll onto your back if you keep an arm around her—or once you're in that position, maybe she can sleep on your chest. Or roll over with your baby to change sides now and then. Try moving your arm to a different position. Straighten out your lower leg and bring your upper knee up a bit. This rotates you slightly towards your baby and takes the pressure off your hip. Or sleep with a small pillow between your knees.
- *I can't work out how to breastfeed on my other side.* Practise during the day, not in the middle of the night. Maybe have someone take a bird's-eye picture of you breastfeeding on the side that works so that you can analyse your position. Most of us have asymmetrical breasts, so maybe you just

need to tweak your position on one side. If some practice on both your parts isn't helping, maybe there's some kink—yours or your baby's—that a breastfeeding helper can sort out with you.

- *My baby wants to hang out all night with my nipple in her mouth.* We have ideas on this in Chapter 22. You're not alone!
- *Wouldn't it be easier to sleep-train/use a cot/put the baby in a different room/hit myself on the head with a board?* As one mother pointed out, "Just because some parts of parenting are difficult doesn't mean they aren't important." Almost all babies would choose bedsharing if they got to vote. But *your* vote matters too. Chapters 9, 10, and 11 offer many ideas and compromises. But if sleeping with your baby is important to you, there's almost always a solution to whatever problem you're having. Those same chapters have many of them. Whichever way you're feeling, it's always helpful to talk with other bedsharing mothers who have been there too.
- *What about hiring a baby nurse?* The trouble with a baby nurse is that her job is taking care of the baby. Which puts a huge strain on establishing breastfeeding and connecting with your baby because you get less face time. A postnatal doula, on the other hand, does all your other work so you can focus on your baby. (Check out Doula.org.uk.)

Something to Sleep On

Responsible bedsharing just means making sure that you, your baby, and your sleeping spot meet the Safe Sleep Seven guidelines in Chapter 2. And you can apply those standards anywhere you and your baby find yourselves.

Smooth nights happen most easily with smooth breastfeeding and easy mother-baby contact. It takes a while to find what works best for your combination of people, personalities, and places, and it will probably change over time. Whatever arrangements you settle on, now or permanently, make your own bed safe for bedsharing. You need a safe place to lie down with your baby, just in case you turn out to be among the two-thirds of breastfeeding mothers who end up bedsharing sometimes.

Lying down and gazing at your peacefully sleeping baby can be luscious. Wakening gently to snorts and stirrings rather than being jolted awake by cries is definitely more restful. And there's a certain natural ebb and flow feeling to shared nights, once everyone—including the baby—has adjusted to family life. It's not wonderful every night, and it's not for every family. But more often than not it works well.

chapter 7

Sleep Personalities and Places

When my third baby, Danny, was two months old, I took him to the doctor in tears. "I think he has brain damage or something," I told her. "If I put him down on a blanket on the floor, he doesn't cry. He'll eat only at specific times every day. And sometimes he falls asleep without eating. I don't know what's wrong with him."

By now my doctor was smiling. She said, "There's nothing wrong with your little boy. You're just comparing him to his older brother and sister, who have very different personalities." They still do today.

—Melissa

Babies aren't blank slates that we write a personality on. Being active or quiet or unpredictable is as built-in as being curly-haired or long-legged or round-faced. It can even start in the womb—many mothers notice that one baby is far more active before birth than another, or is active at different times of day. As you get to know your baby, you'll realize that you can *shape* who she is a little bit, but you can't *change* who she is. Becoming a family is all about fitting your personalities together, day and night. Books may offer a one-size-fits-all solution to nighttime parenting, but you and your baby are unique.

Infant Temperaments

In the 1950s, researchers Alexander Thomas and Stella Chess began studying what they called "temperament".[1] They observed how a group of babies reacted and behaved in different situations, and followed them throughout childhood into the teen years, looking for personality characteristics that seemed to persist throughout life. Since then, other researchers have suggested additional categories and groupings of characteristics, but the basic ones that Thomas and Chess set out are still widely used to help us understand the ways in which children can be different. Their categories are Rhythmicity, Initial Reaction, Adaptability, Mood, Activity, Distractibility, Persistence and Attention Span, Sensitivity, and Intensity. You can think of each characteristic as being rated on a scale. Children are typically high in some traits and in the middle or low range in others.

You may wonder how on earth you're going to figure out your own baby's profile. But think for a moment about an adult you know very well. You can probably work your way through the table below. As you get to know your baby, you may start to see certain profile traits popping through. "Ah, right, he's a ____." It's especially helpful if you're trying to fit opposite personality types together under one roof.

Got a Match?

If you've always happily followed a regular schedule (breakfast at 6.00 a.m., lunch at noon, dinner at 6.30 p.m.), you may find your highly Irregular baby confusing and frustrating. If you're low in Sensitivity, your baby's fussiness over clothes and temperature may seem way over the top to you—can the tag on the back of his sleepsuit really bother him *that* much? Yes, it can. When something about your child is driving you crazy and you're tempted to think

Sleep Temperaments and Traits

Activity	High	Needs to move! Wiggly to hold, wiggly in bed, especially if the day was "too calm". May be harder to nurse in bed because he doesn't want to lie down. May want to play whenever he wakes up.
	Low	Spends more time sitting quietly. Tends to nurse quietly and stay put in bed.
Rhythmicity	Regular	Tends to eat and sleep and wake up at predictable times (although these may not always match the times you'd like).
	Irregular	Eats, sleeps, and wakes at irregular times. May nap for an hour one day, 20 minutes the next, and two hours the next. Finds schedules or imposed routines stressful. Needs flexibility.
Initial Reaction	Approach	New situations and people are interesting and exciting—he wades right in. Happy to sleep in a tent, in a motel bed, or at Grandma's house.
	Withdrawal	Initially reacts to new people or places by pulling back. Sleeping in a strange place makes him cranky at first, but give him some time and he'll settle in.
Adaptability	High	Moves smoothly from one activity to another. Won't mind much if you take him from playing to cuddling in bed, and usually falls back to sleep easily after nursing.
	Low	Changes are stressful, even changes from one good (and familiar) activity to another. May need long feeds to settle at night; may cry as soon as he wakes up because being awake is a "new situation".
Mood	Positive	Typically wakes up happy, moves through day in a generally good mood, smiles readily.
	Negative	Needs comforting more often. People have to earn those smiles. May wake crying. And no, you're not doing anything wrong.
Distractibility	High	Has difficulty settling in to nurse or sleep if there's activity or noise in the room. (Typical of many babies around three to five months; starts earlier or lasts longer for others.)
	Low	Noise, activity, and other distractions don't bother this child. Can nurse or fall asleep in the middle of a rowdy family party.
Persistence and Attention Span	High	Will practise over and over to achieve his goals. May be hard to settle to sleep if his focus is on learning to roll over or sit up.
	Low	Learns new things in frequent, small steps and may become frustrated or give up if he can't accomplish something quickly. Not usually an issue for sleep.
Sensitivity	High	May be bothered by certain sounds or textures, changes in temperature, car seat fatigue. Picks up on your moods and her own internal rumblings; may be up all night teething. You may have to figure out what soothes and what irritates your particular child. Needs to have her environment, including sleepsuit, just right to be comfortable and ready to sleep.
	Low	Not bothered by scratchy sleepsuit or slamming doors, so he can sleep more easily. Teeth may just appear without any fuss.
Intensity	High	His expression of each of his personality traits is strong. When he's happy, he's over the moon; when he's unhappy, everyone knows. (If he's Low Sensitivity, this may not show up too often; if he's High Sensitivity, it may be a roller-coaster ride.)
	Low	Feelings are not strongly expressed. Even if he's High Sensitivity or tends to withdraw in his initial reactions, he doesn't make a big fuss about it.

Name That Trait

What traits do you think the child in each of these stories is exhibiting?

- My middle son woke up grumpy from the time he was a baby. His older and younger siblings would beg me not to wake him up if we needed to go somewhere, because he'd be so grumpy he would make us all miserable—even when he was school-age! —Delia

- New settings, new faces, and group activities were a nightmare for me the whole time I was growing up. Once I overheard my parents talking in concerned voices about my shyness. But I knew I'd be fine if they'd just let me be who I was. Now I'm about to retire from a very successful, very public career. I'm still the one who leaves the party early, the one who doesn't make eye contact on the plane. But sure enough, I've been fine just being who I am. —Erica

- I love the feel of scratchy wool. Neither my son nor his dad can stand it. Our son at three: "Mummy, will *you* get the lumps out of my socks? Daddy has his own problems." —Diane

- My toddler, Jake, asked for a doughnut on a shopping trip and I said no. It was "Doughnut! Want doughnut!" every couple of minutes all through the rest of our trip. He was still asking for one when I put him in the car seat and headed home. He fell asleep in the car and finished napping in the house—but when he woke up an hour later, the first thing he said was *"Doughnut! Want doughnut!"* You have to laugh! —*Esmerelda*

he's doing it on purpose, think about how his innate personality fits (or doesn't fit) with yours. None of these traits is inherently bad or good. They just are.

Life with a Sparkler

Some babies sail smoothly into your family. Other beginnings are stormier. Thomas and Chess described babies with certain traits as "difficult".[2] That's a pretty negative description for some traits with pretty positive aspects. It's not so much that a child is "difficult" as that our society expects children to behave in certain ways. As some mothers say, "The same thing that drives you crazy when he's 2 is the thing you'll admire when he's 20." The High Activity baby who rolled and wiggled in bed may be the adult who impresses you by all he accomplishes in a day. The High Persistent child who kept leaving his bed for yours four times in one night may grow up to accomplish some pretty tough goals through perseverance and determination.

Chess and Thomas themselves added that the parents' response to their babies makes a huge difference. Many cultures have a more relaxed approach to feeding and sleeping that allows different personalities to shine more easily, so let's put a more positive spin on "difficult" babies.

Dr. William Sears has renamed babies at the intense end of the spectrum "high-need".[3] Mary Sheedy Kurcinka wrote about them in *Raising Your Spirited Child.* In *The Womanly Art of Breastfeeding* (eighth edition), they're called "sparklers".

If you never find the reason why your baby resists sleep or is chronically fussy, you can say to yourself, "I have a sparkler." Sparklers need constant input to take their mind off their troubles. They tend to do best with the motion and closeness of carrying. Go with your sparkler's need for action attention, and all that input can pay off in an especially smart little one. Those of us who lived with a sparkler and went with the flow can tell you it was worth the trip.

Sleep Training and Infant Personality Traits

Combine very different sleep personalities and very uniform societal expectations about how babies "should" behave, and you can see why some of the sleep training ideas became popular . . . and why the outcomes are so uneven. Let's say you have a baby who is highly Regular in his sleeping patterns, very Adaptable, not Intense at all, not very Active, and low in Persistence. You decide to try sleep training. You put him in a cot at the time when he's naturally tired—which was easy for you to predict—and he might fuss a little but soon falls asleep. You repeat this a few more nights and soon he's going to sleep all by himself every night with little effort on your part. And you wonder why *all* parents don't do it! But your friend tries the same thing with her Irregular, highly Active, Withdrawing, less Adaptive, Negative-mood, highly Persistent, highly Sensitive child and the process of sleep training is an absolute nightmare for everyone. Same process, different babies, totally different results.

Sleep-training researchers will say that their methods worked because the babies whose parents stuck with their plan started going to sleep alone without much crying. But almost *a third* of parents drop out of a typical sleep-training study.[4] Do they just not follow through? It seems likely that the parents who are happy with the results have the kind of babies who are more able to manage being sleep trained, while the parents whose babies have a different temperament realize that it was just too harsh to continue.

According to a 2001 study that rated preschoolers on the characteristics listed above, children who were less Adaptable, less Regular, and more Intense were the most likely to bedshare.[5] The researcher commented that these children may *need* parental contact in order to get back to sleep when they wake up, and added, "They are likely to be especially resistant to efforts to get them to 'self-soothe'."

Babies Who Speak for Babies

The more intense babies who insist, "This self-soothing stuff isn't working. I need *you*!" may be speaking for *all* babies, because sleep training doesn't fit with human infant biology. Some other babies may be just as stressed and need their mothers just as much, but because they don't have that intensity gene, they don't announce their concerns as loudly. Appreciate the fact that your Intense baby makes sure he gets the attention that all babies thrive on. (You'll find much more research on how sleep training does and doesn't work in Chapter 18.)

> I'm glad I had my first baby first. He was what the books call "high-need". He woke up crying until he was three. His mood would go from 0 to 60 in seconds. He needed nearly constant holding, and he let me know when he didn't get it. He *demanded* responsive parenting. His younger brother was okay with whatever life brought, and I felt just a little silly bouncing him, carrying him around, and talking to him, when really he seemed content without it. Oh, what he'd have missed out on if I hadn't been trained by the expert first! The younger brother automatically got his needs met because his older brother had insisted on it. My older son says my younger son should send him a thank-you card for all the training he gave me!
>
> —Wendy

Baby Sleep Styles

Just as babies have different temperaments, they also have different sleeping styles. And it's amazing how different children can be within the same family. We are sharing these labels and descriptions to remind you that (1) your baby's normal and (2) you have company.

Cuddlers

A *cuddler* relaxes into you, curls around you, sighs happily against your shoulder, and shows you in many ways how much she enjoys being in your arms and snuggled next to you. Cuddlers are surely the original body pillows. Some like to tuck a hand or foot under your body. Maybe they like the extra closeness. Or maybe they just like to know for sure that you're there.

> For some fun with bedsharing-baby sleep gymnastics, *The Guide to Baby Sleep Positions: Survival Tips for Co-Sleeping Parents* by Andy Herald and Charlie Capen is a cute, cartoon-style been-there book.

> Lisa always arranged herself in bed to have maximum contact. She was very skilled at moulding her body to fit against mine no matter what position I was lying in.
>
> —Amelie

Velcro Babies

A *Velcro baby* must be in near-total body contact with you or your partner (or both, if they can manage it) at all times. They seem to relax completely only when they're right up against you. Velcro babies also tend to need more carrying throughout the day. That doesn't mean they're clingy or shy. They just have a greater need for closeness. Take heart: accept and meet their needs at the start, and with that secure "launchpad" they tend to grow up to be highly independent, even adventurous.

> We always called our son the "heat-seeking missile." He would snuggle right into any warm spot. Usually he'd end up with his head under my armpit near the "na-nas."
>
> —Sherrie

Slow to Sleep

Many *slow to sleep* babies take a long time to wind down. Even when you know they're tired, they breastfeed, fuss (sometimes a lot), wiggle around, let go and coo at you, play with your hair, breastfeed some more, hum to themselves, squirm around a bit, breastfeed some more, and—just when you are ready to scream—finally fall asleep. They tend to be the more sensitive children, and seem to need extra time to work off whatever stresses they've encountered during the day before they can relax into sleep. They often benefit from a long walk in a sling or carrier before bedtime, or a relaxing bath with Mum or Dad.

H Is for Hogs—Space Hogs

It's hard to miss the *space hog*—the older baby who persistently shoves people out of the way to claim a large area of the bed for himself. He often ends up in a perfect H with his head against (or on top of) one parent's body and his feet against (or on top of) the other's. There isn't much you can say or do that will keep him aligned in bed. One father even found himself sleeping with his foot on the floor so he didn't fall off the side of the bed. Some mothers find that their wiggle worms are less wiggly in a bigger bed—one of the reasons many families put a big mattress (or two) on the floor. If you have a king-size mattress, so much the better.

Constant Contacters

They're not looking for full-body contact. But *some* part of *constant contacters* always has to touch *some* part of you. Maybe the H position comes from the ones who have to touch both of you.

> Our son used to throw a leg over his father in his sleep. His father, fractionally awake, would throw it back. Over, back, over, back.

His father didn't like it . . . until he didn't have it any more. Now he misses it.

—Kayla

Martial Artists

Martial artists (who are usually older than a year) expend a lot of energy while they sleep. They flip and flop, toss and turn, and twist from one end of the bed to another. They may poke, kick, or jab anyone within arm or foot range. And nothing you do during the day seems to make any difference at night. These children simply have more active sleeping styles. They fling their hands and feet while they sleep—sometimes right into the parent's more sensitive areas. Ow!

Someone once told me that babies who sleep with their mothers from a young age don't move around as much as other children. Ha! I have a couple who were gymnasts once they were older. I don't know what they did in their sleep, but I'd wake up in the middle of the night with the covers all pulled off, and the child facing the wrong way at the opposite end of the bed. These two still sleep in really odd positions sometimes.

—Lara

Cover Kickers

Many children "run hot" in a room that feels just right to the parents. Try dressing your *cover kicker* in lighter-weight pyjamas or just a nappy. Some parents have the baby sleep on top of the bedcovers, with his own little blanket that he can kick off or snuggle with as he pleases while his parents stay warm under the covers. He won't have the closest contact, but that's often fine with these easily overheated babies.

The occasional baby or toddler steals covers rather than kicking them off. Maybe he runs cold instead of hot. If he's a cover grabber, you might try dressing him a little more warmly (without overheating him). Or practise the kind of reverse thinking you'll be using at times for years to come: try changing what *you* wear, so you can adapt to what you can't seem to change.

> I have one child (out of three) who always generated incredible heat in bed, always sweaty and kicking off the covers. He is my athlete, the most intensely physical of my children.
>
> —Kelly

Wedgers

A *wedger* is usually an older toddler or child who climbs into bed with his parents midway through the night and squeezes in between them. Depending on their sensitivity or how deeply they're asleep, the parents may not realize it's happened until they wake up with a child sleeping happily—and snugly—between them.

Boomerangers

The *boomerang child* transitions pretty easily to his own bed, then comes back in the middle of the night to slip into yours. Don't worry: it's a very normal part of learning to sleep alone. It's one thing to fall asleep after a bedtime story and a kiss, and another thing entirely to wake at 2.00 a.m. to a dark and silent world. Your child still needs some reassurance during the night for now, but eventually he'll feel more okay in his own bed. Nightly boomeranging becomes several times a week and then only when monsters loom. Eventually you won't be able to remember the last time he crawled in, and it may leave a hole for a while in both your bed and your heart.

Your Own Sleep Style

Sleep positions are much more varied for breastfeeding and bedsharing babies than for their mothers. You're likely to do the cuddle curl around your baby to protect and nurture her for at least the first few months. That position means you're less likely to move much during the night, and you'll face your baby more than formula-feeding mothers do, though you'll spend time on your back too.[6] As she gets bigger and sturdier, you'll roll onto your back more often and eventually even turn your back to her at times. These gradually evolving sleep behaviours are hardwired for breastfeeding mothers. Talk to just about any breastfeeding mother anywhere and she'll probably describe the same pattern. Research supports this, too.

One Room, Lots of Options

Our partners don't have our hardwired sleep instincts, so they come in more styles. Fortunately, so do beds, and there are lots of different ways to set up a sleeping space with your baby. Many families like to have a king-size mattress on the floor, where everyone can snuggle or separate whenever they want. That's not always practical or affordable, though. Sleeping arrangements change as babies grow and new babies join the family, so most people end up trying out new options as time goes on.

Of course, who we sleep with affects how we sleep. Here are some common sleeping arrangements that may work with different "sleep personalities".

Baby-mother-other: If your other bed partner is a heavy sleeper, flailer, sprawler, or older child, it's best to keep yourself between baby and other. If your bed is high or narrow, you might want to consider a mesh side rail or bedside cot on the baby's side of the bed as a precaution against falls. Or you could try separate beds for a while, for at least part of the night. See "Baby-Mother. Other", below, for some thoughts and reassurance on that one.

Mother-baby-other: If your other is still and self-contained, or clearly a very baby-responsive adult, or if your baby is older than three or four months, you might feel safer and snugglier with your baby between the two of you. Some mothers have a partner who's a true snuggler who even does an automatic cuddle curl with the baby.

Baby . . . mother-other: The bedside cot arrangement. It's useful for about the first five months, or until your baby starts pushing up on hands and knees. Remember to babyproof your bed according to the Safe Surface checklist so that you can feel comfortable whether you slide your baby back into the bedside cot after breastfeeding or just fall asleep together.

Mother-other-baby: Some parents of older babies who are trying some gentle night-weaning or bed-weaning have the partner snuggle the baby. Mum is still available . . . just not quite so available. An older baby may decide it's not worth climbing over the person in the middle in order to breastfeed, and settle back to sleep.

Baby. Mother-other: Baby in the same room, completely separate sleep space. Room-sharing is important for at least the first half year. If you move your baby to another room after that, having a two-way monitor or two monitors (one set up so you can hear the baby, the other so the baby can hear you) can be comforting. Your little one expects the stirrings and mutterings of his favourite grown-ups. Hearing you will help bring a little of that soothing presence into the new setting with him.

Baby-other: You'll probably leave your baby alone with your partner at some point, for one reason or another. It's fine when you get up to pee, fine for a short time when your baby is a little older and a little sturdier, and fine if your partner is happy to help and you need to get something else done. You can do what you need to do in the same room, and go farther afield as your baby gets bigger and you know how your partner behaves with a little one in the bed. It's a gentle part of a "See? There are other safe people besides me!" message in the second half of the first year.

Baby-mother. Other: Sometimes it's just easier for a couple to sleep in separate spaces for a while after the baby's born, especially right after the birth, while the mother and baby are learning how to breastfeed lying down. Some cultures routinely have a separate space for the mother-baby pair at the start. It's not about your relationship; it's about nighttime coping. And you need to make it through the night in order to be on speaking terms in the morning!

A separate bed can work well for the *light sleeper* who's bothered by every wiggle and jiggle. The *early riser* who has to get up for work may be able to squeeze out a little more sleep in a different bed. Some partners go to another room. On some nights even a sofa (for partner, not for mother and baby!) can be preferable to sleeping with an active baby. Sometimes the partner moves the first time the baby wakes and spends the rest of the night in another space.

A partner who's a *flailer* or *sprawler* may do best farther away from you. Like *way* over there. At least for now.

The *snorer* may or may not be hard to sleep with, depending on your and your baby's temperaments. Some people—both grown-ups and babies—aren't bothered by noise at night, but some are very sensitive to it. Earplugs can help (white noise can be too much for these developing ears.) Your snoring partner may also have sleep issues that are worth a trip to a sleep clinic.

The poor *sick sweetie* is a partner who has a migraine or the flu or (please, no!) a stomach bug. Most of us like a little space when we're not feeling well.

Maybe *you* want the whole bed to yourself at first while you learn the mechanics of sleeping with a little one. It gives you all the room you need while you figure out sleeping, breastfeeding, bedside table needs, and reducing nighttime fumbling. Some mothers go with their baby to another room (with appropriate preparations for bedsharing) for the first few months, or set up a flat futon in the living room for easy downtime day or night.

Obviously, sleeping in a different place from your partner has nothing to do with how much love there is in the family. It has nothing to do with avoiding sex. It's about a lack of space or comfort or just a desire to avoid an elbow in your ribs for now.

Which leads us to *musical beds*. Some mothers who didn't consider this with their first child discover how much easier life can be

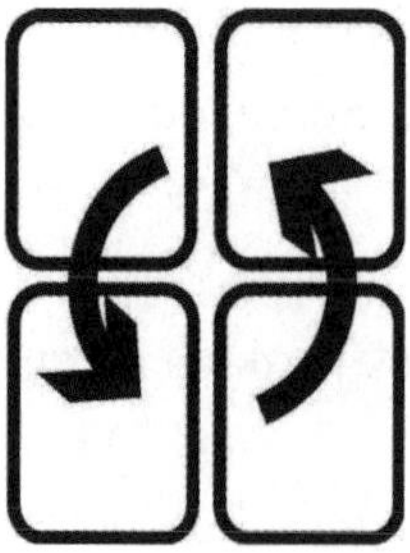

with "freestyle sleep" once there's more than one with nighttime needs to consider.

What about a single or cot mattress on the floor, two single mattresses pushed together, or a king-size mattress with a single mattress pushed against it? Watch out for a slowly widening mattress gap anytime you push two of them together with an under-one-year-old baby in the picture. The "bed connector" mentioned in Chapter 2 may be a big help. The beauty of moving to the floor is that any child who's mobile can get off and on without help and without risk (although it can be awkward for a pregnant mother or one who's recently had a C-section). One of us put a cot mattress on the floor in "the boys' room" and read the toddler to sleep on it each night. When he woke up, he could come across the hall to "the big bed". Mum and Dad had some private space and still got to wake up to a child's smile in the morning. Later on, the little brother sometimes slept in a single bed with his big brother. Later still, they had a bunk bed, and the big brother could escape the little brother anytime he wanted, day or night, by scrambling to the top bunk.

Whatever your nighttime arrangements, they're going to change over time. Tomorrow *may* be different. Next year *will* be different. In fact, one infant sleep researcher dislikes the term "family bed" because it makes bedsharing sound like a very specific, unchanging set up. In the early days, daytime sleep is already pretty free-form. Might as well go with 24/7 flexibility and do whatever works. Keep your options open, stay flexible and creative, and remember that nights are for *sleeping*, not for arranging your family life to please Aunt Agatha.

When we brought our first baby home, we all settled into the back bedroom, which was less draughty and less noisy. We had intended it to be the guest bedroom, but it became our bedroom.

Late in my second pregnancy, my son had night-weaned, and sharing a bed with my husband and child became uncomfortable. So I moved into the front bedroom. After my daughter was born, she and I slept in the front bedroom and my husband and son slept in the back bedroom. After a while, my husband would put my son to sleep and come to "our" bed.

My daughter started sleeping in her own room when we moved to our new house. But it's rare to find her in her own bed in the morning. She still wakes up in the middle of the night and crawls in with someone for the rest of the night.

—Eglantina

Partner Places

- My partner was amazing. He never moved at night when we had the baby with us, or else he'd cuddle him just the way I did. —Cathy
- I just always slept between them. I never really believed my husband wouldn't throw an arm out and clonk the baby the way he's clonked me before. —Nan
- At first I didn't want the baby in our bed, even if my wife slept between us, because I was afraid. By the time our daughter was six weeks old, I was snuggling with her while my wife got ready for work. Now I really enjoy bedsharing. —Paul
- We started out sleeping baby-mother-father. Sarah and my husband had a cordial but not terribly warm relationship. Then, for some unrelated reason, I moved Sarah to the space between us. It was amazing. Father and daughter became best buddies. Once they started spending one-third of their day being right next to each other—even though they were both unconscious—their relationship warmed right up. —Linda

Something to Sleep On

Keeping your child's, your partner's, and your own personalities and sleep styles in mind can help you find ways to improve your nights, which we hope will help your days go more smoothly.

If you're willing to change your arrangements as needs change, you can save a lot of struggle and strife on all sides. Some families' mantra is *whatever gives the most people the most sleep tonight*. Where and how everyone sleeps will settle down eventually, all by itself or with gentle nudges along the way. As your children get older, they'll stake out their territories, and instead of wanting a welcome sign on your door, they just might put a "Private!" sign on their own. Or not. Depends on their personality.

chapter 8

Working

> At the nursery, they kept asking me questions about how well he sleeps. Things like, "Does he have a favourite toy he likes to hold?" But they meant, "Does he need something special to sleep with?" Finally, the lightbulb went on. They were fishing for advice on how to get him to sleep. Well, in fact . . . I just breastfeed him to sleep. He has two parents in bed with him each night. *We* are his stuffed toys, complete with nighttime fresh milk services. Is that special enough?
>
> But in the end, you know a tired baby will sleep.
>
> Before you take your baby to nursery, you freak out with worry that it won't work. But it usually does. Something works out.
>
> —Donna

If you're a working mother, you're not alone. Mothers all over the world work in countless settings and circumstances while their children are tended by family members, a nanny, a childminder or at a nursery. This is a short chapter because you're not that different from other mothers and babies, so most of this book is written for you. But you do have an extra load, so you deserve your own space.

The younger your baby is, the more difficult it can be to work out the logistics. It's especially problematic in the United States, the only developed country in the world with no national paid maternity leave, which often forces mothers with babies just a few weeks old to return to work. (See goo.gl/raqWU1 for a dramatic infographic.)

In the UK women who are employed must take at least two weeks' leave (four weeks for factory workers) and are entitled to take up to 52 weeks of Statutory Maternity Leave (SML). This is made up of two parts – 'Ordinary Maternity Leave' which is the first 26 weeks and 'Additional Maternity Leave' which is the second 26 weeks. Up to 11 of these weeks can be taken before the baby is born.

Most of the weeks that a UK mother is on SML are paid. Statutory Maternity Pay (SMP) is paid for up to 39 weeks and the mother receives 90% of average weekly earnings for the first six weeks and then either £138.18 or 90% of average weekly earnings, if lower, for the next 33 weeks. So, for example, a woman working a minimum wage job (40 hours a week at £6.31 per hour) would receive £227.16 for six weeks and £138.18 for 33 weeks. If she started her maternity leave, as many women do, two weeks before her due date her baby would be eight and a half months old before she moved into unpaid leave. Many employers offer packages for maternity pay that go over and above the statutory requirements although anything beyond SMP may be repayable if the women chooses not to return to work.

UK women on SML are entitled to return to their old job if they return after the period of Ordinary Maternity Leave and to their old job or a suitably similar one after Additional Maternity Leave. There is no legal right to return to work part-time but parents are entitled to request flexible and/or part-time working and the employer must seriously consider it.

In Australia employees with over 12 months' service are entitled to up to 12 months' unpaid parental leave and can request a further 12 months. Mothers can get 18 weeks of this as paid leave which must be arranged with the employer. However, many employers will provide packages over and above the statutory Paid Parental Leave. The Australian mother who doesn't want to take unpaid leave would be returning to work when her baby is four months old.

In New Zealand mothers are entitled to 14 weeks' unpaid leave and, if eligible, extended leave of up to 52 weeks. A mother who didn't want to take unpaid leave would be returning to work when her baby is a little over three months old.

In South Africa mothers are required to take six weeks off after the birth and may take a total of four months' leave, starting up to one month before the due date. Women on maternity leave can claim unemployment benefits for 17 weeks which are between 38-60% of her usual salary. A South African mother not wishing to take unpaid leave would therefore be returning when her baby is three to four months old.

Scandinavian maternity leave is often held up as the world's best. For example, in Sweden parents are entitled to 480 days (15 months) of parental leave, the bulk of which is paid at 80% of usual salary.

Most working mothers have two main sleep-related challenges. The first is how to make napping at day nursery easier for your baby. The second is how to make sure you get enough sleep while meeting your baby's needs. And, of course, you also have to work! You get only 24 hours a day to do it all, and they can't be squeezed or stretched. All you can do is squeeze or stretch what you do with them.

For starters, if you're going back to work or college in the early months, getting as much rest as possible while you're on your maternity leave is really important. It's tempting to try to get everything done before the baby comes, but there really will be time after the birth and it's tough starting off with a sleep deficit. Now is a good time to start delegating responsibilities, and it might help to practice *front-loading* – getting all your jobs done at the beginning of the day to allow time to wind down in the evening when the baby is at his most fractious (see Chapter 10).

Melting into Motherhood

In Chapter 3 we use the phrase "melting into motherhood" to describe giving in to the timelessness and intense demands of early motherhood—taking your eyes off your phone and taking a leap of faith. Enjoy the time between birthing and working, and let those magnets that you read about in Chapter 3 stick together. It's a unique window of time for attaching deeply and securely. Some mothers are tempted to keep a little distance, steeling themselves against the separations to come. But you'll give yourself some wonderful memories and certainly a lot more rest if you can forget about the job ahead and live in the moment. A strong relationship with your child will outlast any job you'll ever have.

Some mothers avoid bedsharing or holding their baby through naps because they know that kind of attention won't be available at nursery. But there's no sense in depriving a child of affection and touch in one part of a day just because he won't get all he needs in another part. That's sort of like having your partner sleep in another room because you're about to take a business trip and you both need to get used to being apart. Building a strong bond with your baby before you go back to work, and continuing it when he's home, can go a long way toward reducing the stress of being there without you.

Going Back

If you have any flexibility, see if you can give yourself an easier back-to-work transition. Rather than starting back on a Monday, ask if you could make your first day back a Wednesday or Thursday, so you have only two or three days before the weekend. Then see if you can take the next couple of Wednesdays off—maybe as a holiday?—so that you're working only two days in a row before you have a day or two to catch up on breastfeeding and sleep. It can go a long way towards helping you and your baby get into a new rhythm.

If that's not possible, ask about other options. Sometimes mothers can arrange to start back part-time for the first few weeks. Be creative. You may not know what's possible until you ask. Reassure your employer that it's not forever—you're just trying to smooth the transition a bit for you and your baby. La Leche League GB have a leaflet on Working and Breastfeeding which is available from goo.gl/vG6tLc. The United States Breastfeeding Committee has a comprehensive list of resources for U.S. breastfeeding mothers at goo.gl/OZXThv and goo.gl/QuK4T5.

UK employers are legally obliged to provide breastfeeding mothers with somewhere to rest. They are not required to provide you with somewhere to store milk, nor a private space or breaks, though many employers will. Maternity Action have an information sheet at maternityaction.org.uk/wp/advice-2/mums-dads-scenarios/6-breastfeeding-rights/continuing-to-breastfeed-when-you-return-to-work. Further information about breastfeeding at work is available from the Health and Safety Executive (hse.gov.uk/mothers/faqs.htm).

In Australia there are no specific provisions but there is general legislation which prohibits discrimination against breastfeeding mothers. The Australian Breastfeeding Association has information at breastfeeding.asn.au/bf-info/breastfeeding-and-work/can-you-return-work-and-still-breastfeed.

In New Zealand employers are obliged to provide facilities and breaks for breastfeeding mothers (although these can be unpaid). More information is available at dol.govt.nz/er/holidaysandleave/parentalleave/infantfeeding.

South African legislation allows for mothers to have two 30-minute breaks per day for breastfeeding until the baby is six months old and employers should provide a space where practical.

Home at the End of the Day

A mother who's home all day is usually happy to hand the little one over to a partner who's been at work all day. You, on the other hand, haven't seen your baby for hours. You get first refusal. Blame your breasts: "Darling, I really need to sit down and breastfeed." If you plan some regular feet-up time with your baby as soon as you get home, and make it a routine, the rest of your family will be more likely to give you that space than if you're hit-and-miss about it.

Your planned bed is an excellent place for that feet-up time, in case you fall asleep. Keep water and some snacks at your bedside for some quick after-work fuel. Even if you're not sleepy, that feet-up time is a chance to reconnect with your baby and can help make up for time spent awake during the night. You might want to tell your partner when you'll be up (and set the alarm on your phone).

If you really can't afford downtime yourself, a babycarrier is a fabulous way to give the baby a nap. What a baby wants most is closeness, not conversation, and you can offer that whether you're lying down or getting things done around the house.

If your baby doesn't want feet-up time and you do, take some time first for a long feed before giving your partner some baby time. You'll rest better and longer if you're empty and he's full. After supper, give *serious* thought to using the "front-loading" approach in Chapter 10—slow down the end of your day instead of speeding it up, even if it means getting up a bit earlier in the morning. You'll be more efficient in the morning and you'll have an excuse for relaxing in the evening. If that doesn't work for you, experiment with mealtime. Does having dinner earlier give you the energy to get through your evening more easily? Does pushing it later give you an hour or so of rest or a short nap before you have to think about it? (If you're going to eat later, you may need a hearty snack in the afternoon at work.) Could a slow cooker help so that dinner's done when you walk in the door?

Speaking of meals, every woman is superwoman after having a baby. Take a look at the pie charts in Chapter 15, and you'll realize how much more you're getting done in smaller slivers of time than you ever had before. All on top of building brains, bones, tiny toes, and smiles. So let go of your before-baby standards, simplify and streamline the meals as much as you can, and know that life will be a little less hectic in a few months.

> I recently started working in direct sales, and sometimes this means I'm on the road for 10 to 12 hours. By the time I get home, all my two-year-old wants to do is breastfeed. All I want to do is sleep! So we do both . . . we snuggle up on her mattress and she breastfeeds while I take a quick nap. It's just a great way to reconnect and recharge. It's also probably the only time she will stay still!
>
> —Susanne

Days Off

The temptation is to spend days off and weekends catching up on errands and housework, but in the early months your time may be much better spent breastfeeding and resting as much as possible. It's a good idea to keep your breastfeeding times flexible. There's structure enough during the week, and mothers who keep their baby on a schedule may find the baby weaning sooner than they wanted. "Snicky-snack" breastfeeding is good for your milk supply, good for your baby's growth, and is actually easier than sticking to a schedule. Napping, breastfeeding, and ignoring the clock when you can will make it easier for you to soak each other up for the week ahead.

Baby Nights After Working Days

However your baby spends her days away from you, she's going to want—need—lots of time with you at home. In fact, bedsharing feels like a necessity to many working mothers. They can breastfeed, pat, settle, and cuddle the baby without getting up. All breastfeeding mothers gain precious minutes of extra sleep time when they bedshare.[1] Mothers in the workforce surely need it most. Your milk supply does best with more frequent feeds, especially since pumping a few times during the day is no replacement for the many little snacks you and your baby enjoyed before you went back. And your baby? She gets to spend a whole one-third of her day in total touch with the person she most wants to be with. More than a few mothers have enjoyed some of their awake time at night as the only time in their busy days when the baby is the total focus of their attention.

Those night feeds are especially important now for maintaining your milk production. And you may find that your baby wakens more than before because night is when he can reconnect. Bedsharing may help; many mothers who breastfeed lying down find that they can fall back asleep while the baby breastfeeds. And if you can't sleep while you breastfeed, remember that lying there awake still gives you much more rest than sitting up or getting out of bed or dealing with a crying baby. If you haven't yet mastered breastfeeding lying down, you might want to check out the pointers and photos in Chapter 6.

And then there's morning—a final feed in bed before you have to get up and start the day. Since most of us have the easiest time expressing first thing in the morning, you might want to have the pump set up beside the bed, breastfeed on one side, and express on the other to give you a head start on that day's milk.

> I'm more aware when breastfeeding happens, say, 15 to 20 minutes before the alarm goes off. Then I feel I've been deprived of sleep. But as long as I get back to sleep, it's like a dream. I don't actually remember doing it at all! —Donna

Days at Nursery or the Childminder

If your baby is under about four months old and already vulnerable, daycare does increase his risk of SIDS (see Chapter 19).[2] It's worth delaying going back to work until your baby is past this highest-risk period if you can. Or see if you can leave your baby for shorter times at first. Four half-day periods a week will probably be easier on him than two full days. Ask about the napping arrangements at the nursery or the childminder. Babies shouldn't be left unattended for about the first six months.

In the UK nurseries must have a ratio of one member of staff for every three babies under two, although many nurseries have higher ratios. One staff member cannot give three babies the kind of attention during a nap that they could get at home. Childminders may be able to give your baby more attention as they often have fewer babies and some will even use slings or hold babies while they sleep.

In Australia the recommended staff:baby ratio in nursery settings is 1:4, in New Zealand it is 1:5 and in South Africa it is also 1:5.

If your child is older when you go back to the workplace, things will probably be easier for both of you. A verbal or nearly verbal child is more likely to understand that this time is naptime—lights down, sleeping mats out, adults quiet, maybe a book being read—and you can help him by talking through the routine.

Owen needed to be with someone while he napped. I often breastfed him in my computer chair and unwound by playing around on the computer, right into toddlerhood. I went back to work when he was about 15 months old. My mum still relishes the naps she shared with Owen after that.

—Lillian

Here are some other thoughts from working mothers:

- Sit down and breastfeed your baby at nursery before you set off home. Having the baby already "tanked up" might allow you to get some things done and plan an earlier bedtime. And being exposed to the nursery's germs means you'll make customized antibodies for your baby.
- If your baby just isn't ready for an early bedtime but you have a partner, those evening hours are a chance for them to get better acquainted while you warm up the bed.
- Give your partner some of the errands you used to run and chores you used to do. Show your partner the pie charts in Chapter 15. You can't do it all. Something has to give, and it can't really be the food shopping (unless you do it online).
- If your baby is over six months old and you feel like something has to give, take a look at the nudging ideas in Chapter 11.
- Find a way to connect with other working mothers. Online will probably fit your schedule best. Two good sites: mumsnet.com and netmums.com.
- Sick days are there to be used! Sleep deprivation is an illness, and it's cured only with sleep.
- Remember how important night breastfeeding is to maintaining your milk supply during the day.

Meanwhile, Back at the Nursery

You're back at work, you've dropped off your baby and your expressed milk, and the caregiver is left caring for a baby for whom Mum is everything. A child's stress hormones are higher at nursery, from infancy right through the preschool years.[3] Maybe he's willing to take a bottle when you're away, but maybe he's not crazy about it. He certainly isn't happy about spending hours and hours away from you. He misses you! It's not easy to be the nursery worker who has to learn how your baby responds. What's a compassionate caregiver to do? There's a page in the Tearsheet Toolkit with some hints for childcare providers to help with naptime and ways to keep your baby safer.

What if your caregiver isn't on board with all this? What if she firmly believes that babies should be put to bed on their stomachs, on a schedule, and that a little formula never hurt anyone? That can be *really* intimidating, but even if she's older than you are, or has more experience, it doesn't make her right. Unfortunately, you can never really know what goes on there when you're at work, no matter what you request. Bottom line, as always: listen to your instincts. And try to remember that she's working for you and not the other way around. If your instincts tell you to look for a different arrangement . . . look for a different arrangement.

> You'll find lots of information on managing work-time issues like pumping in *The Womanly Art of Breastfeeding*, eighth edition. Two great books full of stories of breastfeeding and working mothers supporting one another with real-world tips are *Hirkani's Daughters: Women Who Scale Modern Mountains to Combine Working and Breastfeeding* by Jennifer Hicks, and *The Milk Memos: How Real Moms Learned to Mix Business with Babies—and How You Can, Too* by Cate Colburn-Smith and Andrea Serrette.

Nursery Naps

Babies use different strategies to make it through the day without you. They know very well that a bottle isn't a mother, so don't worry that the feeding schedule at nursery won't match your feed-on-demand breastfeeding style at home. But the sucking and holding that go along with meals may help your baby settle for sleep just as they do at home.

Some babies look for *extra* sucking if they're away from their mother all day. This may be one of those situations where a dummy is a kindness, especially at naptime. It's a very good idea to "lose" the dummy when you're at home, though. A dummy can hasten weaning if it's used to replace or delay feeds or if it's given more freely than your breast is.

If your childcare provider uses a slow-flow nipple and holds your baby fairly upright while she offers it, the milk will come more slowly and gently, giving your baby a more leisurely, less stressful feeding that can help her settle for naps (see the Tearsheet Toolkit from *The Womanly Art of Breastfeeding,* llli.org/toolkit).

Reverse Cycling

Some babies prefer to "reverse cycle" while at nursery or at the childminder's, sleeping the day away with only a couple of feeds, and breastfeeding more at night. The upside with a reverse cycler is that you may not have to do as much expressing during the day. The downside is a baby who'll want some activity in the mornings and evenings and—gulp—at night, to make up for having slept so much during the day. This is a baby who *really* needs to be with you at night, breastfeeding, reconnecting, and breastfeeding—yet another reason for "front-loading". See Chapter 10 for more ideas on getting as much rest as you can.

> When our first son, Gabriel, was a year old, I went back to work as a nurse on the evening shift. The three of us had always slept together and I had always breastfed Gabriel to sleep, but my husband, Paul, knew that now he would have to get our son to sleep without me (and my breasts). He ended up playing his guitar and singing to him until he fell asleep. It worked beautifully. With our next two children, Paul started playing guitar to them right away to help them fall asleep. It became his magic sleepy-time tool whenever I wasn't there. He grew as a dad and his relationship with the children was enriched too.
>
> —Beth

Bedsharing When You're Working the Night Shift

If you have to work the night shift, you probably won't be at home when your baby sleeps, so what about bedsharing? Take into consideration that bedsharing with someone other than you does increase risk for about the first four months.

Here are some ways to keep a bedsharing connection even if you can't be there during the night:

- If possible, ask the daytime caregiver to bring your baby to you in bed when he's ready for a nap or for a feed.
- If you get home before your baby wakes up in the morning, you can bring him to bed with you to snuggle and breastfeed before he's ready to start the day.
- Some babies reverse their days and nights at least partially, which helps.
- You can bedshare on your days off (if you can sleep at night).

For Milo's first two years, I worked part-time at night. Bedsharing really saved our bacon and our breastfeeding relationship. During the day before or after a shift, I would sleep and he would be brought to me when he was fussy or sleepy. It was great that his usual nap space was in our arms or in our bed, so this was familiar. I could keep snoozing and reconnect with him at the same time. I felt better about my time away since we had the close time together. I'm glad I didn't breastfeed him to sleep and then put him in another room—I would have wasted so much sleeping time!

—Michelle

Something to Sleep On

Working away from home when you have a young child is tough. Even though you're apart during the day, your two magnets can stick together—really stick together—at night. Breastfeeding and bedsharing give you an extra power that many working mothers don't have—the ability to reconnect deeply every night at the same time that you multitask feeds and sleep. Breastfeeding and bedsharing can be a mutually beneficial arrangement for everyone.

chapter 9

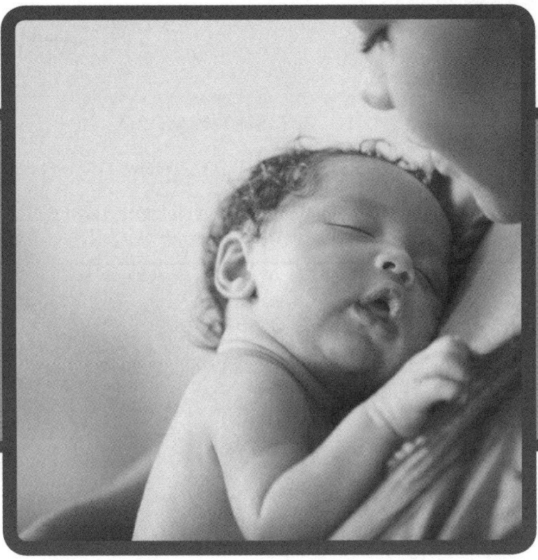

Alternate Routes

> I supplement my baby at the breast for most feedings, usually with donated breast milk. The greatest challenge came at night. It took nearly seven weeks, but I was finally able to master lying down beside my son on the bed to breastfeed. I make sure I have my supplementer on a flat surface and everything ready. Once he's latched on, it's only a matter of sliding the tubing into the corner of his mouth. Of course, late at night I'm groggy and tired, so it isn't as easy as it sounds. It has taken a lot of perseverance and determination. I don't always get it on my first try. Nonetheless, it's been worth it and I am so happy to be able to continue breastfeeding.
>
> —Ali

Most of this book so far has been about why and how to bring your baby into your bed. But along the way we've mentioned some of the reasons and situations when it might not work well. If one (or more) of those applies to you, this chapter is for you.

Maybe bedsharing *isn't* your first or best choice. Or maybe you need some modifications to the usual bedsharing setup. We'll help you explore some of the situations and ways to help both of you stay close and get some sleep. For many of these, there is little or no specific research to guide us, so we need to rely on the experiences of other mothers and their maternal common sense. (And no matter what sleeping arrangements you settle on, be sure to keep your own bed as safe as possible, just in case.)

Are breastfeeding problems the issue? Nights are almost always the hardest part of the day if you're still struggling with nursing. And a book—*any* book—is going to fall short. It's well worth reaching out to a real person, a breastfeeding specialist who can help you troubleshoot. We've given you some starting points in Chapter 23. La Leche League is a great place to start—check out our website (laleche.org.uk) to find a local La Leche League Leader. Even if she can't help you herself, she's likely to know about other local resources.

When Breastfeeding Is Difficult at Night

Alternate routes means the simplest route isn't available to you. After working out the logistics of supplementing and expressing (which we'll discuss in detail below), here are three of the next most common reasons that breastfeeding can be difficult at night and ideas for working through them.

Some babies are more likely to latch easily at night, especially when they're sleepy. More than one bedsharing mother has wakened to find her baby happily breastfeeding with no help at all—yet another good reason for bedsharing if you can. But if nothing's working, nighttime isn't the time to try to fix it. Some issues are just too big to deal with when you're tired. The sections that follow will give you ideas on getting through your nights when you're bottle-feeding and expressing. We really encourage you to find a La Leche League Leader or breastfeeding counsellor in your area, and get some skilled help . . . in the morning.

If Latching Works in Only One Position

Even if your baby latches on fairly easily, he may be good at it only when you're sitting up. That's fine at the shopping centre, but it's not ideal at night. Some thoughts that may make it easier:

- Sit on the edge of the bed to start. Once your baby is doing the slow, rhythmic sucking that means he's really getting into his meal, slowly swing your legs up and your body down onto the bed. Or sit up in bed, latch, and snuggle down. Move slowly and try not to shift your baby's mouth-nipple connection while you do it.
- Make a nest of pillows behind you first, so that you can lean back against it once he's breastfeeding well. Arrange the pillows so that if you fall asleep, your body will relax backward onto the pillows, and your baby can roll or slide onto the bed surface (not a pillow) next to you if gravity doesn't hold him on you.
- One mother had her partner brace her as she gently lowered herself onto her pillows or into a side-lying position, until she could start from a side-lying position on her own.
- If you do need to get up and move to a chair, make sure it doesn't have nooks and crannies or extra pillows, and lean back after the baby's latched. If you're leaning forward to breastfeed, even a breastfeeding pillow is a risk because you're likely to slump forward if you fall asleep.

Once your baby is latching easily when you're sitting up, though, it's well worth learning to breastfeed lying down. There are suggestions in Chapter 6, including that you go to a mother-to-mother group to find out how other mothers do it. Just snuggling together in a cuddle curl is a lovely way for both of you to nod off.

If Latching Works on Only One Side

If there's just one breast or nipple that your baby has trouble with, or if your baby can't breastfeed easily on one side but is fine on the other, you may want to breastfeed on the easier side through the night and focus more on the difficult side during the day until you work out the kinks. Depending on your milk supply, you may have to express from the unused breast some time during the night, and you may need to give your baby the expressed milk if breastfeeding from one breast doesn't satisfy him. If it's tough for your baby to latch on to the problematic side even during the day, it's worth a call to a breastfeeding counsellor for personalized help.

Supplementing at Night

There are lots of ways to supplement your baby's nighttime feeds. The ways that work in the first few days aren't necessarily the way you want to continue, and the ways you supplement during the day aren't always the ways that work best at night.

The bottom line with any baby—what breastfeeding counsellors call Rule Number One—is to feed the baby. But struggling to supplement your baby at night can leave you bleary-eyed. So whatever it takes to get through the night will probably get you more sleep.

If breastfeeding itself isn't going well, you might find it helps to try one of these options, tweaking as needed to fit your milk supply, your situation, and your baby's needs and personality.

- Remember to follow the Safe Surface checklist in Chapter 2 to make your bed safe in case you fall asleep with your baby.
- If you're supplementing, be sure to read the Tearsheet Toolkit pages from *The Womanly Art of Breastfeeding*, eighth edition, on feeding a non-latching baby and on paced bottle-feeding to support breastfeeding (you can find them at llli.org/toolkit).
- Thinking about supplementing with formula? Since using formula has consequences, a breastfeeding counsellor can help you avoid it or balance breastfeeding and supplementing in a way that protects your supply and keeps your baby well-fed.
- Already supplementing with formula? No need to limit it if your baby needs it, so long as you keep your own supply as high as possible with frequent, *efficient* milk removal.
- Keep a cooler box at your bedside with bottles of your milk (or formula if needed). Feed the baby, toss the bottle

back in the cooler box, express your milk, and get back to sleep. Or have your partner feed the baby while you express your milk.

- Don't spend too much time *trying* to breastfeed during the night. If it doesn't work right away, supplement and express your milk.
- Or don't breastfeed at all during the night. Just give your baby the milk that's in the cooler box, express, and go back to sleep.
- Offer the supplement first and use breastfeeding for a sweet little dessert. Many babies relax and go to sleep more easily if they're "topped off" with breastfeeding instead of a bottle. Express afterwards if you need to.
- Breastfeed for several of the night feeds, and if you get to the point where it doesn't satisfy your baby, break out the supplement. Some mothers who are tapering off supplementation find their baby is willing to breastfeed exclusively through all or part of the night.
- Drink a great big glass of water before bed if your baby isn't waking you up. A full bladder will waken you much more gently than an alarm will!

At-Breast Supplementation

Some mothers use an at-breast supplementer, which isn't always easy at night. Here are a few hints from at-breast supplementing pros:

- Have multiple supplementers ready in an insulated cooler bag with ice packs by your bedside.
- There's no need to warm the supplement because it will warm enough as it flows through the tube against your chest. But it will still be cool enough for you to feel it moving so that you can know it's flowing properly even in the dark.
- Keep a couple of towels or cloth nappies next to the bed in case of leaks.

- Keep a small, dim light next to the bed at night to be able to see to get started until you learn to do it without looking.
- Try different styles of supplementers, including the low-cost homemade versions, to see which one is easiest to position when you are lying down.
- If you use a commercial version, there's no need to hang it from your neck in bed. Just put it on the bed next to your baby. Make sure you use tubing that's long enough to reach!
- If you need a faster flow, you may need to keep the supplementer higher than your baby's head. Your arm or a nearby pillow should work.

I think that using a tubing supplementer at my breast brings together all the joys of breastfeeding and all the annoyances of a fiddly appliance. Nighttimes with a supplementer can be especially daunting. It's dark, you're tired, you're all fingers and thumbs, and you just want everyone to get back to sleep as soon as possible. Using a supplementer is a skill. But like any new skill, it got easier with practice, and my baby gave me many opportunities for practice!

—Pamela

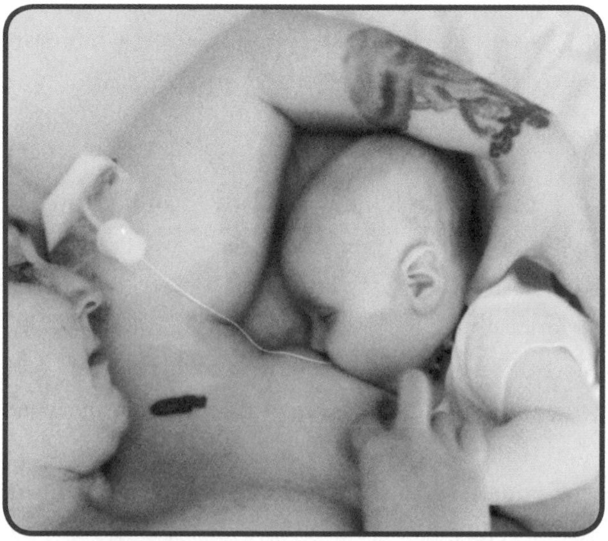

Yes, you can definitely bedshare and supplement at the breast!

Expressing at Night

In the first week or so, all babies consider themselves to be breastfeeding babies and try to stay close to the breast. Whether you're expressing for a temporary problem or plan to express long term, the two of you can bedshare as long as you naturally do a cuddle curl (see Chapters 2 and 4). Once your baby stops looking to your breast for food, or once you stop automatically cuddling him at breast level, he'll be safer in a bedside cot or cot for the first three or four months.

Here are some tips to make nighttime expressing easier:

- It's well worth learning how to hand express. Most of the world's mothers use *only* hand expression. And it's a very good thing to know if your pump fails.
- If you express, your milk production and your baby's health deserve a high-quality model. Look for one that's designed for full-time use, not occasional use. Even if expressing is temporary, it's *well worth* getting a rental-grade or hospital-grade pump (also called multi-user) to provide enough oomph. It's not a substitute for an effectively breastfeeding baby, but it'll do a far better job of establishing and maintaining your supply than a lightweight, inexpensive pump can. The bigger pumps tend to be much quieter too, something you may really appreciate after a few nights.
- Double-expressing—expressing both sides at the same time—is a huge timesaver and helps maintain and even increase milk production. Smaller pumps may not double-pump effectively.
- Using breast compressions and hand expression after pumping can significantly increase the amount of milk you express. See goo.gl/EtlUv6 for videos.
- Put your pump on your bedside table, plugged in, set up, and ready to go.
- Express at least twice at night during the first few weeks while your supply is getting established, and at least once a night until night breastfeeding is going well. A long

stretch (over four hours) without good milk removal, whether it happens during the day or during the night, sends a powerful message to your breasts to cut production back.

- Try expressing every one and a half to two hours during the day until you're ahead by two feeds. We know it can be tough, but getting yourself at least two bottles ahead of your baby's needs will give you real peace of mind.
- Once you're ahead by one bottle, get that bottle out before bedtime and let it warm to room temperature near your bed until the first feed.
- Freshly expressed milk can sit for hours at room temperature and lasts for up to five days in the refrigerator,[1] so storing it overnight in a bedside cooler box with ice packs is fine.[2]
- Have extra empty bottles on hand for nighttime expressing. Even if you're planning to use bags, consider using bottles at night (much less chance of spilling).
- After you've expressed, screw lids onto the bottles you used (or seal the bags), put them in the cooler box, and attach fresh bottles or bags to get a head start for the next session.
- Unless your baby is premature or seriously ill, there's no need to wash the pump parts between nighttime uses. Just wash them well in the morning. Hot, soapy water is fine. So is a dishwasher. No need to sterilize.
- Your middle-of-the-night milk is higher in the sleep-encouraging hormone melatonin.[3] Giving your baby milk that you expressed at night may help him sleep better.

Are you expressing at night because it just seems easier? Is exclusive or nighttime expressing your fallback plan and not your goal? Be sure to check out *The Womanly Art of Breastfeeding* (8th edition or newer) for ideas on latching problems, increasing your milk supply, feeding a non-breastfeeding baby, and overcoming other issues. If you aren't already working with a breastfeeding counsellor or other skilled breastfeeding helper, it's worth giving one a call—there can be some surprising solutions that you won't find online. And if the person you've been working with is out of ideas, we encourage you to try someone else. Chapter 23 lists some good starting points.

If everything you've tried hasn't worked and you've resigned yourself to nighttime expressing, it might be worth trying breastfeeding in bed again in a few weeks or a few months. Babies (and mothers) are always changing, and what the two of you can't do today might work fine in a month or so.

Premature or Fragile Babies at Night

Premature babies are more vulnerable than full-term babies. They weren't expecting to have to manage their own breathing, digestion, temperature, and all the other realities of life after birth quite so soon. This may be why they are at greater risk of various problems, including SIDS.[4]

The American Academy of Pediatrics is quite clear that preterm infants shouldn't bedshare, and there's some research to support it.[5] These very little people may be unable to move freely towards and away from their mother or keep their breathing space clear. Babies with other health issues that make them more fragile may have the same problems.

> I love talking about the science behind bedsharing, skin-to-skin contact, and kangaroo care. I always tell Dr. Bergman's story about the woman who was told her very premature baby was going to die. She instinctively held her baby skin-to-skin, and her baby's health actually improved within a few hours!
>
> —Trevor

Researchers have known for years that hospitalized premature babies and other fragile babies do best when their mothers provide "Kangaroo Care." The mother leans back comfortably, her baby's bare chest against her own bare chest, a blanket over the two of them.[6] Her body keeps the baby's body at just the right temperature, and the familiar sounds of her heartbeat and voice encourage steady breathing and the kind of sleep that promotes growth and brain development for virtually *all* babies.[7] There are graphics in Chapter 4 that show the differences.

When your premature or fragile baby comes home, you can continue Kangaroo Care as much as you like, and even go it one better with Kangaroo *Mother* Care.

Kangaroo Mother Care

In Kangaroo Care, a mother usually holds her baby for a few hours a day. Kangaroo Mother Care (KMC) means your body is where your baby *lives,* nearly 24/7. You sit, walk, and even sleep with your baby secured against your body, using a special wrapping technique that ensures close contact without restricting her airway. She gets all the benefits described above. And the secure wrapping protects against any suffocation risks that she can't yet fend off by herself.

Even if you don't want to wear your baby all the time, wearing her at night can mean the best of both worlds: your baby has all the benefits of bedsharing, with an arrangement that protects her despite her vulnerability. For information on making or buying and wearing a KMC wrap, check out goo.gl/iFaTm4. *It's important to check out the website before you try KMC, to make sure you're doing it safely.*[8]

Whether and how your little one bedshares with you is always your choice. Take your baby, setting, and circumstances into account, and do what feels right for your family.

Preemie in a Cot, Moses Basket or Bedside Cot

If you opt to have your preemie in a separate sleeping space for nights and naps, there can be a real temptation to make the space smaller to fit your tiny little person. But there isn't a cuddle nest or sleep positioner, "snuggle nest", or other sleep gadget that's safe enough. *Every one of them is a suffocation or entrapment hazard.* Instead, choose one of the smaller baby beds that will keep your baby close at hand. And be sure to make your own bed a Safe Sleep Seven surface, just in case.

Daytime naps for your preemie may be easiest for both of you if you just let your baby sleep on your chest or in a sling or wrap while you lean back. She'll probably have more sleep, steadier vital signs, and lower stress if you wear her, and you'll get to know every one of her wiggles and expressions by wearing her through all her stages of waking and sleeping. Be sure to keep her upright, chest to chest. There's more information on safe baby-wearing in Chapter 12. See the website kangaroomothercare.com for a specialized preemie wrap.

Older Preemies

When is it safe to do ordinary bedsharing with your older preemie? There's no research on this. But there will probably come a time when you *feel* your baby is old enough and strong enough to protect herself from covers and other minor safety issues. So follow your head and your heart, see how bedsharing naps go, and take it from there.

Multiples (Twins, Triplets, and More) at Night

Most babies want to be near their mothers at night, no matter how many siblings they have. And bedsharing helps breastfeeding mothers of multiples get more sleep. But the bedsharing dynamics change when there are multiples. So what are some bedding arrangements for you and your new little cuddlers?

For More Information About Bedsharing and Multiples

Karen Gromada, a nurse, lactation consultant, and La Leche League Leader, is the author of La Leche League International's *Mothering Multiples*. She has been actively helping mothers of multiples breastfeed since 1977. You can find her on Facebook on the Mothering Multiples, Breastfeeding, and Caring for Twins or More page or the Attachment Parenting Multiples email list at goo.gl/Wr2043.

Co-bedding

Premature twins are often kept together in the same incubator in hospital intensive care units in North America.[9] A more stable twin can help a less stable twin improve his heart rate, breathing, and sleep states just by being beside him.[10] When parents see their babies being put in the same sleeping space in the hospital, it seems natural to put the babies together in the same bed (a cot or large Moses basket) when they come home.[11] And multiples often seem to feel comforted by sleeping next to each other. But is it safe?

A recent analysis of studies comparing co-bedding of stable preterm twins with twins sleeping separately did not find enough evidence to make any recommendations one way or the other.[12] Based on theoretical drawbacks—the possibility of a larger baby smothering a smaller one, or too much face-to-face "rebreathing"—the American Academy of Pediatrics advises against it.[13] The UK NHS says co-bedding twins is safe and recommends it as beneficial with no indication that doing so is dangerous for premature babies. Australian advice is similar to the US.

On the other hand, a small study of one- to three-month-old full-term twin baby pairs who co-bedded found that the babies had more synchronized sleep cycles than babies who slept separately. They did not have higher body temperatures, squash each other, or block each other's airways. Sleeping next to each other did not change how long they slept or how often they wakened, and there was no evidence of increased risk of suffocation or SIDS.[14] The study looked only at full-term babies, but the results seem reassuring. The sleep synchronization aspect may be helpful for mothers because it helps them streamline the babies' care.

Bedding for Multiples

Twins are often already a bit fragile. Whatever arrangements you settle on, these little ones really need to be in your room for at least the first six months.[15] It also helps you respond quickly and easily when they call. The closer they are, the less ground you have to cover in the middle of the night.

A bedside cot can be particularly handy with multiples because it frees up space in the bed and provides a safe place for one to sleep while you feed and change the other. A three-sided cot pushed tightly against the bed can also work well (see Chapter 6).

No matter where they sleep, if you breastfeed both at once, consider breastfeeding them in the bed you've prepared for "emergency bedsharing" (see Chapter 1). Tempting though it may be, breastfeeding two or more on a sofa or in a reclining chair isn't safe.

Bedsharing with Multiples

Breastfeeding mothers of multiples bedshare for the same reason that breastfeeding mothers of singletons do: it makes night feeds easier and they get more sleep. But adding another baby to the bed changes things. The Safe Sleep Seven and Safe Surface criteria become even more important. The best advice comes from mothers who have been down this road:

- When my girls came home, they immediately began sleeping in a bedside cot. It made night breastfeeding much easier to handle because I could just roll over to whoever was awake and breastfeed. Eventually we upgraded to a king-size bed on the floor with a single mattress pushed up to it.

Waking up to those little faces—even multiple times a night—is one of the greatest feelings in the world.—Olivia

- We bedshared with our oldest daughter and knew that bedsharing would help me get more sleep than I would get going back and forth to the nursery with the twins. And I felt like I could ensure my milk supply better if I was always available. Those nighttime hours are some of our most precious as a family. I love looking over to see our twins sleeping with hands together.—Soña
- Bedsharing was the only way I could actually get any sleep at night. I put a bed rail up on the left side of the bed and laid the twins on that side of the bed next to each other, while I slept on the right side of the bed. Then I rotated the babies as they woke to breastfeed.—Clare
- I like to say that we bedshared because I'm lazy; it was the easiest way to get everyone breastfed overnight, and it made me feel more secure to be able to feel them breathing. There wasn't much management involved, honestly; that was one of the best things about it!—Cory Ellen

And here are some specific tips from other MOMs (mothers of multiples):

- A partner or a nighttime helper is handy when there's more than one baby, especially when it comes to breastfeeding. If you're breastfeeding one baby at a time, the second (or third) may not be able to wait patiently, so someone carrying and singing and providing a finger to suck on may help to keep the peace until the first baby is done.
- If side-lying hasn't become easy for you yet, it may be simpler to get the baby to latch on in a leaning-back position with the baby lying across your body. Sometimes you can even get a second baby to latch on that way while the first is still breastfeeding.
- Once your babies are bigger, you may be able to lie on

your back with one baby on each side of you, on or next to your body.
- A big bed is great. A bigger bed is even better. You might even need to use a bedside cot to make enough room. Bed rails may give you some peace of mind about accidental falls with so many babies in the bed.
- A mattress on the floor may be the best bedsharing solution of all: lots of space for everyone, and no concerns about rolling off the bed if the mattress is low and the floor beside it is cushioned.

Online groups can be especially appealing to mothers of multiples particularly in the early months when it's hard to get out of the house. We know one mother who came to La Leche League meetings enthusiastically . . . until her twins were born. Then she just couldn't get out of the house on time, so she stayed in touch through the La Leche League forums until she was ready to attend meetings again. You might also find like-minded parents at a local twins club. A quick Google search should help you turn up resources in your area. There's also a good list of clubs in many different countries at goo.gl/Jz3Q7t.

In parenting organizations for multiples you may hear the cry-it-out technique recommended as a way to manage the babies' schedules. If it sounds tempting, we encourage you to read Chapter 18 to see the reasons and research behind those kinds of sleep-training methods. You'll find more gentle ideas in Chapter 11.

> My boy-girl twins are 16 months old now and were born at 39 weeks. The first night home, we put them both in the cot by themselves and they screamed, so that was it—they went into our bed. For the first few weeks, I was paranoid about squashing them. About four months in, we took the side off the cot and put it next to the bed to give us more space in the bed.
>
> It has definitely made breastfeeding loads easier, particularly in the early weeks when my son had reflux and was very unhappy and just wanted to suck all night. It is lovely to wake up to gently sleeping

babies with little fuzzy heads of hair. Or their smiling faces looking at me. I've gone back to work now, and these nighttime cuddles have helped with that transition. —Susannah

Adopted Babies at Night

Finding ways to bond and build your connection with your new baby is probably one of your first and most important goals when you adopt. Since nights take up about a third of every day, bedsharing gives you an automatic way to spend long stretches of intimate time together. It also taps into your baby's basic need to feel protected at night. She wants—and needs—to have you near, to trust you, to feel she can rely on you in the new world she's trying to adjust to. A relationship built on constancy and trust can help to heal any trauma she experienced before she came to you. And sharing a bed, even for a little while, can really help you soak up each other's scents and smiles.

How safe is bedsharing if you aren't exclusively breastfeeding your adopted child? There's no research on this. If you and your child are mostly "breast-focused", whether the milk comes directly from your breast or from tubing at your breast . . . well, isn't that what breastfeeding is all about? And once your baby is older than about four months, all you need to worry about with bedsharing is having a responsible, non-smoking adult and a safe surface.

I thought I would never bedshare. I thought that I wouldn't sleep well, or that we'd never have the bed back to ourselves, but that just isn't what's happened. After we brought our adopted newborn home, I was exhausted and he would not sleep in the bedside cot. He looked at me with these big brown eyes and a look that said, "I'm trying to figure out who you are." I picked him up and snuggled in bed with him and let him know that I was his mummy. We both slept beautifully. It felt so right, and it bonded the two of us together fiercely.

—Elizabeth

When we adopted our daughter at six months, her fear that she might be abandoned again seemed evident in her inability to sleep without touching me. She used a leg, a toe, an arm, or her head to send out feelers that I was still there, a constant for her. It seemed only natural that a child who had gone through so much loss would want to be next to her mother. The natural relationship of bedsharing helped to cement our bond, mending my infertile heart of many years, and healing a child who had lost her birth mother, foster mother, and first adoptive mother. Little by little the snuggling and warmth we shared while sleeping seemed to bring the missing pieces back.

—Alexandra

If you opt for a cot, Alyssa Schnell, author of *Breastfeeding Without Birthing,* suggests starting with the bedding that your baby came to you with, without washing it, so that she smells those familiar smells in her unfamiliar bed. Alyssa also recommends setting up the new bed as close as possible to the way it was set up in the previous home (unless it was unsafe, of course). As your baby begins to feel more comfortable with you and in your environment, you can transition into other sleeping arrangements.

Many children come to adoptive homes from less-than-ideal situations. Some babies crave the safety and love that you're offering and don't want to let you out of their sight. Others are not immediately ready to sleep next to another person because they have come from institutionalized care and aren't used to close contact.[16] Honour your baby's need to make the transition in whatever way is right for her. If your child isn't ready for bedsharing, it can be more respectful of her feelings to put her in a cot for now, but it may help ease her into the new situation to put the cot near your bed. Since touch is

For More Information About Breastfeeding an Adopted Baby

Alyssa Schnell, a lactation consultant and La Leche League Leader, is the author of *Breastfeeding Without Birthing: A Breastfeeding Guide for Mothers Through Adoption, Surrogacy, and Other Special Circumstances.* You can find her on Facebook on the Breastfeeding Without Birthing page.

important for everyone, keep moving gently toward normal closeness over the next days or weeks or months.

What about your baby's exposure to smoking, alcohol, or drugs during pregnancy that you may not be aware of and that may increase your baby's overall risk of SIDS? You may be able to gather some information from the adoption agency or from the baby's medical records after birth. Ultimately, you'll need to decide on the best course for your particular baby. Yet another of the gazillion decisions parents have to make for themselves. You'll have plenty more to come.

When You're Not Bedsharing

There are plenty of reasons why a mother can't or doesn't want to bedshare. Here are a few of them.

"I *Can't* Bedshare"

A bedside cot can be a good compromise in a lot of situations. It keeps your baby on a separate surface but within easy touching distance. A Moses basket set up next to the bed, or a cot fastened securely to the bed with one side removed can be excellent options. When smoking's involved, though, the further from the smoker (but still in the same room) the lower the risk.

"I Don't *Want* to Bedshare"

Maybe you just can't sleep well with a baby by your side. Maybe it's too much snuffling and squeaking and squirming, or you're too worried about the baby, or you have another sleep issue that means bedsharing doesn't work for you.

If overstimulation or waking up with every sound or wiggle is what keeps you from bedsharing, you might try giving it a full week before deciding for sure that it won't work. Many mothers have found that it doesn't disturb them as much after a few days. It's just like adjusting to sleeping with a partner—over time, you get used to the way your partner moves and breathes.

If you're simply too worried in your circumstances, a bedside cot can give you peace of mind but still keep your baby nearby.

If you have a sleep issue that prevents bedsharing, Chapter 10 has stories from mothers who can absolutely relate. They were realistic about their situation while keeping in mind the importance of responding to the baby.

Bottom line: Even if you can't bedshare, any responsible arrangement that keeps your baby in your room for about the first half year can work, especially if you respond quickly and willingly to his nighttime needs. Use the Safe Surface checklist in Chapter 2 to make sure that if you fall asleep with your baby, it's going to happen as safely as possible. Family life is always a compromise, and you can usually find solutions that consider everyone's needs.

"My *Baby* Doesn't Want to Bedshare"

Sometimes even Safe Sleep Seven babies don't bedshare comfortably. Diana's son Alex had sensory difficulties from birth and couldn't sleep well when anyone was too close to him. When Diana and her husband realized that this was just the way Alex was, they put him in a Moses basket next to the bed. Keeping him near the bed made her feel much better and kept him safer than if he had been in a room down the hall. He did need extra effort to help him become comfortable with touch. It's worth the patience and persistence it may take to help your baby accept more cuddling.

Babies with Special Needs

One of the criteria for the Safe Sleep Seven is a healthy baby. But there are subtleties that come up with a special-needs baby that may not have been covered in that general discussion. So where does that leave you?

Many mothers believe bedsharing has saved their baby's life. Several mothers told us they discovered their child's seizure disorder because of their nighttime contact. One mother whose son stopped breathing seven times during his first year found she responded to his sudden lack of motion more reliably than his apnoea monitor did.

The critical factor about a baby's health when we talk about bedsharing is that he has the ability and awareness to move or roll himself towards and away from you, and can use his arms and legs to bat away something that covers his face, so that he can fine-tune his position and airway. If your baby can do that, then other physical limitations are less likely to be a problem for bedsharing. Every situation is different, so you'll need to use your best parental judgment.

One thing to keep in mind with a child with special needs is that he may need the reassurance of bedsharing even more than other children, especially if he has sensory deficits or difficulty with social interactions. Some special needs, such as autism, don't show up clearly in infancy, but close contact with a mother at night from his earliest days can help strengthen the non-verbal—and very important—part of your relationship.

Bottom line: Every child could benefit from the closeness, contact, and easy access to breastfeeding that bedsharing provides, but for some babies it includes some risk. You know your own child, his physical limitations, and your home situation best. Think through his mobility and capabilities very carefully and rely on your mothering instinct to guide you to the best sleep arrangement for you and your baby.

> My son Quinn has Asperger's syndrome, diagnosed when he was five years old, just after he had weaned. None of his Asperger's traits showed up until after he stopped breastfeeding. I wonder if his sense of humour, ability to make eye contact, and comfort with cuddles and snuggles were helped by his having breastfed for so long and bedshared with me through his toddler and preschool years. It seems that those years of continual personal connection and interaction may have made him comfortable with social interactions that many children with Asperger's find difficult. Autism is a complex and poorly understood disorder, but I believe that giving a child with physical or mental challenges more personal connection and interaction through bedsharing may make a difference.
>
> —Diana

Something to Sleep On

If bedsharing isn't easy or practical, you might need to get creative in planning a nighttime strategy that will work for you, your family, and your new baby or babies. We hope this chapter has given you the raw materials to put that strategy together. You know the factors that make some sleep arrangements safer and some less safe, and you know the importance of being responsive to your baby during the night. You also know what restrictions you might be dealing with in terms of bedroom space, any unknowns about your baby's past, and your unique circumstances. There's no one, perfect way to deal with these situations. You may have to try a few approaches before you find something that works. And you may need to change your strategy as your baby grows.

If we haven't addressed your situation specifically, you may find answers in Chapter 22. If it's not there, don't hesitate to reach out to a La Leche League Leader or other breastfeeding helper, or post a question on our forums at forums.llli.org.

Alternate routes can get you where you want to go. The scenery may be a little different along the way, but the destination is still amazing.

Welcome to Holland!

For a been-there-doing-it take on life with a differently abled child, you might want to read this wonderful essay that's resonated with many, many families: goo.gl/P3nuDc.

chapter 10

Your Own Sleep Needs

> I have a condition that permanently affects my sleep. The slightest movement wakes me up. Even if I'm exhausted, it's hard to fall asleep and stay asleep. When Grady was born, I powered through the early weeks of bedsharing, drawing from some mummy reserve of strength, but it was clear early on that it couldn't be a long-term arrangement.
>
> So I go to bed very early to maximize my sleep, and he starts out sleeping in a Moses basket beside our bed. He wakes more fully in the basket since he has to be louder to get my attention, and I have to get out of bed to pick him up. But sometimes I drift back to sleep while breastfeeding, so I guess we still do bedshare part of the night. Our arrangement isn't perfect, but I know this time won't last forever, and I figure that I am growing my "mummy muscles" big and strong.
>
> —Susanna

Most newborns sleep for more than half of every 24 hours, so in theory we should be well rested. (Of course, some perfectly healthy babies sleep considerably less than that.) The problem is the tug-of-war between *our* quest for long stretches of unbroken sleep and our *baby's* need for frequent breastfeeding, day and night. And most of us are *already* sleep-deprived because of our fast-paced lives and the ragged sleep of late pregnancy (which may be Mother Nature's way of getting us ready for broken sleep after the baby comes).

Sleep is essential. It can affect our mood, our weight, our blood pressure, our heart, and our insulin levels, and the average new mother looks for sleep any way she can get it. Fragmented sleep goes with the mothering territory, but there are some ways to make the territory a little less rocky. Bedsharing is a good place to start. You know from the preceding chapters that it's good for sleep, good for breastfeeding, good for lowering your own and your baby's stress levels, and—did we say this already?—good for sleep.

This chapter explores some of the other issues that affect your own sleep. The first part has ideas for getting more rest while still meeting your baby's needs. (You might want to share some of these ideas with your partner; new mothers aren't the only ones operating on a sleep deficit.) But maybe you have reasons for being sleep-deprived that go way beyond just being a fast-paced woman and brand-new mother. The second part of this chapter covers sleep problems that are totally separate from babies, with some ideas that may help.

Front-Loading

This statement from a University of California breastfeeding clinic got us thinking: *"More time is often spent trying to fix the baby's sleep 'problems' (which are normal waking and short sleep periods) . . . rather than finding ways to deal with the resulting (and inevitable) sleep deprivation."*[1]

We already have a shorter sleep time than our biology expects and we try to force our babies into our modern mould at an age when their biology just doesn't allow for it. What if we turn the whole baby "sleep problem" upside down and look at *our* sleep problem instead?

It turns out that some very productive people "front-load" their days, doing more work early in the day and—here's the key—winding down earlier in the evening.

Give front-loading a try!

The Basics

You probably already have a favourite winding-down spot. For many couples, it's the bedroom or living room. To front-load, get everyone (including you) *ready* for bed an hour or more before you plan to *go* to bed, right down to night clothes and brushing teeth. Then just chill out with your partner and baby. Conversation, a book, texting or online time, knitting, mindless TV or a film—anything low-key. Leave the washing and the hard thinking for morning. Head for the bedroom or for bed when it starts to call to you instead of when you're ready to collapse. If your baby isn't ready when you are, the slower pace may help.

Advice on insomnia often includes the suggestion that you reserve your bedroom for nothing but sleep (okay, sex is allowed). The difference here is that you're using your bedroom to move *towards* sleep, to let yourself wind down for a seamless slide from day into night. This extra restful time can help make night waking feel less stressful.

Our secret—it happened out of necessity—is a busy morning routine and relaxed evenings. I make sure I get at least one load of washing done every morning. Next, I learned to always unload the dishwasher, make phone calls, and clean and tidy during the happy morning hours. I've found that if I put my baby in a sling and play some music it has even become fun! I save Internet surfing and texting for naptime and bedtime.

My baby and I retire for the night around 9.00 p.m. with my phone and computer at hand. I do some catching up with the outside world, watch TV with my husband, and then snuggle in next to my baby around 11.00 p.m. He breastfeeds, I change his nappy with the supplies ready on my bedside table, he breastfeeds some more, and then he drifts off again.

Everything runs much more smoothly when I'm more efficient in the morning. It's never perfect, but it's *much* better than waiting until 11.30 p.m., when you're dog-tired, to get through the essential, never-ending to-do list. I've even learned to do my supermarket shopping online from the comfort of my family bed! By front-loading my day, I have time to relax in the afternoon and evening with my family. We are peaceful.

—Monica

Is It Realistic?

When we backload our days, we pile up things that really need to get done all through the day, and then stay up late to clean up the pile at the end of the day. As a new mother, you can probably feel your productivity, patience, and logic starting to go by dinnertime. You look forward to "putting the baby down" so you can get some of that work done. But you really just want to go to bed. So you rush it, call it "good enough," and—probably your most logical thought—decide that "it can wait until tomorrow." As one mother said, "I got more accomplished in an hour in the morning than I did in four hours late at night."

Being able to have relaxed evenings depends on getting more done *early* in the day. Of course, some days have more obligations than others: "I haven't spent much time with my older children today." "My in-laws are coming tomorrow and I need to make lasagne." We know, we know, we know. But maybe it *can* work for you. What if you build your day around enough rest, rather than around squeezing more into a too-busy day? What if you make the lasagne in the morning? Or maybe your mother-in-law can help you make it. Or just buy it!

Your partner is probably every bit as tired at the end of the day as you are, and might feel an enormous sense of relief at getting to unwind for a while in the evening and head to bed a bit earlier. "It can wait until tomorrow" can become your first, not your last, response to the day's backlog. You'll probably have more energy and time for each other, for conversation or . . . whatever.

> My mother read to us every night when we were little, to wind down before we went to sleep. I wanted to keep the tradition after I got married. I started out reading books to my wife after we were in bed. I kept it up after our first baby was born. We read whatever we wanted until he got a little older. Then we switched to children's books that we all liked. Now he sleeps in his own bed for the first part of the night. One of us reads to him there, and in our own bed we're back to reading whatever we want, this time with our baby girl listening in.
>
> —Richard

Some of us are at our most productive late at night and just *know* this isn't for us. We're *sure* we're more productive if we stay up later. But maybe we night owls are missing our "first sleep" (Chapter 4), making use of that clearheaded middle-of-the-night interval that seems to be built into all of us, and then bunching first and second sleeps together at the end of the night. Desperate times call for desperate measures, so maybe front-loading is worth a shot just in case it *does* work.

The How-To's

Consider giving it a trial week. You can adapt your approach if you decide you like the overall concept.

Prepare the Space

You don't have to redecorate (although a decluttered space may help you relax). Just add whatever equipment you consider helpful for low-key living: a TV, a comfy chair or backrest for the bed, baby stuff, lower-wattage bulbs in some of the lamps, e-gadgets, books and magazines.

Establish an Earlier Wind-Down Time

Aim for a time that's well ahead of your usual bedtime. Take several days or a week to get there if you need to. When wind-down time starts, turn off the other lights in the house and retire to your wind-down zone—the place where you can be low-key and deadline-free.

Keep It Simple, Keep It Calm

It doesn't much matter what you do. Sprawl on the bed or sofa. Talk together, get up and walk the baby, lie down and breastfeed the baby, make lists, knit, daydream together. Your baby may not let you go to bed exactly when you want. Still, you've had at least an hour, preferably more, of rest before your actual bedtime, which can help relieve the stress of having to get to sleep so you can wake up.

You'll still wake up in the night. That won't change. But try to reframe it as a normal human pattern. It's okay. You've had that longer, more leisurely winding-down time, and that counts for *a lot* in terms of overall rest. The chances are both you and your partner will feel better in the morning. Maybe your baby will sleep better too.

> My eight-month-old was waking a lot at night. I started winding down and going to bed earlier and things improved drastically. Now she only wakes twice a night. I get *so* much more done by doing it early in the day, and that means that she gets much more rest and sleep at night.
>
> —Nancy

Make It Your Own

Front-loading isn't a specific arrangement. It's more like a revised attitude. Take the idea of lower-key evenings and adapt it in any way that makes you and your partner—and just possibly your baby—happier.

These mothers did their own versions of front-loading by making sure that they were ready for bed before they were ready for bed.

- If I tried to stay awake to have an "evening" after the baby was asleep, I would end up falling asleep anyway and waking up several hours later, fully dressed, feeling cheated and not at all rested. What worked best was to put on my pyjamas when I went to feed the baby to sleep. Occasionally I would stay awake and feel like I had a couple of bonus hours of time to myself, but if I fell asleep, I slept well.—Kirsteen
- I finally learned this lesson after too many mornings waking up in my clothes, feeling terrible!—Holly
- I would put on my pyjamas just in case. . . . —Mary Alice

Banishing the Sleep Robbers

Take a look at each of these sleep robbers to see if they're having any effect on your sleep.

Caffeine

Consider cutting back on caffeine, especially if you've been using it to help you get through the day. For some mothers, the more caffeine they have, the less sleep they get and the more they feel like they need caffeine. Caffeine not only makes it hard to fall asleep; it can also keep you from sleeping deeply. To make things worse, some sensitive people find that their sensitivity increases over time. Babies can be sensitive to caffeine too, especially during their first month, and it stays in their system longer than it does in yours.[2] The last thing you need is an overstimulated baby!

You might try avoiding caffeine after the middle of the afternoon so that it's out of your system by bedtime. Cutting it out altogether could make naps more likely. (If you've been a heavy coffee drinker, though, be sure to cut down slowly to avoid withdrawal symptoms such as headaches.)

There's caffeine in coffee, tea, and certain carbonated drinks, but look for it in unexpected places too, including some medications and anything with "energy" on the label. The Energy Fiend website (energyfiend.com) keeps an up-to-date list of caffeine amounts in most foods and beverages, listed by world region.

Alcohol

Alcohol may help you fall asleep, but it can also keep you from sleeping deeply or well. When sleep is in short supply, alcohol is not your friend. And, of course, alcohol and bedsharing don't mix.

Bright Lights and Electronics

Intense light and electromagnetic radiation (EMR) from electronics, including TVs, tablets, and even backlit e-books and smartphones, can reduce natural melatonin levels in your brain, which can make it harder to fall asleep and stay asleep.[3] Consider "turning off and tuning out" an hour or so before bedtime, and switch from an e-reader to a paperback book. Breastfeeding (or expressing) without turning on the light may help your baby sleep better too, by keeping your natural melatonin level—and your milk's melatonin level—higher.[4]

On the other hand . . . see the bullet point on page 161 about *using* electronics if that's your habit.

Clutter

Most people sleep more readily in a room that's not too cluttered. Even just a smooth bed surface can be calming when you crawl in. If your room's clutter is daunting, try doing a little organizing each day. (Check out FlyLady.net for a fun—and free—system for getting organized. *The Eight-Minute Organizer* by Virginia Leeds shows you how to declutter and sort out in eight-minute chunks.)

Racing Thoughts

When you finally get to bed at night, do you start thinking about everything you have to get done the next day, one thought jumping quickly to the next? Racing thoughts are natural when you're overwhelmed, but you won't be able to get as much done tomorrow if they keep you awake tonight.

Try putting a notepad and pencil by your bedside. Not an electronic version, ideally, because of the light. Even in pitch blackness, you can scrawl a helpful word or two. "Cat" can keep you from missing the vet appointment; "MIL" can remind you to remind your mother-in-law to bring the whatever when she comes. There—your scribblings will remind you in the morning, so you don't have to remember it tonight.

> I put a piece of paper under my pillow, and when I could not sleep I wrote in the dark.
>
> —Henry David Thoreau

Catastrophic Thinking

That's the circling fears and panicky thoughts that always loom way larger at night than in the morning. Just being able to put a name to it can help. You can lie there thinking, "Okay, this is just catastrophic thinking." It's a reminder that you're not being logical and things aren't really as bad as they seem.

Let Go of the Clock

There's nothing worse than being wakened by your baby, looking at the clock, and thinking, "Great, I have to get up in an hour and a half," or "But it's only been an hour since the last time." Somehow, knowing the time can make you feel more tired and stressed, and many mothers find that their nights go much better if they don't know when they wake up or for how long. Doing the maths and thinking about what it means can make you feel more tired than if you didn't know it at all. If your partner needs to see the alarm clock for work, put it where *you* can't see it. Or maybe putting the alarm on his mobile phone to vibrate is enough to wake your partner up.

> With my second baby, I decided that I would never put on my glasses when I woke in the night. Without my glasses, I couldn't read the clock. So I never knew when my baby last woke me.
>
> —Marianne

Sleep Aids

Here are some ideas to make sleep happen more easily when it's elusive.

- Take a nightly walk outside in the dark with or without your baby (weather permitting). Even in a city, night has a different feel that can calm the chaos in your heart and mind.
- Maybe some *daytime* changes would help. Do you have a partner or family member who can help with some of your day-to-day stressors? Maybe cook dinner or bring a meal home? Daytime help can make for better nighttime rest.
- Breastfeeding and cuddling release oxytocin and prolactin, both of which tend to make you sleepy. And snuggling with your grown-up bed partner can be soul-soothing for both of you.
- An old-fashioned but effective way to wind down is sex, especially with an orgasm. It releases oxytocin, which makes you feel sleepy. That's why men are so renowned for falling asleep afterward!
- If you're not ready for sex yet, would your partner be willing to give you a massage—even just a foot, shoulder, or scalp massage? A good massage releases oxytocin.
- Maybe you're someone who sleeps *better* when there's music or a TV in the background. Most babies aren't bothered by noise or light, but white noise machines can harm little ears (see Chapter 12). Just make very sure any cords can't tangle with your new little bed partner.
- Exercising a few hours before bed may help.[5] It can also help you function better during the day.[6] Finding it hard to exercise with a new baby? Try going for a late-night walk with your baby in a babycarrier or in the pram. A little fresh air and natural light can really brighten your frame of mind and soothe your baby. And sex counts as exercise that can help with sleep any time.
- A hot shower or bath as part of the bedtime routine seems

to help many people fall asleep more easily. Time for a leisurely bath can be tough to come by, so try bringing the baby into the bath with you. Even five minutes in the shower while the baby watches you from a safe spot outside the shower may help trigger sleepiness.

- Many people find the scent of lavender soothing and relaxing. Try putting some crushed blossoms or essential oil inside your pillowcase, in a dish on your bedside table, or try a lavender-scented lotion.
- A simple, standard bedtime routine can help you wind down—teeth brushed, earrings out, comfortable clothes, into bed, reading for a few minutes before lights out. You'll probably do it with your toddler; it can work just as well for you.
- A nightly baby massage can be a happy, relaxing routine for both of you. Good starting points: the *BabyBabyOhBaby: Infant Massage* DVD and *Infant Massage: A Handbook for Loving Parents* by Vimala McClure. There are more thoughts and resources in Chapter 15.
- Meditation during the day can help with sleep at night. If you've never done it before, there are pointers at wikihow.com/Meditate-for-Beginners. The simplest may be the mental repetition, with each exhalation, of a soothing word or phrase. Or focus on relaxing the toes on your left foot, then the sole, then your instep, ankle, lower leg, and on through your body in any pattern and at any speed that works for you. When your mind wanders (and it will), just bring it gently back. Relaxing your shoulders, neck, jaw, lips, tongue, and other "head parts" can be especially helpful, if you get that far.
- Deep breathing is almost a form of meditation. It drops your blood pressure and calms you. Try 10 to 20 slow, deep breaths several times a day and any time in the night that you need it.
- Daydreaming about things you want to do or things you enjoy can help sleep happen more easily.

- Writing in your diary before going to bed can help you record random thoughts so you can stop thinking about them.
- Some people get sleepy thinking of a flower, fruit, or even car model for every letter of the alphabet. If you don't get to the end of the alphabet, all the better.
- Remember that even broken sleep counts as sleep. And there might be time for a nap tomorrow.

Daytime Changes for Better Nights

How well we sleep at night depends partly on how our day went.

- Would your partner like a "baby fix" after work? You could hand over the baby while you curl up and read or catch up on your social networking, take a long shower, or go for a walk.
- Try putting your sleeping baby in a Moses basket or infant seat in the bathroom while you take that shower.
- Getting outside helps! Even just long enough to throw your shoulders back, look up at the sky, and take a few deep breaths. Or take a walk or go to the shops. Try putting your baby in a sling or babycarrier and you can have your mind away from your baby without having your baby away from your body, and your baby has a snug, secure nap.
- Visit a friend. Adult time and new surroundings are mood lifters.

Maternal Medications That Help and Hinder Sleep

Medications can go a long way towards helping you sleep . . . or making it more elusive.

Medications That May Help

Melatonin is a sleep-inducing hormone that's sometimes used as a sleep medication, though research suggests that it's only mildly effective for adults.[7] There aren't many studies, but the theoretical dose through your milk if you take no more than 1 mg (the maximum recommended dose) is less than the dose that's been given directly to newborns.[8] At that level, no negative effects on babies have been reported.[9]

Camomile tea has been used for mild relaxation for generations. No negative effects for the baby have been reported through breastfeeding.[10]

Beware the Medications That Make You Too Sleepy

If you need a sleeping pill—or *any* medication with sedation as a side effect—bedsharing becomes riskier. It would be safer to have someone else who isn't sedated available to take care of the baby until your medication wears off.

Valerian root and kava kava are problematic for bedsharing. Studies disagree on the effectiveness of valerian as a sleep aid,[11] and its safety in humans has been called into question.[12] Kava kava carries a number of side effects for adults, and its use has been discouraged in pregnant and lactating women.[13]

Oral allergy medicines can have drowsiness as a side effect, even when they're labelled "non-drowsy". Some decongestants can also reduce your milk supply. A nasal allergy spray may work just as well as a pill, usually without the side effect of drowsiness or lower milk supply.

You can check lactmed.nlm.nih.gov for information on specific medications or the Breastfeeding Network (Drugs in Breastmilk helpline 0844 412 4665).

Single Parenting

You may have read some of these previous sections with frustration if you don't have a partner who can help. And with the double load of responsibilities you're carrying, you could really do with some uninterrupted sleep.

It can be *incredibly* tough. Which is why it's important to cut yourself a whole lot of slack. Some thoughts (there are also ideas in Chapter 8):

- *Let go of perfect.* Nobody gets there anyway.
- *Prioritize.* You and your child(ren) first: keep a roof over your heads and food on your plates. It doesn't matter how orderly things are or if the meals are home-cooked.
- *Be present.* Do your errands with your baby in a babycarrier and you're doing the exact kind of excellent parenting your baby needs, even when you're not focused on him. Later, he'll need a combination of your touch and your mind. (Bedsharing meets a lot of a young child's need for touch.) Older children don't lose their need for touch, but mostly they need your availability.

Without a partner to turn to, you may need to seek out other resources to help you care for yourself so you can care for your baby. Needing more touch to reduce stress and relax? Perhaps you could schedule a regular massage. To gain some time to rest or catch up, consider hiring someone to to look after your baby for a bit. Or look for another mum or two who would come to your house some days if you go to hers on other days.

When you're tired and struggling with caring for a new baby on your own, you can feel really alone. But there is help out there, and you deserve to be supported and cared for. For more information on connecting with other mothers, see Chapter 23.

Underlying Causes of Poor Sleep (Other than New Motherhood)

There were over 100 identified sleep disorders at the last count! It can be a lose-lose situation: You need good sleep because of your health problems, and your health problems keep you from getting good sleep. We understand what it's like because two of us coped with significant sleep challenges during early motherhood, just like so many other women around the world.

Returning to Work

Adding work responsibilities on top of baby care can make getting enough sleep much more difficult. See Chapter 8 for some approaches and strategies for working mothers.

Physical Causes

Pain from an injury or from a caesarean or other birth intervention can certainly affect your sleep. So can chronic conditions and diseases. If you have a known condition, you might want to check with your doctor to make sure your treatment or medications take the changes of new motherhood into account. If your condition is hormonal, especially if you have a thyroid condition, it's a very good idea to have your levels checked about two weeks after birth and then more often than you normally would, because antenatal and postnatal changes can significantly affect them. Thyroid levels, both high and low, can also affect how well you can release your milk, potentially reducing your milk supply.

> I had begun feeling extreme daytime sleepiness. I fell asleep just sitting on the sofa. My husband told me I had started snoring at night and sometimes stopped breathing and gasped for breath. My doctor sent me for a sleep study.
>
> The sleep study indicated that I had severe sleep apnoea, and I started using a CPAP (continuous positive airway pressure) machine, a lightweight nose-and-mouth mask that provides a room-air "breeze" at night. My daughter (and my husband) quickly got used to the white noise it makes, and my daytime sleepiness disappeared.
>
> —Marianne

If you snore (and sometimes even if you don't), there may be times during your sleep when you stop breathing temporarily (apnoea) or breathe too shallowly (hypopnoea), so you get less oxygen and therefore less restful sleep. Teeth grinding, irregular sleep rhythms, night terrors, sleep walking, involuntary limb movements, sleep paralysis, narcolepsy, and insomnia are all sleep disruptors. There's a whole new medical specialty, *sleep medicine,* that addresses those issues. Sleep dentistry is another specialty that has developed to address sleep issues that can be affected by oral structures. Consult your GP or dentist if you are experiencing dental or oral problems. In the UK mothers are entitled to free dental treatment for 12 months after their baby is born.

If your sleep is disrupted because your *baby* has a chronic problem like reflux, see Chapter 22 or ask your GP or health visitor for advice.

Medications, Medical Procedures, and Breastfeeding

Take a look at the medications you use on a regular basis. Are there any that could be contributing to either insomnia or drowsiness? Even if that wasn't a side effect you experienced before or during the pregnancy, it could be happening now.

If you need medications for a short-term or chronic problem, you may also be worried about whether it's safe to take them during breastfeeding. Remind your health care provider that you're breastfeeding if you need prescription drugs. The good news: *most* drugs pass into human milk in only tiny amounts.[14] The American Academy of Pediatrics agrees that most drugs are appropriate at their standard dosages for use by breastfeeding mothers.[15] Taking the medication you need in the full dosage you need is especially important if your medication controls pain or other symptoms to help you sleep. So, instead of assuming you can't take any medications while breastfeeding, it's worth looking up the drug in a reliable lactation medication database, such as Lactmed (toxnet.nlm.nih.gov). Other information can be found on Kellymom (kellymom.com) and also the UK-based Breastfeeding Network (breastfeedingnetwork.org.uk) who have factsheets and a UK 'Drugs in Breastmilk' helpline on 0844 412 4665.

Taking Care of Your Own Health

If you're wondering whether you have an underlying condition that's affecting your sleep, it's worth getting it checked out. You're the mother of a new baby, and that means you need—and deserve!—all the sleep you can get. Most disorders have effective treatments. The sooner you get treated, the sooner you'll get better sleep.

Sometimes getting help can be hard. If your health care provider is inclined to chalk your symptoms up to new-mother fatigue, you might need a strategy to get across why you and your symptoms should be taken seriously. It often helps to write your concerns down before you go. Could you bring a partner or friend along to take notes? If your doctor suggests formula supplements as a solution, you may need to explain that not breastfeeding is likely to make things worse.

Emotional Causes

Most of us have emotional baggage of some kind. A significant number of new mothers in Western societies experience trauma from birth interventions,[16] which can bring up past traumas that we thought we'd healed from years ago.[17] And some emotional difficulties are caused by chemical imbalances related to shifting hormones, inflammation, and other changes in the postnatal period. Any resulting anxiety, depression, mood disorders, panic attacks, or post-traumatic stress disorder can create a downward spiral—the less sleep you get, the less you *can* sleep. Or you may feel a need to sleep too much. Either way, you're trying to care for a new baby too, which can make your sleep problems seem worse or even tempt you to take out your frustrations on your baby.

> I had a complicated labour and then a caesarean. Nipple pain from the start, thrush at three weeks, hand-foot-and-mouth disease at five weeks, thrush again, and then a letter saying my maternity leave had been shortened. I was horribly sleep-deprived. It was a set up for a postnatal mood disorder.
>
> The next week my mum brought me new sheets. Perfect colour and pattern, softer than any I had ever owned. I washed them, went to put them in the dryer, and realized that a single red pillowcase had got mixed in. And the perfect, new, never-used sheets were *covered* with pink streaks.
>
> I lost it. I had a complete meltdown in front of my husband, just standing in the kitchen. For about 45 minutes it all came pouring out. *Nothing* had gone right since I was 36 weeks pregnant. I couldn't even do the washing properly. Even my perfect baby didn't make up for what I was feeling. Which made me feel worse.

> The breakdown wasn't about the washing; that was just the trigger. I had reached the point of depression and severe sleep deprivation when nothing seemed normal and everything felt incredibly wrong.
>
> —Michelle

This isn't a time to be stoic. Your doctor can help you investigate therapies, treatments, or medications that might help you feel better. More and more psychologists and therapists recognize the seriousness of birth traumas and traumas brought to the surface by birth. There are new and better treatments and medications developed all the time, and there is a very good chance one of them will help you. *Most* medications are compatible with breastfeeding. If it turns out that the drug you need is too sedating for you to bedshare safely, you can still sleep in the same room with your baby, which will help you keep your breastfeeding connection. Two good resources for further information are birthtraumaassociation.co.uk or tabs.org.nz.

Stress

For many people, sleep problems come from the stress of making ends meet and the burden of all their obligations and responsibilities. Sadly, there's nothing we can say that will take the load off your shoulders. We can only tell you that you're *definitely* not alone. If you reach out to others, either in person or online, sharing your worries can make your burden feel a whole lot lighter.

Real, live people can offer a sense of relief and belonging that can be hard to find online. Think about contacting a La Leche League Leader at laleche.org.uk. La Leche League Leaders are mothers themselves who understand sleep challenges with breastfeeding babies. They are also a wonderful gateway into your community's resources. La Leche League meetings provide a roomful of caring and sympathetic mothers, some of whom have probably walked where you're walking.

If sleep issues are making breastfeeding difficult, a LLL leader or skilled breastfeeding counsellor from one of the other UK voluntary organisations such as the NCT, Breastfeeding Network or the Association of Breastfeeding Mothers, or an NHS infant feeding adviser or IBCLC lactation consultant can give you tailored help in finding the right tools and techniques, sorting through medication issues, maintaining your breastfeeding relationship, and devising a plan that works for you right now and that changes as your needs change. Try Lactation Consultants of Great Britain (lcgb.org) for help near you. Many women find support and help from both La Leche League and an IBCLC. For more resources, see the sidebar on page 172 for help when you're feeling down.

> As a newborn and infant, my daughter woke frequently during the night. Bedsharing was great for that, but my husband couldn't take it and moved into another bed in the house. I also am an extremely light sleeper and was not getting any sleep or even rest.
>
> I ended up moving her to a cot in our room at six months. I got more sleep by responding to her cries, breastfeeding her, and putting her back down than I did sleeping next to her. My anxiety reduced greatly with her in her own space. I carried her in the sling during the day to help make up for the lack of connection at night.
>
> —Chana

Blue and Bluer

The baby blues are fairly common in our culture when new mothers don't feel supported and cared for. The blues usually hit within the first week or two and last only a few days, but they can interfere temporarily with your sleep.

If you're more than a week or so into new motherhood and things seem worse than ever, it might help to talk about how you're feeling with someone you trust, maybe starting with another mother, because motherhood has got most of us down at one time or another. Or post on breastfeeding support forums or social media groups like Facebook.

Some of us don't feel depressed or blue, but we do feel anxious, maybe even frantic—as if we have to keep control of everything or we won't be able to control *anything*. Like the baby blues, postnatal anxiety is most likely temporary, easing gradually as you realize that, instead of being responsible for the whole ocean, you can just ride the waves as they come along.

Postnatal depression can happen any time in the first year. It's a deeper depression than the baby blues and it can hit you really hard. Sometimes friends, family, or even doctors recommend stopping breastfeeding and getting the baby out of your bed as ways to help you feel better, but research has shown that depression is more likely to be the cause of broken sleep than your baby,[18] and continued breastfeeding tends to relieve depression better than weaning does.[19] Most medications for depression are compatible with breastfeeding.[20]

Your doctor or health visitor may also be able to refer you to a breastfeeding-friendly mental health specialist or specialist health visitor—someone who won't tell you to stop breastfeeding, since that can actually make things worse. Immediate help is also available at the phone numbers and websites listed in the sidebar on page 172.

It can be hard to talk to a doctor when you're feeling so down, but the baby blues, postnatal anxiety, and postpartum depression are very common. Most doctors will understand right away and be able to guide you to effective treatments. It's really worth reaching out to them. Some UK maternity service providers have a postnatal debriefing service for women who experienced difficult births where a midwife will look at your birth medical notes and talk you through what happened. Referral is usually via health visitors.

Fish Oil Supplementation

According to recent research, one cause of depression is inflammation, which often results from stress.[21] New mothers certainly know all about stress! Fish and fish oil products contain EPA and DHA, long-chain fatty acids (omega-3s) that may reduce inflammation.[22] (There are also vegan sources of omega-3s.) There is some evidence that EPA and DHA supplementation can help with depression, though more research is needed.[23] The standard dosage for treating depression is 1 g of EPA and 700–1,000 mg of DHA,[24] moderate doses that are considered safe for pregnant and breastfeeding women.[25] EPA and DHA transfer into milk but have no known negative effects on breastfeeding babies.[26]

Help When You're Feeling Down

Your health visitor or GP are often the first place to go for help. Below are a selection of other resources:

Hotlines

UK

PANDAS 0843 28 98 401 pandasfoundation.org.uk

House of Light 0800 043 2031 pndsupport.co.uk

MIND 0300 123 3393

APNI (Association for Postnatal Illness) 0207 386 0868 apni.org

PNI (no phone but have website and forum pni.org.uk)

NCT 0300 330 0700 nct.org.uk

Australia

PANDA 1300 726 306 panda.org.au

Beyond Blue 1300 22 4636 beyondblue.org.au

New Zealand

PND Support Wellington 04 472 3135 pnd.org.nz

South Africa

PNDSA 082 882 0072 pndsa.org.za

Online

Breastfeeding with depression: uppitysciencechick.com

Crisis Chat: crisischat.org

Kristin Brooks Hope Center for Postpartum Depression: 1800ppdmoms.org

Postpartum Progress: postpartumprogress.com

Postpartum Support International: postpartum.net

Psych Central: psychcentral.com

The Postpartum Stress Center: postpartumstress.com

Books

After the Stork: The Couple's Guide to Preventing and Overcoming Postpartum Depression by Sara Rosenquist, PhD

Depression in New Mothers: Causes, Consequences, and Treatment Alternatives, second edition, by Kathleen A. Kendall-Tackett, PhD, IBCLC

Dropping the Baby and Other Scary Thoughts: Breaking the Cycle of Unwanted Thoughts in Motherhood by Karen Kleiman and Amy Wenzel

The Hidden Feelings of Motherhood, second edition, by Kathleen A. Kendall-Tackett, PhD, IBCLC

Overcoming Postpartum Depression and Anxiety by Linda Sebastian

Excessive Fatigue

Excessive fatigue is the technical term for having had less than four hours of sleep in the previous 24 hours. Constantly broken sleep for weeks on end is almost as debilitating. With either kind of sleep deprivation, the world can start to look stranger and stranger, and you can't seem to feel good about anything. It's more likely if your baby has had a rough start. Maybe breastfeeding has been difficult, maybe you've been supplementing or expressing, maybe she has reflux or another problem, maybe she's been feeding a lot during a growth spurt, maybe she's been really fussy, or maybe you just haven't found a good sleeping arrangement yet. Maybe it's something else altogether.

How do you know if you are *excessively fatigued* as a result of the sleep challenges you've faced? Here are some of the signs:

- *Constant* yawning
- Aching eyes
- Severe headaches
- Body aches
- Head feeling heavy
- No appetite
- Clumsiness
- Irritability
- Delayed reactions
- Short-term memory problems
- Difficulty thinking clearly
- Impaired judgment
- Microsleeps (nodding off for very short periods, from part of a second up to 30 seconds)

If some of these are happening to you regularly, you may be severely sleep-deprived. But when you're in that state, *you may be unaware of how tired you really are.* So you think you can do the things that need to be done, but you can't do them safely. In fact, being awake for 24 hours straight can cause as much impairment as having a blood alcohol concentration of 0.05 per cent, near the limit for drink driving in many areas.[27] That's why a lack of sleep is a factor in a significant number of car accidents.[28] Extreme fatigue affects much more than just your mothering; there is no distance that you can drive safely with that level of exhaustion. When it gets this bad, you need sleep. Now. And you need to have your baby in a separate space until you're more rested. You need an emergency sleep break (ESB).

> When we finally headed home from the hospital after Adam's birth, I was totally sleep-deprived. I started to say, "I think I should feed Adam . . ." My eyelids drooped, and I had a microdream of being on the tube, before I finished my sentence with, ". . . before we get to Oxford Circus. Wait, I think I just fell asleep." James swears that there was no more than a tiny pause in my sentence, but I'd managed to fall asleep and have a dream in that moment.
>
> —Shelley

Emergency Sleep Break (ESB)

An ESB works like this:

1. Breastfeed your baby (or express thoroughly if the baby is not breastfeeding effectively).

2. Go to a quiet, secluded, dark room to sleep.

3. A partner, family member, postnatal doula, or someone you can trust takes full care of your baby out of earshot while you sleep.

4. If your baby needs feeding before you wake up, he's given the expressed milk in any way that works for the baby and the person taking care of him.

5. You sleep until you wake up—fully—on your own and/or you can't sleep any more.

6. If your breasts wake you up because they're bursting, you breastfeed or express and then go back to sleep until you wake up on your own and/or you can't sleep anymore.

ESBs aren't to be taken lightly or done very often because they can undermine breastfeeding and reduce your milk supply. But when they're used judiciously, most mothers who have to take an ESB wake up the next day saying they feel like a whole new woman. The improvement in the way they feel both physically and emotionally can be amazing.

If sleep deprivation gets to be a chronic problem, it might help to build in a regular opportunity to sleep in, at least until the nights get easier. Maybe Saturday or Sunday morning. Your partner or a friend can take the baby when she wakes up and you can sleep for a few more hours.

Expressing for Nighttime Feeds

Once breastfeeding is going smoothly, mothers almost always say that nighttime expressing would make their nights harder, not easier, because they've learned how to breastfeed lying down and can drowse through breastfeeding instead of sitting up to express. But when breastfeeding at night *isn't* easy, either physically or emotionally, nighttime expressing is a temporary or long-term option that some mothers have used. Remember that if your nighttime routine involves long stretches without either breastfeeding or expressing, it increases your risk of mastitis—an inflammation or infection that you really don't need right now—and can decrease your milk production.

> I just couldn't be a mother all day and all night too. I was already battling depression, and something had to give or I was going to go crazy. So I started expressing for nighttime bottles. The pump didn't tangle up my emotions the way breastfeeding did so my partner went on night duty. When Olivia woke up the first time, I'd express while he gave a bottle. If she woke up again, he'd either use milk I'd expressed the day before or wake me up to express again. If it was a bad night, he'd put the baby in the bedside cot and I'd go and sleep in the other room.
>
> —Anna Luisa

When You're on the Edge

Sometimes thoughts can get truly dark and overwhelming. You may not want to tell anyone you've been thinking or feeling this way, but it's important to get help. Is there anyone you trust enough to talk to who won't overreact but who'll take you seriously and listen with kindness and empathy? It's possible that saying the words out loud to someone like that will be enough to dispel the darkness. If it's not, that person may be able to find someone to help. If you can't talk to anyone you know, we've listed good hotlines in the sidebar at the end of this chapter. There really is help out there, and it really can make a difference, even if it's hard to believe that right now.

My husband was out of town, so I was a single mother of two. My toddler had an ear infection and had been crying for hours. At one o'clock in the morning I called a friend for help.

Me: Nancy, I just almost threw Hannah across the room. Help!
Nancy: Take a deep breath. I'll help you right now. What's going on?
Me: [Long, frantic story interspersed with tears]
Nancy: Wow, that must have been scary!
Me: Yes!
Nancy: Are you ready to hear some ideas?
Me: Yes!
Nancy: What do you need to get everyone through the next few hours?
Me: To know you're there and I'm not crazy.
Nancy: You're not crazy. You're smart to call for help. You sound calmer now, so can we make a plan for the rest of the night and the morning?
Me: Yes.
Nancy: Can you get Hannah into the clinic tomorrow to see a doctor?
Me: Yes.
Nancy: If she's in pain, could she have some baby pain medication?
Me: Yes. I hadn't thought of that.

Nancy: Can you handle breastfeeding her or giving her some apple or orange juice on and off till morning?
Me: Yes.
Nancy: Is there someone to manage your four-year-old when you take Hannah in?
Me: No, I can handle both if I bring some toy cars for him.

By then I was rational again. We made it through the night and saw the doctor the next day. I was *so* close to really hurting her that the memories are still scary.

—Lynne

You're *So* Not Alone

Whatever is keeping you from sleep, there are things and people that can almost certainly help if you can summon the courage to ask. We've listed some; you probably know others. In the meantime, you need to take care of yourself at night in order to be there for your child during the day. It's okay to let go of the image of the perfect mother. It was never real anyway. Perfect is never necessary; good enough is *always* good enough. You're not walking this path alone.

Immediate Help When You're on the Edge

Samaritans 08457 90 90 90
samaritans.org

Australia Samaritans 13 52 47

New Zealand Samaritans 0800 726 666

South Africa Suicide.org 1-800-784-2433

chapter 11

Gentle Sleep Nudging Methods

> When our little guy was born, we decided to do everything we could to support his natural sleep rhythms and trust in his own capacity to sleep. Which isn't to say we didn't help—when he seemed like he was rousing but it was still early in his sleep, we'd pat him back down. We learned which peeps we could ignore to extend his sleep. We did all the little "tricks" you hear about, but never sleep-trained him. And, in what truly felt like a miraculous process to us, he eventually slept through the night. At first the stretches got longer. Then they combined to only one waking per night. And when he was ready, he stopped waking to breastfeed during the night.
>
> —Heather

Are you getting tired of hearing "Is he sleeping through the night yet?" Are you just getting plain tired? That's understandable. Waking up to feed and connect through the night is normal for babies and young children.[1] But it can be hard on mothers. Is there any way to make it better? Maybe a starting point is understanding your *baby's* starting point.

Growing up is hardwired into babies. You don't have to teach them to crawl or walk or sleep. They're getting there as fast as they can. Even knowing how normal your nights are, though, you may be ready for a change. You're feeling fed up with interrupted sleep or tired of explaining to all your relatives why your three-year-old is still in your bed. If *you* want your nights to change *and* your little one's developmentally ready, here are some gentle things you might try. We call the process "nudging".

Nudging towards more mature sleep is all about *letting* it happen or *helping* it happen, but recognizing that it's not always best to *make* it happen. Who needs confrontation at 2.00 a.m.? With the right approach at the right age, you may be able to tip your on-the-brink baby or child into the next stage. Gently, and within his comfort zone. You'll find nudging approaches for different stages in the second half of this chapter, or you can put the books aside, look at your child instead of someone else's advice, and invent your own.

These nudges are completely different from sleep training methods, especially the kinds that involve leaving the baby to cry, which work against a mother and baby's instinctive, magnetic pull toward each other. Sleep training can make a baby stay quiet at night.[2] But Chapter 18 reviews the significant immediate and long-term consequences of sleep training, in the form of a baby's future emotional maturity and ability to cope with stress.

This chapter offers some basic nudging ideas that you can adapt to your situation any way you see fit. The common thread is respect for your child's feelings, competence, and personal timetable. Nudging means taking the lead, but only when she's ready to follow.

And don't ever feel you *have* to nudge. At any stage, if you and your family are fine with what's going on, that's all that matters. Even if you never nudge at all, your child will one day sleep longer at night, stop breastfeeding in the night, and, yes, move out of your bed.

Babies Under About Six Months: The Un-Nudgeables

Infants aren't ready for any kind of nudging. They need round-the-clock, responsive mothering. Night feeds are essential because babies are growing faster than they ever will again. And they don't start consolidating sleep (sleeping longer stretches) until somewhere between six weeks and three months.[3] So at this stage it's not so much a matter of nudging them as maximizing your own sleep. You'll find some ways to improve your own sleep in Chapter 10. "Front-loading" can be a good place to start.

Even though it's too early to nudge, relaxing and reassuring your baby will help to maximize his—and your—ability to sleep. Here are some possibilities:

- *Bedsharing.* You already know that bedsharing mothers get the most sleep.[4] Bedsharing babies have a gentle waking and falling back to sleep that translates to greater calmness for them and more sleep for you.
- *Skin contact.* Most babies sleep longer with physical contact. Chest-to-chest or body-to-body contact works best, but even putting a hand on the baby can help.
- *Moving and dancing.* There's wonderful research showing that baby mice and kittens relax automatically when they're carried.[5] Human babies tend to do it too. Side-to-side movement usually works better than head-to-toe, but your baby will let you know his preferences.
- *A pre-warmed surface.* If you hold a lightweight blanket or small pad against your baby's back while you breastfeed him, you're more likely to have him stay asleep if you shift him—and it—to another surface.
- *Breastfeeding more often during the day.* Sometimes daytime feeds drop off when a mother's days get really busy. It can also happen with easygoing babies who don't fuss when they're hungry. Most babies are happy to breastfeed more often, and any excuse to breastfeed is a good one. It may help reduce nighttime "hunger-waking".

Matt was breastfeeding very frequently at night. My La Leche League Leader said maybe he wasn't breastfeeding enough during the day, so he was making up for it at night. Not for the food—he was growing fine—but for those other things that they get from breastfeeding (closeness, comfort, etc.). She suggested I breastfeed him every time he seemed at all willing during the day. And he started breastfeeding a *lot* more. I had been taking advantage of how easy it was to keep him busy with other things during the day. Once he was breastfeeding more in the daytime, he cut way back on his night breastfeeding.

—Stella

What About Formula or Solids?

Giving formula at night may help your baby sleep longer,[6] but introducing formula is a serious step with serious consequences. It doubles the risk of SIDS,[7] impairs your baby's immune response,[8] and raises his lifelong risk of health problems.[9] Mothers who mix formula and breastfeeding tend to breastfeed for a significantly shorter length of time[10] and tend to get *less* sleep overall.[11] There's a page in the Tearsheet Toolkit with some of the differences between your milk and formula.

In the past, baby cereal was suggested for young babies to get them to sleep longer. Filling your baby up with solid food might seem to make sense, but research finds that it doesn't work.[12] If night waking were just about hunger, then no babies on solids would wake up at night, and we know that many *toddlers* still do. (In fact, we adults waken in the night too, despite eating plenty of solids.) Babies also want the comfort of sucking and being close to you in the night, not just calories. And introducing solids too early increases the risk of infection, allergies, early weaning, and obesity.[13] Commercial baby cereal isn't even a nutritious food. It makes more sense to wait until your baby can pick up bits of real food and feed himself. Bottom line: unnecessary formula opens the door to a host of other problems, and cereal doesn't work.

Babies over About Six Months: The Barely Nudgeables

Nudging works only if your child is developmentally ready for the stage you're nudging him into, and the second half of the first year is pretty early for most babies. Breastfeeding several times at night is still normal for a baby over six months. It doesn't make him any less mature and it doesn't mean he's too dependent or "hooked" on breastfeeding. Why limit a baby's access to comfort and breastfeeding when he's growing fast and learning about relationships? A baby this age is still at risk of premature weaning or slowed weight gain if his night breastfeeding is restricted. Even so, many mothers are thinking, "Enough already!"

So how do you know whether to nudge or not at this age? Since it's such a gentle, good-natured approach, if you get it wrong, there's no harm done. Really. Life's little ragged patches actually build resilience,[14] so being the perfect parent would make you, well, less than perfect.

If your under-one-year-old child puts up more than a token fuss, then it may be too early to push the issue. Pushing too hard and too fast usually backfires by making a child anxious, irritable, or clingy. Just back off and try again later. Or just "let nature take its course". Some not-even-nudging nudges:

- *Topping him up.* You may be able to reset your baby's hunger clock by breastfeeding him just before you go to bed, even if you need to rouse him. He'll start his night with his tummy full, and that can buy you a longer first sleep.
- *Exposure to sunlight during the day and to the outside at night.* Exposing your baby to as much natural light as possible and making his day active (as one mother puts it, "places to go, people to see, things to do") helps ensure better sleep at night.[15] And as Chapter 15 describes, it can give him the reassuring sense of a village at peace. Older children benefit from playing outdoors too, every day if possible. Outside time with nature is calming in general and can even help with attention deficit disorder.[16] The sounds of a village at peace are different in the evening. The darkness, the hush, and the feeling of being outside at night can calm both of you before you turn in.
- *Bedtime routines.* Those babies who like predictability may enjoy a bedtime routine almost from the start. Lulla-

bies and favourite bedtime stories, especially ones that have rhythm, such as Dr. Seuss's books or Margaret Wise Brown's *Goodnight Moon,* can be started as early as you want and can last for years as part of a bedtime routine. Baby massage, long or short, can be a lovely part of the routine (see Chapter 15).
- *Being emotionally open and available at bedtime.* Research has found that responding promptly and willingly to babies helps them sleep better with fewer awakenings,[17] and helps them get back to sleep more quickly when they wake up crying.[18] It makes sense. We *all* sleep better when we feel secure and loved. It's a starting point that makes it easier for you to nudge later.

At about nine months, your baby may start waking up more, not less. And here you thought you were seeing the light at the end of the tunnel! But it's a normal, almost predictable developmental stage, and it passes.[19] Babies at this age are learning all sorts of new things, and sometimes it's so exciting—and maybe a little scary—that they don't sleep as well. Meeting his needs now by responding to him through the night may be all it takes to reassure him that his world is okay, so he'll start sleeping longer stretches again . . . until the next stretch of frequent waking, which will *also* be temporary.

If a pattern of frequent waking has been going on for much longer than a few weeks with your older baby and it's a problem for you, look at the section below on nudging towards fewer or shorter feeds, and see if any of them feel right for the two of you.

Toddlers and Up: The Increasingly Nudgeables

You may be surprised to read about toddlers and even older children who still have a nighttime need for their mothers. Yet it's totally normal and much more common than most people think. It just isn't discussed much, and all of their families, no matter what they thought at first, got to where they are one day—and one night—at a time.

Nudging is a whole lot simpler once you're dealing with a verbal, reasonably rational young person. Here's an example of nudging a four-year-old: Alanna wants you to lie with her every night until she's asleep. You might start off lying down with her, then say, "Oops, I have to go to the toilet—I'll be right back." You leave for a minute or two and return. The next night you might say, "I have to put some washing in the tumble dryer—I'll be right back." And you come back after a few minutes. Maybe you leave again in a bit, and return again. (Make sure you really *do* those things that you leave the room for. Children are very, very good—from birth—at separating the real you from some script that you're following. In fact, you might want to mix nights when you slip away for a few minutes with nights when you stay without leaving, because that *is* the real you.) Eventually you'll find that your child starts falling asleep while you're gone. Then it's "You lie down and I'll come in as soon as I finish cleaning up the kitchen. You can look at a book until I get there." The night will come when she's already asleep by the time you get there. No tears, no stress.

These goings and comings—with a reliable return each time—reassure your child that you are absolutely there for her. The key to it all? It happens very close to your child's natural "independence day", and you've built her big success from a series of small, real-life successes.

As for when a child leaves your bed or your bedroom, some cultures expect it at birth and others don't expect it until a child is well into his teens. The range of normal is so wide that whatever your sleeping arrangements and timetables, you're on the charts.

Clearing the Storm Clouds

Sometimes a child goes through a phase where she just can't wind down enough to sleep. She gets more and more irritable, less and less soothable, until it seems like something has to give . . . and it does. She cries even though you're holding her and reassuring her. But your loving presence helps more than you'd think. The quick storm clears, and everyone relaxes. We can't explain it; we just know that even adults can feel calmer after they cry. Fortunately, most babies grow out of needing to release tension this way after a few months.

> Andrew's a lively toddler who just can't wind down if he gets overtired. I've tried singing, rocking, lots more breastfeeding, but sometimes the thing that works is to hold him calmly, just enough to keep him from wriggling off the bed. It's not what he wants. He'll complain and cry, but I know that he's in a safe embrace that's distressing to him only because he wants to be up and playing. After maybe five minutes he feeds himself to sleep and stays asleep.
>
> —Laura

Nudging Towards Independent Sleep

There's independent and there's independent. It can mean independence from night breastfeeding, or from sharing your bed or room, or from falling asleep with you. Let's take them one at a time.

Night-Weaning

Night-weaning an infant is unlikely to go smoothly and always risks permanent weaning. Babies can very logically see your now-you-can, now-you-can't approach as a breach of trust, especially babies who are still sorting out their days and nights. Many nighttime parenting books recommend night weaning in babies who are far too young to manage it, with negative consequences for breastfeeding and even for the child's long-term emotional health (see Chapter 18). With an older child, moving gradually away from night feeds is part of a natural progression towards independence. Be aware, though, that for every child who stops breastfeeding at night before she stops during the day, there are probably *several* whose last feeds are during the night or at least at bedtime. It all comes back to reading the child (not the book) for readiness and then testing the waters.

The ready-to-night-wean child has probably already started lengthening her sleep stretches or shortening her feeds. Maybe sometimes a pat and reassurance is all she needs to settle back to sleep. Maybe sometimes she breastfeeds for a minute or less before drifting off again. *Something* lets you know that she's backing off on her own. Here are some ways you can encourage the trend:

- See if you can pat and reassure a little more often, breastfeeding her if reassurance isn't enough, and sometimes just going straight to breastfeeding. If she's on the brink of not needing to breastfeed, she may decide that convincing you to breastfeed isn't worth the effort.
- Wear something that's hard to get your breast out of. The fumbling delay may be more than she wants to stay awake for. *She* becomes the one to turn it down, not you.
- Get up to go to the toilet, promising to breastfeed when you come back. It's another amiable "in a minute" approach.
- If your supply is already lower from fewer feeds overall, you could use the same side all night and explain that the other side is sleeping. The slower flow can be less rewarding.
- Start your child in his own bed and let him come into yours when he wants. This is a common scenario with preschoolers and older children. Eventually they just stop showing up.
- Just let it go. All children eventually stop breastfeeding at night, and sometimes the simplest approach is to let go of the "should" and go to bed a little earlier.

As always, if you've chosen a nudging approach and guessed wrong—if there are tears or if she's more anxious or clingy during the day—you can back off and try again later, or try some of the ideas below.

Nudging Toward *Shorter* Feeds

Your agenda involves longer stretches of sleep; your *toddler's* involves as much breastfeeding as she wants. Wants? Needs? Which is it? One way to find out is to nudge, and to back off if your child has more than a mild objection. Among the ways mothers have shortened feeds:

- Try slipping a finger into the corner of her mouth to slide your nipple out a little before she would normally roll away.

- If she starts to rouse, or right after breastfeeding, try rolling her over and "spooning" with her, her back against your front. It's a cosy, reassuring position that might help put her back under.
- If your child is verbal enough—18 months or so—you can sing softly, count slowly, or say the alphabet slowly. Gradually sing, count, or talk a little faster, or skip verses, so that the feeds become shorter without her being aware. Or maybe only say the numbers or letters in your mind. (Some savvy little ones will start their feeds with "Don't count!" That means it's time to reconsider your timing or your method.)

Shortening feeds before your child is well established on family foods can shortchange them on calories at night. That's reason enough to wait until after her first birthday.

> When my older son was about three and a half, we started trying to night-wean, explaining to him that he wouldn't be able to breastfeed until the sun came up.
>
> We all had several *miserable* nights. What finally worked was shorter and shorter sessions any time he woke up. I told him that night breastfeeding was "just for a second". I'd let him breastfeed very briefly, and then gently tell him that was it. He would unlatch and be able to go to sleep. I kept making it shorter and shorter and shorter, until he just stopped waking and started sleeping all night. The concept of "never at night" was just too sad and scary for him, but this way he night-weaned without realizing it.
>
> —Antonia

Nudging Towards *Fewer* Feeds

If you think your one-year-old or older child is ready for fewer night feeds—if he's eating and drinking enough during the day—you may want to try some of these nudges. Keep in mind that if your child relies on your milk, he may need to breastfeed more during the day. Keep an eye on his weight gain at first, just in case.

- *Spooning.* An older baby may settle for this snuggly position instead of breastfeeding. It has the advantage of facing him away from the milk. Out of scent range, out of mind?
- *Turning your back.* By now, you're probably already doing this some of the time. If you're trying to stretch out feeds, you can make a point of rolling over while he's asleep. If your breasts are "on the other side", there may be fewer requests to breastfeed.
- *Partner in the middle.* If there are three of you in the bed, consider putting your partner between you and your baby. A baby on the brink of longer stretches of sleep may decide it's not worth the effort of getting your attention, but there's still a reassuring someone to snuggle with.
- *Verbal reassurance.* Using it without any body contact isn't likely to work until well after a year, when your child can make a satisfying connection in his own mind between your voice and your presence. But you can start it along with patting, reducing the patting over time but hanging on to a familiar, softly repeated song or poem.

Nudging Towards Falling Asleep Without You or Without Breastfeeding

This can mean different things—and can happen at different stages. Falling asleep without breastfeeding? Without breastfeeding if you're away for the evening, but breastfeeding when you're home? Falling asleep alone in the room? You can use just about the same approaches for any of those.

Changing the old routine can be happy for both of you if you nudge respectfully, as Alanna's mother did earlier in the chapter. It may be that the transition has to happen slowly, blending gradually from shorter and shorter feeds to new routines. Some ideas:

- *Substitution.* Extra stories? A later bedtime? A massage? At some point your child may be happy to swap breastfeeding for something cool. On the other hand, are you substituting something that actually takes more time and energy than just breastfeeding?
- *Snuggle time.* Parents often end up taking turns with this.

One gets a stretch of free time, the other gets story-and-snuggle time. Everyone wins. (And if you fall asleep, that's not so bad either!)

- *New person.* Sometimes it helps if the new routine comes with a new person, maybe a partner or grandparent.
- *Massage.* Any loving adult can do it, and it can help a child relax into sleep (see Chapter 15).
- *Leaving home.* It's not at all unusual for a toddler or older child to need his mother when she's home but to be content to go to sleep with a special other in his life who has a totally different routine, if he knows Mum just can't be there. Do you have an errand to run? See how he does. As always, keep it real. Your child will figure it out if you're standing in the driveway waiting. (Don't ask us how he'll know. He just will.)
- *Talking it through.* You can't really make a deal like "Yes, we can breastfeed, but not until the sun comes up" with a baby. But the time comes when a series of daytime conversations can open the door to some nighttime changes.

> I always breastfed Dan to sleep. One night, when he was about three and a half, we got into bed and I undid my shirt, ready to breastfeed him. He looked up at me and said, "Let's just talk."
>
> —Francesca

Nudging Away from Your Bed or Room

Lots of families share a room long after they've stopped sharing a bed. They may add a cot or single mattress or even a sleeping bag on the floor. There tends to be considerable ebb and flow to and from the parental bed, either nightly or occasionally, but the parents are on track to get their space back. Many mothers lie down on the child's bed for the bedtime breastfeeding and breastfeed in their own bed after that.

It's common to have "Sam's room" long before Sam actually spends his nights there. Just having the room available is nudging.

Most breastfed children still come back for night feeds, but the effort they have to make provides yet another nudge.

> My three-year-old daughter is excited about having her own bed, and wants to sleep in it, but she still wakes several times per night. I would hear her crying for me, so I'd go running down the hall to get her and bring her into our bed, where she spent the rest of the night. A little while ago, I was just exhausted and didn't want to go and get her. I called to her, "Come here, Annie, come here!" She kept crying. I called her again and waited. After about 30 more seconds, the crying died down and I heard the pitter-patter of little feet. Now she gets up and slips into our bed when she wakes at night.
>
> —Zöe

> When my toddler needed to start sleeping in his own room, I put him there and told him he only had to stay for an hour (or whatever). I set a little light on a timer so he knew that once the light went on, he was free to relocate to our bed. I kept moving that time forwards little by little until it went on just an hour before our own alarm.
>
> —Felicia

> Towards the end of our bedsharing years, Thomas would start out in the boys' bedroom and come into our bed only occasionally. A couple of years later, I asked him why he stopped. "Well, you know," he said, "it's a funny thing. Whenever I needed you, I woke up. But then I stopped needing you, so I stopped waking up." We adults think children wake up and then think they need us. From this child's perspective, he didn't wake up *unless* he needed me.
>
> —Anne

Backsliding Is Normal

If your child has been breastfeeding for shorter periods, sleeping longer, or staying in her own bed, but then suddenly things go back a few paces, don't worry. It's normal for children to take two steps forward and one step back as they develop new skills. If you're

Our sleep nudging ideas are just starting points. If you need more help, look at one of the books listed below. Better yet, read at least two books, because there really is no one-size-fits-all approach, and the way your child—each of your children—transitions from newborn to longer sleep stretches is going to be unique to that child and to the mother you are at that point.

The Baby Sleep Book: The Complete Guide to a Good Night's Rest for the Whole Family by William, Robert, James, and Martha Sears

Baby Sleep Guide by Marci Jones and Sandy Jones

The Family Bed by Tina Thevenin

Good Nights: The Happy Parents' Guide to the Family Bed (and a Peaceful Night's Sleep!) by Maria Goodavage and Jay Gordon

Helping Baby Sleep: The Science and Practice of Gentle Bedtime Parenting by Anni Gethin and Beth MacGregor

How Weaning Happens by Diane Bengson

The No-Cry Sleep Solution: Gentle Ways to Help Your Baby Sleep Through the Night by Elizabeth Pantley (Note: LLLI does not endorse the recommendations in this book not to let babies fall asleep at the breast.)

Sleeping with Your Baby: A Parent's Guide to Cosleeping by James McKenna

Sleeping Like a Baby by Pinky McKay

Sweet Dreams by Paul Fleiss

Three in a Bed by Deborah Jackson

Kiss Me! How to Raise Your Children with Love by Carlos González always there to reassure and comfort her, like the mother at the beginning of this chapter, your child will be able to move forward with confidence when she's ready.

When Nudging Doesn't Work

What if you try nudging at what seems to you like a reasonable age, and you end up with a sad, clingy, and frantic child? What went wrong? Maybe you wait a few more weeks and try something else, with the same result. Here's the thing: as you read in Chapter 7, babies come with all sorts of different personalities that are absolutely hardwired, meaning they were born that way, and nudging works a lot better with some personality types than with others. The beauty of nudging is that your attunement to your child lets you know right away if you're helping or coercing. If it feels like too much, it probably is. Nudging shouldn't be a battle. For some very sensitive children, even a little nudge feels like a big push (just as the tiny seams in socks feel like painful ridges to a High Sensitivity child). They really need to accomplish things when they are ready, and probably not a day before. One study found that bedtime resistance and trouble falling asleep seem to be pretty temporary, whatever the child's age.[20]

> I think nudging is *so* baby/toddler-specific. We would read nudging techniques, look at May, and literally laugh out loud. Nudging, if anything, would have produced a higher-need baby. For Jack, it felt like watching a miraculous flower unfold. When it seemed like he was getting ready to sleep a bit longer, you could "help" the process along . . . and it worked! With May, it felt like we were coercing her. With Jack, we felt like we were helping him.
>
> —Cullen

At any age, wakeful nights can be a response to restless days. There's a list of physical sleep stealers in the Tearsheet Toolkit. But maybe it's as simple as keeping your child electronics-free for more of the day. Getting outside for some vigorous play can be a big help.

An earlier, later, or less structured bedtime may help. And maybe your own preoccupations—the necessary ones, like work, and the less necessary ones, like a magazine-quality home—mean your child uses nights to catch up on mum time. Sometimes rethinking the day means you don't have to rethink the night.

One of the best ways to ease your way through the ever-developing patterns of normal baby-and-child sleep is to find other breastfeeding mothers. Our society has forgotten what those normal patterns are. Is your family nagging you about your still-waking baby (or toddler or preschooler)? It's enormously reassuring to see other families walking your same path. Any attachment-style parenting or La Leche League group can be a source of ideas, support, and reassurance. It's well worth finding one. You may also make some really good friends there. Two starting points are attachmentparenting.org/groups/list and laleche.org.uk/find-lll-group.

Something to Sleep On

As more than one family has said, "We do whatever gives the most people the most sleep *tonight*." All children move out of your bed and your room and sleep through the night, without your having to do a thing. Sometimes you can make it happen faster with some well-timed nudging. Sometimes you need a change for your own sake. And sometimes the best approach is no approach . . . yet (or maybe ever). The essence of nudging is that you can always relax about it for now and trust that time—with or without a little nudge—will take care of it. It will.

chapter 12

Sleep Gadgets

I had the whole gamut of baby gear. A small fortune in stuff that "they" tell you that you need. The only things we used more than once or twice were the car seat, the rocker, and the changing table. After the first few weeks, we bought what we *really* needed: a sling (the first of several). When our daughter was about nine months and active at night, we put her in the cot in our bedroom, but before that I mostly used it as a safe place for her while I went for a wee!

So now I tell mums not to get anything but nappies and wipes, a few sleepsuits, a few blankets, and a car seat before the baby comes. Once the baby's here, you can see what else you really need.

—Nan

Baby sleep is big business, and what's an easier sell than something that makes big promises to tired parents? "From screaming to dreaming in 60 seconds!" "Build a better brain through better sleep!" "Quietly off to dreamland!" But do they work? Some really are helpful, but many are unnecessary or even harmful. Here's our take on some of the common baby sleep gadgets on the market today.

Babywear

All babies come in their birthday suits. The lucky ones stay like that for hours or days, right there with their mothers. After that, though, the clothes go on. Here's a look at some of the special clothing.

Swaddling Devices

Swaddling—tightly wrapping and restricting a baby with a blanket or specially designed device—goes back at least 6,000 years, though the reasons for swaddling have varied widely over time and across the world. One popular sleep book recommends tight swaddling as one of its no-fail ways to soothe a baby.[1] Many hospitals still routinely teach parents how to swaddle, which makes them think it's important to do. Swaddling does tend to produce quieter babies who will accept sleeping on their backs alone for longer periods. Only recently has current knowledge of infant development given us a different look at what babies really need.

Babies who are swaddled immediately after birth are only about half as likely to breastfeed right away.[2] This may be part of why swaddling can affect later feeds and milk production.

Because their movements are so restricted, swaddled babies are less able to defend themselves against even the smallest problem. Swaddling may help a baby accept being on his back, but it also keeps him from drawing his hands in and bending his knees in the "fetal tuck" that is his natural position. The jury is still out on whether it increases or decreases the risks of SIDS and suffocation. There *is* agreement that tight swaddling may be linked to overheating and breathing issues,[3] and to hip dysplasia.[4] But the biggest issue for the average baby is that a swaddled baby isn't a body-contact baby. And body contact is what babies are designed for.

If you choose to swaddle at times, it's a good idea to use it sparingly. Keep it loose so that his hips and legs are free to move and his hands can be on his chest, or better yet able to reach his mouth for normal self-comforting and hunger cues. Loose swaddling is more likely to come undone, but your baby's efforts to get his hands free and loosen the wrappings may be telling you he wants something different. For one lactation consultant's take on swaddling, see goo.gl/YOs1LI.

Mittens

You may have been told to put mittens on your baby to keep him from scratching his face. But mittens mean sensory deprivation. Touch is a powerful sense for babies. Babies experience the world through touch even more than through vision. The feel of your baby's own hands on his face organizes him and triggers more effective feeding.[5] Have you noticed that his hands sometimes stroke and push against your breast right before feeding? Like kittens kneading their mother's teats, the movements actually help your milk release. Your baby's hands can even mould and shape your breast to make it easier for him to latch on to.[6]

Almost all scratching seems to happen when babies are stressed, because stressed babies often bring tensed hands to their face. It can happen when they're separated from you, or hungry, or feeling unstable from lying unsupported on their backs. Put your baby's chest on your own, breastfeed him effectively, and the scratching usually stops. If you're still concerned, just file his nails with an emery board—or easier yet, just nibble them away.

Sleeping Bags

Sleeping bags are a healthier alternative to swaddling or thick blankets and are used in some newborn facilities for that reason. A cot-sleeping baby can wear one over his regular clothes so that he stays warm without a blanket that could cover his face or be kicked off. That does mean he can't kick his covers free if he's too hot, so a sleeping bag can overheat a bedsharing baby, who's already warmed by your body. If you use one for your separate-sleeping baby, make sure it fits well so that it can't slide up over his face and the bottom can't flip onto his head.

Soothing Devices

A lot of the go-to-sleep gadgets are designed to imitate or replace a mother's soothing. But imitations are never quite as good as the real thing.

Dummies

Mothers today may be urged to consider a dummy (also called a soother or a pacifier) after the first month of breastfeeding to help reduce the risk of SIDS.[7] There are significant problems with that rationale, though (see Chapter 19). Dummies have been linked in numerous studies to breastfeeding problems, though it's not clear whether dummies cause problems or mothers with problems are more likely to use dummies.[8] One study found that using a dummy less often than once a day was not linked to problems.[9]

If you're concerned about your baby's weight gain, you might want to rethink giving your baby a dummy instead of breastfeeding because he might not gain as well if he uses one. Dummies are like chewing gum instead of eating when you need to gain weight fast. So if you feel breastfeeding isn't going well and think a dummy might give you some relief, you'll probably find that getting breastfeeding support helps more in the long run.

Is your baby just "using you as a dummy" to go to sleep? Of course not. Breastfeeding is nature's automatic drowsy-maker. It also provides warm milk, the feel of your skin, the sound of your heartbeat and voice, comfort, and security. All your baby's senses are involved as he drifts off, not just his mouth. A dummy is a substitute breast, not the other way around.

Comfort Objects

Some children get attached to inanimate objects—in fact, some have been known to go off to university with a soft toy secretly tucked into a pillow case.[10] If you have to be separated regularly from your baby—if you're going back to work or your child is in the hospital, for instance—then having something soft may help reassure him, especially if it smells of you.

Mothers often want their child to have a comfort object, since some psychologists call it a "transitional object" and say that it's a normal part of development from mother-dependence to independence. But in cultures where mothers and children breastfeed and sleep with or next to each other, the mother *is* the security object, from whom all children move away in their own time. Children who sleep alone are more likely to use a comfort object.[11] And of course any child who truly wants one will choose it for himself.

> I tried valiantly to help my son Mark attach to a particular stuffed toy that I knew I'd be able to replace if he lost it. But he never cared about a lovey at all, until his younger brother Zach was born and he had to move out of our bed. Soon after, he met Turtle, a stuffed turtle that had belonged to his late grandmother. Turtle is still a fixture on his teenage bed.
>
> —Danielle

Aromatherapy

The use of aromatic herbs and essential oils as childhood sleep aids goes back thousands of years. They're believed to affect emotions and stress hormones, and to have antibacterial or anti-inflammatory properties. Lavender, geranium, rose, and camomile are most commonly used to help babies relax and sleep. (A small study that linked lavender to breast growth in boys[12] has been debunked.)[13]

Some studies have found benefits.[14] In one study, very young infants whose bath water contained lavender-scented oil looked at their mothers more during the bath, cried less afterward, and slept more deeply than those bathed in plain water. Both the mothers' and the babies' cortisol (stress hormone) levels were lower.[15]

Undiluted oils can be irritating to children. A 1 per cent dilution—five drops of essential oil to two tablespoons (30 ml) of base oil—is appropriate for children under two years old and a 2 percent dilution (ten drops essential oil to two tablespoons base oil) for children two and older. Because of the potential for skin irritations, avoid spraying any on the bedding. Eucalyptus oil, even diluted, can be toxic to children.[16]

Nightlights

A low-wattage nightlight or dimmable light in your bedroom, bathroom, or hallway helps you check on your baby, change a nappy, or use the bathroom without turning on a light. A burst of bright light wakes everyone up more and can make getting back to sleep more difficult.

There's no need to use a nightlight to keep your baby from being afraid of the dark. It was dark before he was born, and having you nearby helps him feel secure.

Sleep Apps

New smartphone apps designed to help babies sleep or to help parents manage their babies' sleep appear on the market every day. Unfortunately, most are made by people who don't understand how normal mother-baby interactions develop.

Some apps try to track your baby's sleep so you can see patterns. But numbers and tracking draw your focus away from learning from and with your baby. (And some babies just don't *have* patterns; see Chapter 7.) Apps can only categorize, generalize, and follow a checklist. That's about as helpful as having an app for marriage. You'd be looking in the wrong direction all the time.

Another group of apps provides "white noise", womb sounds, or lullabies to help your baby sleep. But these electronic sounds can actually be harmful to tiny ears.[17] Most breastfed babies fall asleep pretty easily (and with a full tummy) just from breastfeeding.

One type of app becomes a video monitor. But there are too many ways it can fail, from a drained battery to an incoming text that hangs up the app. Monitors in general need to be used with caution.

Baby Monitors

You won't need a monitor at first, and you may never need one. It's not a good idea to leave a baby under six months alone, day or night.[18] He can always sleep in a Moses basket in whatever room you or his carer is in (see Chapter 5).

What about naps in another room just around the corner in the early months? They're fine, if you look in every few minutes. But a monitor is likely to reduce your own monitoring. The main concerns with monitors are that they can make you think you're keeping an eye on your baby better than you really are, you can misinterpret what you hear, and they can stop working without your noticing.

A "movement monitor" that clips onto your baby's clothes or uses a pad under the baby and sounds an alarm or vibrates if your baby stops moving or breathing is never recommended. Movement monitors are too unreliable and their false alarms desensitize parents, just as car alarms don't make anyone think about car theft any more. Even medical-grade aponea alarms (for detecting gaps in breathing) are prone to too many false alarms, so parents tend to tune them out.[19]

After the early months, infant sleep researcher Dr. James McKenna recommends using either a model that has a bidirectional feature or two sets of monitors so your baby can hear *your* sounds too. Hearing your sounds may help keep a baby from going into a deep sleep state that's harder to rouse from.[20]

Older baby? That's when monitors come into their own. But be aware that longer-range monitors may allow strangers to pick up on your family's sounds and conversations and, if you use a video monitor, maybe even see what your own monitor sees in your child's room. Digitally enhanced cordless telecommunications (DECT) technology may reduce the possibility of this kind of invasion.

As always, just keep in mind that any gadget can fail without letting you know. They're mother aids, not mother replacements.

> Maybe he would have been safe with the monitor system, but in those first few months I felt very deeply that he needed to have my presence when he was asleep and for me to be right there when his eyes opened or even when he stirred and breastfed himself back to sleep without ever opening his eyes. It was a matter of trust and security that I was always there.
>
> —Pam

Humidifiers, Vaporizers, and Air Purifiers

Humidity levels below 50 per cent can cause babies to wake up more frequently with dry or stuffy noses, and can cause static electricity that can be . . . well, shocking. So a humidifier or vaporizer can be helpful in the room where you and your baby sleep, especially in the winter time.

The oldest vaporizer was a pot of water simmering on the fire, sometimes with herbs added. The second-oldest—and most effective of all—is probably the bathroom shower. More than one mother has sat in the bathroom with a croupy or stuffy child, door closed, room comfortably steamy. Some weary mothers have even made up a bed on the bathroom floor.

If you want a machine to increase humidity, it is best to use a cool mist humidifier because a warm mist can cause burns. Follow the guidelines for safe use with infants if it has an aromatherapy feature. A whole-house humidifier can be a good choice if it fits your budget. Air quality can also affect sleep, especially in the homes of allergy and asthma sufferers or in high-pollution areas. Air purifiers with a HEPA filter are highly effective and don't produce ozone, a potential lung irritant that ionizer-type purifiers produce. No air purifier protects your baby from the chemicals in secondhand smoke. (Be aware that the noise of the motor can be too loud for still-developing ears.)

Baby Carriers

Mothers' tired arms have led to lots of baby-transport inventions. Here are some of the options you might be considering.

Babycarriers

We think a babycarrier—sling, wrap, tie-on, buckle-on, or strap-on carrier—is an essential for almost every mother and baby. Babies are calmer and cry less when they are carried,[21] often sliding in and out of sleep without making a fuss. Favourite carriers can end up faded and worn—old friends that the mother and baby both love.

The simplest babycarrier style, used for thousands of years, is just a wide strip of sturdy cloth. Today there are hundreds of brands, patterns, and innovations, with instructions and videos online about how to put them on, use them, and take them off. Mother-to-mother groups like La Leche League are great for checking out what mothers in your area use, learning how to use them, and trying out several styles before settling on the one—or two or three—that you want for yourself. There are tips on the safe and comfortable use of babycarriers in Chapter 5. There are also many YouTube videos showing you how to use them, and great books such as *Babywearing* by Maria Blois and *Babywearing Safely and Securely* by Beate Frome, as well as the darling children's book *A Ride on Mother's Back: A Day of Baby Carrying Around the World* by Emery Bernhard. And see the "Hands-Free Baby Holders" section below for a special kind of wrap just for naps.

Prams and pushchairs

The pram or pushchair—basically a baby chair or bed on wheels—may seem like essential baby equipment. We would say the babycarrier is *the* essential piece of equipment, especially for the younger baby, and that the best use for a pram or pushchair is to carry all your bags when you go shopping. But if you can't carry your baby, it helps to have something that rolls. Your baby may be less stressed if he can face you in the pram or pushchair, and if no hood or cover blocks his view of your face.[22] Touching and talking to your baby frequently also helps. Keep any cold-weather blankets below your baby's chin, and keep toys and dangling objects away from his head. If your baby falls asleep in the pram or pushchair, recline the back if at all possible to open his airway more.

Car Seats

Babies and children are well-known for falling asleep in car seats (thank goodness!), lulled by the motion and vibration of the vehicle. Some reminders:

- *Install the car seat properly.* Your local council or mums' group may have car seat safety events where experts check the installation. In the United Kingdom, you can also check goo.gl/5UNQuw. In the United States, you can check goo.gl/kEOSDu.

- *Dress your baby for the car temperature, not the season.* If you think he will be cool while the car warms up, add a blanket on top of the harness.
- *Keep toys, padded seat belt covers, and unrolled blankets away from your baby's head.* If your newborn's head needs support, you can put tightly rolled towels or tightly rolled small blankets alongside his head but outside the harness straps, or use a commercial U-shaped head support recommended by the car seat manufacturer—not all types work safely with all car seats.
- *Bring your sleeping baby along whenever you leave the car, with or without the car seat, even if it wakes him up.* Even for a short trip. No matter how nice the day is.

If you're carrying a fussy baby in a car seat, try swinging it gently from side to side and letting it bump lightly against your leg on each swing to imitate a walking stride. It's an almost instant calmer for many babies, and usually more effective than rocking the seat backwards and forwards.

Coming in with groceries and baby asleep in the detachable car seat? Most of us have set the car seat on the floor while we unload. Use it *only* on the floor, and not as a routine napping spot. The angle is designed for the tilted seat in a car, and on a flat surface it can cause a baby to slump too far forwards. So consider resting the front edge on a book or towel to give it more tilt for temporary indoor naps. Unbuckling the straps lets him shift his position, a basic kindness and maybe a help for head and spine.

Baby Furniture and Holders

As cute as they are, most of us don't hold babies 24/7. We talked about many types of baby beds in Chapters 5 and 6. Here are some of the other places babies sit and sleep.

Hands-Free Baby Holders

Holding a baby doesn't always mean *holding* a baby if you use a device that keeps your baby attached to your body but allows you to have your hands free to do other things. As we mentioned above, babycarriers are wonderful for this purpose.

Babies can sleep safely in most slings and babycarriers on the marke-t. Stretchy slings and wraps can be adjusted to hold the baby's head in place on your chest/ back. Buckle carriers and shaped carriers like Mei Tais often come with a sleep-hood which fixes over baby's head when they sleep. Follow the advice on page 270 if you feel like you need a nap yourself and are using a sling.

Infant Seats (Bouncers, Sleepers, Rockers)

There's an almost infinite number of infant seat designs on the market today, from simple fabric-on-a-frame types to models that vibrate and play lullabies. Although they are usually intended for sitting, not sleeping, manufacturers sometimes market them as "sleepers". The seat usually reclines far enough that the baby's back stays straight and his airway open. If your baby's head slumps forwards, look for a safer model. Keep the seat on the floor, never on a table, work top, sofa, or bed, and never put it in a container like a cot or playard.

The stationary play centres that are surrounded by a circular plastic table with attached toys aren't safe for sleep.

Swings

Infant swings are designed to be used until babies can sit up on their own, as a way to keep a baby happy while you rest your arms or get something done. The ones that swing from side to side are much more relaxing for babies because the backwards-and-forwards motion can disturb their sense of balance. (Maybe that's why cradles have always rocked from side to side.)

The Consumer Products Safety Commission recommends side-to-side swings for babies younger than four months if a backwards-and-forwards swing can't recline to about 45 degrees, halfway between vertical and horizontal. If the seat is too upright, babies can slump forwards and compress their airway. Whatever the swing style, stay nearby and remember that babies napping in swings are at higher risk.

Playards

Playards, popular in the US, have replaced the "playpen" of previous decades, but the purpose is the same: a contained space to keep a sleeping or wide-awake child out of harm's way. They can be a place to play or sleep. As always, a sleeping baby should have only a light blanket in the playard with him.

Many newer models come with all sorts of attachments. Some even have two bassinet sections for twins. But only the playard and suspended bassinet are for sleep; the infant seat can curl the baby forward and restrict breathing, and both the seat and the changing table are falling risks. Most "newborn napper" attachments are designed for babies under three months who are not yet able to turn over. The bassinets are for babies up to 15 pounds (6.8 kg).

> I was rocked in the antique wind-up cradle that my mother and sister were rocked in. My two babies used it too . . . in another room, no less! It didn't meet code, but the main reason I got rid of it was that I didn't want to model detached parenting for my children and grandchildren. I didn't want to send the message that *I* had gotten: that a cradle—and a wind-up one at that—was an honoured family tradition. But my grandmother's snowman candle? That's a family tradition we're keeping.
>
> —Julia

Bedside cots

If you want your baby close at night but aren't bedsharing, a bedside cot (also known as a sidecar or co-sleeper) is an excellent compromise. It's a cradle-size box (sometimes larger) that attaches to the bedside. Your baby is within arm's reach but still on a separate surface, and the sides are high enough to keep a non-mobile baby from falling out.

If the cot mattress is at the same level as your own mattress, you can move your baby back and forth from your sleeping spot to his more easily. It's like having a wider bed. If the cot mattress is slightly below your own, shifting him from your space to his means you have to rouse more, but it still beats going to a separate cot. And if he should roll or drop from your bed into the cot, no harm done.

Some parents convert or build their own bedside cots. A cot, with one side removed, can be secured against the bedside. There's detailed information with pictures of how to convert a standard cot into a bedside cot at drmomma.org/2010/01/turn-your-crib-into-cosleeper

A bedside cot

.html. There's also a YouTube video at goo.gl/5Uw4Xl.

Diana's husband, Brad, built a bedside cot from leftover pieces of wood for their third baby because the bed was getting too small for their expanding family. Their cot mattress was the same height as their own mattress; it could also be made slightly lower. The combination of heavy wood and carpeting below meant that the cot stayed put.

No matter what kind of bedside cot you use, make sure it can't move, and remember to fill the gap between the cot and your bed if necessary (see Chapter 2). The cot should have a mattress that fits tightly against the sides. Use a fitted sheet without extra folds or scrunches. No pillows, padding, bolsters, or toys, but there can be a light blanket.

Baby Hammocks

Baby hammocks have had some recalls in recent years. Until there's more known about what does and doesn't make for a safe sleep hammock, your best bet may be to avoid them.

Sleepy-Time Accessories

There are lots of products designed for use with a baby's bed or cot.

Sleep Positioners, "Nests," and Wedges

In 2010, the U.S. Food and Drug Administration (FDA) and the Consumer Product Safety Commission (CPSC) issued strong statements warning parents never to use sleep positioners.[23] In 2011, the American Academy of Pediatrics warned against the use of wedges and sleep positioners.[24]

Any positioner that's used inside another container—inside a cot, playard, bassinet, sidecar, or even in your own bed—can block a baby's breathing if he wriggles himself out of it or presses his face too far into it. You'd be amazed what even a very young baby can do when you're not looking. There's also a soft-sided "nest" that's designed to be put in the centre of the bed, between the parents, as a "protected" space for a "bedsharing" baby. The trouble is, it presents the same kind of suffocation risk as other sleep positioners.[25] And because it separates the two of you, your bedsharing "mother radar" isn't turned on, and your baby can't orient toward your breasts.

If you want a wedge because your baby has reflux and does better on an incline, he can sleep with his shoulders on your arm or sleep on your chest with you leaning back against pillows. If he's already sleeping in a cot or sidecar, you can put a foam wedge designed for that purpose *under* the mattress.

What about the beanbag—sometimes shaped like a hand—that's designed to comfort a baby like a parent's hand so he'll sleep better? Like any other positioner or cot toy, it's just not safe for a healthy, full-term baby. Instead, try gentle hand pressure that you *veeery* slowly lift off your baby after he's sound asleep.

Breastfeeding Pillows

Most breastfeeding helpers have seen breastfeeding pillows cause more breastfeeding problems than they solve. It's well worth getting breastfeeding help if you think you need one.

And here's something that might surprise you. A breastfeeding pillow can be a suffocation risk when you're really tired. Picture the exhausted mother who has her baby on the pillow in her lap. Sitting upright in her chair or even in bed, she starts to droop forward more and more, until enough of her body or breast weight is on the baby to interfere with his breathing. Without the pillow, there's more room for the baby to slide into her lap and there's lots of body contact to waken her if that happens.

Bed Rails

Many bedsharing families use a bed rail on their adult bed as a "tumble barrier". There are two main types: mesh and slat. Mesh rails are safer for bedsharing. They typically have a metal frame with nylon mesh fabric stretched firmly across the frame, instead of slats that tiny bodies can slip between. Mesh rails have extensions that slip under the mattress to hold the rail in place.

Any gaps between the bed and the rail can trap a baby, which is why the U.S. Consumer Product Safety Commission (CPSC) issued a warning against their use with children under two years old in 2012.[26] Parents who use them typically fill the gap tightly to avoid that problem (see Chapter 2). Some mesh models have a flap that locks down on the bed to eliminate the gap, but make sure your setup fits your comfort zone.

Mesh rails come in both a short size for toddler-length beds and a long size for adult-length beds. Many bedsharing families use the adult-size rail because it adapts more easily to a standard bed.

Inflatable tube "rails" are marketed as bed rails, but even small babies are able to get over them, and they're useless if they deflate. They don't provide enough security for an infant, but they *can* be an edge-of-bed reminder for a toddler. Some parents use a pool noodle for a less expensive "here's the edge" guide for older babies, tucking it under the bottom sheet (maybe using safety pins on the outer edge to keep it positioned).

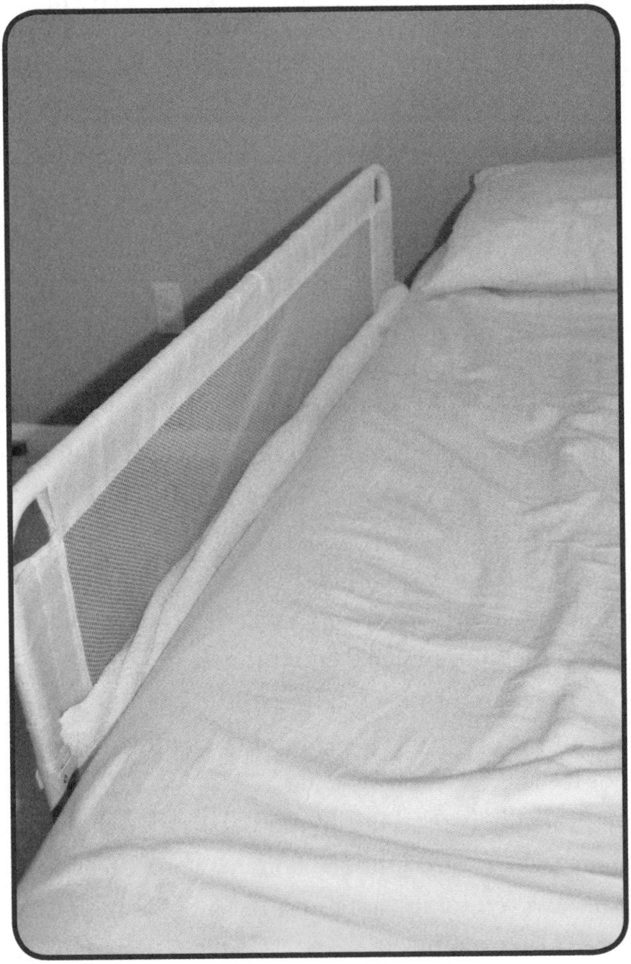

Mesh bed rail on an adult bed

Vibrating Devices

Some parents call their car the most expensive baby sleep machine ever built. Vibrating cot and infant seat attachments are intended to mimic that sleep-inducing effect, and manufacturers even claim that these gadgets help release trapped intestinal gas that makes babies cry, but there's zero research so far. Part of what makes a car so effective is probably the constant *changes* in motion as well as your continuous presence. The level of vibration produced by these products isn't really similar to a car's. There's a fine line between soothing a baby and causing him to shut down from stress. It probably makes more sense to get out the car keys. Or try breastfeeding again. Hunger isn't always the problem, but breastfeeding is usually the solution.

Cot Toys

Mobiles and cot gyms suspended above the cot, stuffed toys, and toys that attach to the cot rails provide sounds, movement, and colours intended either to soothe babies to sleep or entertain them while they're awake. They're mainly for babies who spend time awake in a cot before or after they sleep. Some versions help entertain a baby on a changing table.

Cot mobiles and cot gyms should be securely attached, kept well out of your baby's reach, and removed by five months or when he can push up on his hands and knees and grab them, whichever happens first. Stuffed toys, including those with recorded heartbeats and/or lights, are always considered a suffocation risk. Toys that attach to the cot rails, like aquariums with plastic fish, should be well out of reach, firmly attached to the cot, and with no small parts that can come loose. Toys shouldn't be attached to a cot with any type of tether.

You've probably figured out by now that asking a baby to go to sleep on his own is stressful for both of you. Breastfeeding and sleep are interwoven for most babies. For most of the rest, it's still a parent's touch that soothes them best. It beats a cot toy every time.

What about when a baby wakes up? Consider your child's personality type (Chapter 7). Some babies are happy to spend some time entertaining themselves when they wake up. The baby who typically wakes up crying needs you *now,* and cot toys won't cut it. And your baby will enjoy any entertainment much more with you there.

Cot Bumpers and Padding

As one study points out, "The use of crib [cot] bumper pads is strongly discouraged because the possibility for serious injury, including suffocation and strangulation, greatly outweighs any minor injury they may prevent."[27] Babies who don't have the motor skills or strength to move away from bumper pads can be trapped or smothered by them or choked by the ties. Instead, make sure cot slats are no more than 2³/₈ inches (6 cm) apart. Those unprotected slats may be less than cuddly, but a baby can't really hurt himself on them.

Infant Sleep Machines

"White noise" has come up in this book several times, always with a concern about harming a baby's developing ears. There's been research on the subject for years, but a recent study looked specifically at infant sleep machines and issued a caution.[28] We're so accustomed to background hums that we don't even notice them. But our babies do. "Village noises"—voices, breezes, dogs, and soft music—are fine. Steady, unreleting noise isn't.

Something to Sleep On

Many of the promises the manufacturers of baby gadgets make are just savvy marketing. They know how tired and vulnerable you are. Keep in mind that gadgets can't anticipate or react to your baby's actions. No product is completely safe without a loving, responsible, adult brain connected to it. "New and improved" models are often the result of something bad having happened to at least a few babies with the old one. And sometimes the fancier the gadget, the greater the potential for problems. Set the advertising aside and judge for yourself what's best for you, your baby, and your family.

part four

Sleep Ages and Stages

chapter 13

The First Few Days

> I guess the thing that I keep going back to is that it was a truly excellent hospital, but bedsharing in the hospital meant a sleep-deprived mother (me) attempting to hold my baby sitting upright in bed, post-caesarean, and biting my tongue to try to stay awake. After not sleeping the previous night either!
>
> We tried to rig something so I could put the baby in bed with me. It would be so easy to manufacture slide-in side rails so the mum and baby could bedshare! But they don't. So for an hour, when I couldn't stay awake, Michael sat there with his hand on the baby. That was the most wonderful restful hour of our stay, and we had to time it between nurses' visits.
>
> —Donna

You've worked your way through pregnancy, labour, birth, and a whole lot of issues and decisions along the way, and you've earned the reward at the end: the best baby in the entire world, and he's yours to keep. But if you've had your baby in a hospital, he may not *feel* like he's yours yet.

When you're awake, your healthy baby belongs in your arms or snuggled on your chest most of the time, his bare skin against yours, and it's *usually* the right place for a not-so-healthy baby as well.

Sleeping with your baby isn't usually an issue after an unmedicated birth. You just snuggle into your own bed from the start or go back home to start snuggling in a matter of hours. And it may not be an issue in hospitals that have bedside cots that fasten to the hospital bed to give new mothers free access to their babies day and night.

The Staff Want You to Be Comfortable

At least one part of you is probably uncomfortable right after giving birth, and the midwife, maternity care assistant or staff will know what to do about it. So that's some common ground, right from the start. You can tell them you'll feel best if you dry your newborn yourself. It's an important part of bonding for all mammals—an intimate shared reward after the work of giving birth. And then soak in every aspect of your incredible baby in those first hours and keep his skin against yours. No need for clothes yet!

If you're in pain, don't hesitate to ask for pain medication, especially if you've had a caesarean. Starting it early can keep pain from escalating, and most pain medication is okay to take when you're breastfeeding (check lactmed.nlm.nih.gov if you want to know specifics about any particular drug).[2]

Baby-Friendly Hospitals

The Baby-Friendly Initiative (BFHI) certifies hospitals and birth centres that provide research-based support for breastfeeding. Be sure to check the hospitals and centres in your area to see if you are lucky enough to have one with a BFHI designation. These facilities have worked hard to implement evidence-based practices that support breastfeeding and mother-baby togetherness.[1]

They Want You to Be Able to Sleep

Research shows that new mothers tend to sleep best when they have their babies with them to cuddle, stroke, admire, and breastfeed.[3] And of course having your baby near and breastfeeding is what gets your milk supply off to a good start. The staff may encourage you to let them take care of the baby because they think that will help you rest. You're totally within your rights to refuse. Breastfeeding raises your oxytocin level, which helps make you content, comfortable, relaxed, and loving, and it helps prevent excessive bleeding. Just having your baby on your chest does the same. Breastfeeding and touching also raise your prolactin level, which contributes to that feeling of peace and affection while it boosts your milk supply.[4] Having the baby in another room, tended by strangers, tends to make new mothers *more* anxious, not less anxious.[5] With all the research that supports keeping mothers and babies together (see Chapters 3 and 4), you can say with confidence that being apart isn't healthy for you or for your baby.[6]

Someone does have to keep an eye on the baby if there's no bedside cot and no way to make the bed safe. In the story that opened this chapter, Michael was Donna's "Sleep Sentry". That's someone who *expects* to be on call at night for whatever you need, because you planned it ahead of time. A Sleep Sentry, even for an hour or two, is an enormous help if you're trying to share sleep in a setting that doesn't make it easy. In the hospital, a Sleep Sentry is typically a partner. It could also be a relative or a close friend, or even a paid doula, who's willing and able to be awake whenever you want to sleep.

They Want Your Baby to Be Safe

Hospital beds are often narrow and high, with movable rails and a hard floor underneath. So the hospital staff's concerns about safety are understandable. And they can be addressed. Some of the ideas below may work for you.

Hospital staff are sometimes intimidating, but it's worth asking for what you want. A baby-safe side rail? A bedside cot? Ask! And it doesn't hurt to put on your best "surprised and disappointed" face if they don't have one. The first step towards change is helping the staff recognize that change is expected.

Don't Take It Personally

Any rebuffs you experience in the hospital aren't about you. Between hospital regulations and overworked staff, your requests and needs aren't always going to be met. But as the saying goes, you make more friends by being nice than by being rude. If you push against the staff, they may push right back. On the other hand, if you request rather than insist, if you let them know that you understand their workload and concerns, if you compliment where compliments are due, the staff may find a way to accommodate your requests.

> When Phoebe was born, they scared me about not having her in that acrylic cot when I wasn't breastfeeding her. When she was a few days old, I was sitting in my bed breastfeeding her and feeling really tired. Slowly, slowly I scooted down until we were side-lying. I was a new woman!
>
> When my other two were born, they knew I was an educated mum and helped me to build up pillows around the rails and do a variation on what we are now calling the laid-back position. I did have a couple of nurses shake a finger at me, but I smiled and told them I would not fall asleep and they left me alone. A smile goes a long way!
>
> —Leah

Use a Real (Wider) Bed

Some birth centres now have double beds for mothers after birth. Talk to the centre in advance (maybe while you're visiting) about arranging yours for bedsharing. Check out the options in person, so it's *planned* bedsharing. They may already have a side rail arrangement in place for you and your baby.

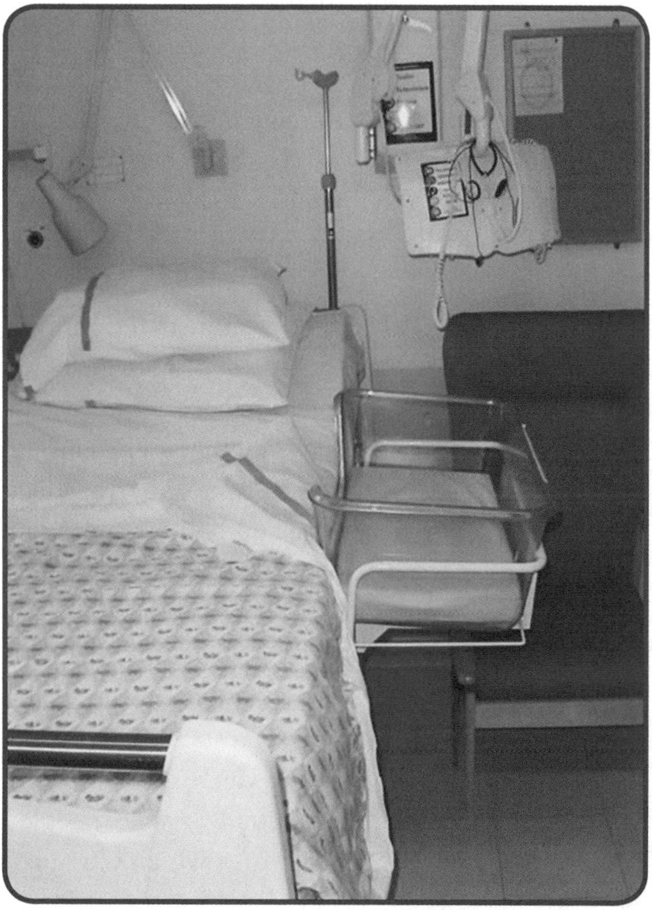

A bedside cot in a hospital

Ask for a Bedside Cot

There are special bedside cots designed for use with hospital beds. They're an excellent compromise between bedsharing and the standard clear plastic cot on wheels. Research indicates that mothers who bedshare in the hospital do the most breastfeeding during their stay. Mothers who use a bedside cot are a close runner-up, and mothers who use a cradle or Moses basket on a stand breastfeed considerably less.[7] In the United Kingdom, where the research was done, bedside cots are now available in many maternity facilities, and the idea is catching on elsewhere.[8]

What are the problems with the regular hospital cot?

- The baby gets less stimulation and is less likely to rouse when he needs to.
- Same with you. Video footage shows new mothers, their backs to the cot, snoozing through the arm-waving signals of their newborns. That means the baby has to waken more fully—often to the point of crying—to get your attention, which makes him harder to feed and harder to settle again.
- It's not easy—especially after a caesarean—to sit up and lift your baby up and over the side of a cot to get him out, and then over and down to put him back. Research videos show mothers clonking their elbow or the baby's head trying to get up and over, and babies being plonked back into the box because their mothers' arms just don't bend that way.[9]
- The physical effort involved in using a standard hospital cot means you're fully awake too. Two totally awake people instead of two drowsy people. And all that extra effort might mean you'll need more pain medication.

Easing the Path for the Next Mother

Hospitals tend to be receptive to consumer comments. At some point, *even years from now*, it would help other mothers if you let your facility know what was and wasn't helpful to you. Your hospital may not have heard about bedside cots or know where to get them, so here's a couple of websites to share with them. You might want to tell your doctor and midwives too. And your antenatal class teacher can remind other families to ask for them.

kododo.fr/berceau-de-maternite

nctshop.co.uk/bednest-bedside-crib/productinfo/4364

Putting your baby in a bedside cot lets both of you drift off to sleep safely, whether or not you slide the baby into the cot first. Bedside cots just can't catch on fast enough! If the staff don't have a side rail or bedside cot and are unwilling to allow you to have your baby in the bed when you're asleep, and if you don't have someone who can be your Sleep Sentry (your partner may be almost as tired as you are), you can always mention it to the staff anyway. With enough requests, they may eventually change their policy.

Adjust the Box or Bed

Maybe you just don't feel comfortable sleeping with your baby in your bed. Maybe you just don't have it in you to make waves. Your simplest, lowest-resistance option is to go with 24/7 rooming-in, or as nearly full-time as you can make it, with your baby's separate cot next to your bed. If the height of the cot is adjustable, you may be able to lower it so that the open top is as close as possible to your mattress height. That way, you'll be able to lay him back in the cot more easily when you're ready to sleep, without having to lift him up and over and plop him in. If you can't lower the cot, maybe you can raise your own bed. Go for whatever arrangement makes the putting in and taking out as comfortable as possible, and remind yourself that you'll be home soon.

Cover the Rail

A flat sheet can be laid sideways across your bed so that more of it hangs off on one side than the other. You and your baby lie on the sheet with the free end running up over the rail and back under the two of you again. Put some slack in it so it lies flat on the bed, and put your baby between your own body and the now-solid rail.

Wear a Wrap

Another possibility is a wrap. Many hospitals have adjustable soft elastic "girdles" for postnatal abdomens. Even though there's no research on this, many mothers and professionals have used these to hold a newborn gently on his mother's chest. Put your baby inside and Velcro the fabric loosely to keep your baby in place, head nestled under your chin. Not too tight! Your goal is gentle containment, not compression. Nurses from a past generation sometimes had the mother lie on a sheet folded like a triangle, the point towards her feet, and brought the other two points up over mother and baby, knotting them to keep the baby in place.

Ask your midwife if she can wrap a sheet around you and your baby so that he can rest safely on your chest, and make sure your curtains are open so the staff can do routine checks without bothering you. Have the head of your bed somewhat elevated, *not flat*. Babies breathe most easily when their chests are higher than their bottoms. Make sure your baby's face is open to the air.

Using a wrap for skin-to-skin care

No Swaddling

Swaddling is not the same as having the baby held snugly against your chest. Swaddling is designed to quieten a baby *without* adult contact. It's popular in hospitals that separate babies from their mothers. Swaddled babies are less of a problem for the staff, but as you read in Chapter 12, wrapping a newborn at birth can compromise breastfeeding,[10] and a swaddled baby can't wriggle out of trouble. So it makes sense to say no to swaddling and keep your baby with you instead.

When Elizabeth was born, the nurses made a point of swaddling her and putting her in the cot to sleep. We had a double bed room, so we took her out of the cot to snuggle in between us. We left her swaddled because she seemed okay with it and we thought that maybe the nurses were right and it made her feel secure. Then, in the middle of the night we woke up to see that Elizabeth had spit up some milk. She had a look of total panic on her face. She was choking slightly and couldn't move to fix it. We quickly unswaddled her and she has never been fully swaddled since. She has also never had that panicked face since.

—Scott

The First Night in a Hospital

If you gave birth in the middle of the night, like many mothers, you're already into your first night. Keep your baby close, cope as best you can, and that's quite enough for tonight! Tomorrow, you can start resolving any snags you may have run into.

In hospitals that still separate mothers and babies at night, the night nurses may be accustomed to having all the babies in the nursery at night, and they may be accustomed to supplementing with formula or sugar water, believing that this will "help the mothers rest." It could be that you or your partner will spend part of the night in discussions with well-meaning but poorly informed staff. Ask them what you need to do to keep your baby with you. If there's no *medical* reason for your baby to be somewhere else, there's zero *need* for your baby to be somewhere else, and there's plenty of need for him to be with you. A lot of new mothers are surprised at how protective they become when someone tries to take their baby away. It's a great instinct.

Your next day is likely to be a mosaic of people, poking and prodding, feeding the baby, information, feeding the baby, meals, more poking and prodding, feeding the baby, more people, and feeding the baby. Did you see *rest* on that list? Hospitals are notorious for emphasizing the importance of rest and then not letting new mothers have enough.[11] You might want to have your partner or the staff put a sign on your door, "Please knock first" or "Mother and baby resting—no visitors," or any other phrase that will minimize the number of nonessential visits. It's your space, after all. You get to say who comes in and when. Most new mothers are too focused on new motherhood to be able to advocate for themselves effectively. And it's easy to forget, in the face of "this is how we do it", that *they* are there to help *you* and not the other way around. Do what feels best to you, and know that you'll be home soon.

> When our first was born, the hospital made a big deal about her sleeping in the acrylic cot. She cried when she was alone. I held her and breastfed her. I remember being so tired. Around four in the morning Mike took her and slept with her on his chest on the little pull-out bed next to me. The second night Mike and I took turns holding her, despite the nurses. She just cried in that cot.
>
> —Mary

Early-Days Breastfeeding

Sitting up and holding a baby to breastfeed—especially after a caesarean—is tough for a brand-new mother whose physiology is saying, "Sleep! Sleep! You just had a baby! Cuddle him and sleep!"

Letting Gravity Help

You've probably heard lots of rules and instructions about breastfeeding. But as a starting point, try stripping them away and trusting gravity. You and your baby can figure this out. Just get yourself comfortable to start. Lean back, supported and a little reclined—as though you're watching TV on your favourite sofa. It's usually easy to adjust the hospital bed (not flat, of course, or you couldn't see the TV).

Once you're comfortable, lay your baby on your chest and stomach, and gently move her arms out of the way so her chest is flat against your own. As long as your baby's chest and tummy are against you, it doesn't really matter where her legs go, though she may be calmer with her feet touching something. Whatever feels comfortable to you both. Now gravity can do most of the holding. Most of us like to gather an arm around the baby. Just make sure that if your arm drops away in sleep, your baby will stay in pretty much the same position or will roll into a safe position.

Let her find your breast. Help her as much or as little as you want, no rules. It may take some time, but fumbling around is a normal and even important part of the process. You might even see some head bobbing—that's a normal latching reflex that means she's on the right track. Skip the mittens and leave your baby's hands free to explore.

Experiment with ways to be totally comfortable and relaxed holding your baby. If you want to change positions, go ahead and do it, then settle back into something comfortable that supports you both. It often works best when three things are in place:

- Your baby's whole front is flat against you.
- Your baby's head is higher than her bottom.
- Your baby's feet are touching something—your thigh, your hand, or your bedding.

You'll find much more about breastfeeding in of *The Womanly Art of Breastfeeding* (8th edition or newer).

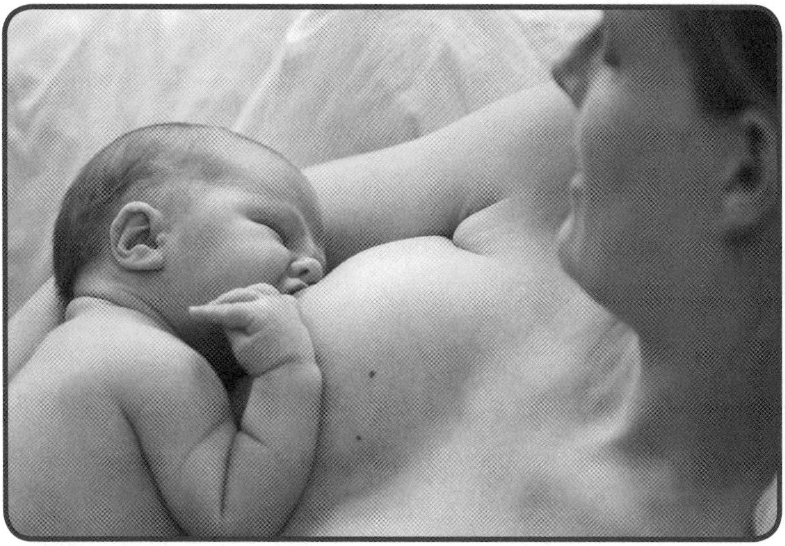

Using gravity to help your baby latch

When It Sucks

What if this whole breastfeeding thing isn't turning out to be as simple as the books said? Your baby wobbles and screws up her little face and shakes her head and fusses. Or she latches and sucks like there's no tomorrow, and your nipples are feeling it. Or she takes half an hour to latch on each time. Or she latches but then comes off and cries. Or she doesn't latch on at all.

Sometimes the midwives and health care assistants are a big help, but sometimes everyone tells you something different and *nothing* helps. You're sore, confused, scared, and looking frantically for the exit sign.

Many mothers and babies have been through this kind of rough start and gone on to breastfeed just fine. What can make all the difference is finding good help to sort through the problems. Finding a local La Leche League Leader through laleche.org.uk is a good first step. You can make contact before you leave the hospital by talking to your local Leader on the phone or ring the Helpline (0845 120 2918). If you are employing a doula, she may be able to help with breastfeeding challenges. If you need more help and don't mind paying for a private consultation, you can contact an International Board Certified Lactation Consultant (IBCLC) through lcgb.org. If the first person you reach isn't as helpful as you'd hoped, it's worth trying again.

Hang out with your baby. Just keeping your baby's bare chest against your own bare skin actually helps him save calories and reduces his risks of hypoglycaemia and hypothermia. It also puts your baby in the "restaurant", which allows him to breastfeed more often, especially in the first two hours after birth. Those rich drops of colostrum are all he needs for now; newborns need very, very little food in their very, very little tummies at first.

Give your baby expressed colostrum meals two or three times in the first six hours if he hasn't started breastfeeding, and keep up that skin contact on your leaning-back chest. You can express into a plastic cafeteria spoon and tip the golden drops into his mouth. He might even smack his lips over it. With two people and two spoons, you can start an assembly line: you express into one while the other person feeds with the other. Several spoonfuls holding a thumbnail-size puddle is a full meal. If you collect more, offer that too.

Once you have a way to feed your baby your colostrum every few hours, you can relax a bit. There's almost nothing you can do "wrong" that can't be patched up later, and you can get some more intensive assistance from a good breastfeeding helper when you get home. Keep your baby near your breast, and you may see him perk up after a spoon-feeding, find his way to your breast, and latch on.

A medical need for any kind of supplement in the first few days is rare. Formula is useful only if he truly needs more food than you're producing yourself right now, and only if there's no donor milk available. (There's information on formula risks in the Tear-sheet Toolkit.) You can discount any weight loss in the first 24 hours, especially if you've had IV fluids,[12] so gauge his weight from the 24-hour mark, keep expressing those rich drops of colostrum, and keep your baby's bare skin on your own bare skin, with a blanket over you both. Ask a midwife, or call or ask for a breastfeeding helper for more help if you need it.

Once your baby has some colostrum in his tummy and has spent some time on your chest, once you've both relaxed a little bit, you might start feeling better about things. Your baby *is* totally cute, isn't he? So here are some ideas that might make those early breast-feeding attempts a whole lot easier on your mind and body than the sit-up-and-follow-the-rules approach that the mother at the beginning of this chapter struggled with.

Baby First at First

You may want your best friends or colleagues to see your new baby in the first few days. But wait a bit. You and your baby have been through a huge, life-changing event, birth, that's supposed to be followed immediately by another life-changing event: breastfeeding. Unless you're an old hand at both, to the point where you can breastfeed comfortably with other people in the room, you and your baby will both benefit—really, really, really benefit—from asking the world to go away for a few days. That includes tweeting, texting,

The Second Night (or Whatever Night Your Baby Really Wakes Up)

Contributed by Jan Barger, RN, IBCLC, FILCA

All of a sudden, your little one discovers that he's no longer in the warmth and comfort of the womb, and it's *scary* out here! All sorts of people have been handling him, and he's not accustomed to the new noises, lights, sounds, and smells. He *has* found one thing, though, and that's his voice . . . and you may find that each time you take him off the breast, where he comfortably drifted off to sleep, and put him down, he protests—loudly!

So you put him back on the breast and he nurses for a little bit, and then goes to sleep. As you take him off and put him back to bed—he cries again . . . and starts rooting around, looking for you. This can seem to go on for hours. A lot of mums are convinced it's because their milk isn't in yet and the baby is starving. What's *really* happening is that your baby has realized that the most comforting and comfortable place for him to be is at your breast. It's the closest to "home" he can get. Breastfeeding helpers all over the world have seen babies do this even when a mother's milk came in early. Here are some ways to reduce the crying and increase your rest:

- *When he drifts off to sleep at the breast, don't move him except to pillow his head more comfortably on your breast. Don't try to burp him—just snuggle with him until he falls into a deeper sleep where he won't be disturbed by being moved. You'll see his breathing become even and there'll be no eyelid movement.*

- *If he starts to root and act as though he wants to go back to the breast, that's fine . . . this is his way of settling and comforting.*

- *Babies feel comforted when they touch with their hands. Sometimes babies just need some extra snuggling at the breast, because your breast is his home!*

and Facebook. Now is a once-in-a-lifetime experience for the two of you, and you need time to "soak into each other's skin". You'll never have these special days to yourselves again.

Rest when you can, maintain or improve on your sleeping arrangements, and rest some more. Your second night is likely to be more straightforward, but it's also likely to involve a lot of breastfeeding.

"How Do I Cope After a Caesarean?"

Maybe you're doing fine, except for postsurgery discomfort. Or maybe you're recovering from a caesarean that you hadn't planned on. You may feel like you're trying to hold yourself together (literally, it seems!) and getting to know your baby, take care of her, and breastfeed, all at the same time. Not fair! But not endless either.

After a few days your body may be more comfortable, but your mind might not be. Your incision may be hard to accept—maybe even harder for you to show to your partner. Flashbacks may occur when you're falling asleep. The lights are out, everyone else is asleep, and you're wide awake, feeling vulnerable and alone, reliving events that were out of your control. Knowing that one in every three women today has a surgical birth doesn't help. Your psyche may have as much healing to do as your body.

Some thoughts by mothers who've been there:

- *Pain.* Stay ahead of it. You've just had abdominal *surgery,* for goodness sake! Use whatever pain medications are suggested, in whatever amounts and frequencies you need; the ones used after a caesarean have been approved for breastfeeding. Pain itself is depressing, but pain that's well managed is likely to go away sooner.
- *Rest.* All injuries, including surgical sites, heal faster with adequate rest. So rest whenever you can. Sleep when the baby sleeps. Rest when the baby's calm. Go to bed early.

Get up late. Rest, rest, rest. You'll feel better that much sooner.
- *Bedshare?* This one's tough. You *are* compromised. But you aren't *able* to roll over, and you probably can't lift your baby from a hospital cot. A cuddle curl, even if you could do one, isn't safe with the sedating medications you'll be on, and your baby could even slip from your chest without your awareness.

Welcome Home!

Your baby is in the outfit you picked out before you knew each other. You've had your discharge instructions and packed up your belongings. Your car seat gets its very first use. And you're heading for home. You probably can't wait. And you may be totally intimidated by the night to come.

> I started out thinking I was not going to bedshare. Ever. The reality turned out to be much different. The first night home, I tried to put my son to sleep in his Moses basket. It lasted all of an hour. When he woke up and realized he wasn't in my (or someone's) arms, he wailed! I sat up, breastfed him back to sleep, then laid him down between me and my husband. We all slept for a few hours after that.
>
> —Cheyenne

Your First Night Home

If you've read the previous sections, you may already have done the maths: your first night home, which may be your baby's second or third night, could be the roughest night of all. So ask for a morning or early afternoon discharge to give you time to settle in and get as much rest as you can *before* bedtime. No matter where or how your baby is born, that day or two between when your baby really wakes up to the world and your milk volume really increases can be intense. But at least you'll be in your own bed tonight, with no one popping in to feel your uterus or take your temperature. On the other hand, there's no nurse to call if you need help. Even if someone's within earshot, it's still a little scary.

Your baby's sudden increase in breastfeeding is just her way of trying to (1) feed herself, (2) figure out how to make that happen easily, and (3) soothe herself. Birth was a major event for her too. Your low but growing milk production is a gentle introduction for your little novice, and her frequent breastfeeding is a potent call to your breasts to get full production under way. Your baby needs all that breastfeeding, and your body needs her to be doing it.

Now that you're home and quiet, you may notice how much noise your baby makes. But you've done this before—slept with a new and unaccustomed partner. Remember how you had to get used to it? New sounds, new routines, even the smell of a new person. Give it some time.

> I had never shared a bed with anyone before I met my partner. When we began living together, I couldn't sleep at all—not in the same bed as someone else—and definitely couldn't fall asleep with someone touching me. My partner always fell asleep with one or more limbs draped over or around me. I got very little sleep for several months, until we spent a night on the road together. Our hotel room had two beds. After a couple of hours of not sleeping, I moved to the other bed. When my partner woke up on his own, he finally understood that I *needed* some space to sleep. After that, we would snuggle until ready to sleep and then he would move away a bit. Now I am much better at bedsharing and don't think I could sleep alone anymore. Our baby always sleeps touching me, and my partner often does too.
>
> —Trevor

The Three Keeps for Plan B

1. *Keep your baby fed.* That means some kind of efficient (for everyone's sake!) feeding method.

2. *Keep your milk flowing.* That means expressing milk at least twice during the night in addition to daytime expressing if your baby isn't nursing effectively.

3. *Keep the two of you together.* That means you stay close, with as much holding as you can manage.

If You Go Home with Plan B

Maybe you've arrived home with a baby, a car seat, and some breastfeeding challenges. Is your baby being supplemented or not latching? Maybe you're expressing exclusively or trying to build up milk production. Any of these will make your nights more complicated at first.

Tonight may not be the night you expected. For instance, you might have to be the one who wakes the baby, instead of the baby waking you. If you keep three goals in mind—milk in, milk out, stay together—you'll still get some sleep. In the morning you can check in with your breastfeeding helper, and the two of you can tweak your arrangements in whatever ways might streamline your Plan B. For lots more information on the nitty-gritty of expressing and supplementing, see Chapter 9 and *The Womanly Art of Breastfeeding* (8th edition or newer).

Your Sleep Sentry

Once you're home, if you have the chance and feel the need, you might want to assign someone the role of at-home Sleep Sentry for the first few nights. It could be a relative who stays in another room, fully expecting to be wakened for questions, company, reassurance, refills of food or water, help to the bathroom, anything at all. If your Sleep Sentry has experience with breastfeeding, so much the better. But it's mainly about just having someone kind and helpful nearby. Your baby stays close at night so you can take care of all the baby stuff, and your Sleep Sentry is within easy earshot, ready to wake up if you call.

Remember, your job isn't to give your overnight visitors a restful night's sleep; it's *their* job to help *you* when you need it, or there was no point in their coming. The opportunities they get to hold the baby here and there are a delightful bonus in addition to helping you. In some places you can even hire a nighttime doula—*not someone to do the baby care,* but someone to help *you* do it.

From Plans to Reality

All the forethought you've given this homecoming is real now. You may decide on a different arrangement tomorrow, but for tonight, if you had time to plan ahead, you're all set. (For a baby whose arrival date surprised you, you can check Chapters 1 and 2 for how to get a safe spot ready right away.)

The Set up

Wherever everyone plans to sleep tonight, have your nightlight on, water and snacks laid out, and nappy and clothing changes available. Using a cot? Have a chair ready to breastfeed in, and make your bed safe too, just in case. Bedside cot? If your bed is set up to be safe too, it will be very easy for you to use one arrangement for part of the night, and another for the rest of the night if you want. Just knowing that you can fall asleep safely without putting your baby back can give you more rest. Planning on bedsharing? It's a good idea to sleep between your baby and your partner until you know how everyone's going to do. There's more on sleep arrangements and personalities in Chapter 7, but remember that for tonight at least, keeping the big bed for yourself and your baby and having your partner sleep elsewhere is a time-honoured tradition in many parts of the world.

Keep in mind that pets aren't likely to understand your newcomer's place in the family at the start, and the best arrangement for now may be to have some distance between baby and pet at night, as life is confusing enough for all of you as it is.

Get to bed as early as you can tonight. You're likely to get at least one stretch of good sleep (maybe two hours, possibly as many as four), especially if you bedshare.

Should you set your alarm to feed the baby? Not usually. Unless there's some specific issue that you've been cautioned about, you can trust your baby to let you know what she needs and when.

Normal newborns sleep best when they're right next to their mothers, and they waken when they need to, just as puppies and foals and all other mammal babies do.

> During the days, there was always someone around to help me, to take the pressure off from it being just me. But at night, I was all there was. This was my job, and I discovered that I could do it. When I was pregnant for the first time, I remember staring at my face in the mirror and thinking, "Someone is going to look at this face and to them, it will mean 'mother'." It seemed impossible. But during those long nights, I earned it and I became it. I discovered that my old limits were not my limits any longer. I could respond again and again and again—without feeling angry. I was this baby's *mother* and he needed me, and that was that. I was a little bit in awe of myself, and am still.
>
> —Traci

Milk on Tap

Somewhere in the midst of all the comings and goings of the steepest learning curve of your life, your breasts are going to "wake up", like your baby probably did on that second night. A suspicion of heaviness, a little more firmness, some white drizzle at the corner of your baby's mouth after breastfeeding, and . . . oh my! Move over, colostrum, the tide is rising!

The more your baby nurses, day and night, the more she keeps the balance of milk and gearing-up fluids in balance. Your milk will come in faster and painful engorgement is far less likely. (If you're using Plan B for now, frequent expressing can perform the same functions, though not as well or conveniently as an efficient and eager baby.)

As your milk supply increases over the next day or so, you'll probably find that your marathon breastfeeder fills up faster and cuts back a little on her breastfeeding time. Expect her to breastfeed again soon, though. Many newborns breastfeed almost hourly.[13] "Cluster feeding" is a baby's tendency to breastfeed, take a quick nap, breastfeed, take a quick nap, repeat this a couple of times, and then crash for an hour or more. It's all normal, it's all good.[14]

Your First Night Home After a Caesarean

If you've had a caesarean, you'll probably be a day or two later coming home than the mother who had a vaginal birth. And you'll probably be pretty sore, and really protective of your incision. The bullet points in "How Do I Cope After a Caesarean?", earlier in this chapter, might be worth another look.

Milk may "blossom" a little more slowly for some mothers who've had a surgical delivery, so even though you come home later, you may still have your most intense night on your first night home.

So here you are, having trouble getting up and down and rolling over and holding your baby and protecting yourself from pain . . . and you may have more wakeful nights than the other mothers. *Definitely* not fair! It might help to remind yourself that your baby's fussy first nights, like everyone else's, are temporary, and so is your postsurgery pain. You can get through this! And you deserve all the extra help you can get—friends, partner, family, paid postnatal doula, and so on.

Your First Night After a Home Birth

If your baby was born at home, one day slides into another much more easily, each with its ups and downs but with the very comforting thread of being at home running through them. A home birth tends to be both unforgettable and uneventful. Your first night home after a home birth will happen on your first night, of course. If you're bedsharing, you'll just continue doing what you're probably already doing—snuggling in bed, mostly or completely skin-to-skin, learning to breastfeed (maybe with the support of your midwife at first), and sleeping. You'll probably hit your stride sooner rather than later, and your recovery is likely to be straightforward.

Odds are that your nights will be reasonable right from the start, maybe with a not-so-easy night or two while your baby cranks up your milk supply. Take a look at "The Second Night" sidebar, which may be just as valuable to you as it is to the mother who's only now coming home. And if you've started out using a bedside cot or cot, remember the Safe Sleep Seven guidelines and feel free to change your mind at three a.m. You'll probably all sleep better if you don't try to shift the baby away from you after you breastfeed.

Nighttime Nappy Changes

After the first few days, newborns start pooing a lot, including during the night, so you can expect to be doing nighttime changes for at least the first few weeks. Have on hand wipes, all the components of whatever nappy system you're using, a couple of changes of clothing for the baby, a couple of changes of clothing for you, and a place where you can make those changes without going more than a few feet from the bed. Remember that you can always use the bed itself as your changing station, with supplies at the bedside and a waterproof mat to lay the baby on.

Your First Night Home with Your Second (or More) Baby

Thankfully, you know your way around babies now. But this baby is different, and this time your attention is going to be divided. Expect plenty of "help" with the baby, and maybe some extra visitors in bed. And expect some jealousy. Happily, body contact with you is one of the easier ways to spread your attention around, and an easy place to do that is in bed. Remember that it's safer to stay between any older children and the baby.

If you don't want older children in bed with you at night, consider having everyone nap together. Sometimes the older children will sleep with the other parent in a different bed at first. Or you and your older children can snuggle on the bed and read or talk while the baby sleeps next to you. Many families decide this is a good time to push a single mattress or cot mattress alongside the bed to give everyone more space.

The Morning After

You did it! You made it through the night! You were up every hour, it seems like—breastfeeding, or fretting, or being amazed, or changing a nappy, or soothing a crying baby, and doing things that sort of worked that no one ever suggested to you . . . and now the sun is up! You may even have had a couple of hours of unbroken sleep toward morning! Amazing!

But you're dragging. Even if everything went great, last night wasn't the most restful night you've ever had. And now you're facing a new day. So you regroup, breastfeed the baby again, grab a little breakfast, and . . . why not go back to bed, where you belong?

Settling In

No matter where or how your baby was born, you'll do your brain, your body, and your baby a big favour if you spend your first week (or first few weeks) taking it easy as much as you can. You'll be surprised how much it helps just to be lying down, whether or not you're asleep while you do it. And at this stage your baby will almost certainly appreciate hours and hours of close contact, not just at mealtimes. In fact, hang out in bed as much as you want unless you or your baby gets restless and wants to be up and around.

From the start, it may help to keep a bottle of water, some snacks and downtime favourites—phones, tablets, laptops, magazines, books, remotes—near where you sit or sleep. You can rest and make use of the goodies—electronic, entertainment, intellectual, and caloric—until you really, truly want to get up. Some mothers stow it all in a basket that they can move from spot to spot.

A Few Nice Ways to Say "Go Away"

"Shhh! Baby napping!"

"We're resting and nesting. Call after Tuesday."

"Leave a message and we'll call you back in a couple of days" (or "after we've had more than three hours of sleep in a row" or "some time before she starts school" or "in this lifetime").

"Visiting hours are 11.00 to 11.30 a.m. Other than that, we're comatose!"

"For now, please visit us on Facebook and not face-to-face."

"Admission ticket: clean something or bring food."

If you're going to have visitors, the first couple of weeks are when they're most likely to show up. Put them to work doing whatever it is *you* don't want to do! (Not the baby care, though. You and your baby need to "fuse".)

Unless you'd feel better getting a shower and getting dressed, you'll decrease everyone's expectations of you, including your own, if you don't get dressed at all today. Wearing a dressing gown is a reminder to everyone that you need to be treated tenderly. Don't be a hostess. Act tired. Move slowly. Don't put on makeup or do your hair. Put a sign on the door and a message on your phone to . . . well, see the box on the previous page for some possibilities. Most people will get it. And of course, some days it may feel like you couldn't get showered or dressed if you tried. (How can a baby sleep 18 hours a day and still keep you up 20 hours a day? It's a time warp thing that no one can explain.) So lounge around and have someone else pull together snacks and drinks for you (or if you really have to, do it in quantity yourself when you have a free minute, probably with a baby in one arm).

But wait a minute. Isn't it better to show the world or at least your family that you've got this mothering thing under control by getting your office-worthy clothes on, and your makeup and shoes? Nope. There's a time for that. Right now, take all the time you need

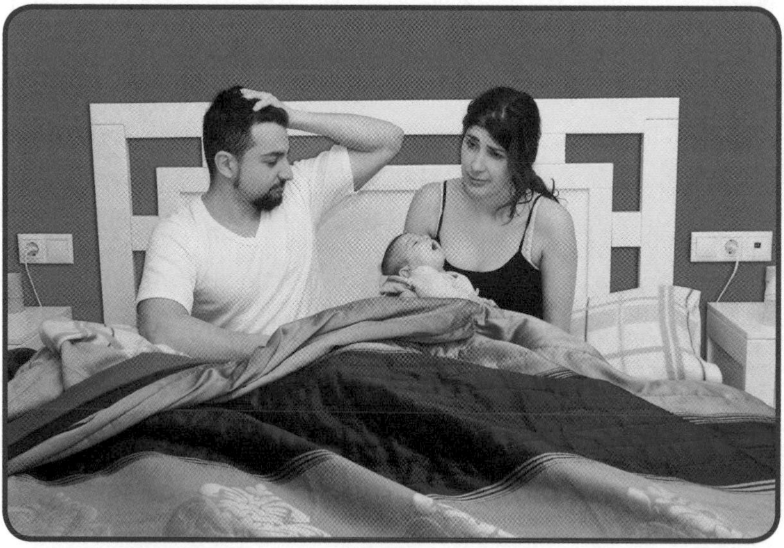

to recover from the birth, get breastfeeding going smoothly, and get to know your baby. Let everything be about tending the baby and resting whenever you can. Use the sleep spaces you've set up, and use them as often as you can. Everything that isn't immediate—housework, email, even bills—can probably slide for at least a few days. A possible mantra: "Hey, world, give me a break. I've just had a baby."

And so you start your life at home, with a shrinking body and a growing baby. And maybe with a sense, on some level, that you might be able to make this work for at least one more day.

Something to Sleep On

The good news is that everyone in your new family will survive this first stage, with all its inevitable ups and downs. Try to do at least one tiny-but-nice thing for yourself every day. (This might sound trite if you're pregnant, or surprisingly challenging if you're in your first couple of weeks of motherhood.)

Probably the single best tip is to step outside each day, even if it's raining or snowing. Throw your shoulders back, look up, and take a couple of deep breaths. You're one of billions of mothers, now and across time. You're built strong, and you're built competent. You're going to find happiness and skills that you never knew you had in you. Even if it doesn't feel like it yet.

chapter 14

The First Two Weeks

> The first two weeks were incredibly intense. I am so grateful that David had arranged to take two weeks off work so that we were in the same boat, slumming it in our pyjamas, unshowered, ordering take aways, and revelling in the beauty and havoc of our newborn. As David says, "That time is a *blur*."
>
> I will say that every single day for at least the first two weeks (and then on milestones thereafter) David and I shook hands and heartily congratulated each other on having kept an infant alive another day. The whole experience made me want to endow a postnatal doula grant because no parents should have to be without a village of support. This culture is in no way realistic when it comes to newborns.
>
> —Rosie

Maybe you've read the chapters on normal sleep, naps, and nights. You *have* information. These early weeks are when you start to *live* it. In your first two weeks, you'll change well over 100 nappies and get to know the person who's wearing them. And sleep? Well, you and your baby are probably still working that out.

Healing

You have a lot of healing to do, inside and out, while you're juggling all these new parts of your life, especially if you've had abdominal surgery.

Your baby has healing to do too. His head, moulded by birth and maybe by a ventouse or forceps, has to get back in shape. He's still dealing with any birth medications you may have had.[1] Lights are bright, sounds are loud, limbs are stretching. Even gravity must feel odd.

Breastfeeding can help with all his pains. Literally. It's natural, research-confirmed pain relief.[2] But breastfeeding is a new skill for you, and as with any new skill, there's a learning curve. Be sure to get good breastfeeding help if latching isn't going smoothly, if you have nipple pain, or if your baby isn't gaining well or is just fussier than you expected.

There are ways around virtually every glitch, large or small. Many mothers have gone from having to express full-time for a while to effortless breastfeeding for the next few years. But it often takes an experienced helper to walk with you through the beginning. The same two excellent sources of help we mentioned in the last chapter are there for you now: La Leche League (laleche.org.uk) and Lactation Consultants of Great Britain (lcgb.org).

Getting Your Feet Under You

You're up and around more, maybe getting outside for longer stretches. But you're certainly not yourself yet. You're probably still running on adrenaline to compensate for lack of sleep. And every night is going to be different for a while, which produces its own kind of fatigue. One night you get a couple of chunks of heavenly sleep and feel great, while the next night feels like a shambles again. There are great nap days and awful nap days, and they're not predictable.

But it's possible that even now you're starting to see a trend towards easier nights. If you are, a good bit of what's driving it are things you're not even noticing. You're doing your own bedtime problem solving. Your shoulders get cold at night so you come up with a different sleepwear or bedding arrangement. These nappies are too loose, so you use the other style. The nightlight is too bright, so you put it on the other side of the room. Little errors get remedied, and every remedy brings you that much closer to a smooth-running night. No, you're not starting to sleep through the night. But yes, within these first couple of weeks you'll probably start feeling a bit more rested—because you'll probably be getting more rest. Probably.

Your baby is a little bit more organized every day, more settled into her new world. Those billions of brain cells are firing up, wiring together, and turning her from a bundle of reflexes into a bundle of reflexes plus some experience. You're tuning in more to her squirms and sighs, and you have increasing competence and confidence with all the baby basics. At five days, the little stranger who came to stay is a full 25 *per cent older* than she was at four days! At 11 days, she's 10 per cent older than she was the day before. What a difference a day makes when you haven't had very many days!

Reach for the (Baby)moon

Traditional cultures often give mothers a month or so of dedicated time—a "babymoon"—to get to know their babies. If you can't manage that traditional full month, maybe you can swing two or three weeks before you have to jump back into your responsibilities. Do you have family who can run the house and take care of your needs for at least a while? Maybe you have a friend or relative—or a take-turns group of them—who can come for an hour or two every day for a couple of weeks to help you do whatever needs doing. Or maybe you can afford to line up some paid resources in advance, such as a local postnatal doula.

Postnatal doulas help with housework, cooking, and the care of older children, and are on hand to answer new-mother and new-baby questions as they come up. They also know the best breastfeeding resources in your area. To find a postnatal doula near you check Doula UK (doula.org.uk) or the National Childbirth Trust (nct.org.uk).

One helper who *isn't* likely to be useful to you is a baby nurse. She's usually trained in formula-feeding, not breastfeeding, and she's trained to take over all the baby care "so you can rest". It's a recipe not only for causing and prolonging breastfeeding problems but also for interfering with the raw, awkward, sleep-depriving, critically important job of falling head over heels in love with your baby by spending lots of time with him. We can't urge you strongly enough to look instead for helpers who will take over your *other* jobs so you can focus on what's *really* important right now: your growing connection with your baby.

It does help to get in touch with other breastfeeding mothers. The sooner you can connect, the smoother your days and nights are likely to be. You'll be amazed at how similar the questions are and the number of good ways there are to answer them. In person is usually much more satisfying than online, because you can *see* how they mother. Check out Chapter 23 for more resources and thoughts on finding other mothers and building friendships.

"Please Make Noise—the Baby's Asleep"

What happened to "Shh, the baby's asleep"? Well, before birth, our babies are accustomed to a whole lot of racket—our lungs whooshing, our blood swooshing, our voices booming. And they're very good at sleeping through it. In fact, they expect it; it was their world for nine months, even when we were asleep. They're accustomed to movement too, day and night. So what do they think when both the noise and the movement stop? It's got to be disturbing for them. If there's no noise, there's no one there to take care of them. So don't try to have your baby sleep in a silent room—he's better off with some sound and movement.

Breastfeeding Lying Down Revisited

Hospital beds let you choose your own angle and help you use gravity to hold your baby on your body. But you won't be taking the adjustable bed home with you, and your own bed is just flat. Side-lying is an absolute sleep and sanity saver for almost all breastfeeding mothers. Some don't figure out how to do it until their babies are several months old, but you can bet that they'll breastfeed lying down right from the start with their next baby. Unless you've had a caesarean (which often makes side-lying difficult at the start, although sometimes pillows can help), there's no time like the present to start practising! There's a full description in Chapter 6. It's *definitely* worth taking the time to learn, and getting help if it's not comfortable. If you practise while you're awake and thinking, you can figure it out with a reasonably working brain and remember what worked best for you. Then you can apply it to naps as well as nights.

Napping, Day and Night

During the day it's called naps. At night it's called broken sleep (as in broken into segments, not broken needing to be fixed). At first, these two kinds of short sleeps run into each other.

Stopping the Startling

You've probably seen the startle (Moro) reflex by now. Your baby is asleep on his back, you start to move him, and his hands jerk up, arms stiff, fingers spread. And then he relaxes again, often without waking up. Our guess is that the reflex helps a baby find something solid to grab (for other primates it's fur) so he can feel secure. Startles don't usually happen when a baby is already on solid ground, especially on your chest. Like any other mammal newborn, he has some degree of competence when he's on his chest. The flailing and startling happen when he's on his back.

When Do They Nap?

You've already discovered when your newborn takes naps: all the time. Never. Unpredictably. All of the above. This little person was born with very little concept of time, and a couple of weeks aren't going to do a whole lot to move him towards adult sleep patterns.

You can try to look for patterns at this point, but you could drive yourself crazy trying to find them. On Monday, you see him take 5- and 10- and 20-minute naps. So you plan Tuesday around that notion, and then he sleeps for more than two hours. So on Wednesday you assume there'll be one long daytime sleep stretch, and there isn't. Might as well try to herd cats.

One way to cope is to go back to the notion of sleeping, or at least resting, when the baby sleeps. As we said in Chapter 5, it's an old, old rule, and it *sounds* good. But it won't always work unless you can clone yourself. The reality is that when your baby falls asleep—and maybe you do too—your phone rings. Or a friend texts to see how things are going. Or you need to go to the loo. Or you remember that the sink is really dirty. Or you don't fall asleep because you don't know how long the baby's nap is going to last. Or, or, or. The old wishful thinking rule isn't going to work every time.

So if you can't sleep, your next best coping mechanism may be to spend some time experimenting with the soft babycarrier or sling that can make your days so much easier. The first few times with a babycarrier aren't always easy for a tiny, floppy baby and an inexperienced mother, so check some online videos or ask an experienced friend for suggestions. Once you get the hang of it, that carrier is likely to become a good friend itself.

Nights

They're pretty much the same as days, as far as your baby is concerned. So at first the two of you compromise. During the day both of you nap here and there, with plenty of feeding and short periods when your baby is in a quiet, alert state—those delightful times when she is awake, alert, and not asking for anything but a chance to gaze into your eyes.

If you can get outside most days to experience the bright light of day, it may help "set her clock".[3] Then at night, the lights stay low, and everything stays gentle and quiet. "Breastfeed as often as you need to, but then let's get back to sleep!" Gradually, gradually, your baby's physiology will begin to agree with that notion.

In the meantime, a few things may help. In the early weeks, your baby may sleep best on your chest at night, while you're slightly propped up on your pillows. If the propped-with-baby-on-chest position is what gets you the most sleep in those early days or weeks, make it commonsense safe and go for it.

At some point, though, you're going to want to change positions. Oozing the baby off your chest works the same at night as it does during the day. If you're sliding your baby into a bedside cot after time on your chest or after breastfeeding, you might try the blanket-on-the-back approach so that the new surface—cot or Moses basket—isn't cold and unfamiliar. That's probably not important if you're just oozing the baby onto your own sleep surface.

If your baby's in bed with you, she'll sometimes lie on her side while breastfeeding and may fall asleep that way, or roll onto her back. It's unlikely that she'll roll onto her tummy. Make sure to lay your baby on her back if she isn't by your side.

Milk May Wake You Up

Needing milk is what wakes your *baby* up. *Having* milk can be what wakes *you* up! For the first several weeks (maybe for the first month or two) you may have breasts that are ready to feed the multitudes. Don't worry: part of what goes on in these early weeks is that your baby adjusts your milk production up or down to meet his needs.

At the start, too much milk makes life easier for both of you than not enough milk. But if your baby takes a longer-than-typical nap, you may feel as if you're about to burst! You have every right to give your baby a nudge and say, "I need you. Now!" just as your baby has every right to say it to you. But sometimes the baby's answer is, "Too sleepy. Call back later." Can she be coaxed into breastfeeding anyway? If you pick up and drop an arm and it's totally limp, probably not. If there's a little muscle tension as it falls, you can probably convince her to eat, especially if you lean back with her tummy side down on your chest, mouth near your nipple, and stroke and talk to her. (You could change her nappy, but it's nice to try a more gentle awakening first.)

She's still not ready to breastfeed? Here's where it's reassuring to know how to express by hand (see below). An electric or hand pump will also work. Take out only as much milk as you need to in order to stay comfortable. It's probably little enough that there's no need to save it—remember, you're just letting off some pressure, not settling in for a pumping session. You have plenty more where that came from; that's the problem right now! Diane remembers stumbling into the bathroom in the night to spray some of the aching extra into the sink while Eric slept, oblivious and full. If you do want to save the extra, you can freeze it in any clean (sterile doesn't matter) container, and add more chilled milk to it whenever you like.

And then there are those of us who are struggling to provide enough. It may be that your baby isn't sucking as efficiently as he needs to, or there may be some other issues. If your baby isn't gaining roughly an ounce (30 g) every day, it's well worth talking to someone with training and experience in helping breastfeeding mothers.

Hand Expression

One of the best ways to learn is to lean over the bathroom sink or put a cloth in your lap, and see what you need to do to your breast to get milk out. (You can even learn while you're pregnant; several studies have found it improved milk supply after birth.[4])

- First of all, move your breasts around and gently massage or shake them a bit, just to wake them up.
- Put the pad of your thumb on top, near the edge of your areola (the dark area around your nipple).
- Put the pads or tips of the pads of your index and middle fingers under your breast, near your areola's lower edge.
- Press back towards your chest, then press your fingers gently together and draw them forward as you press.

- Instead of sliding your fingers over your skin, slide your skin over the underlying tissue while you're compressing. What you're trying to do is get behind the milk, move it forward, and squeeze it out. Stop at the base of your nipple.
- Relax.
- Repeat, shifting your thumb and fingers to other places around your areola after every few cycles: press back, compress, draw forward, relax.

It may take some practice to get a milk release right away, so give yourself time to learn. You'll probably get drops fairly quickly. The idea is to make the milk *spray.* (Don't expect colostrum to spray. It's too thick.) Every breast is different, so it's a matter of trial and error. If you find you just can't get the hang of it, ask a La Leche League Leader or an experienced friend to show you how. There are also good videos online. Three that mothers have found helpful: newborns.stanford.edu, goo.gl/VIC4fj, and goo.gl/iUN15U. Any video that you find online that shows milk spraying also shows a good technique. If your baby can get milk out, you can too, once you find your personal "sweet spots".

Sleep Deprivation

If you have a clock beside your bed, try turning it to the wall and don't look at your phone. As we mentioned in Chapter 10, it only makes you feel worse to think "I have to get up in three hours" or to add up the number of hours you've been awake.

Broken sleep is a reality at every stage of life. It's how we *handle* it and how fully we have to wake up that can make a difference. A few things that may help: (1) accepting the reality of fragmented sleep so that you can put your energy into creativity and flexibility instead of resentment, (2) grabbing rest and sleep whenever you can because every little bit counts, and (3) giving "front-loading" a try (see Chapter 10). Remember, rest speeds healing! It also improves your mood along with your ability to function. Your patience is better, the sun looks brighter, and the day looks more doable when you have some rest under your belt.

One of the best antidotes to new-mother fatigue, outside of sleep itself, is to go to a mother support group and ask how everyone's handling sleep. That may be the only question that gets asked at that meeting! Almost everyone is either going through or went through the stage you're in now. If there could be a little blue light on the rooftop of every home in your town where a mother is awake when you are, the town would be lit with little blue lights, coming on and off, but always lots of them. It might even help to picture it when you're feeling awake and alone in the middle of the night.

There is an old song that begins with "Sleep my child, and peace attend thee," and ends with, "I my loving watch am keeping / All through the night." It's a gentle song, and a gentle notion. You might discover that those stolen nighttime minutes and hours alone with your baby, when he's awake but calm, are just about the only chance you have to give all your attention to the newest family member.

Evening Fussies

Your baby's most likely source of bedtime blues is just plain end-of-the-day frazzling. You're probably feeling it too: it's been a long day, you're tired, and your tolerance for just about anything is practically nil. What makes it tough is that the day's end is when most babies have their fussy time, if they're going to have one. It's been a long day for them too. They typically alternate their evening fussiness with marathon breastfeeding, but eventually most will zonk out.

You may feel that evening is when you have the least milk . . . but it's also when you're making milk the fastest, because milk is made most quickly when the breast is most empty. It's just that your marathon baby is taking it out as fast as you're making it. That does two good things. First of all, although your baby wants to breastfeed, she doesn't necessarily want tons of milk. A lower volume lets her comfort herself without overstuffing. And because she keeps your breasts so empty, they respond by cranking up production for the night and the next day. So if you find yourself saying, "I've run out of milk," but your baby has been gaining okay and isn't unhappy, maybe more breastfeeding for less milk is exactly what she wants to soothe her soul at the end of the day. (If it seems your milk supply is truly lower than what she needs, see the section below.)

> Because we had a lousy start, my milk supply was low for about six weeks. I gave my baby extra food at my breast with a supplemental feeder—tubing that ran from a bottle to my nipple. My baby took the tubing along with my breast and got milk from both. What was interesting was that, in the evening, I had to use a smaller size tubing. He wanted to breastfeed all the time, and if I used the standard daytime size, he just threw up. He wanted to breastfeed and breastfeed and breastfeed; he didn't want to be stuffed and stuffed and stuffed.
>
> —Allison

Not Quite Enough?

In these first few weeks, your technique, your baby's technique, and your milk supply are all sorting themselves out. If your baby tugs at your nipple, bats or scratches at your breast, rarely breastfeeds with her eyes open, falls asleep after just a few minutes, and never seems to come off your breast relaxed and satisfied, or if your baby isn't gaining weight well yet, you might want to look into how well milk is getting into your baby. There can be three very different reasons—technique, baby issues, and mother issues, probably in that order. Trying to work out which it is often takes more breastfeeding training than most health care professionals have, so it's well worth talking to a La Leche League Leader. She can help you keep it together while you sort things out. You may also like to consider talking to an International Board Certified Lactation Consultant.

Changing of the Guard

Sometimes an evening change to a partner's arms helps, especially if it's combined with a quiet walk into other rooms or outside. It can be almost magical what stepping out of the door can do to settle a baby. Or try the Magic Baby Hold below to give him a whole new perspective on the world.

Magic Baby Hold

The Magic Baby Hold

This all-purpose parenting tool is soothing for most babies if breastfeeding again doesn't help. And it frees one hand at the same time. Partners usually love it too. Hold your upright baby's back against your front. Bring your left arm over your baby's left shoulder, so that one of his arms is on each side of yours, and grab his right thigh. (This is much less complicated than it sounds!) Your baby is snuggled up against you, totally secure, with a little pressure on his tummy. You can hold your left hand with your right for support if you want, keeping your baby either fairly vertical or fairly horizontal. When he's a little older, you can rest your thigh-holding hand on your hip to totally free your front.

If you see the back of your baby's head begin to wrinkle, or if you feel him tensing, add the "baby dance" (a little sway and bounce) and turn to give him a slightly new view.

Most babies who aren't hungry will relax at least for a while in the Magic Baby Hold (though, as with everything else, there'll be a few who hate it). The big advantages:

- Your shoulders can relax.
- Your baby faces away from the milk for a change of scenery.
- The right side of your baby's stomach—where his oesophagus enters—is on the uphill side, so any air bubbles can get out easily.
- There's a little pressure on his front, which makes him feel secure and helps those air bubbles rise.
- You can have one hand totally free if you want.

If your baby starts to relax into sleep, gradually slow and stop the baby dance and enjoy the quiet.

Bedtime Troubles

You've planned ahead, you climb into bed with your beautiful new baby, you're looking forward to some calm . . . and the problems don't stop, they start! He's miserable! Is bedsharing the problem? Almost certainly not. More likely there's some discomfort on your baby's part. Here are a few likely culprits in the first two weeks; Chapter 6 has a longer list.

Check the Temperature

Babies are more likely to be too hot than too cold, and a too-hot baby who fusses about it just makes himself hotter. He doesn't have to have toasty-feeling hands and feet to be warm enough. You can experiment with lighter layers and see if it helps.

Check the Nappy

Some babies just can't sleep with a damp nappy, others really don't care, and no wetness indicator is going to tell you which baby you have. Breastfeeding didn't work? It's worth a nappy check.

Food Sensitivities

Despite the "diet anxiety" breastfeeding mothers may feel, food sensitivities aren't common in the first couple of weeks, but they do happen. Your baby's evening or nighttime fussiness is most likely just the general frazzling we mentioned earlier, so you might want to wait a bit. If it doesn't get better, it might be good to check with a breastfeeding helper for other causes before adjusting your diet.

Who Knows Why

Some perfectly healthy, ordinary babies are agonizingly hard to get to sleep, for no reason that anyone can figure out. Maybe it's temperament, maybe not. The single most important tip? Time passes. Your one-month-old will be *four times* older than your one-week-old, and things will be different.

"Undercover Agents" and Outsiders

A baby's temperature stays the same, awake or asleep, for another few months, and ours drops at night.[5] So most of us assume at first that our babies are likely to be cold at night, when they're more like little furnaces, at least compared to us.

At night, you may find yourselves in disagreement over who's going to be how warm. Mum wants warmth . . . and contact with baby. Baby wants cool . . . and contact with Mum. Chapter 6 has thoughts on bedding arrangements and clothing arrangements to keep your two different thermostats happy.

Partner at Home

Ideally, your partner will be able to get some time off work for all or part of these first two weeks. That can make life much easier at first! Babies love short times in another pair of arms. They love the different voice, the different way of holding. And mothers usually love having someone take charge of meals and household chores while they do their basic recovering. It's great having someone who can find you the right help—breastfeeding, healing, whatever—when you need it. And both partners can say to each other, "*I* don't know; what do *you* think?" (Plus, of course, "I love you.")

The tricky part for a partner is knowing when to step forward and when to step back. When you were learning to ride a bicycle, you wanted your parent there to stabilize as needed. When it finally clicked and you could balance on your own, you probably *didn't* want that helping hand any more. But how was your parent to know? You had to yell, "I can do it now! Let go!" Same thing now. Your partner can't read your mind, and vice versa. Good communication skills can help. If you aren't good at communicating already, some books that can help are *How to Talk So Your Kids Will Listen, & How to Listen So Your Kids Will Talk* by Adele Faber and Elaine Mazlish (great for anybody anytime); *People Skills: How to Assert Yourself, Listen to Others and Resolve Conflicts* by Robert Bolton; and *Nonviolent Communication: A Language of Life* by Marshall Rosenberg.

Grandmothers and Others

Here's another reason to brush up your diplomacy and communication skills. Grandmothers and other visitors seem to come in three styles: helpers, baby junkies, and guests.

Helpers understand what it's like with a new baby, and they're there to smooth your path. Give them a spatula, vacuum cleaner, or dirty nappy and they're good to go. Baby junkies just *love* babies and want to be in charge of yours, maybe even to the point of wanting to offer a bottle "so you can rest or sleep". It's a wholly understandable impulse from a bottle-feeding generation, but right now is when you and your baby need lots of time together. Everyone else can admire from afar until you're ready to share.

And then there are the guests, who just came to have a holiday and *see* the baby, not to help. If you know in advance who the baby junkies and guests are likely to be, maybe you can schedule them for a shorter stay. If they're on your partner's side of the family, you might want to say, "Darling, could you . . ." Most likely, your partner can do a better job of stopping them from interfering than you can.

Whoever the unhelpful visitors are, it'll be easier for *you* to keep from waiting on *them* if you can remember to *be the queen*. From your very first contraction, this has been your show. No one else is the mother. No one else knows this baby the way you do. No one else knows better than you what it is that you need in order to be a good mother for your baby. Your home is your castle, and you are the queen. Put your crown firmly on your head, and remember that while a good queen is always gracious and grateful to her subjects, everyone still remembers that *they* work for *her*. At least that's the way it should be. You'll be back in your old role soon enough. For now, you're royalty, even if you and your baby are the only ones who know it.

Food: Need It, Can't Cook It

A queen shouldn't have to cook her own food. Sometimes, yes, but there are ways to get around it in the short term. Freezer foods, fast foods, friends' foods, and foraging in the fridge all work. Even though you're breastfeeding, nutrition isn't critical in the short term. Easy definitely is!

You'll find some quick and easy snacks in La Leche League International's book *Feed Yourself, Feed Your Family*.

Some high-energy snacks:

Granola and cereal bars

Leftovers from breakfast, lunch, or dinner

Crudités or vegetable sticks with hummus, tahini, or Greek tzatziki (yogurt-cucumber dip)

Hard-boiled eggs

Anything at all that's easy to grab and tastes good to you is a good choice. Calories trump perfect nutrition in these early weeks. But do try to get plenty of protein, fibre, and fresh foods when you can.

Baby Blues

You may wonder why you cry so easily, why your wonderful baby doesn't put you over the moon with happiness, why you feel so inadequate or fragile. It could be a case of the baby blues—not uncommon in cultures where new and breastfeeding mothers are routinely separated from their babies and aren't well understood or well supported.[6] You might be part of this fairly large club, which includes lots of mothers who never, never let on—or who honestly don't remember—that they ever felt that way.

Even at the best of times, tears are a normal part of new motherhood, and baby blues make them flow all the more. The A-list celebrities who show up on magazine covers, glowing and beautiful and cuddling their new babies? You can be sure that after the photo shoot some of them are in tears before they even hit the limousine. The baby blues don't discriminate.

And then there's postnatal anxiety. Some of us feel a low-level anxiety that seems hard to shake off. We worry and ruminate about things that really aren't a big deal.

The good news is that the baby blues and postnatal anxiety typically start to clear within a week, maybe ten days, most of the time. So give in to some good cries. You're entitled! Talk through your birth story to another woman who wants to hear it. If you aren't starting to feel more like yourself by the ten-day mark, take a look at Chapter 10 for more help.

Riding the Waves

Becoming a mother can be a tough adjustment, especially for those of us who have worked in management positions. We've become used to making daily decisions and seeing them carried out, putting together schedules, feeling confident and in control of our days.

Babies aren't interested in schedules and plans. They live from moment to moment, without clocks or calendars. Their needs are immediate and strongly expressed. As mothers, we can take one of two approaches: we can try to take charge and push our baby to follow our schedule, or we can bend and respond to our baby's needs.

For some of us, it feels more like breaking than bending. Preconceptions come crashing down. The real baby isn't at all like the dream baby. We finally give in and ride the waves. And then, amazingly, mothering gets easier. Accepting broken sleep, accepting the baby's *intense* early needs, trusting our instincts—it all helps not only with mothering but also with sleeping.

Getting Out

Whether or not you're going back to work soon, for the moment you're definitely a stay-at-home mother. Doesn't mean you have to stay *at* home. By the end of the second week, leaving home may feel wonderful! "Ahh, fresh air! Ahh, my legs still work!" Going for a leisurely short walk, a quick trip to the shops—your horizons will probably expand quickly.

Your baby's going to enjoy those outings too, and they'll help him start to organize his days and nights. In the next chapter, we'll look at your baby's expectation of being born into a village. These early outings reassure him that the village really does exist. And they're likely to make a difference to your mood too. Exercise and sunlight are mood brighteners, and getting outside even briefly can brighten the mood for you both.[7] It just might help both of you to sleep better tonight too!

Doctors' Appointments

If you had a homebirth, your midwife will probably do the early checkups in your home. If you had a hospital birth, one of your first outings is likely to be an early-days checkup for you or your baby or both. (At least it's a great chance to get out and get moving.)

This visit is your chance to get your questions answered . . . and possibly to face your first real questions about your sleeping arrangements. Before that happens, check out Chapter 21 and think about where the person you'll be talking to is coming from. There's a page in the Tearsheet Toolkit with talking points if sleep comes up.

Breastfeeding in Public

It's very likely that your baby will want to feed while you're out. Which means you'll have to deal with breastfeeding in public.

There are some hints on breastfeeding in public in Chapter 5. And for more than a few of us, the first draw-a-deep-breath-and-do-it feed outside the home was in a health centre. Most places (and every friend's home) will have a private spot where you can ask to go if you'd rather not be *truly* public just yet. (You'll probably find it a whole lot easier, and a whole lot less visible, if you forgo the breastfeeding cover-up gadget that Aunt Edna gave you and just go for it.) Whether you breastfeed in the waiting room, in your car, or in your friend's spare bedroom, you may emerge with a happier baby, and feel very proud of yourself for having managed to get out *and* feed your baby. If your baby is still fussy, try a little distraction, like a nappy change, a walk around the room, or a pat on his back in case a burp wants to come up. And then another feed may finish calming him (and you) down.

Something to Sleep On

Maybe your love affair with your baby hasn't even begun yet. Love comes as a tsunami for some, a gently rising tide for others. But the urge to protect usually comes very quickly, and that's enough for now. By this point, you may be starting to see your baby's personality emerge, a hint of a pattern taking ragged shape in your days and nights, less pain from the birth, and at least a few steps back into the wider world.

By two weeks, you've gone from having a baby you never met to knowing a lot about how to take care of him or her. You've been keeping your baby fed, keeping yourself fed, recovering physically, getting rest when you can, getting better at breastfeeding or getting help with it, and just plain getting used to this very small, very needy, very charming, and sometimes very scary new person. And a good thing, too. As three-year-old Elizabeth told her grandmother about her new baby brother, "He's going to be staying with us for a while."

chapter 15

Two Weeks to Four Months

My third baby doesn't "breastfeed on demand", he "breastfeeds on request", very politely. The baby wakes, then wiggles more and more. He taps me gently, either on purpose or randomly. Sometimes he makes sweet little cooing noises. I eventually roll over and breastfeed him, and fall back to sleep. As long as I get back to sleep, it's like a dream-feed.

When he was a couple of weeks old, I took him to bed to breastfeed and sleep. Four hours later, I woke in a panic. "Honey! I slept for four hours and forgot to breastfeed the baby!!!" My partner reassured me: "You were breastfeeding him most of that time! I knew you were exhausted, so I checked on you several times. He's fine. Don't worry!"

—Donna

We can start this chapter with some reassurance. If you're reading it around the two-week mark with your first baby, you're probably *not* where Donna was with her third. Not yet and that's normal. But odds are that by the time your baby is two months old, life—including nights—will have some stability to it. "Two months!" we hear you saying. "That's forever!" Hard to believe you'll look back and think it went by in a flash. Rough or smooth, you'll probably remember these early weeks through something of a haze.

"This Mothering Thing"

"I just don't feel like I'm very good at this mothering thing," the mother of a one-month-old told her friend. She was standing beside her car, her baby in the car seat at her feet. She glanced down, saw the sun in his eyes, and moved a few inches to put her shadow over him. Without even realizing it, she was doing this "mothering thing" beautifully. You are too. You're getting to know your baby a little better every day, and you're beginning to see the world through two sets of eyes automatically now—yours and your baby's, both at the same time.

Ask a first-time mother who had a tough start how long it took her to start feeling competent, and she'll probably say six to eight weeks. Ask a first-time mother with an *easy* start . . . and she'll probably say six to eight weeks. It just takes time to learn to juggle the many unaccustomed parts of motherhood.

Getting in the Habit

Before the end of the first month, you'll probably have most of your nighttime supplies where they work best for you: a bottle of water *there* and filled before bed, covers like *this* and baby dressed in *these*. You've learned how to change a nappy in a nighttime daze. By six to eight weeks you'll have developed lots of little habits that let you manage a whole lot of motherhood without having to think.

It's sort of like moving into a new home. Maybe you do some renovating in advance, but you don't discover most of the changes you want to make until you've done some living there. The same with nights. You might not realize until you try it that the changing table needs to be on the other wall. Or that you don't need one at all. You might use a cot, a bedside cot, or a breastfeeding chair for just a couple of nights (sometimes a couple of hours!) and decide it's making life harder instead of easier. Maybe the new maternity nightdress doesn't open far enough and your old T-shirt works better, or you take a pair of scissors to the nightdress. You automatically breastfeed *this* way, because it just works better than *that* way. When you start to develop quirky routines that aren't in the books, you're definitely sliding into motherhood.

> My favourite milestone was at about six weeks when Dylan stopped pooing at every feed so we didn't have to change him every time he woke to breastfeed overnight.
>
> —Julie

Breastfeeding Lying Down

Part of the slide into motherhood is becoming comfortable breastfeeding in any position. Maybe you started out needing three pillows and four hands, and now all you need is the baby. If the lying-down hints in Chapter 6 didn't help during your three-pillow phase, you might try them again now that you're both more experienced.

Even if your baby sleeps separately at night, you might find that naps together in a Safe Sleep Seven bed feel so good that you end up taking a nap yourself. If you bedshare at night too, you'll have a more easily maintained milk supply because breastfeeding is less of an event for you both. So what you'll probably get, once you learn to breastfeed lying down and especially if you bedshare at night, is more sleep for you, not waking up as completely to breastfeed, measurably less stress, more sleep for your baby, an easier time getting him back to sleep after he breastfeeds, and an overall breastfeeding experience that's less likely to end before you wanted it to. It's definitely worth learning to breastfeed lying down!

If Everything Is Still Hard

If you're still working out the breastfeeding kinks—and that's a whole lot of new mothers—take another look at *The Womanly Art of Breastfeeding* (8th edition or newer), and stay in touch with your breastfeeding support networks and helpers. Even though breastfeeding is still not quite where you'd like it to be, your baby will probably follow the patterns in this chapter. And think back a mere two weeks. Isn't it amazing how much you've learned?

> I had an emergency C-section with my first, and had such bad abdominal pain that I couldn't lie down. I couldn't lie back even the slightest bit because it hurt too much. I slept sitting up towards the middle of the bed with pillows behind me, and I would just hold her in my arms. If she was asleep, I would put her down in bed between me and my husband. If she woke to feed, I would just pick her up and breastfeed her. I did this for four months and honestly don't remember much of it, except that it always took me about 15 minutes to get up on my feet and walk normally after I was sitting up trying to sleep all night. I don't know how I managed to cope, but I just took it one day at a time. When I was able to lie down and breastfeed her on my side it was *so* much easier. So I had no complaints after that.
>
> My second caesarean was so different! I could walk, lie down, and breastfeed lying down, all from the start!
>
> —Toni

Your Baby's Village

We don't give birth to a 21st-century five-year-old princess or an eight-year-old superhero. We birth a simple little cave baby who expects the village we lived in aeons ago.

What did that ancient village offer? The sound of adults at peace. If they're talking, laughing, and working, the village must be in pretty good shape. No danger nearby. A village also offered leaves blowing, children shouting, dogs barking, streams running, birds singing, all with a mother nearby.

Babies tend to calm down when they're held by a reassuring adult who moves, jiggles, strokes, talks or sings, and goes about the day's business. What do many of our babies get? A stationary cot. A pram that rolls along too smoothly. An infant seat that keeps them in one position. A mother who often isn't within touch or sight. Only one or a few adults, all day long! And four walls. Those four walls get pretty isolating for mothers. They get pretty isolating for babies too. And it can be pretty boring for both of them.

More than one mother has brought a very young infant to the shops or a La Leche League meeting "just to get out". And more than one fussy baby is an angel there. "He's not like this at home!" his mother says, almost feeling betrayed. A very little one may arrive asleep from the calm jostling of getting there and stay asleep the whole time, very likely from the noise of the "village" around him. It's as if he goes to a party and never even knows he's there. When you want your baby to sleep, day or night, you're usually better off thinking "village", not "shh".

Village Days, Sleepier Nights?

One of the things a village baby gains is sunlight. And no surprise, sunlight is one of the things that "sets our clock" and helps us sort out day and night. Keep a baby indoors in shaded and artificial light, and it's going to take him longer to adjust. So one of the things you can do to encourage his day-night rhythm is to get outside with your little one, right from the start.

And it's not just the daylight. One of the best sleep-producers for anyone may be time spent outside or even just . . . out. These first four months may actually be one of the easiest times for outings. You have a non-mobile but increasingly social baby whose limited abilities mean he's especially eager for out-of-the-house excitement, and especially non-critical of the venue. Going for a walk, visiting friends, going to a mother and baby group, or going to the shops or a café—any place where there's movement, light, life, and action—can pay dividends at bedtime. Probably for both of you.

Any kind of exercise helps. Easing back into a favourite exercise routine or even just going for a walk can make it easier to sleep later. There are exercise classes designed for mothers and babies—slower-paced and understanding of baby needs. Park some distance from the gym, and you'll get a bit of outdoor time as well. Look out too for mother and baby outdoor exercise classes in your area.

Some Babies Aren't Village Babies

If your baby was even a few weeks early, you might want to keep the village toned down for a while. Premature babies and even late preterm babies (born between 34 and 37 weeks) usually do better in a soothing environment. So do certain full-term babies—the High Sensitivity ones. Some don't even settle in the car. These babies may prefer to breastfeed in a quiet room at first, and respond better to gentle swaying than to enthusiastic bouncing. Give them a few weeks, and they'll probably be able to join in with village life. Until then, you might want to think "evening village"—not silent, but not boisterous.

Patterns, Not Schedules

What's the difference between a pattern and a schedule? Let's say you usually get up to go to the loo, some time between 2.00 a.m. and 3.00 a.m. That's a pattern—a little vague, not every night, and not tied to a clock. In the morning, maybe you always wake up to an alarm. That's certainly a schedule.

Right now, your baby is what Chapter 11 calls an "unnudgeable"—a baby who's not ready for much compromise in his sleep behaviours. But soon some patterns may begin to emerge. He starts to get his days and nights sorted out. He starts having the occasional longer sleep stretch. He might give you a generous four- or five-hour stretch at times. There's a hint of things to come.

Evening Patterns

Through the first few months you may find your evenings given over to a whole lot of feeding, maybe mixed with fussing. Those breastfeeding marathons, which may even have begun in the first two weeks, are one of the most common evening patterns for breastfeeding babies. Some of them fuss in the evening way more than they breastfeed. It's an extension of that frazzled time we talked about in Chapter 6. If you're lucky, you have a quiet, calm Other nearby who can hold and rock the baby while you regroup.

If you're having to manage without an Other, and if you have one of those babies who just has a really tough time in the evening during the early months, front-loading can help take the pressure off so you're not worried about getting things done. The Magic Baby Hold described in the last chapter may help. And you'll find other baby-calming hints in the section below, "When Your Baby Just Can't Sleep", as well as in the Tearsheet Toolkit at the end of the book. Even if fussy evenings continue for weeks on end, it might help to know it's normal, it's common, and it ends. Often by around three months.

Even with a calm baby, your evening pattern right now probably involves a fair amount of baby care, which can fit nicely with Chapter 10's "front-loading" idea. If you can move most of your other responsibilities into the earlier part of your day, you'll probably be much less frantic on those evenings when your baby needs you more than usual, and you'll get more pleasure out of the quiet stretches when she doesn't.

Starting the Night in a Cot?

There's a difference between bedsharing all night and bedsharing by bringing the baby from crib to bed the first time he wakes up. Research shows that babies who sleep alone sleep more deeply and waken less often, and that's not healthy (see Chapter 4).[1]

One mother found that her three-month-old (peak SIDS age) slept up to 11 hours straight when he started the night in a cot—putting him at higher risk.

Nighttime Patterns

Does night start when your *baby* goes to bed or when *you* go to bed? Or do you both go at the same time? For about the first six months, if your baby goes to bed first, it's a good idea for that bed to be wherever you spend your evenings. A Moses basket, or even a blanket on the floor is fine. When you head off to bed, just take him along with you. Most babies sleep just as well in the living room as they do in the bedroom.

Even if your baby wakes four or five times a night, within a month or two your familiar patterns probably mean it isn't the huge deal that it was in the beginning. One day you may find yourself saying, "He slept for five hours straight last night! I feel like a new woman!" It's almost as if babies know. Just when you start to despair about some aspect of baby care, they give you a gift: a first smile or giggle, or that blissfully longer stretch of sleep. On the other hand, babies do tend to be a little stingy in the longer-stretch-at-night department.

When Your Baby Just Can't Sleep

There's probably no baby who *always* falls asleep breastfeeding. Just like their mothers, babies have days when they're off, days when they're edgy, and days when they just can't get comfortable. *We* can sort out whether it's our heads or our bodies that are keeping us awake, but our *babies* can't. So we need soothing ideas for their brains *and* their bodies.

Most of the ideas below involve your being out of bed. But then, we're likely to be out of bed with a fussy baby anyway. Maybe your partner can help with some of these, except of course for the first one. We also have a list in the Tearsheet Toolkit of both causes for wakefulness and ways to calm babies.

- *Breastfeeding.* It usually puts a restless baby to sleep.
- *Lullabies.* We're not sure why they work. Maybe it's the reassurance of repetition. Maybe it's the soothing tones. Maybe we just plain bore them into sleep. But almost all of us drift into some form of lullaby as we pat a fussy baby at bedtime or in the middle of the night. There are the standard ones, of course, and the ones that our families hand down. There are our own favourite songs, jazzed up or softened to fit the occasion. Even "mmmmmm-mmm-mmmmm" qualifies as a lullaby. Some of us, desperate to soothe a baby in the car, for instance, come up with countless silly and simple verses to a simple melody. Even if it doesn't put the baby to sleep, it gives *us* some distraction!
- *The baby dance.* You may already have figured this out: most but not all babies are calmed more by a sway with a slight hitch or small bounce each time than by a smooth sway. Maybe the little hitch helps trigger the reflex that

causes babies to relax when someone walks around while holding them.[2]

- *The Magic Baby Hold.* Described in the last chapter, it relaxes lots of babies. Others may love an over-the-shoulder hold with patting. Your baby has probably already let you know her preferences.
- *The other room.* Sometimes babies need a change of scenery. You can try walking with her in other parts of the darkened house while you talk or sing quietly. Is there a light with a dimmer switch? Sometimes just showing her the beautiful soft lights and telling her about them quietly will captivate her and help her settle.
- *The outside.* On a warm night, you might even be able to walk outside, or stand just outside your door. The darkness, the hush, the night sounds, often leave a baby quiet and spellbound. Even in a city, night has a different quality and a subdued mood that you may be able to carry back inside.
- *Baby massage.* This is more likely a settle-*for*-the-night idea than a settle-*during*-the-night idea, but it can be soothing to both of you. You don't need a book on baby massage, just warm hands and maybe a little olive oil. But the websites, books, and videos listed in the sidebar have some lovely ideas in them. A couple of general thoughts: keep your strokes firm enough not to tickle and smooth enough not to startle. If you use any oil or lotion, use it on just one limb for a few days to make sure there's no reaction. Younger or fussier babies may do better lying on their fronts throughout. And watch out: you both may enjoy it so much that you have to find a way to squeeze it in every night.
- *Breastfeeding . . . again.* If breastfeeding didn't work, and the other ideas didn't work, be sure to offer again! As one mother said, "Hunger isn't always the problem, but breastfeeding is almost always the solution." If it isn't right away, it probably will be soon.

Baby Massage Resources

BabyBabyOhBaby: Bonding with Your Brilliant and Beautiful Baby Through Infant Massage DVD: BabyBabyOhBaby.com (sample video available online)
Baby Massage: Soothing Strokes for Healthy Growth by Suzanne P. Reese and Bill Milne
Baby Massage: The Calming Power of Touch by Alan Heath, Nicki Bainbridge, and Diana Moore
Infant Massage A Handbook for Loving Parents, revised edition, by Vimala McClure
Pinky McKay's Baby Massage DVD
Massage for Happy Babies Helen Pritchard (DVD)
Also try YouTube!

To find a class try International Association of Infant Massage iaimbabymassage.co.uk/index.html or look in local sources of information such as Health Centre noticeboards, local magazines or the local sections of online forums such as Mumsnet or Netmums.

Naptime Patterns

Having read this far, you know that it'll work best if you keep up a certain amount of noise and activity during your baby's naps if you're not holding her. That's easy enough to do since a baby this age ought to be in whatever room you're in. It might also help if you nap together where your baby can sense you.

> Some of the best sleep I got was while she was breastfeeding. The rest of the time I was waiting for her to wake up.
>
> —Cindy

Your Baby's Naps

Your baby's naps tend to get simpler and simpler as you move through the first few months of her life. Breastfeeding her to sleep isn't the complicated ritual it felt like at first. In fact, you can sometimes *encourage* a nap by breastfeeding her to sleep when *you* want her to have one. She may also fit in short feeds (and often naps or catnaps) all through the day. All that breastfeeding sounds like a lot of work, but you'll be surprised. A bunch of short feeds tend to free up your day a lot better than infrequent but l-o-n-g sessions on the sofa. Sometimes you may take advantage of one of her catnaps to hold her and just admire her. Having time just to breathe her in is one of the perks of holding her while she naps.

Babies tend to be very good at fitting their naps into your own activities. You shop, your baby sleeps in the babycarrier, pram or pushchair. You can breastfeed in the car park, in a shop or a bench in the street to top her up and keep going. (There are thoughts in Chapter 5 about making public breastfeeding easier.) Most babies love being away from home (although some more sensitive ones may find it stressful). It's the "village" notion again. Babies tend to thrive on being with other people, awake or asleep. If you have a fussy baby who doesn't nap easily, you might find some more insights in Chapter 5.

Your Own Naps

It doesn't take long after the birth before everyone, including you, thinks you should be able to keep going all day. But it's the wise culture—and in the past there were many of them—that gives mother and baby a full month of idleness. That's probably not going to happen unless you make it happen. If you're not part of that culture, relatives can help or maybe you can hire a doula. (If relatives do come, remember that their job is taking care of you and your job is taking care of your baby.)

You're probably going to have to carve out your own naptimes. You may find that you can feed her to sleep when *you* need a nap. Napping with your baby—both of you horizontal on a Safe Sleep Seven bed—can be a blissful part of your day, maybe even a daily or weekend routine. Some couples like to make it a Sunday afternoon threesome.

> The summer that my son was about four months old, we lay on the bed, barely dressed, on a beautiful, sunny, afternoon, with the breeze blowing across us as we breastfed. I can clearly remember my inner dialogue: "With all the pleasures of the flesh this world celebrates,

why is it that no one has ever talked about *this* bodily pleasure before?"

—Jean

Napping on the sofa with your baby in a Moses basket on the floor is another idea. Consider breastfeeding her to sleep on a baby blanket and holding her until her arms go limp before laying her down, still on the blanket. You can even lie there with a hand resting on her while you settle yourself into sleep.

Or you can sit upright on the sofa, slouched back enough that gravity "sticks" your baby to you, or with your baby in a sling or wrap that's snug enough to keep her on your chest but loose enough for her to move her head and hands freely. And revisit Chapter 5. It's all about naps.

Life After Baby

Even though it seems like your world is all baby, baby, baby right now, there's a real world out there, with other family members, your partner, your job, your to-do list. But there are also limits, and those limits can be a wake-up call. Here's life *before* baby.[3] It's a 24-hour pie, and all 24 hours are full. No empty spaces anywhere.

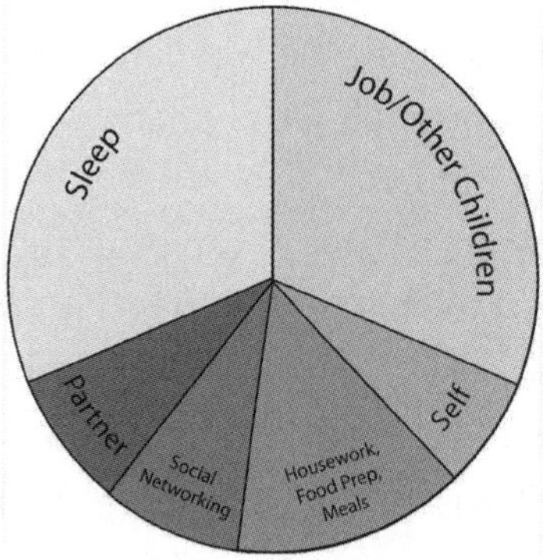

Dividing up your time before baby

And here's life *after* baby, at least for months.

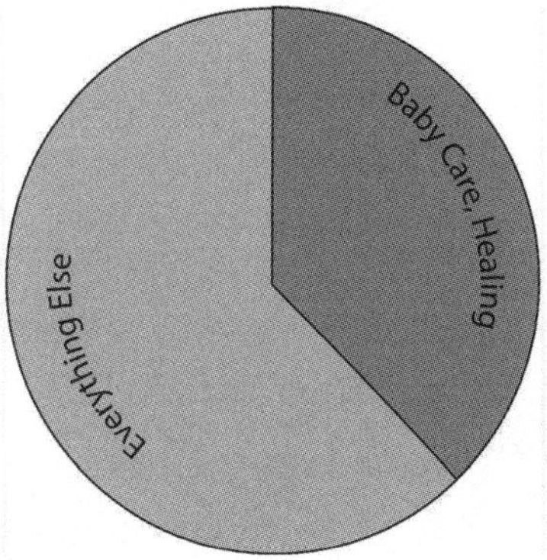

Dividing up your time after baby

Same 24 hours, same things filling it . . . plus two more—your baby, and your own mending and temporary inefficiency. You can keep *all* your original slices and make some or all of them smaller, in order to make enough time for those new elements. Or you can drop some slices out altogether. Or both. But that great big chunk for baby and recovery can't be made smaller by more than a little, even with supportive help. And the infamous baby nanny is *not* a good idea for any mother or baby. You need someone who'll *support* breastfeeding, not compete with it.

The after-baby pie chart isn't a permanent condition, of course. But it's a reality at first. Lots of mothers tuck their accustomed social networking in and around that big new pie wedge. Holding the baby for a nap? iPad. Nappy changes? Speakerphone and Bluetooth. And so on. Some mothers find they're actually more connected than before.

Partner Time

That's another big one. To some extent, right now, it has to be baby, baby, baby for your partner too. Some partners get all wrapped up in parenthood right along with you. Others very quickly begin to feel elbowed out. Probably most partners feel a bit of both. They don't have your breastfeeding hormones. They don't have that breastfeeding connection (and no, giving the occasional bottle isn't going to create it the way that *doing* things with the baby and *sleeping* with the baby will).

Some good conversation, squeezed in where you can, may help the two of you figure out what the other one really needs. And one surprising help can be your babycarrier. When you wear the baby, your eyes and attention can focus on your partner. And when your partner wears the baby, it's an attention-getter and bond-builder.

Sex

How soon mothers are ready for sex is all over the map, from a few days post-birth (yep) to a few years (yep). It depends a lot on the birth and other stresses and strains. You might be feeling "touched out" by days and nights of intense mother-baby contact, while your partner may be longing for some touch. Vaginal dryness is an issue for many breastfeeding mums, but lubricants and extra foreplay can help. The touched-out feeling can be relieved to some extent when your partner helps you get some time for yourself. Almost all mothers love hearing those three little words: "I'll clean up." You and your partner can compromise too, maybe enjoying each other in ways other than intercourse. And maybe a lingering massage for either one of you, anywhere that feels good(!), will remind you of feelings you'd sort of forgotten about.

So where exactly do parents make love, especially if there's a baby in the bed? Well, naptimes when you're both at home are pretty easy to work out. Nights need more creativity. Some couples are fine with a new baby right there in the bed. More than one mother has breastfed through an orgasm, probably surprising the baby (and her partner!) with a spurt of oxytocin-triggered milk.

Some couples leave the bed. As one mother said, "There's always the floor . . . and the walls." Some couples move the baby, if the baby's easy to move without waking. Bottom line: where there's a will there's a way.

And if there's no will or you're feeling "No way," that's very normal too. But we're straying from sleep here. Sex can be a surprisingly fun topic for La Leche League meetings. Discussions usually start with some halting comments and end up getting . . . well, we women can match the locker-room talk when we want to.

Back to Work

This can be really hard for a lot of women, especially if you have to go back to work before you are are ready for it. Chapter 8 has some ideas about how to manage your nights with your young baby when you're separated during the day, but you may find yourself in the tough position of balancing a pattern-based baby with a schedule-based workplace. Remember that perfect isn't possible or even healthy.

Naps After the Newborn Weeks

As the weeks go by, you'll probably begin to see a gradual shift towards longer naps at longer intervals. And your own "mandatory naps" will gradually become less mandatory. Your baby doesn't seem nearly so fragile now, but his need for watchful tending is still strong.

When your baby begins to separate his days and nights, it makes much more sense to go with his flow, figure out his emerging personality and patterns as best you can, and stay flexible.

Your body is still your baby's "natural habitat" through these months (see Chapter 4). The more you carry him and wear him, the less fussiness you're likely to see and the more relaxed his sleep is likely to be. You'll be his favourite napping spot, by far, for a while to come. So wearing him can make your days and his naps easier.

Time to Nudge Towards Longer Sleep?

There's not much point in nudging this soon. It would probably create a whole lot of trauma for very little gain, and it could mean he misses out on calories and contact. If you've been bedsharing and want to start using a bedside cot, it might buy you a bit of sleep—or it might cost you some. As with all nudging, if your idea doesn't sit well with one of you, it's a good idea to back off and try again later. Chapter 11 has lots of tips on the hows and whens.

Something to Sleep On

Your first four months are a very steep learning curve, day and night. You learn motherhood on less sleep than you're used to, and you learn it every day of the week, every hour of the day. You're amazing! Your baby is amazing too, and the team you make together is amazing.

If you're like most of us, though, your nights still aren't very amazing. But you're probably getting used to them, and certainly they're more relaxed than they were at the start.

Eventually you'll all sleep well *almost* every night. (Don't forget, there are years of midnight conversations ahead of you, from "I feel sick" or "What a great party!" right up to the time when you hear the words "Your grandchild's here!")

Our wish for you is that somewhere along the road you can feel what Jane felt—not always, of course, but sometimes: *"I remember when I finally figured out how to sleep* well *with my baby, and thought,*

'She is the best *little teddy bear I can imagine!' and having it feel* So Good *with her in my arms, next to my heart! I felt so totally content. I can still remember it, the wonderful feeling, and it makes me go, 'Awwwwwww'."*

chapter 16

Four Months to Toddlerhood

I used to nap with my eight-month-old on a futon on the floor of her future room. The room was totally babyproofed and practically empty except for some toys. I could usually feed her to sleep there and sneak away. She'd sleep for an hour or two, and when she woke up I knew she'd be fine even if I didn't get to her for a minute or two.

She was crawling at that point, and didn't always want to nap when I thought (hoped!) she would. Those times, we'd breastfeed and she'd quieten down, and I'd pretend to be asleep—totally still, heavy breathing. But she would crawl around me, pat my face, and try to pry my eyes open to breastfeed her or play with her! I was shaking with laughter when she was doing it—little rascal!

—Marlina

By the time your baby is around four months, the new-mother pressure is wearing off. You're more likely to be thinking, "Let's breastfeed so I can get some Facebook time." You may already be able to cook dinner and breastfeed at the same time. And hopefully you've developed—or are developing—the oh-so-valuable talent of dozing and breastfeeding at the same time.

You've passed the time of greatest risk for SIDS too, though it's still important to keep your baby in your room for a couple more months.

Features Around Four Months

Any getting-started problems probably have been mostly ironed out. But babies are always changing, and there will always be new pleasures and challenges.

Wiggle Worm

Nighttime breastfeeding may be easier in some ways—if she sleeps with you she can pretty much attach herself by this point so you don't have to wake up completely—but now she's probably moving around more in the bed. What if she rolls deliberately onto her tummy and stays there? It's okay. Once a baby is strong and mature enough to roll off her tummy and back whenever she wants to, she can pick her own positions.

If she's a real wiggle worm and you haven't bothered with a side rail before, you might want to consider it now. Make sure you fill in any gaps between the rail and the mattress (see Chapter 2). Some Safe Sleep Seven parents just move the baby in between them.

Teething

Around four to six months many babies start getting teeth. It's a slow process. Your little one's gums may be sore and swollen *long* before any teeth actually appear. That can mean trouble falling asleep and more frequent waking. ("*More* frequent?" we hear you say.) Those teeth keep coming in over the next year or so, and each new tooth can mean some miserable nights. If you've ever had a toothache, you probably noticed that it was worse at night. You're lying down, which can make it hurt more, and there's nothing to distract you. That may be true for babies too.

If your baby has a hard time falling asleep because of tooth pain, you can try putting ice cubes in a flannel and letting him chew on it before bedtime, or giving him a cold teething ring to chew on for a while. If it's really bad, you can ask your doctor about pain relief medication.

Not all babies are bothered by teething, though ("Look, honey! A tooth!"), and some find certain teeth more uncomfortable than others. Whether your baby works hard for every tooth or springs them on you as little surprises, teething has a definite upside. It's called "Well, *you* know, *teething*", and it excuses any situation you want it to. Is she throwing a tantrum in Grandma's arms? "She's teething." Kept the couple next door awake at 2.00 a.m.? "She's teething." Most people will back off with an understanding nod, even if they have no idea what you mean. It can even work on you. She spent the whole night feeding and fussing and feeding and fussing? Take a deep breath in the morning and remind yourself, "Well, you know, teething."

> Some grandparents—even some doctors—say that four months is a good time to start solids, and suggest cereal at bedtime. But a baby isn't physiologically ready for solids until he can pick food up and feed himself. That's usually around the six-month mark. The National Health Service and the World Health Organization endorse exclusive breastfeeding until then (and of course continuing to nurse after starting solids).[1]

Four-Month Fussies, Five-Month Fidgets

Whenever the fussy fidgets hit, nothing about babies goes by the books and breastfeeding can get a little quirky. Your newborn breastfed with intense concentration, not knowing or caring what else was going on. Some time between about three and six months he's likely to get really interested in the world around him. But he doesn't yet have an organized enough brain to "walk and eat at the same time". He can feed, or he can watch and listen to his fascinating surroundings; he just can't do both at the same time. More than one mother has retreated to the bedroom, or even a bathroom with the fan on for feeds for a while until her baby's ability to multitask improves. Some babies cut back their daytime feeds because they can focus only at night. If that's your baby, then this isn't a good time to work towards night weaning. At least you can blame your nights on "teething".

Sense of Humour: Hers and Yours

Your baby's developing horizons include a sense of humour that grows by leaps and bounds. She may wake up in the morning ready to play peek-a-boo. Fingers in your nose, examining your teeth while you feed her—she thinks it's all fun. She may find being up in the middle of the night amusing too. (Parents, usually not so much.)

Your own sense of humour is developing as well. Who knew that you'd share jokes as simple as baby toes in your mouth, or bicycle legs, or boop-boop-boop-boop-*beep*? (Though they aren't quite as funny in the middle of the night.)

Sleep Consolidation

At least there *is* a middle of the night now. Almost all babies, in your bed or in a cot, are on track towards a real day and a real night. Though naps may still be frequent, awake times during the day are longer, and nights may be much more about sleep than they used to be, even if it doesn't feel that way.

Waking Patterns at Four to Six Months or So

"Patterns" is a pretty loose term. La Leche League meetings are full of mothers whose babies didn't read the books or who have forgotten what they read.

In fact, they *did* all read a book. The title is *Normal Sleep in the Four- to Six-Month-Old,* and most of the pages are blank. "Normal" is just all over the map.

Still Breastfeeding Frequently

Some babies were feeding five times a night as newborns, and they're still feeding five times a night at four to six months. If this is your baby, you might wonder if it's just a bad habit at this point.

Do they really need the calories? Maybe. Every breast and baby is different. It's absolutely normal for a baby to be feeding several times a night at this stage. After all, nights are a full one-third of their day. That's a long time to go without food when you're growing so fast.

If your breasts can store more milk than average, your baby may not need to breastfeed *for food* as often and may be able to go four or five or six hours between feeds. Mothers with less storage space in their breasts (and you can't tell by looking) need to breastfeed more often. They can make more than enough milk over a 24-hour period, but their babies need to feed frequently to keep it coming and get enough.

And of course breastfeeding is more than food and drink and antibodies. It reassures a baby who is feeling lonely or scared or who's uncomfortable for some reason; it helps him get to sleep when he's tired or can't calm down; it's even a painkiller![2] There may be times when you or your partner can replace a feeding with, say, rocking the baby or patting his back. At 2.00 a.m., though, it's usually easier just to breastfeed and not try to figure out what else to do.

Waking More Often

Last week you may have been saying, "Oh, my baby hardly breastfeeds at all in the night," and this week you're wondering what changed.

Many people who don't actually have babies are under the impression that baby sleep is a steady progression from waking frequently at night to waking less at night and then to sleeping all night. But like most aspects of infant development, it's rarely that simple. There are lots of reasons why a baby's sleep patterns change from night to night and week to week. Teething, illness, growth spurts, and being somewhere new can change sleep patterns. Often you never do figure out the cause. The same thing may happen with *you*. Toothache? Less sleep. Bills due? Less sleep. And sensitive babies may wake up more if you're going through a stressful time yourself. (There's a list of some reasons for frequent night waking in the Tearsheet Toolkit.)

One of the biggest causes of increased waking is that your baby is learning or has just figured out some new developmental skill, like rolling over, crawling, or sitting up. The excitement seems to cause the baby to wake more at night and have more trouble getting back to sleep.

Whatever this week's pattern is, we do a baby a real disservice when we call it a "sleep problem". True sleep problems in babies are extremely rare. Babies are just doing what would have come naturally in the long, leisurely, two-part night pattern they were born "expecting" (see Chapter 4, "Normal Sleep"). It's just going to take a while for them to grow into the non-normal patterns of 21st-century, short-night, fast-paced living.

That doesn't mean *you* aren't craving sleep, though. Chapter 10 can be just as helpful now as it was a few months ago. And now *might* be a time when you consider some gentle nudging techniques to help your baby sleep for longer stretches. Check out Chapter 11 for some insights.

Night Breastfeeding Means Longer Breastfeeding

If your goal is to breastfeed for at least a year, you might want to reconsider any plans to night-wean at this age. It can be surprising and disappointing to find that the baby who is prevented from breastfeeding at night against *his* wishes returns the favour by not breastfeeding as much during the day, against *your* wishes. Babies don't see their breastfeeding relationship as something that turns on and off according to the light switch, and some of them just opt out altogether. Or maybe the missed feeds at night lead to a lower milk supply, so the baby turns more and more to other food sources and less and less to breastfeeding.

Night Breastfeeding as Contraception

The method of birth control that's used around the world more often than any other is night breastfeeding, and not because the baby keeps you from having sex. Good research shows that if (1) your baby is under six months old, (2) your periods haven't returned, and (3) he breastfeeds freely both day and night—no long stretches without breastfeeding, no dummy all night, no patting back to sleep, and no routine solids or supplements—then you have about 98 to 99 per cent protection from pregnancy.[3] The no-long-stretches part isn't essential for everyone, but many mothers find that their periods return as soon as they stop breastfeeding at night.[4] Your body assumes that if he's breastfeeding less, it must be because he's independent enough and eating enough solids that both of you can handle the stress of another baby. It's a pretty good system for child spacing, but if you're not open to a new pregnancy, you'll want another birth control plan by about six months.

How soon your periods return is really variable, assuming they haven't started already. Some women get a year or more without periods. A few unlucky ones start their periods at six weeks even if they're breastfeeding twins. (Sometimes life just isn't fair.)

Maybe your biological clock is ticking. What about night weaning so you can get pregnant? This one's tough: you're balancing a real baby's real needs against a theoretical baby. If you've had several periods, your fertility is probably back. If not, cutting back a little on night breastfeeding might nudge you into fertility. But your milk is designed to be your baby's *main* food source for at least the first year, and your own body needs about two years to recover fully from pregnancy and birth. A pregnancy now could shortchange both of you. If you can, you might consider waiting until your baby is at least a year old.

Around Nine Months

This section could be about your baby at 7 months or 11 months, but you'll probably recognize it somewhere in the second half of that first year.

Waking Up More Often

Around nine months, just when your baby seemed to be sleeping longer stretches, he may start waking up more often. He's not alone. Just like the four-to-six month stage of increased waking, this is something that many nine-month-olds do, often when they're going through big developmental changes like learning to crawl or walk.[5] No one sleeps very well when there's a big project in the works.

More Teeth

You may find that breastfeeding lying down isn't as comfortable as it was, but it can be. The first thing to check out is his position. As he gets longer, he may end up tucking his chin to reach your nipple. If his chin tucks, he's likely to clamp to hold on, because a tucked chin can pull his lower jaw away from your breast. "Cliff-hanging" can hurt! Whether you're sitting up or lying down, try sliding him more towards his own feet, so that his head tips back slightly, the way it did when he was younger.

Breastfeeding Strikes

Sometimes a baby just suddenly stops breastfeeding. Maybe he's had a cold, or there's been a big change in his world. Usually it involves a baby who has either bottles or solids to fall back on. Sleepy times can be your ally during a strike. Often a baby on strike will do some breastfeeding at night to make up for what he just won't do during the day, or a baby on strike may be willing to breastfeed while he's asleep or very drowsy. There's more on coping with breastfeeding strikes in *The Womanly Art of Breastfeeding* (8th edition or newer).

When Huck was about eight months old, his reflux pain was so bad that he went from being tricky to breastfeed to being unwilling to breastfeed at all. I had trouble releasing my milk to the pump, and Huck would take only a cup. Once we got the reflux under control (much body work, dietary changes, and, to my great dismay, medication), the only way to coax him back was by breastfeeding him in his sleep. I'd settle him in on his left side and "sneak it in" while he was fully asleep. I later added breastfeeding in light sleep, then when he was drowsy. Finally, he was back on track, even while fully awake. Huge relief! It really made me appreciate what we have, and we've breastfed now for several more years.

—Jeanette

Crawling Off the Bed

Your newborn stayed pretty much where you put her. As babies get older, though, they roll over, push themselves around with their feet or knees and elbows, creep or crawl, and generally find ways to get where they want to go. Some roll over effectively at six weeks, while others don't master this skill until they are past six months old. Some are crawling at four months, while some walk at seven months or not until well into toddlerhood. Somewhere in the midst of this you might want to reconsider or reconfigure a bed rail, remembering again to fill in any gaps.

If you have a high bed, you might want to get a step stool to put next to he bed. Tumbles can happen anyway. A folded blanket on the floor makes a reasonable crash pad. Just make sure it's nothing squishier than a cot mattress. If you take your own mattress off its frame and put it on the floor, you'll have a solution that many mothers use and many others secretly envy. Gaps and traps are still an issue at this age, so look at your bed through your baby's eyes. Don't forget to take his ever-increasing strength and wandering into account.

Rob is a great teacher. He taught each of our children at seven months to get off the sofa safely. He had them roll onto their belly and then wriggle down onto the floor. We used a bed rail on our bed, and eventually they all learned to get on their bellies and wriggle down to the floor.

—Kay

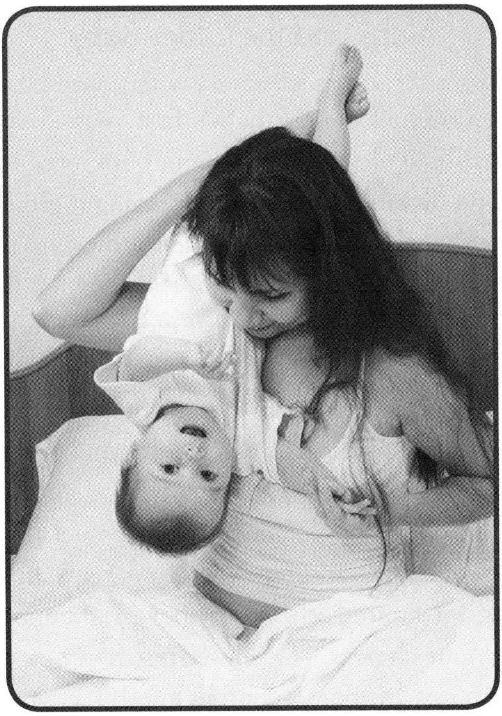

Crawling over *You*

Towards the end of his first year you may start to see "athletic breastfeeding"—hanging on to your nipple as he assumes some very creative positions. One of the benefits of sleep consolidation is that you're more likely to see this at bedtime and in the morning than you are at 3.00 a.m. If your sense of humour is at a low ebb, try pretending to be asleep. There's always a chance your little gymnast will give up and do the same.

Pretending to Be Asleep

In fact, as we saw in Marlina's story at the beginning of the chapter, feigning sleep is right there in the standard mothering toolkit along with oozing. You can use it to discourage the baby who wants to breastfeed but doesn't want it enough to put any energy into it. You also can use it to help your baby to fall asleep at bedtime or to encourage a longer nap or at least a little quiet time during the day.

Naps and the Older Baby

During the second half of your baby's first year—maybe sooner—your baby's naps may decrease in number, increase in length, and become semi-predictable. You may start using a phrase that didn't exist in the early weeks: "It's almost time for his nap." (Of course, if you have one of those Irregular babies, this may not be happening. Sorry.) As a baby moves towards a year old, many of us start incorporating simple books into official naptimes, a first step towards a lifetime of reading for pleasure. Lots of mothers use naptime as their own fairly predictable baby-free time and use a monitor to keep track.

But these more mobile babies are able to get themselves into other kinds of trouble at naptime. Not *during* naps, but if they wake up and you're not around, they can move right into search-and-destroy mode. Your choices: stay close (put him in a sling, or work in the same or a nearby room), confine him (to a cot or playard), or babyproof the room and keep a close ear out for waking (put a cot mattress on the floor, or even set up a low toddler bed; if your own mattress is already on the floor, you're all set). When you're babyproofing, try to think like a baby. Even a chest of drawers with the bottom drawer ajar can give a climber a way to pull the chest over on himself. And be aware that babies can develop new skills—like climbing—overnight. A common comment is, "I can't believe it. He just started to [pick any skill or risky behaviour] just like that!"

Don't feel that your baby *has* to nap away from you. Sharing a nap with your baby—even just holding him through naps—will be one of the things you'll remember fondly from this stage of babyhood.

> Max started out as a cat-napper, but around ten months he became a champion napper. He started taking two- to three-hour naps in the middle of the afternoon. He napped the way he slept at night, waking enough to want to breastfeed and then falling asleep again. For a two-hour nap I would breastfeed him back to sleep once, and for a three-hour nap twice. I always considered these to be one nap.
>
> —Kasey

The One-ish-Year-Old

Child still not sleeping through the night? Join the club! At this age, night-waking is still common.[6] In one study, a majority of one-year-olds were still waking up at night, even if they slept in a cot, and half of those tended not to be able to get back to sleep on their own. In fact, they were actually more vocal about it than the typical six-month-old and tended to wake as often as they did at three months.[7] So is your nearly-one-year-old starting to backslide? Nope. Totally normal child. Better yet, consider him a clearly superior child, developing obvious and not-so-obvious skills at such a pace that it keeps him awake. That wakefulness won't last (though of course the brilliance will). Your eight-year-old probably won't be waking like this, though maybe he'll have the occasional nightmare about zombies.

If you want some reassurance that bedsharing is still a good thing as you approach toddlerhood, read the beginning of the next chapter. Bedsharing at this age has a lot going for it. A Swiss study found that nearly half of children aged between two and seven years old crawled into their parents' bed at least once a week![8] Bedsharing, it seems, even helps repel zombies.

Common Issues from 4 to 12 Months

Nighttime issues aren't just about how long your baby sleeps. They're about the ongoing meshing of your old life and your new one, especially when a bed is involved.

How Can I Get More Partner Time?

By now, it's been well over a year since your body and your life started to change. Maybe you were queasy during the first part of your pregnancy, so sex seemed unappealing, and as your body changed, sex may have been increasingly awkward. Then in the first few weeks after the baby was born, both of you might have been too tired or overwhelmed to think much about sex. But now you may be really missing the connection you had, especially the sex part. Is it time for things to get back to normal? Some of you might laugh at this question—you've been having sex for months. Others are feeling a bit panicky because you still don't have much interest in sex at all. The range of normal is wide enough that you're in it either way.

For most of the history of the human race, babies have slept with their parents well past the first year of life. And most of those parents went on to have second or third or fourth children, so sex was happening somehow. How did they keep their relationships strong? Almost every longer-term relationship will go through times when sex is lower on the priority list for one or both people involved, or times when, even though both partners are interested, the times and opportunities for sex are limited. Illness, different working hours, travelling for work—these things happen.

You might be feeling uninterested because you're tired, because you're getting enough (or more than enough) touching and cuddling from your baby, or maybe because you're hormonally still at a low ebb. This is one of those times when "it's not you, it's me" really is true, and it often helps to talk it through.

Your partner needs to feel loved and cherished, even if there isn't a lot of sex happening. Touching as you walk past, saying "I love you," saying how much you value your partner's help and relationship with the baby, talking about the future—there are lots of ways to show affection without draining your already low emotional reservoir. When you need to, remind yourself (and your partner) how things were and how things will be. You're in one of the most intense parenting phases of your life, but there *is* life beyond babyhood.

You may find you're more interested in sex when your partner can help tend the baby for a while (much easier by four or six months than when you had a newborn) while you have a relaxing hot bath and maybe a nap. Take the warm-up to sex slowly, to give you time to get in the mood. If hormonal issues are making sex physically uncomfortable, check out the lubricants available at the chemist or online.

Is the problem that you're both hot for each other but can't figure out how to do it with the baby there, especially now that he's bigger and might wake up and watch you with those big, thoughtful eyes? If that's become an issue, your baby doesn't have to be in the room any more. Once he's asleep, either the two of you or the baby can be somewhere else. Feed him to sleep in place A, and you have place B all to yourselves, at least for a while. Or maybe you can get a friend or Grandma to babysit in her home for an hour or two while you "go out to dinner".

Sex isn't the only kind of intimacy you might both be missing. Even the nightly conversations that used to happen may have been reduced to a few whispers when the baby's nearby. Remember, though, that babies enjoy peaceful background noise. Just keep the loud laughter and other abrupt sounds out of the way, and go ahead and talk . . . or whatever.

How Can *I* Get More Sleep?

Still feeling sleep-deprived? Maybe you have a baby who simply needs less sleep than most, while you need more. Maybe you're back at work so napping during the day isn't an option, and you're just not getting what you need at night. A quick recap: go to bed as early as you can. Even if you don't fall asleep right away, lying down is restful. If your baby isn't ready to sleep yet, maybe your partner could tend her until she is, while you rest/doze/sleep. On weekends or other days off, maybe your partner can take the baby for a bit after that first morning feed.

And you can always give the front-loaded day a try—or another try. You can look at the details in Chapter 10 and adapt the suggestions to your household. And look through the other ideas in the chapter. Maybe something that didn't seem to fit before will make sense now.

Does Anyone Else Understand?

Yes. Any mother-to-mother group will be chock-full of mothers who are living your life. Look for a group that matches your style. A breastfeeding one, of course. One that sits well with your instincts. One where you think you could make some friends. They'll have lots of ideas, and some of them may work for you. Even if they don't, you can have caring people keep you company on your own particular path.

Something to Sleep On

You started out with a baby and now you're on the brink of toddlerhood. It's a fun, amazing, overwhelming, exhausting time. Approach it all with a sense of humour and involve yourself with like-minded parents, preferably in person. Check out Chapter 11 if you need to help your baby move towards longer sleep stretches, and keep your bed arrangements flexible. Between 4 and 12 months, you're going to see a whole lot of changes. Just when does your baby become a toddler? As one mother said, "If you think you have a toddler . . . you do."

chapter 17

Toddlerhood and Beyond

> I lie with Rosa as she falls asleep in our bed. Before we go to sleep Brad or I move her to her sleeping bag on the floor of our room, then she crawls back into our bed in the early morning. (The only reason she waits until the early morning to come into our bed is because I've asked her to.) She has a beautiful room across the hall from ours. I just bought her some pretty pink flowered sheets to entice her to sleep in her bed. She was excited about the sheets, but still wants to sleep with Mum and Dad. I know that this will pass and that we will have our bedroom back to ourselves again one day. Until then, I will gaze down at that lovely sleeping angel before I turn out the light each night.
>
> —Alyssa

Maybe your toddler is already out of your bed. Maybe you're sure your 9-month-old won't be there much longer. Or maybe your preschooler's there every night. We all get to where we are one night at a time, and we often don't end up where we thought we would. Whatever your plans, learning more about long-term bedsharing may be validating and even eye-opening.

> I looked forward to my school-age son Thomas's nocturnal visits, because he'd snuggle in with his dad while I left to snuggle into *his* warm bed, which I felt was the most comfortable one in the house!
>
> —Janine

Long-Term Outcomes of Long-Term Bedsharing

People may tell you it's not good for toddlers to sleep with their parents. And sleep programmes sometimes warn that long-term bedsharing will lead to later sleep problems or psychological problems. The research says something different. In Chapter 3 you saw a list of positive emotional outcomes for children who bedshared in the early months. Here's what the research has shown about children whose bedsharing is measured in years.

In a recent study in Singapore, parents of children aged 2 to 19 were asked where their children slept and how often they had various sleep problems. Nearly three-quarters of the children were *currently* bedsharing with no reported increase in sleep problems.[1] In that same year, a study of 3- to 10-year-olds in India, where more than 90 per cent of school-age children bedshare, found significantly *more* nightmares, teeth grinding, bed-wetting, and other sleep problems among those children who had *never* bedshared, compared with those who were still bedsharing.[2]

More than half of Japanese children under four bedshare. Sleep problems among them are less frequent than in the United States, and one of the researchers commented, "Resisting the intense desire of young children for close proximity with caregivers at night may set the stage for bedtime protest and persistent night waking in the United States."[3] A Swiss study found that nearly a quarter of all three-year-olds woke up enough every night to want contact with their parents, and more than half of all four-year-olds still woke in the night at least once a week.[4] A study of 175 cultures found "co-sleeping" rates of 10 to 100 per cent.[5] It seems that all over the world children sleep like, well, children—which means they wake up now and then at night and may bedshare at least part-time for years, not just weeks or months.

A study of sleep-wake patterns in the first two years of life did find that weaned children and children who slept separately woke up less often than bedsharing children. But it also pointed out that their infrequent wakings don't reflect normal biology.[6]

These studies can reassure you that any length of time that your children share your bed is normal and healthy, and no negative consequences have been found.[7]

> When my son was about two years old, I would lie down with him until he went to sleep, then go to my bed, and go back to him when he woke for comfort. He would have nightmares, saw monsters in his room, so we had the light on in his cupboard and even had the dog sleeping with him for company. One night when he again awoke with a bad dream and I was comforting him, I told him he was safe, the dog was beside him, and I was going back to my bed with his father. He looked at me and said, "But *you* get to sleep with somebody!" It hit me hard. Such wisdom from a small child.
>
> —Gabriela

Nights with Toddlers and Preschoolers

So it's perfectly normal for toddlers (ages one and two) to wake up and want their parents at night—whether it's to breastfeed, to be comforted after a bad dream, or just to feel cosy and loved.

Think back to Chapter 4. Normal sleep for humans incorporates an awake time in the middle of the night, and many small children naturally fall into that pattern. As one four-year-old told his mother when she woke at 3.00 a.m. to find him playing with his building bricks, "You might as well go back to sleep, Mama. I'm just not tired." After making sure the area was safe, she did. He joined her later.

Some toddlers do sleep all night long—though even those may wake and need your comfort when they're not feeling well or have a nightmare. It's no surprise that parents find bedsharing helps them all get more sleep at this age too. Many toddlers or preschoolers (ages three to five) start the night in their own bed and then come padding into their parents' bedroom—or crawling into their parents' bed from a bed just beside it—at some point in the night. And some toddlers and preschoolers can slip into any tiny space in the bed and quietly go back to sleep; when the parents wake up they wonder, "When did Emma join us?"

> Our four-and-a-half-year-old leaves her room and climbs into bed around midnight and shoves her way in between us or sleeps right across our pillows by the headboard. She is so cute about it! Ooh, here she comes again.
>
> —Laura Elizabeth

Preschoolers generally sleep a bit longer than toddlers (can you see a general trend here?). They might still wake up, but they are more able to settle themselves without help from an adult. They do often like to sleep with their parents if they're given the opportunity. For many families, bedsharing allows them to reconnect after being apart during the day.

Of course, sharing your bed with a three-foot-tall preschooler is wildly different from cuddling with a tiny baby. That cuddle curl you used with your infant? Long gone. Preschoolers kick and wriggle and snore and usually manage to take up far more room than you'd imagine given their size. (And many, many of us miss them when they start staying in their own rooms.)

As your child gets older, you gain one great advantage: you can communicate with each other better and better. You can negotiate your sleeping arrangements, and, maybe even more importantly, your child can talk to you about what *she's* feeling and needing. She's not always very articulate at first, of course, but this growing skill may help you find solutions to interrupted nights. For more insights into changing routines, see Chapter 11.

"I Don't Wanna Go to Bed!"

One of the challenges with toddlers and preschoolers is what some sleep gurus call "sleep resistance". Your child insists he's not tired, even though you know he's exhausted. When you tuck him under the covers, he comes up with a dozen reasons why he can't doze off yet: just one more story, one more drink, what's that thing lurking in the wardrobe? These are challenges more often seen in young children who sleep alone. Remember Javier's story at the end of Chapter 4? And, of course, some children have a personality that doesn't shift gears easily. (Time to take another look at the chart in Chapter 7?) But your child may just be enjoying the day's activities too much to want to go to bed. Even adults sometimes stay up until they feel "too tired to go to bed".

What can you do when your tired child resists bedtime? This is one of the times when breastfeeding can be a huge help. Persuade him to breastfeed and he's almost guaranteed to fall asleep. If he's weaned, maybe you can get him to lie down in bed if you promise to lie down with him and tell him a story in the dark. Another option is to invite him to come sit with you on the sofa for a bit, and you watch something calm on TV or listen to music and cuddle together until he drifts off. "Clearing the Storm Clouds", in Chapter 11, describes those children who may just have to cry to decompress.

Maybe it's just too early for bed. Sometimes in our desire for downtime, we aim for too long a nap, too early a bedtime, or both. Plenty of time outside and plenty of time without electronics or TV have helped many families towards easier bedtimes. And children, like adults, often just need downtime of their own—a chance to look at books in bed and fall asleep in their own good time.

Every family comes up with its own strategies for helping older children sleep. We do much better with examples than rules, and you'll find a bunch of them in Chapter 10. Whatever helps all of you get more sleep and feel connected is good.

> One toddler I know is always out like a light. You could put him down and then go about your business until you were ready for bed yourself and he would stay nicely asleep. When he did stir, you could just snuggle up to him a bit and he'd go back to sleep. Our own toddler is an intense teether and an insanely light sleeper. Even in his sleep, he seems aware. A few nights ago he insisted on going to sleep wearing his football boots. After he'd been out for a decent amount of time, we tried to take them off. In his sleep, he said very clearly, "No! On!"
>
> —Ian

Bedtime Routines

Many of the bestselling sleep books tell you that following a strict bedtime routine is crucial for healthy sleep. Usually the list includes things like a bath, a snack, getting into pyjamas, brushing teeth, reading a story or two, and then leaving the child alone in his cot or bed. The routine starts and ends at the same times every night. The idea is that these activities prepare the child to go to sleep and create an expectation that once he's tucked up in bed, he'll naturally fall asleep promptly and wake up in the morning cheerful and ready for another busy day. Lots of parents follow this pattern, at least as much as they can. And for some toddlers or preschoolers and some families, it works well.[8] One of us even had a list in the form of pictures, to remind our children what they needed to do to get ready for bed. For others, depending on personality types and household schedules (see that chart in Chapter 7 again), that approach is more frustrating than helpful. Both of those can be true at different times in the same family.

When a friend came to babysit, I told her, "Jodie (age 5) goes to bed about 7.30. Ned (18 months) may or may not go to sleep until we get home. It doesn't matter." She was scandalized. A few years later I babysat for *her* children, and she told me, "Teddy (6) goes to bed about 8.00. Molly (2) doesn't really have a bedtime." Aha!

—Hazel

Some families might watch TV in the evening, go for a walk, play outside, or do some chores. They help their children brush their teeth and get into their pyjamas, and then they might play or read books or listen to music or chat for a while. The toddler joins in or plays with his own stuff, and at some point gets tired and wants to breastfeed. Mum might breastfeed him on the sofa while watching TV or surfing online. Once he's asleep, she might leave him there until the parents are ready to go to bed, or she might carry him off to the bedroom right away. Or she might take him into the bedroom—his or hers—and breastfeed him to sleep there. A weaned child often gets a story and some time lying with a parent. Maybe they'll talk a little in the dark, and then the child will fall asleep. Still a routine, just a different style. Come to think of it, it sounds a lot like front-loading!

The part that's left out in these variations on the bedtime routines is the part where the child is put in bed to fall asleep alone. Being put to bed awake and alone is scary and unpleasant for most young children, and many will do all they can to resist. When adults want to fall asleep they read, or they review, or they plan. Unless they're anxious, and then they can't sleep. A three-year-old doesn't have those falling-asleep skills. He can't read, can't review, can't plan, at least not very well. But he does have anxieties. It's no wonder he doesn't want to fall asleep alone.

Trying to stick to a standard bedtime routine can be especially frustrating with a child who has an Irregular temperament (Chapter 7), because some nights she'll go right to sleep and you think the routine is working brilliantly. Other nights, even though you've done everything the same, she's just not tired or sleepy. Or she's pretty sure there's a monster in that dark corner.

If you're sharing your bed with your toddler, it's a whole lot easier. Tired or sleepy toddlers naturally ask to breastfeed, and the breastfeeding tends to put them to sleep. Three-year-old Keagan used to ask for "sleepy milk" in the evening. Sometimes he'd want to stay up: "Don't give me the sleepy milk!" But that's what came out of her breast anyway, and he'd fall asleep. And then there are those bedsharing toddlers and preschoolers who actually ask to go to bed when they're tired. Three-year-old Xavier would ask for "upstairs na-nas" when he was ready to go to bed. Lucky family!

Routine? No routine? Whatever works, it will probably change over time, so it helps to be flexible. Just a hint if you've decided to use one: be aware that children can be pretty insistent about what they think the good parts are. One mother, on an especially difficult evening, wrote out a dream for her little boy while she told it out loud, and put the dream story in an envelope on his bedside table. (The idea was to prevent a repeat of the previous night's bad dreams.) Naturally, each night after that the little boy wanted another dream thought up, written out, and put in the envelope on his bedside table. You can be sure there were tears when this "new routine" was vetoed.

And then there are parts of Guatemala where Mayan children don't bother with pyjamas, brushing teeth, bedtime stories, or lullabies . . . and where going to bed doesn't seem to be a struggle and childhood sleep problems don't seem to be a problem.[9] There are all kinds of cultures, families, and systems, and all of them work at least some of the time with at least some of the children.

> When mine were little, we spent at least an hour, usually two, playing outdoors after dinner (rain, snow, whatever). Then we'd have a short and simple approach to going to sleep: snack, "top and tail" wash, teeth, story, breastfeed. They fell asleep more easily, and it helped with the night waking too.
>
> —Trish

> There's no way I could manage all that.
>
> —Rhianna

Breastfeeding Fidgets

Lots of toddlers have quirky little sleeping or breastfeeding-to-sleep behaviours that can be really frustrating for their mothers. Some breastfeeding toddlers like to stroke, pull, or even pinch the nipple of their mothers' opposite breast while breastfeeding on one side. Or pick at a mole on Mama's neck or chest. (Ouch!) Or smear her glasses. Or rub the fabric of her nightdress.

Breastfeeding doesn't mean you have to put up with being tormented. You may be able to persuade your child to stop by gently moving his hand each time, but you may have to do it over and over before he gets the message. It's easier if you start the process with a younger baby or toddler before it becomes routine. It sometimes works to put something else (like a special toy or chunky bead necklace) in the child's hand instead. Wearing clothes that make the area less accessible can help too. One mother put an adhesive bandage over her child's "favourite" mole. And another wore a loose-fitting bra to bed until the nipple-fiddling habit disappeared.

Bed-wetting

It isn't much fun to fall asleep next to a warm and cuddly two-year-old and wake up a few hours later to a cold, wet bed. Some children will signal (with a little fussing or crying perhaps) before they need to go, which gives you some lead time. Others don't seem to get (or give) much warning.

Remember that your child is not doing it on purpose. He's asleep when it happens. He can't help it or control it. Experts assure us that bed-wetting is common and normal until around age seven, especially in boys.[10] Consistent bed-wetting in children may have a genetic factor, be a sign of an infection, stress, hormone imbalances, fragmented sleep, sleep apnoea, constipation, or several other medical or neurodevelopmental issues.[11] In some cases, an overproduction of urine at night combined with deeper-than-average sleep makes for wet beds. If he was dry for several weeks or months and this is a new issue, be sure to check it out with your doctor.

Try to treat it in a matter-of-fact way: "Yes, lots of children wet their beds sometimes—let's work out what we can do so we can all sleep better." Some other ideas:

- Some toddlers, preschoolers, and older children are willing to wear nappies (or pull-ups) at night even if they are dry in

the day, especially if the nappies have illustrations of their favourite cartoon characters on them.
- If your toddler goes to sleep earlier than the adults, the last one to bed can carry him or walk him to the toilet and say, "It's time to go for a wee." Many children can comply without really waking up.
- If you know he typically wets at a certain time, you can set an alarm an hour earlier for a quick bathroom run.
- If your child wets only occasionally, you can cover your mattress with a clean bottom sheet, then a plastic mattress cover, then another sheet. If the first layer of bedding gets wet, you can strip it and the plastic off and have a dry bed for the rest of the night.
- You can even keep a potty in the room.

Through the early years, a soggy bed may be unpleasant, but it's not at all uncommon. If your child is edging up towards six or seven, your doctor can help you explore the causes and many options available to address this common problem, including no treatment at all.

> My son Ross slept very deeply and occasionally wet the bed. Sometimes he'd sort of wake up, go looking for the toilet while still half asleep, and wee in the wrong place: the bath, the wardrobe, a wastebasket. If we were lucky, we got to him first.
>
> —Gaby

Toddlers and Preschoolers and Naps

Your toddler or preschooler probably naps pretty soundly now . . . when she naps at all. The overnight trip to Grandma's was so exciting that she didn't sleep well, so she fell asleep in the car on the way home and was wide awake hours past her typical bedtime, so she took a morning nap the next day, which meant her usual nap . . . well, you get the picture. Each day seems like its own universe, distinct from yesterday and tomorrow, because the out-of-the-ordinary seems to happen every day.

But just as before, a quiet time is a much needed period of silence in the hum of life. Some days you'll need it more than your child will. If your child goes to a nursery, naptime is built into his day, of course, and probably at a set time. It may make sense to stick to the same time as naptime or "quiet time" on weekends too, just to keep the week's rhythm in place. For those of us who are with our little one all day, there can be regularity there as well, very likely in a time slot of your choosing. But one of the many advantages of continuing to breastfeed is that you can still feed her to sleep much of the time. It's a mothering tool you may really miss one of these days.

Creative Napping for Toddlers

Maybe your toddler (or preschooler) just can't nap at all. Doesn't mean you can't have a break. There are all sorts of ways mothers have managed a toddler who might or might not nap. Here are a few.

- When I needed a nap too, I taught her that if she could look at a book or play quietly (while we were both in a closed, safe room), that she could have a treat of watermelon or custard once I got my catnap. It helped that she was old enough to reason with.—Nan
- Milo will take me upstairs and lie in bed for pretend naps that involve many stories and tucking in, then him popping up and saying, "Great nap! Now I'm tired again. Tuck me in and read a different story." But then, we both love our reading times.—Michelle
- The TV sound would wake her up, so I'd turn on the subtitles to watch my favourite show.—Jeanette
- We never had set naptimes. Our children could nap just about anywhere and often fell asleep wherever and whenever they got tired. This meant I could go just about anywhere at just about any time. Car? Great place to nap. Shopping? They all loved the sling, awake or asleep. Friend's house? I'd bring a blanket for the floor or hold them while my friend and I continued chatting. I don't

remember ever going home "because it's naptime." Very freeing.—Helen

- As a toddler, my middle son wasn't big on naps. From an early age he loved to build and be inside forts, so for his second birthday I bought him a red play tent. We set it up in a quiet room and made it our napping castle. I covered the tent floor with blankets, pillows, and his favourite stuffed animals. We started a ritual of reading *The Napping House* by Audrey Wood inside the tent. Then we would lie down together and he would feed to sleep inside the very cosy, red-glowing "womb" that we had created. (There was plenty of air circulation because the top was a mesh fabric.) I would often fall asleep briefly too. Or I'd turn on the monitor, leave the room, and have time to myself. My prince slept blissfully and woke up happy and calling for the queen (me) to come back to the castle. Looking back, I think that not being in a fully darkened room but having the dim red glow of the light filtering into the tent added greatly to his sense of peace. This worked for us for at least a year. Writing this makes me miss those days. . . . —Beth

Naps on the Wane

Two naps a day are too much, but one isn't enough. Then you realize that any day there's a nap, your child stays up late that night. And if there's no nap at all, you have a cranky child by suppertime.

No easy answers here. Time will take care of it, of course, just as it resolves most early parenting issues. But in the meantime, dropping a nap can be a ragged, irritable time for mother and child both. You may even find that the nap that you thought was gone for good returns if your child starts preschool or nursery, or a new baby arrives. Making your child's life more predictable for a while can help, but the waning nap period isn't always something you can *manage;* it's just something you have to *get through.*

Even a minute or two of breastfeeding lulls many a child to sleep whose age is counted in years, not months. Many mothers replace fading naps with a "quiet time" of reasonable length—

maybe a half hour with picture books and calm toys or drawing options—and they don't concern themselves too much with whether or not their child actually sleeps. If your older child does still nap, you have some fairly reliable time to yourself. If the best you get is a quiet time, you may still be able to make it a soul-restoring part of your day.

For an older child, a timer with a soft tone may help *you* get some sleep. Diane remembers her mother napping, with instructions to "wake me up when the big hand is on the 12".

Quiet time has advantages even if there's no nap in it for either one of you. Reading to your child is one of the great privileges and luxuries of motherhood. It's a time when you can sit quietly together. That ritual may continue well into primary school or beyond, and is a chance to revisit your own favourite childhood books.

And Then There Were Two (or More)

Second baby? Third? Once you learn to juggle, you never really forget how, even though each new baby means putting several new balls in the air. Part of what you don't have to learn a second time is basic new-baby behaviour: nappies and dressing, how tough and smart a baby really is, carrying and using a car seat—you already know all that. Each baby's going to give you some surprising new balls to juggle, including how much smaller this new baby is than your "old" one. But by now you're pretty good at coping with surprises. First babies teach you how.

"Sleep when the baby sleeps" can be tough enough to pull off with one child. Add a second baby and you have to hit the ground running. Your toddler needs both your body and your brain, which takes most of your day. And your baby needs your body almost constantly, which *also* takes most of your day. Help in the early days can be a real sanity saver, especially if it's someone your older child enjoys doing things with. It takes a while to slide into the new family dynamics. This is another of those ragged parenting stages that you just have to learn by doing.

Beds Revisited

If your bed is big enough, you and your partner can certainly sleep with two children, maybe more. It's safest to keep your body between your baby and your older child. Children can sleep very deeply and don't have enough awareness to keep from rolling on or against the baby.

Bed too full? Here are some things other parents have suggested:

- Bring in a second bed and push it up beside yours (or against the bottom of the bed, if there's more room that way) for your older child. You might put a flat sheet horizontally across both beds so that there won't be a gap for the child to fall into. Or use a "bed connector" (see Chapter 7).
- Put a mattress on the floor beside your bed or at the foot of your bed, or put a blanket or sleeping bag on a carpeted floor. Your toddler or preschooler may be willing to sleep there, although you might have to get up and down a few times in the night.
- Have an "open-door policy" for your toddler to join you at his first waking, after starting the night in his own bed. Or your partner could lie with him when he wakes up, leaving the big bed for you and the new baby.
- For the first few weeks, have mother and baby sleep together in one bed while partner and toddler sleep together in a different bed.

Whatever arrangement you think will work, you might want to start sliding into it before the baby's born, so that your older child isn't hit with two big life changes at the same time. Check out the nudging ideas in Chapter 11 for more thoughts. As always, expect that your arrangement will change—maybe on that very first night, maybe not for months or more.

Naps Revisited

Since babies tend to nap well anywhere that includes Mum, many mothers find that baby number two naps on the fly most of the time. Taking the toddler to preschool? Baby naps in the car. Playing with bricks on the floor? Baby naps in your lap. Preparing a meal with the toddler? Baby naps in the sling. Sadly, none of these involves *you* taking a nap! Two or more children can have very different needs and there may be times that stretch you pretty thin.

> I wish that I could lie there for every nap so my baby could see my face when he wakes up, but that would mean having my three-year-old watch videos for hours alone in the other room, and he has needs too. He needs me to do things with just him sometimes so he knows that, while there is this new and enormous presence in our lives (a sibling), something can still stay the same. That need has to be balanced against the baby having to wait for an instant to see me when he wakes.
>
> —Deb

Sometimes group naps can help cement your duo that has become a trio. You can lie down with one on each side and read a story out loud until all three of you doze off. Your older child gets ample cuddle time, and your baby gets everything she was looking for: you. It's a nice idea, and sometimes it even works! One mother of toddlers proofed her bedroom so her toddlers could play while she napped with the baby. She kept a selection of drinks and snacks in the room together with a basket of "nap toys", and a hook on the door so they couldn't escape, and the four of them had a low-key stretch of time even if Mum didn't sleep.

> When my son was a baby and my daughter was four, we took a nap every afternoon together in the big bed. It became such an anticipated part of the day that any interruption would leave me feeling that my life had fallen apart. This seems melodramatic in hindsight, but it was very real at the time. One Monday afternoon, just as we had slipped into a deep sleep, a dustbin lorry with screeching brakes came stopping and starting along our street. There went my hopes of getting through the rest of the day peacefully. And it happened again the next Monday. Insanity is close to the surface in sleep-deprived new mothers!
>
> One phone call to a sympathetic manager was all it took for

the brakes' maintenance to be attended to. After that, we enjoyed our Monday afternoon sleeps uninterrupted, sanity and restfulness restored.

—Barbara

As Time Goes By

Maybe some of your children are weaned. Maybe some aren't. Maybe you have some settled routines, maybe not. But your family is probably finding what works, for now, and is developing the flexibility to change when change is needed. One continuous thread: We're a social species, and we love to be with the ones we love.

- When our children were four and two years old, we decided to wallpaper our bedroom. When we had fewer beds available during the renovations, we put the two older children in the same bed. Miraculously, sleeping together turned out to be the perfect nudge. They slept through the night with a warm body by their side and didn't call for me at all.—Lesley
- My husband has always travelled a lot on business, and my children used to take turns sleeping in our bed when he was away. One night when my son was about 12, I said to him, "Do you think you're too old to sleep in Mummy's bed?" He thought about it for a moment, said, "Yes," went back to his own room, and that was that.—Rowena
- When Lisa was about 16 and out of my bed for many, many years, she came home one night and walked into my room, where I was already in bed. She said, "Can I sleep with you?" I said, "Of course you can," and lifted up the edge of the duvet. She climbed in and said, "Rob and I broke up," and started to cry. I hugged her and we lay together like that for a bit, then she rolled over and went to sleep.—Margot

Something to Sleep On

Parenting means saying good-bye over and over again. You say good-bye to the newborn, infant, crawler, toddler, preschooler, school child, and teen you've come to love, and then you have to get to know someone new. But your bedroom, for all its rearrangements and transitions, will collect a lot of sweet and silly memories along the way.

And yes, some day they'll sleep through the night, but that doesn't mean they won't come back to your bed: "Mum," says the teenager sprawled across the bed one evening, "I've met this girl. . . ."

part five

Safe-Sleep Science

chapter 18

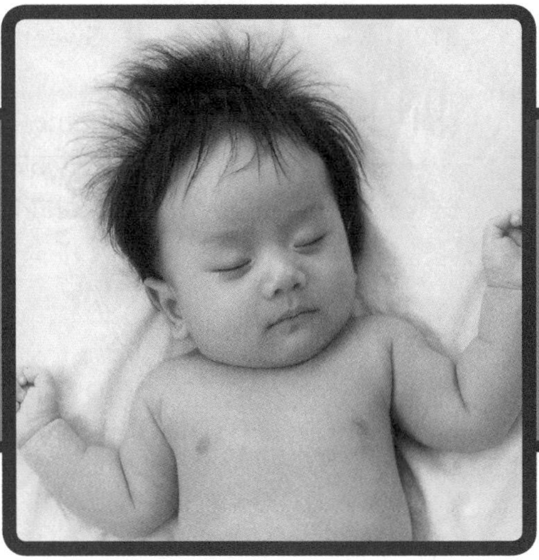

Sleep-Training Concerns

> Night waking is normal. Your baby shouldn't wake up at night. Your baby needs to be in his own room for independence. Your baby needs to be in your room for safety. Your baby needs flexibility. Your baby needs a schedule. Your baby relies on you. Your baby is manipulating you. Your baby needs to learn trust. Your baby needs to learn discipline. You should be more patient. You should be more firm. Boy, do we have the answer for you!
>
> —The Sleep Experts of
> 1750, 1842, 1880, 1923, 1954, 1989, 1997, 2003, 2014

The recipes for getting babies to sleep go way back. Add the following ingredients: a sleep-deprived mother + a crying baby + an expert who offers (and maybe even promises) a good night's sleep and a happy baby. Mix in a new book or video or app that makes the same old promises, and what do you get? Cha-ching! A sale!

Millennial parents spend millions of pounds (and euros and dollars and yen) each year on sleep methods and programmes. It's not surprising. Before the birth, they pictured a baby who goes to sleep happily all alone in a beautiful cot, sleeps all night, never cries, and wakes up smiling the next morning, delighted to see them. Then reality hits. And those programmes, including the latest cry-it-out and controlled-crying ones, start to look tempting. They promise it's better for you and healthier for your child. Could the solution really be that simple? No, it's not. And the ideas themselves aren't at all new.

Advice Before the 20th Century: Certainty Without Science

Parents have always wanted their children to turn into responsible adults. But culture, era, family background, baby personality, the strength and certainty of the advice-giving voices, and the persuasion of friends and role models have probably always had a strong influence over how people parent. The pronouncements from today's sleep experts are only the newest versions of "expert" advice that go back at least 300 years.

> Sleep-training advice is usually for the parents of babies less than a year old, so those are the ideas we'll focus on in this chapter. You'll find further ideas on meeting your own and your baby's sleep needs in Chapters 10 and 11.

Village Voices

In the *very* earliest days of human history, there were no clocks, no artificial lights, longer nights, no cots, no experts whom you'd never met. Parents tended to rely on local traditions, their own parents or older family members, and religious teachings for parenting advice. Right up until the 1700s, those who advised and those who listened lived side by side—an important and ongoing reality check for both sides.

Enter the Experts

Mass printing inventions in the 15th century in Europe, and several hundred years earlier in Asia, allowed self-proclaimed "experts" in any subject to share their opinions more easily and widely, without having to witness or evaluate the consequences. Once household clocks were commonplace, much of the parenting advice included very specific numbers and times. Other advice stressed long-term child development over short-term convenience. Today's researchers call these two approaches "parent-centred" and "child-centred."[1] Parent-centred methods value *external behaviours* and seek near-immediate behaviour changes by controlling affection, food, or sleep. Child-centred methods value *internal processes*—promoting the emotional and physiological bonding that supports long-term healthy development.

From the earliest printed leaflets, the pendulum of child care advice has kept swinging from parent-centred to child-centred and back again. Bedsharing has been alternately encouraged and discouraged. As early as the late 1700s, baby massage was recommended to help babies sleep.[2] The belief that touching spoils children appeared in print in the early 1800s.[3] Some writers encouraged responding to babies' cries, while others said that "crying is good exercise for their lungs".[4]

These early voices—both parent-centred and child-centred—were almost exclusively male, and many felt that men needed to bring reason and order to the more emotional way women manage child care.[5]

In the early 1800s, further advances in printing technology allowed for less expensive, more widely distributed publications. Women's magazines became the first far-reaching forum for women's voices. In 1829, Mrs. William Parkes wrote, *"The cry of the infant ought never to be disregarded, as it is Nature's voice, which speaks of some pain or suffering."*[6] Lydia Child wrote in 1839: *"An infant's wants should be attended to without waiting for him to cry. . . . Who can blame a child for fretting and screaming, if experience has taught him that he cannot get his wants attended to in any other manner?"*[7] In 1838, Lydia Sigourney wrote: *"Are you a novice? I am one also. Let us learn together."*[8] Their writing was often lyrical, almost drenched with oxytocin, as they urged mothers to cherish their time with their babies and not to let servants take over their care. These women spoke with the wisdom and experience of motherhood.

At the same time, male voices such as Dr. Pye Henry Chavasse's recommended breastfeeding on a strict feeding schedule, with separate sleep and no night breastfeeding after a certain number of weeks. Rocking a child to sleep was discouraged because the baby might become unable to sleep without it. And babies were never to be coddled. *"Never reward a child for crying by giving the article desired; wait till it stops,"* Dr. Chavasse warned.[9]

By the mid- to late 1800s, many middle- and upper-class new parents were hiring "baby nurses" for the first month, either full-time or only at night, to tend to the baby and mother and help establish a routine and rules. One child care expert of this time claimed, *"Babies who are tended entirely by the mothers are, almost without exception, troublesome by reason of their ceaseless exactions [demands]."*[10]

By now, science had shown that germs cause illness, so it seemed logical that keeping a mother and baby apart would be healthier. (It wasn't until decades later that we learned that the best way to *prevent* illness in babies is through breastfeeding with lots of contact.)[11] But by the end of the 1800s, ancient instincts were out, and pseudo-science was in.

> Isobel Crawley: Were you a very involved mother with Robert and Rosamund?
>
> The Dowager Countess: Does it surprise you?
>
> Isobel Crawley: A bit. I'd imagined them surrounded by nannies and governesses, being starched and ironed to spend an hour with you after tea.
>
> The Dowager Countess: Yes, but it was an hour *every day*.
>
> —*Downton Abbey*, Season 3

Advice in the Early 20th Century: Standardized, Sanitized, and "Scientific"

With World War I came a multitude of inventions and social changes that transformed the lives of young families. Electrical wiring in more and more homes extended productive working days and active home life beyond the daylight hours. Homes were better-heated, so the mother's body wasn't needed to keep her baby warm. Improved transportation increased people's range of travel. Young families began moving away into separate—and now affordable—modern homes, leaving behind the experience and child care help their extended families had offered. The invention of tinned milk and home-mixed "formulas" meant other people could feed the baby.

Parents were unaware that those babies were up to seven times more likely to die.[12]

A new wave of experts appeared, marketing tightly packaged child care programmes wrapped in the sparkle of the fashionable new "scientific" approach. Doctors such as Truby King and Emmett Holt published popular child care books with rigid feeding and sleep schedules and uncompromising rules, similar to those of earlier decades but now elevated to "scientific" status. Their advice was based on "behaviourism"—a school of thought that focused exclusively on actions, not emotions. They believed that a child's developmental progress and obedience could be judged by how well he slept alone and that the needs of the child were the least important priority in the household.[13] Too much affection weakened character, though handshakes for older children were acceptable. They urged a separate room for each child when possible.

The trouble with this "scientific" approach for children was that it had no *science* behind it. The first half of the twentieth century was a dark age of seriously detached parenting. But it also ushered in the first solidly scientific look at child development.

Truby King dial[14]

Advice After World War II: Research and Retreads

Beginning in the 1930s, Anderson and Mary Aldrich (a husband-and-wife team), Arnold Gesell, and others studied and described the physiological and emotional stages of maturation and the approaches that seemed to foster them. In the 1940s, Dr. Benjamin Spock became the public and very popular face of the burgeoning science. Like the approach of almost all child care experts of the day, Spock's was based on formula-feeding, but he began to introduce some flexibility into the strict feeding and sleep schedules of the time: *"Don't be afraid to trust your own common sense—you know more than you think you do."*[15] The Aldriches, Gesell, and Spock were all moving toward the fundamentals of human attachment that an explosion of new research was about to confirm.

Among the most important research discoveries about maternal-infant attachment and the consequences of poor attachment was the series of studies conducted in the 1950s and 1960s by Dr. John Bowlby, a British psychiatrist who developed the concepts of "attachment theory". He believed strongly that *"the infant and young child should experience a warm, intimate, and continuous relationship with his mother (or permanent mother-substitute) in which both find satisfaction and enjoyment and that not to do so may have significant and irreversible mental health consequences."*[16]

In the 1960s, child psychologist Dr. Haim Ginott introduced new ways of communicating with young children that promoted respect for their feelings and attachment to their parents as being more motivating than an authoritarian approach for good behaviour and "emotional intelligence".[17]

In the 1970s, Drs. Mary Ainsworth and Silvia Bell published their observations on the differences between children who were securely or insecurely attached to their mothers: *"Mother and infant form an interactional dyad: the more responsive she is the less likely he is to cry and the more likely he is to develop more varied modes of communication. . . . Infants whose mothers are responsive to their signals have less occasion to cry—not only in the first few months but through-*

out infancy."[18] Their work has since been confirmed by a rapidly growing body of research.

Advice from the next wave of attachment-oriented child care experts, Drs. T. Berry Brazelton and Penelope Leach in the 1980s, and Dr. William Sears and Martha Sears in the 1990s, was based on this same research. Bowlby's observations have held up: "*The strength of the bond between a child and his primary caregiver (who may or may not be his mother) determines a child's ability to cope with problems and form intimate and reciprocal relationships later on.*"[19] Bowlby's term "attachment theory", far from being a new-age invention, is the cornerstone of modern child development research.

There have been many other child care experts and sleep experts since the 1990s, with both parent-oriented and child-oriented approaches, and many of them have huge followings today. Most child-centred approaches today have a loose structure and are accepting of bedsharing, but they also recognize that there are times when parents need or want to change something, and usually emphasize flexibility. Some recent authors have offered no-cry child-centred approaches involving positive reinforcement that takes the baby's developmental stage into account. You'll find recommendations for some good ones near the end of Chapter 11.

Parent-Oriented Sleep Training "Works" . . . at a Price

Books urging a parent-oriented, controlling approach still crowd the bookshelves, despite the growing evidence against it. They tend to offer very specific techniques promising to work for the majority of mothers and babies, and often use the same terms and schedules that were proposed in the past, usually focused on creating and maintaining distance between mothers and babies.

Sleep Training for Beginners

Sleep-training programmes operate on the assumption that babies can be taught to sleep, wake, and be hungry on someone else's timetable, and to understand that they really are safe and cared for even when they're left alone and untended. Phrased so bluntly, it might sound odd. But sleep training assumes that babies can and should adapt, almost from birth, to their parents' desires rather than the parents adapting to the babies' needs. The programmes typically use what behaviourists call an *extinction* technique, eliminating (extinguishing) an unwanted behaviour by not rewarding it. Cry-it-out sleep-training methods usually involve ignoring a baby's crying until he falls asleep and stays asleep without complaint. Babies are to be put to bed awake, so that they can "learn" to put themselves to sleep.

Programmes may recommend that any baby monitors be turned off and that parents go somewhere where they can't hear the baby, relying on the clock to tell them when to interact with him instead. Parents may be told that vomiting in addition to the expected hard crying is not unusual but isn't harmful. Most programmes assume that the baby will be in a separate room. That kind of nighttime separation before the middle of the first year greatly increases the risk of SIDS in vulnerable babies, and it makes breastfeeding more difficult and weaning more likely.

Two common sleep-training variations are *controlled crying* (also known as *controlled comforting*) and *scheduled awakenings*. Controlled crying is a form of *graduated extinction*. Rather than going cold turkey, parents are "allowed" to spend a minute (or some other specific amount of time) talking to or patting the baby while he's awake in his cot. Some programmes don't allow eye contact or facial expressions. Parents are supposed to leave

Research-Based Infant Sleep Websites

The Centre for Attachment (Lauren Lindsey Porter and Kate Dent Rennie), centreforattachment.com

Infant Sleep Information Source (Dr. Helen Ball and the Durham University Parent-Infant Sleep Lab), isisonline.org.uk

Harvard Center on the Developing Child, developingchild.harvard.edu/topics/science_of_early_childhood

Dr. Kathleen Kendall-Tackett, uppitysciencechick.com and praeclaruspress.com/Sleep-resources.html

Dr. James McKenna, cosleeping.nd.edu

the room for a certain number of minutes, then return to the baby's room for another specific amount of time to pat him and reassure him verbally before leaving for a longer time. The comforting period stays the same; the ignoring period keeps getting longer. The same procedure is followed if the baby wakes up in the night. The process promises to work within a few days to about two weeks.

Scheduled-awakening programmes involve waking a baby or child before he typically wakes up on his own. Once he has learned not to wake up until he's scheduled to, the parents start moving his wake-up times further and further apart until he no longer wakes up at night. The process requires that parents set an alarm for *themselves* several times in the night for three or four weeks.

In most cry-it-out and controlled-crying programmes, parents may take care of some of their babies' physical needs—nappy changes, pain relief—but the babies' emotional needs and hunger needs are to be ignored.

Sleep-training techniques work, at least temporarily, for about 80 per cent of babies.[20] Many babies stop crying within a few days.[21] And parents who are able to stick it out are generally pleased with the short-term results.

So What's the Price?

Like the behaviourists, sleep-training fans and researchers focus on *surface* outcomes. The baby is quiet all night. The parents get a full night's sleep. Problem solved. But researchers in many other fields have looked *beneath* the surface, at what goes on *inside* the baby, now and in the future. They've studied behaviours and physiological responses. They've used electroencephalograms (EEGs), positron emission tomography (PET) scans, and magnetic resonance imaging (MRI). They've measured hormone levels and developmental stages, they've recorded the behaviours of both parent and child, and they've looked at long-term physical and psychological outcomes.

Who is "they"? Neurologists and neurophysiologists. Child psychologists. Biologists. Scientists who study blood pressure, stress hormones, brain development, and emotional states. Their conclusions are pretty compelling: cry-it-out sleep training, controlled crying, and scheduled awakenings can all be damaging in the long run, and aren't actually doing what they claim to be doing in the short term. At least one well-known proponent of sleep training has softened his position on crying it out in light of ever-growing research.[22]

> [Sleep-training] strategies have not been shown to decrease [overall] infant crying, prevent sleep and behavioral problems in later childhood, or protect against postnatal depression. In addition, behavioral interventions for infant sleep . . . risk unintended outcomes, including increased amounts of problem crying, premature cessation of breastfeeding, worsened maternal anxiety, and, if the infant is required to sleep either day or night in a room separate from the caregiver, an increased risk of Sudden Infant Death Syndrome. . . . The belief that [sleep training] in the first 6 months of life improves outcomes . . . is historically constructed, overlooks feeding problems, and biases interpretation of data.[23]—Pamela S. Douglas, MBBS, FRACGP, IBCLC, PhD, and Peter S. Hill, MBBS, DRACOG, PhD

A great many parents don't need to hear the evidence. They know there's something wrong with such an adversarial approach to parenting. One researcher commented, *"The parents were concerned about the possible effects of treatment on emotional development. . . . The researchers were surprised by the severity of the parental resistance."*[24]

Solitary, Prolonged Crying Is Harmful

When your baby is with you, she has lots of ways to communicate: stiffening her body with stress, smiling in relaxation, bringing her fists to her mouth, or twisting open-mouthed towards your breast with hunger. Alone, she has only her voice. Crying is normally her last resort, but the baby alone learns to go there sooner.

A baby's brain changes when she is separated from her mother and cries for more than a few minutes.[25] Prolonged solitary crying sets off a fight-or-flight response that floods her body with the stress hormones cortisol and adrenaline.[26] Cortisol raises heart rate, blood pressure, and pressure inside the skull, and decreases blood oxygenation.[27] Adrenaline increases blood sugar, heart rate, and blood pressure. Digestion, kidney function, and the immune system are temporarily impaired.[28] Prolonged stress also raises a baby's levels of thyroid and vasopressin hormones. Vasopressin also increases blood pressure and can cause nausea and vomiting, which may be why many babies throw up after crying for a long time.[29] It may be common with sleep training, but it's not harmless.

The stress of being separated from a beloved carer can hurt—really hurt in a physical way.[30] Some babies are affected more profoundly by the effects of separation and stress than other babies because they have more Sensitive, Negative, or Reactive temperaments.[31] The problem is, it's hard to know which baby you have until later.

Some babies may cry for hours a day, even in the arms of their loving mother. But there's a huge difference between crying and *crying alone.* The baby who cries from physical or even emotional distress in your arms doesn't have that same cortisol rise.[32] It's *separation* that is linked to those intense physiological responses.

Many mammals, including humans, have what's called a "separation distress call".[33] In historical survival terms, that's good, because the better babies are at expressing their needs and getting them met, the more likely they are to survive. From the sleep trainer's perspective, the crying baby is learning independence. From the baby's, he's just trying to survive.

Protest and Despair: A Baby's Only Defence

Nils Bergman, MB ChB, DCH, MPH, MD, describes a baby's response to separation this way: A baby has two physiological programmes—nutrition and defence (self-protection)—that run in the background all the time. Yet she can run only one at a time. When her nutrition programme is running, she's eating, digesting, resting, sleeping, and growing. When her defence programme runs, she's not happy, she's not eating, and she's not growing.[34]

There are two parts to her defence programme: protest (hyperarousal) and despair (dissociation). Protest is easy enough to spot. It's a crying baby, fists clenched, face screwed up, trying to get someone's—*anyone's*—attention, because solitude leaves a baby completely vulnerable.

Protesting takes a lot of energy. A baby who's been abandoned can't afford to use up *all* her energy calling for help that may never come. So in the midst of her protests, she has to shut down periodically and put herself in power saver mode—despair. She goes quiet, lies still, and may even seem to sleep, but she may keep a slight frown on her face, and her fists may be clenched or her fingers splayed—signs of continuing stress. She'll alternate these two defence programmes—calling for attention and conserving energy—as long as she can. The more time a baby spends in either part of her defence programme, the less time she devotes to growth and maturation.

Babies who are "trained" to be quiet seem only to have discovered that there's no point in crying.[35] Research shows that the baby's cortisol stays high, even though she's not crying.[36] She's still in defence mode. She just stops telling her mother about it.

Prolonged Crying Is Traumatic for Parents, Too

Most emotionally healthy adults are stressed by hearing a baby cry.[37] Just watch the faces of people on an aeroplane with a miserable two-month-old. A mother who is well-bonded to her baby feels even more stress when her baby cries.[38] This stress is especially strong if she is a breastfeeding mother,[39] and especially if she gave birth vaginally.[40]

Parents can often tell the difference between different types of cries,[41] and the "separation distress call" type of cry can be particularly disturbing to hear.[42] It raises a mother's own cortisol levels[43] and can hurt to the point of physical pain.[44] Truby King had a team of nurses, part of whose responsibility it was to restrain mothers during his baby training sessions.[45] That says a lot about how powerful a mother's instinct is to protect her baby.

> Given the new body of sophisticated, cross-discipline research on attachment and brain development . . . it is clear that a baby's willingness to accept sleep training after reportedly brief periods of protest is no less than a cycle of hyperarousal [protest] and dissociation [despair] responses that is damaging to its development.
>
> To think that since the infant has passively accepted the new sleep system, the sleep training is thus "successful", is to misunderstand the workings of the infant brain. No longer can we accept the conventional wisdom that babies are merely "exercising their lungs" when they cry; nor can we tolerate interpretations of babies' cries as "manipulation".
>
> Babies cry to signal distress in an effort to engage caregivers to help meet their needs and foster their healthy development. It is an attempt at communication, not manipulation. Their goals are survival and optimal development. This is achieved through secure attachment.[46]
>
> —Lauren Porter, MSW, founder and codirector, New Zealand Centre for Attachment

Why do we feel such a primal drive to go to our baby when he cries? Because we're hardwired to respond.[47] There may not be a saber-toothed tiger in the nursery, but a baby feels the age-old stress of separation and his mother hears that stress in his cries. She may not know the biochemistry of what's happening, but her gut knows that it's not good for him, it's not good for her, and they need each other. That vasopressin rise that may make distressed babies throw up? Maybe that's why some mothers throw up too when they're told not to respond to their babies.

Responding to your baby isn't weakness. It's an important, powerful, *healthy* protective instinct.

Verbal Reassurance Is Not Enough

Because controlled crying allows for periodic reassurance, it can seem like a good compromise. But while adults who are upset can be soothed by words ("I know how hard that must have been for you. I'm here for you"), babies can't understand language or abstract concepts. Even a soothing tone doesn't do it. Babies need sustained *physical* reassurance, not words.[48] Those verbal visits to the cot, even with a little patting, offer much more reassurance to the parent than to the baby.

> I watched hospital nurses doing a painful procedure on a baby in a cot. The baby screamed for a while, was silent for a while, screamed for a while. The whole time, the nurses were trying to calm *each other* because it was so awful but they felt they had to keep doing it. The baby, of course, ignored their soothing. I had to leave the room.
>
> —Diane

Sleep Training and Breastfeeding

Separate sleep has been shown to lengthen the intervals between feeds,[49] and decrease the number of night feeds,[50] which can decrease a mother's milk volume and her baby's intake. Breastfeeding is a take-and-make arrangement: if your baby doesn't *take* much milk, you aren't going to *make* as much milk.[51] It's one of the main reasons that weaning tends to happen sooner when a mother and baby sleep apart.[52] The risks of poor weight gain and early weaning are a significant part of the high price of sleep training.

> When Rachel was about four months old, my husband heard about a new approach that could get her sleeping all night in six weeks and teach her the importance of order and routine. We were told we should start it right away, because she'd already been breastfeeding at night far too long.
>
> We put Rachel in a cot in the other room, and the first few nights she did cry a lot. But, just like they said, she soon stopped and was sleeping all night. Rachel seemed to be doing fine too, but she started looking thinner and always had this worried expression on her face. She ended up gaining only one ounce in two months. Her doctor wanted me to start her on formula right away. I began supplementing and added solids earlier than I had with my older children.

Rachel's weight gain picked up, thank goodness, but she stopped breastfeeding within a few more weeks. I really miss that connection.

—Maria

Old Books with New Covers

You can see from the history above that the "latest" theories on sleep training approaches are just retreads from centuries past. Today, *more than half* of the sleep-training books are written by first-time authors who, like authors of the past, base their recommendations on nothing more than opinion, personal experience, and selected parent testimonials.[53] Medical schools spend very little time teaching non-medical subjects such as discipline or managing infant sleep, so even the most experienced doctor may be relying heavily on personal opinion and personal experience rather than on research. And sleep-training research tends to gauge success by adult satisfaction and the speed and extent of infant compliance, not by the physiological effects and long-term consequences. Check it out. You won't find the effects on infant development, breastfeeding outcomes, or the parent-child relationship in their literature, or even a nod to what's normal for children around the world. What you'll find is the same old same old.

"Our Programme Gives Parents More Sleep"

This claim is probably true—if parents can survive the training. We've already discussed the high cost of that extra sleep. Are there alternatives? In one sense, no. Babies and young children wake up at night and need parental comforting. On the other hand, mothers who bedshare stay in bed, transition gently from sleeping to waking and back, may not remember all the feeds . . . and retain that irreplaceable bond that research finds to be the best route to emotionally healthy adulthood.

"Our Programme Cures Sleep Disorders"

Those "sleep disorders" are a *perceived* behavioural problem that's just part of the normal range of infant development.[54] According to one sleep-training researcher, *"Overall 20% to 30% of young children . . . are reported to have significant bedtime problems and/or night wakings. For infants and toddlers, night wakings are one of the most common sleep problems, with 25% to 50% of children over the age of 6 months continuing to awaken during the night."*[55] Those numbers sound like an acknowledgment that night waking is normal for babies and small children. You'll find plenty of studies on normal patterns in Chapters 3, 4, and 17. What you *won't* find in the studies of normal is pseudo-science like this, from the same study: *"The etiology of bedtime resistance and night wakings in childhood involves a multifactorial pathophysiologic mechanism and represents a complex combination of biological, circadian, and neurodevelopmental factors."* It might have been simpler to say that Javier in Chapter 4, like normal children all over the world, is most secure and sleeps best when his mother is an integral part of his nights.

You are not managing an inconvenience. You are raising a human being. —Kittie Frantz, RN, CPNP-PC

Babies do need a certain amount of sleep in order for their bodies and brains to grow, but they're born knowing how and how long to sleep. Increasing their nighttime stress can actually *inhibit* normal brain development.

How much sleep do babies need? There's a wide range of normal, and your baby will let you know where his "normal" is. No author has met your baby. It makes more sense to cure your own twenty-first-century "sleep disorder" by going to bed sooner.

Here's what one "expert" says: *"Sleep aids (dummy, teddy bear, etc.) during the night seem to reduce the occurrence of sleep disorders whereas prolonged breastfeeding and co-sleep with the parents interfere with the normal development of sleep."*[56] Say what? Normal sleep behaviours interfere with normal sleep development?

"Our Programme Teaches Independence, Self-Soothing, and Solitary Sleep"

How do you help *yourself* fall asleep? Read a book? Count sheep? Watch a video? Meditate? Your baby can't do *any* of these things. Babies don't have the brain pathways to control their emotions and reactions.[57] When you calm your baby, you're modelling how to become calm, which helps make those pathways. Insisting on "self-soothing" and premature independence can ultimately cause a baby to be *less* secure,[58] which can make it harder for him to feel secure in his future relationships.[59]

As you saw in Chapter 3, breastfeeding hormones induce sleepiness in both mother and baby. Sleep training fights Mother Nature in a very big way. Breastfeeding a baby to sleep is totally normal and totally healthy. You're meeting your baby's most basic physical and emotional needs . . . and you're making life a lot smoother and simpler for yourself.

> It is the nature of the child to be dependent and it is the nature of the dependence to be outgrown. Begrudging dependency because it is not independence is like begrudging winter because it is not yet spring. Dependency blossoms into independence in its own time.[60] —Peggy O'Mara

As for solitary sleep being beneficial, take a look at Chapters 3 and 4 for the physiology refuting *that* one.

"Our Programme Puts You in Charge and Stops Manipulation"

Babies are neurologically incapable of manipulation. Their brains aren't well enough developed to have such complex thoughts.[61] Plus, as we've seen, crying is way too stressful for a baby to use on a whim. What is he manipulating you for? Food? A nappy change? Comfort? These are basic, unsophisticated, completely reasonable needs. Your baby is no more manipulative than a friend who just needs a hug.

> Babies, we know, cannot survive on their own. All basic needs must be met through a relationship with a caregiver. What this new [attachment theory] research tells us, however, is that these needs go far beyond the simple ones of food and sleep, and are intimately tied to the emotional world.[62]
> —Lauren Porter, MSW, founder and co-director, New Zealand Centre for Attachment

Parental authority is more effective when it's based on strong emotional attachment rather than fear.[63] When we love someone wholeheartedly, we try hard to please that person. When we fear someone, we may do what they want, but only when we have to. Model kindness, and children learn kindness. Model distance, and they learn distance. There's a time for *kind* limits and boundaries, but not in infancy. If you model empathy, responsiveness, trust, kindness, and compassion, there's a good chance that's what you'll get when you're elderly and dependent on *him*.[64]

> My mum found an online programme for getting babies to sleep on their own without "props" like breastfeeding. The woman didn't have any credentials or qualifications, but she had a lot of testimonials from people who swore her programme had changed their lives. Alex clearly hadn't read her book. He would cry inconsolably while I verbally "comforted" him. If staying in the bedroom wasn't working, we were to leave until he "learned" to stop crying and sleep.
>
> It lasted three weeks (I'm ashamed to say it got easier and easier to ignore his cries). By the end, if I took Alex near the bedroom he panicked and would start crying. His sleep was worse, his naps were worse. Our solution was to bring him into our bed. He sleeps so much more soundly and longer, even compared to being in the same room but separate. Of course, that means we sleep better too.
>
> —Mimi

"Our Programme Teaches 'Sleep Hygiene' and the Importance of a Schedule"

Sleep hygiene is a popular term for keeping regular sleep hours—not too little, not too much—by establishing bedtime routines. The concept might make some sense for older children and adults who are having trouble getting to sleep because of stress or erratic schedules. But babies are born knowing how and how much to sleep, and they're very good at sleeping wherever they are. We know of no research to show that scheduling a baby's sleep leads to better sleep later in life.

In an era when most of us live by our calendar, a predictable schedule for your baby's naps and bedtime can sound pretty appealing. But in reality, life with a baby is usually less stressful when it's less scheduled. Women of another generation remember watching the clock tick slowly towards 2.00 a.m. while a little one screamed from the cot in another room. Most of them did not breastfeed successfully.[65]

Imagine having to go to the toilet on a schedule, as some of us have to at work. It's much more complicated than just going when you need to. It becomes a major event in your day. It goes from an unremarkable event to downright annoying. Breastfeeding on a schedule is similar. It messes with both your physiologies, and the struggles and time-clock-punching all tend to result in early weaning. Instead, letting babies feed when they need to and fall asleep when they're tired may help them tune into their bodily needs better and is less stressful for both of you.

One Father's Perspective on Sleep Training

To everyone who said things like "My children always slept in their cribs and slept great": Screw you. Screw you to the left, screw you to the right, screw you upside down. (Also, congratulations.)

We tried letting our son cry it out. He would cry. And cry harder. And cry even harder. And somewhere around the 45-minute mark, he would vomit. Every. Single. Time. And then we'd have to go in, pick him up, strip him, get him in the bath, change the sheets in his crib, dry him off, get him in a clean diaper and jammies . . . and then start all over again. Or just say "f——it" and let him nurse down in bed with Mama.

This went on for a couple of weeks. And you know what? We got to the point where we realized that he just needed to be in bed with us. Some children may need other things, but ours needed *that.* Peace in our home and a content family have meant accepting that he sleeps with us for now. (And honestly, part of me will miss him when he's not there next to me all night anymore.)—Andy

If your baby seems to be taking longer to develop a more consistent sleep pattern than other babies you know, it may be related to his personality (or to other mothers' exaggeration or wishful thinking). Take a look at Chapter 7 to see if you recognize any traits that might explain your baby's approach to sleep. If your child has a higher-need personality, one of the very best things you can do is find places where you can vent and get empathy instead of advice (see Chapter 23).

Most importantly, keep in mind that today isn't how it will always be. Your pattern of baby care—whatever it is—will get easier and much more efficient over time.

"Our Programme Cures Your Baby of the Night-Waking Habit"

As we discussed in Chapter 4, we all wake up several times at night as part of our sleep cycles. So do babies, even those who "sleep through the night".[66] Although it may be inconvenient, it's not a "habit", it's normal. And it's healthy.

"Our Programme Prevents Spoiling"

There's no science behind the notion of spoiling a baby. Bell and Ainsworth wrote in 1972, "*Those infants who are conspicuous for fussing and crying after the first few months of life, and who fit the stereotype of the 'spoiled child', are those whose mothers have ignored their cries or have delayed long in responding to them.*"[67] Since then, hundreds of studies have confirmed and extended their findings.[68] In order to solidify his emotional balance and sense of security, a baby needs his mother to be consistently affectionate and responsive to his needs.[69] Your closeness during the night

From the Mouths of Babes

Some toddlers can put their feelings about sleep training into words. Dr. Jack Newman, director of Toronto's International Breastfeeding Centre, shared this experience: "*When our son was over two years of age, we thought we would try [sleep training] again (we were slow learners . . .). We finally gave in, as we heard him cry from his cot, 'This is your little boy, Daniel. Why are you doing this?'*"

gives that security. Instead of being spoiled, a bedsharing baby is more likely to be more emotionally secure.

Does Sleep Training Matter in the Long Run?

A baby's nighttime cortisol stays high throughout sleep training and beyond, but his mother's doesn't. She has a mother's normal stress hormone reaction to the crying, but once her baby stops crying, his cortisol level stays high. Her own cortisol level drops.[70] Now you have a mother and baby who have lost the synchrony of responsive mothering and the easy, automatic, intuitive relationship that goes with it. When she's *responsive* to his distress for two-thirds of the day but *ignores* it for the remaining third, it's like a three-legged race, with two people trying to pull together but unable to synchronize, and it must be very disorienting for the baby. Sleep training runs counter to the kind of read-each-other's-mind relationship that's normal for the breastfeeding dyad.

> If then, parents are primed to an infant's cry and infants are communicating needs to be met, should we encourage parents to ignore these cries and thereby refuse to meet their infants' needs? Moreover, should parents ignore this developing prelinguistic form of communication? Despite these important questions, families who follow extinction techniques [crying it out] purposefully ignore their infant's cry. Is it ethical for health professionals to encourage this ignorance?[71] —Sarah Blunden, Kirrilly Thompson, and Drew Dawson in *Sleep Medicine Reviews*, 2011

The mother's own internal tug-of-war about whether to listen to her baby or her book affects her responses to him in subtle ways. Her uneasiness and uncertainty come through, and that in itself can affect their relationship.

Early Stress Can Affect a Developing Personality

People laugh about how their traumatic childhood landed them in therapy, but there's often some truth to it. Research on mother-baby attachment shows that babies' personalities are moulded in part by how their caregivers respond—or don't respond—to their needs.[72]

Children are most sensitive to stress in the first few years, and their experiences help create lifelong nerve pathways.[73] As neuroscientist Carla Shatz put it, "Cells that fire together, wire together."[74] The more a pathway is used, the easier it becomes to use, so when a child's early relationships are chronically stressful, he feels stress more quickly as an adult.[75]

People who as babies had affectionate, attentive, and empathetic mothers tend to be more resilient under stress, and they tend to be more compassionate and secure.[76] If we ignore or reject babies' attachment-seeking behaviours, they may lose some of their ability to trust and connect to other people,[77] and even become less kind themselves.[78] Being less securely attached as a baby can also impair a person's ability to take care of his or her own infants.[79] Which means the effects of infant stress can echo through another generation.

A 2011 study looked at the relationship between mother and child at 8 months, and then at the same child's mental health at age 34.[80] Mothering styles at eight months were categorized as negative, occasionally negative, warm, caressing, or extravagantly affectionate. The adults with the least emotional distress and anxiety at age 34 were

Further Reading and Viewing

The Science of Parenting by Margot Sunderland

Grow Your Baby's Brain by Jill Bergman and Nils Bergman (DVD)

Why Love Matters: How Affection Shapes a Baby's Brain by Sue Gerhardt

Touching: The Human Significance of the Skin by Ashley Montagu

The Vital Touch by Sharon Heller

BabyCalm by Sarah Ockwell-Smith

A collection of 39 videos on attachment and infant brain development: goo.gl/Ak40Rv

Nils Bergman on the social and emotional intelligence of infants: goo.gl/wMKLE8 those whose mothers had been among the fewer 7 per cent judged to be "caressing" or "extravagantly affectionate".

To what extent are such long-term outcomes affected by sleep training? All that's known for sure at this point is that sleep training creates sustained, elevated cortisol levels, which in young children can have long-term consequences. But we also know that relationships don't come with on-off switches. It can be very difficult to withhold affection and responsiveness for one-third of the day and compensate for it in the other two-thirds. The on-again-off-again mothering that sleep training promotes makes it more difficult to have a 24/7 deeply affectionate and responsive relationship.

The What-Ifs

This has been a pretty scary chapter. It's probably left you with two big questions: What if sleep training *works* with my baby? And what if I've *already* done it?

What If Sleep Training Your Baby *Works*?

What if you have one of those easy-going babies who accepts separate sleep if that's what you want? No problems, no stress—why not? Back to those same two issues: separation from her primary caregiver increases a baby's stress levels even after her mother's stress levels drop,[81] and prolonged increased stress can cause significant neurological changes.[82]

Even if she's sleeping? The charts in Chapter 4 showed that even when babies are asleep they have measurable changes in heart rate, breathing, and stress levels when they are away from their mothers.[83] It's amazing how strong and important that connection is.

What If You *Already Did* Sleep Training? Will Your Baby Be Okay?

It's the rare parent who doesn't look back, years later, and regret some decisions. We all do the best we can with what we know at the time. But normal parenting is neither boot-camp sleep training nor total self-sacrificing attention.

Remember that every new day brings a new chance to recon-

What's a Mother to Do?

There are much gentler alternatives to sleep training in Chapter 11. Chapter 10 is all about ways to maximize your own sleep.

nect with your child and rebuild trust. The more we treat our children with affection, respect, and trust, and the earlier we do it, the fewer long-term consequences there are likely to be from any parenting mistakes we might make.[84] Children are resilient. In fact, having some less-than-wonderful times here and there teaches resilience, and is important for our children's development.[85] Children don't need perfect parents. They just need to be loved and respected around the clock.

Something to Sleep On

We started writing this book knowing that there were two broad attitudes toward infant sleep training—parent-centred and baby-centred. And we knew that the research supported a baby-centred approach. We knew we'd find connections to physiology and developmental stages. And we knew there'd be links between an infant's experiences with his mother and his adult experiences with the world. What floored us was the *sheer volume* of research that supports responsive mothering. The newest studies use advanced technology to reveal what's going on inside the brains of babies and parents. Attachment is not a fringe theory. It has become the cornerstone of our current understanding of child development. We now know that there's real potential for long-term loss when we push too hard for short-term gain.

Nights can be hard for new parents. But it makes much more sense for us to adapt a short span of our own lives to responding to our babies' needs than to force our babies to adapt to our needs during such a vitally important and once-in-a-lifetime part of their development. Children need their mothers when they are vulnerable, and they're never more vulnerable than before they have words to understand and express themselves.

Nearly 200 years ago, Lydia Child wrote, *"I have said much in praise of gentleness. I cannot say too much. Its effects are beyond calculation, both on the affections and the understanding."* Responding to your baby through the night helps build an emotionally strong and resilient personality—the kind of person you'll like to have around when you grow old.

chapter 19

Suffocation and SIDS: Reality and Risks

> I didn't know *why* my baby would die if I slept with her. I just knew that my bed was a SIDS risk. When I woke up one morning after falling asleep with her, I was amazed that she was still alive.
>
> —Ella

This is a tough chapter. No one likes to think about babies dying, and words like "SIDS", "suffocation", and "death" make all of us shudder. But we want to be very clear about this: current research indicates that Sudden Infant Death Syndrome (SIDS) happens only in a very small group of babies who *already* have a very specific health issue—a rare brain disorder that interferes with a baby's arousal centre, for instance. We don't know what all those pre-existing health issues are, but the current understanding of SIDS is that *only* those babies are at risk for SIDS. The problem is knowing whether a baby is in that tiny group. What we know for sure is that the vast majority of breastfed babies are *not*. That can be hard to believe when the warnings against bedsharing are loud, convincing, and everywhere. But those warnings have misinterpreted the very science they're based on.

Keep in mind that *suffocation* risks don't have *anything at all* to do with SIDS. They're two separate issues, and we'll tackle them separately. Nighttime safety, for the Safe Sleep Seven mother, is all about the surface, so we'll go there first.

Suffocation and Other Breathing Hazards

Preventing breathing hazards is just common sense. This section is most likely just a review of what you're probably already doing.

There are five reasons why a person might be unable to get enough oxygen:

- *There isn't enough oxygen in the air.* A major fire, excessive amounts of carbon monoxide, or drowning can all make oxygen unavailable and result in *suffocation.*
- *The nose and mouth are blocked.* There's enough oxygen in the air, but it can't reach the lungs. That form of suffocation can also be called *smothering.*
- *The lungs can't expand enough to draw in enough air.* A person may be wedged somewhere, for instance, and be unable to breathe freely or wriggle free. That's *entrapment.*
- *Something wraps around the neck and prevents breathing.* That's *strangulation.*
- *Something small wedges in the throat.* This blocks the airway and causes *choking.*

Accidental Suffocation and Strangulation in Bed

Accidental Suffocation and Strangulation in Bed, or ASSB, is a new term that's been introduced by researchers to describe infant sleep risks other than SIDS.[1] It's not a catchy name. But we're hoping everyone gets to know it, because for the Safe Sleep Seven mother—and that's a whole lot of us—it's a *far* more important issue than SIDS. Here's how it looks if you plot it out:

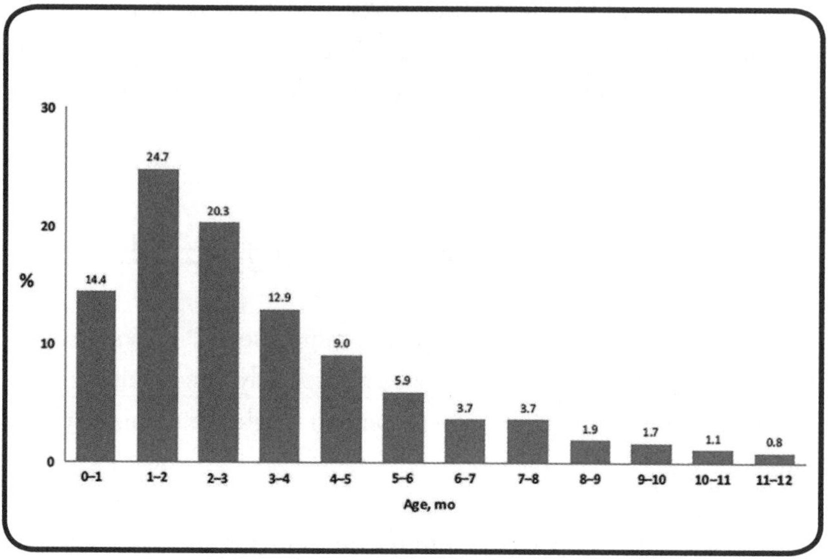

Percentage distribution of deaths caused by ASSB according to age at death: United States, 2004–2008. Reproduced with permission from Pediatrics *vol. 28(5), pages e1341–e1367. Copyright © 2011 by the AAP.*[2]

Babies are skilled at going where they aren't supposed to be able to go and doing what they aren't supposed to be able to do, especially when they aren't even supposed to be awake. It's just a matter of keeping a baby out of trouble in the first place.

Avoiding Breathing Hazards

It's not rocket science. Keep the suffocation risks away, and ASSB—in all its forms—is *extremely* unlikely. But you need to think like a baby to spot those risks.

The Safe Surface checklist in Chapter 2 addresses the most common potential breathing and injury problems in short form. That same chapter describes how the breastfeeding cuddle curl and heightened awareness of a breastfeeding mother make it almost impossible for her to roll onto her baby.

And that leaves SIDS, which should take far less of the average mother's attention than ASSB.

SIDS: A Perfect Storm

Back in 1994, two researchers created a model for how and when Sudden Infant Death Syndrome (SIDS) can happen.[3] Their triple-risk model has been the cornerstone of how SIDS researchers have thought of SIDS ever since. According to this model, it takes three key pieces for SIDS to occur: (1) a baby is already in the vulnerable group, *and* (2) he's in that period of rapid nervous system development that happens between birth and about six months during which 90 per cent of SIDS events occur, *and* (3) some sort of outside stress is put on him—maybe he starts at day nursery, or maybe he's away from adult supervision and stimulation. With rare exceptions, *it's only when all three factors overlap* that SIDS occurs.

The researchers produced a diagram showing this "perfect storm" of all three factors and how they overlap, which we'll get to in a minute. But first, here's an example of overlapping risks that may make it clearer. (We apologize in advance to *all* the people who have suffered tragic losses from hurricanes, no matter where they live. This is only meant as a greatly simplified, theoretical example.)

Let's say that the biggest hurricane risk for people who live in Florida comes from not being prepared during hurricane season. We could diagram the potential for damage this way:

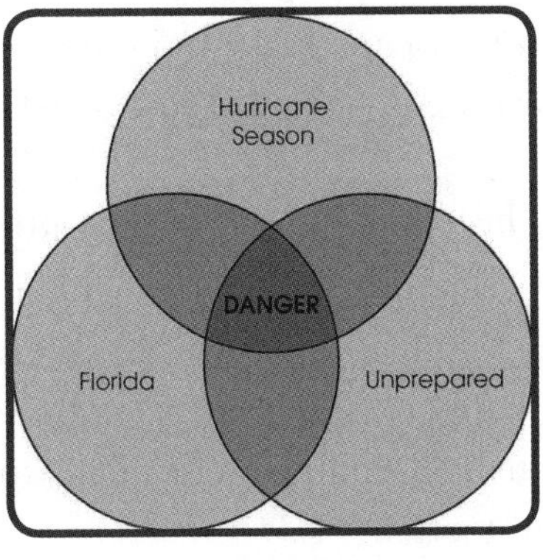

The top circle represents hurricane season, from 1 June through to 30 November. The left-hand circle is everyone who lives in Florida.

The right-hand circle is the precautions that residents could take but don't necessarily. Drop any circle out of the diagram and there's no problem. It's not hurricane season? No hurricane damage. Everyone is prepared? No damage to people or property. Now let's form the Hurricane Protection Committee (HPC) and find ways to keep as many people as possible as safe as possible.

There's no way to control the calendar, so that's out. And if you live in Florida, you live in Florida. So let's try to control what we *can* control and launch a massive campaign to get people prepared: make sure you have fresh batteries! Get a generator! Have some wood on hand for boarding up your windows! The campaign spurs almost everyone to action. Those who don't act at least feel guilty about it. After all, it's for their own protection. And of course everyone worries. But there's no doubt that many lives and homes will be spared with this kind of campaign.

Oops—our HPC has campaigned nationwide, even though the great majority of people *don't* live in Florida. Why should June to November make people in Colorado fearful of hurricanes? Why should people in Utah have to hoard wood? The HPC made the mistake of focusing on what people could do to help prevent damage, without recognizing *who* needed to take hurricane precautions. They focused on the circle they could change—how well everyone prepared. But they needed to focus first on the size of the smallest circle—who exactly needed to do the preparing. When *everyone* prepares, hurricane damage drops dramatically. It's just that lots of people end up with hurricane fears and precautions to achieve results that could have been achieved just as well with a more targeted campaign.

In fact, making everyone think they're at risk can *cause* damage in other ways. For instance, buying a generator unnecessarily can mean a low-income family in America can't afford needed medical care. Bad storms happen, sometimes totally unpredictably. But being overly cautious can diminish our quality of life without providing significant protection.

Now let's look at the triple-risk SIDS model that's used by most researchers today,[4] and think like the HPC.

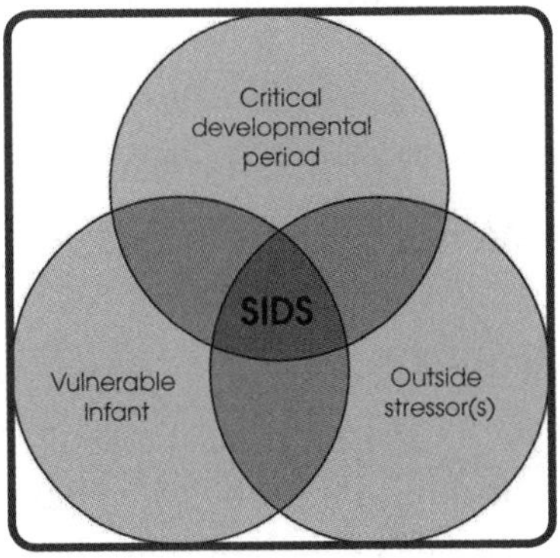

The top circle is the period of greatest risk, which peaks between about one and four months. The left-hand circle is babies who are already vulnerable. And the right-hand circle is all the stresses on a baby that can increase the risk of SIDS for a vulnerable baby. If you take away any one circle, SIDS becomes wildly unlikely.

Well, there's no way to bypass the critical period. And a baby who's vulnerable is vulnerable. So let's focus on what we *can* do: encourage people to eliminate known risk factors—baby asleep on his stomach, baby left alone, and so on. SIDS prevention campaigns around the world have focused nearly all their energy on teaching *all* families how to avoid SIDS risks. But casting the net so widely has resulted in greatly overblown fears in families that are at *extremely* low risk, including those with babies older than about four months, the point at which even groups against bedsharing agree that the risk for bedsharing is the same as for cots and Moses baskets.[5] It has interfered with the normal nighttime behaviours of mothers and babies, raising stress in both groups and shortening breastfeeding duration. All because the campaigns haven't focused their efforts on the smallest circle: the babies for whom it really matters.

We can never say for sure whether a given baby is inside or outside that small "vulnerable baby" circle. We wish we could. Babies die sometimes, and sometimes we don't know why. But there are things you can do to make life a whole lot safer. That's what this chapter is all about. If you live in Denver, you don't have to worry about hurricanes.

What Exactly *Is* SIDS?

It's easier to say what SIDS *isn't.* If a baby under a year old dies suddenly and no other cause of death can be found, it's considered a SIDS death. Sudden infant death syndrome is not suffocation or an underlying health problem that anyone can find. It isn't an accident or a birth defect, and nothing shows up after a thorough autopsy and toxicology screening. A seemingly healthy baby just . . . dies, and no one knows why.

A small percentage of babies have probably always died of SIDS. Your grandparents most likely called it "cot death". It didn't have its official name until 1969. Research increased, conferences were held, organizations were formed, funds—and consciousness—were raised. In the early 1990s, the definition at the beginning of this chapter became the official, internationally accepted one. (We'll talk later in the chapter about the newer term "SUID".)

How does SIDS connect with bedsharing? Not very well, unless smoking is involved. *No one has proposed a physiological mechanism that would cause a baby to die of SIDS just because he's next to his non-smoking mother.* It doesn't make any sense that there *would* be since mothers and babies are hardwired to be together.

What Are the Numbers?

Nearly three-quarters of SIDS cases happen between birth and four months. Ninety per cent occur before six months. Only 2 per cent occur after nine months. The peak SIDS period is usually considered to be one to four months. (Deaths after one year of age fall outside the definition for SIDS.)

Here's what it looks like, plotted out. Looks a lot like the ASSB graph, doesn't it?

The lowest SIDS rates in the world are in countries where bedsharing is traditional—parts of Asia and South Asia, for instance.[6] It doesn't seem to be a matter of geography; when people from a low-risk culture move to a developed country, they also tend to bring along a low rate of SIDS, so long as they bring their traditions with them.[7]

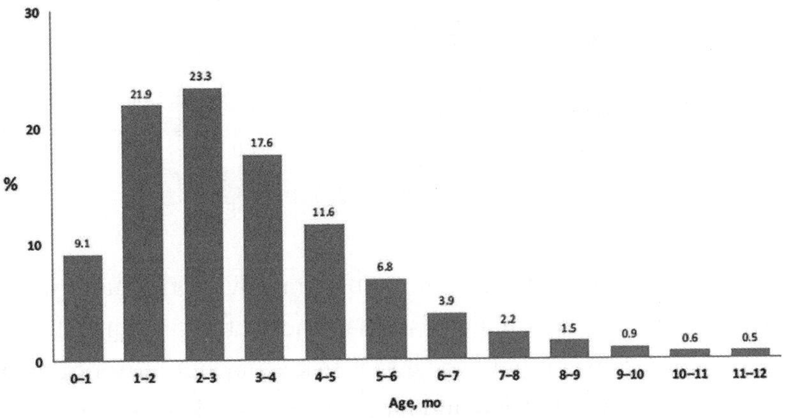

Percent distribution of SIDS deaths according to age at death: United States, 2004–2006. Reproduced with permission from Pediatrics *vol. 28(5), pages e1341–e1367. Copyright © 2011 by the AAP.*[8]

The United States has a higher rate of SIDS than just about anywhere else. Why is the U.S. rate so high? Four big risk factors are household smoking, putting a baby on his stomach to sleep, leaving a sleeping baby unattended (which includes nursery or all types of childcare during the peak SIDS period), and formula-feeding.[9] Note that bedsharing isn't one of them.

In a 2005 comparison of developed countries, the Netherlands and Japan had the lowest rates. New Zealand was highest, at eight times the Netherlands rate. The United States was second highest, at more than five times the Netherlands rate.[10]

What Do the Numbers Mean?

During the three-month peak SIDS period (one month through to four months), when almost two-thirds of SIDS deaths occur, the risk in the United States is currently about 0.27 per 1,000, or one in about 3,700.

2005 SIDS Deaths per 1,000 Births	
New Zealand	0.80
United States	0.54
Argentina	0.49
Germany	0.43
Scotland	0.39
Ireland	0.38
Australia	0.32
England/Wales	0.30
Norway	0.30
Sweden	0.23
Japan	0.16
Netherlands	0.10

The loss of any baby is an immense tragedy for that family. But one in 3,700 is a far smaller risk than most of us imagine. If you want to get a sense of how small that risk is, lay out in front of you one pack of cards (shuffled and face down), two six-sided dice, and one coin. Now write down on a piece of paper what single card you think you'll draw at random. Then write down your guess for the first throw of the dice. And the second. And then write down whether you think the coin will land heads or tails when you toss it. Got them all written down? Now start the drawing and tossing. The odds of a baby dying of SIDS in the United States *during the most risky SIDS period* are about the same as the odds of your guessing right *on every single card draw and dice throw and coin toss with your very first try.* If this sounds easy or even likely, try it for real. You'll draw that first card and say, "Oh."

There's more. That SIDS figure includes all the babies who are *already* at the highest risk of SIDS—the babies whose parents both smoke around them, for example. If you're a Safe Sleep Seven mother, your baby might as well live in Denver during hurricane season. Add another couple of coins to the analogy above.

What if your baby has a totally unforeseen vulnerability? If you're in the Safe Sleep Seven column, then you've eliminated the biggest stresses by far. So your baby's risk is *still* tiny. Life is always a gamble, but one researcher referred to the Safe Sleep Seven baby's SIDS risk, even during the peak months, as "vanishingly small".

Amazing.

Not everyone slides automatically into the Safe Sleep Seven model. So let's move on to vulnerable babies and the known SIDS risks that can affect them.

Vulnerable? Outside Stress? What's the Difference?

There are issues that make a baby vulnerable to SIDS, and there are issues that *stress* an already vulnerable baby. It's sort of like the way having allergies can make pollen season miserable for certain people. The pollen itself isn't a stress for people without allergies. But having seasonal allergies can leave some people vulnerable to the stress of a high pollen count. A vulnerable baby is sensitive to certain stressors in his world that aren't particularly stressful to other babies. Sometimes we just don't know what stresses a vulnerable baby that isn't a stress for the average baby. And sometimes we just don't know what makes a baby vulnerable. But we can reduce *any* baby's SIDS risk hugely with just a few precautions.

The Biggest SIDS Risk Factors

The four biggest issues associated with SIDS are smoking,[11] laying a baby face down for sleep,[12] leaving a baby unattended,[13] and formula-feeding.[14] Let's take them one at a time.

Smoking

We were surprised to find that some safe sleep brochures don't even mention smoking, and very few emphasize it. Yet study after study since the 1990s has shown that smoking, either before or after the baby's born, increases SIDS risk anywhere from two times to *well* over ten times, depending on the study.[15] The risk depends on how much the mother smokes, how many smokers there are in the home, and how many hours a day the baby is exposed to smoke both at home and away. Smoking, either before or after birth, causes a number of changes in a baby's brain, including his ability to rouse from sleep, which may be the reason for the increased SIDS risk. *Smoking—prenatal, postnatal, and second-hand—is the biggest SIDS risk of all.*

Tummy-Down (Prone) Sleeping

Before the 1990s, almost every health authority recommended that babies be put on their stomachs (prone) to help them sleep longer and to prevent aspiration if they vomited. It turns out that aspiration isn't an issue.[16] And because of surprising and overwhelming research in the 1990s, mothers around the world are now advised to put their babies down for sleep on their backs.[17] Between 1990 and 2005, the "Back to Sleep" campaign dropped the U.S. SIDS rate by 40 percent; other Western countries with similar programs had similar results. The recommendation refers only to babies who are too young to roll front to back and back to front whenever they like.

Putting a solo-sleeping baby on her back is the risk-lowering suggestion that's at the heart of all the baby-on-back campaigns, including "Back to Sleep", "ABC (Alone, Back, Crib)", "This Side Up", and "Back Is Best", and it really is well researched.[18] Babies seem to sleep too soundly on their stomachs,[19] which may be part of why tummy-down sleep increases the risk of SIDS. Sleeping on their stomach also compresses their chest, which may restrict breathing.[20] Sleeping tummy-down is one of the biggest SIDS risk factors.

But wait a minute! The baby in Kangaroo Care is on her stomach on her mother's chest, and there are decades' worth of solid research to show that that's an extremely *good* thing.[21] You know from Chapter 4 (and all through the book!) that newborns do best on their mother's chest, head higher than bottom. That position, with the movement of the mother's chest as she breathes and the sounds of her heartbeat and voice, stabilizes vital signs, promotes growth for all newborns,[22] and can be lifesaving for premature babies.[23] Some researchers, recognizing the mother's role in soothing and stimulating a sleeping infant, question whether being tummy-down *beside* her mother is a risk factor for an already low-risk baby. It's a line of thought that's likely to gather momentum when researchers start separating safe and unsafe situations. All we know for sure is that tummy-down during solitary sleep increases the risk for certain babies.

You may have heard about a 2013 study on sudden unexpected postnatal collapse (SUPC)—a rare, sudden, and unexplained death of an infant who's only hours or days old.[24] It has prompted some hospitals to take a newborn from his mother after a brief time prone (tummy-down) on her chest and lay him on his back in a cot. But the authors didn't define "prone". Were the mothers lying flat on their backs, or were they sitting partially upright with their babies on their chests? Were the babies exposed to birth medications? Were their umbilical cords clamped before the placenta downloaded their full complement of oxygen and blood? Too many unknowns, and no physiological reason offered. This needs more research with better clarification of potential risk factors.

Baby Unattended

The risk of *all* baby problems, day and night, is far greater when a baby is in a separate room.[25] And the great majority of SIDS deaths happen out of sight of adults.[26] That's why the American Academy of Pediatrics and UNICEF recommend that babies share a room with a responsible caregiver at night.[27] Various health organizations recommend room-sharing for at least the first six months.

And then there's naptime. SIDS happens during the day too. That's why we encourage you to have an easily portable napping place, so that your baby can be with you wherever you are. A babycarrier is the best solution. A Moses basket works well too. There are more ideas in Chapter 5. Bottom line: if the napping spot is not portable, you're liable to walk away, get busy, and not check back for a while.

"Attended" means more than just being physically present. It means being both competent and caring. Alcohol is a SIDS risk at least partly because an adult under the influence isn't going to be attentive to a baby's well-being. Neither is a child. Babies need a responsible adult or near-adult around them for the first half year. Not a baby monitor, but a real live person.

Does that mean you can't step around the corner? Of course not. It's a real world, and you're hardly going to move a Moses basket if you're ferrying plates from family room to kitchen. But baby napping alone in a room down the hall increases a baby's risk for at least the first six months.

Formula-Feeding

The U.S. Surgeon General's 2011 *Call to Action to Support Breastfeeding*[28] reports a 56 per cent increased risk of SIDS for the formula-fed baby. A number of studies have found double the risk.[29] Astonishingly, safe sleep brochures don't even mention the risks of formula-feeding. Some say to breastfeed "if you can". What about partial formula-feeding? It depends on how partial it is. The more formula-feeding, the higher the SIDS risk.[30] The number one rule, no matter what your milk supply, is "feed the baby". So use formula if you absolutely need it. But don't use formula if you can avoid it. (You'll find sources for breastfeeding help in Chapter 23.)

Unavoidable SIDS Risks

There are other things besides those four big ones that increase a baby's risk of SIDS, of course. Some of the risks you really can't do anything about. Some you can. And remember that these are *SIDS* risks, not breathing hazards or bedsharing risks.

- *Being a boy.* Baby boys are at greater risk for SIDS than are baby girls.[31]
- *Sleeping.* Most SIDS events happen during a baby's sleep,[32] even though you'd swear sometimes that your baby never sleeps at all.
- *Night.* SIDS is more common at night.[33] There's less stimulation for a baby at night, less parental attention and holding, less motion, less noise, and more sleep time.
- *Day of the week.* In the United States, SIDS rates are

higher on Saturday, Sunday, and Monday.[34] Alcohol is probably involved; the highest SIDS risk in the United States is on New Year's Eve.[35]

- *Babies with immature or altered arousal patterns.* In one study, babies who died of SIDS already had more trouble rousing themselves, especially during the second half of the night, when SIDS is most common.[36] Some researchers now believe that an "immature arousal pattern" prevents certain babies from waking.[37] Prenatal smoking is linked to impaired arousal.[38] So is prenatal alcohol, especially binge drinking in early pregnancy.[39] (Prematurity[40] and formula-feeding affect arousal as well.[41] If your pregnancy included smoking and alcohol, those are SIDS risks that can't be changed. If formula-feeding is a risk you can't avoid, you can minimize it by using as little formula as possible.) Abnormal arousal patterns may turn out to be the underlying cause for most SIDS cases.
- *Premature babies.* Preemies aren't entirely ready for life outside the womb yet, and their immaturity increases their risk of SIDS.[42]
- *Not-quite-healthy babies.* A baby with a cardiorespiratory or brainstem problem is at higher risk for SIDS. A common illness in a baby who's not otherwise vulnerable isn't known to be an issue.
- *Babies in transition.* There are developmental periods when babies undergo a neurological "upgrade". A big one is the move towards sleep consolidation (sleeping in two or more cycles without waking fully, especially in the nighttime), which has its beginnings some time around two to four months.[43] SIDS is more likely during these normal periods of growth spurts in the nervous system.
- *Major life changes.* According to one study, a major life stress in the family—a death, divorce, losing a job—increases the risk of SIDS in already vulnerable babies. There was one exception listed: when a mother leaves full-time employment, her baby's SIDS risk *drops.*[44]

SIDS Risks You *Can* Change

You can lower your baby's risk of SIDS *hugely* by not smoking, by laying your baby on his back when he's not being held, and by keeping your baby nearby and breastfed. You can get it even lower if you address these other categories.

- *Overheating.* Many babies are born at night. Many of them are born nearly bald. All of them are born wet. And in our long past they were born outdoors. Put that all together and you can figure that babies are built to handle periods of cool temperatures, though of course we want them to be as cosy as we are. What they *aren't* built for is overheating, which research suggests is a risk factor for SIDS.[45] If you're bedsharing with a vulnerable baby, you might want to go lighter on the bedding.
- *Child care situations.* Non-parental care appears to double the risk of SIDS during the hours that the baby is there, with the highest risk occurring during the peak SIDS months and often during the first week of day nursery. Caregiver ignorance and neglect don't appear to account for the added risk.[46] Childcare may not be something you can avoid, but you can be aware of the potential risk when your baby is at a vulnerable age.
- *Unvaccinated babies.* Studies have found an increase in SIDS when a baby isn't immunized.[47]
- *Many children.* It may be that the risk of SIDS increases somewhat with each birth.[48]
- *Lack of antenatal care.* Good antenatal care seems to reduce the risk of SIDS.[49]
- *Alcohol.* This one's interesting. Antenatal alcohol, especially binge drinking during pregnancy,[50] is a risk factor for SIDS, probably because it alters brain development. Alcohol is also a risk factor if the adult caring for the baby drinks, but in that case it may be because alcohol causes inattention and an unattended baby is at higher risk of SIDS. But alcohol is also implicated in suffoca-

tion deaths with a compromised adult sharing sleep with a baby. So alcohol is a double whammy, increasing the risk of both SIDS and ASSB.

Possible SIDS Risks

There are several possible risk factors that are still controversial. Let's take a look at them more closely.

Not Having a Dummy

The American Academy of Pediatrics (AAP) says to consider offering a dummy at night after the first month, once breastfeeding is well established, for a *possible* reduction in SIDS risk. They add that the data aren't clear yet, that there's no need to insist that a baby learn to use a dummy, and that there's no need to put it back in if it falls out, as it usually does soon after the baby goes to sleep.[51] The UK Department of Health recommends not using a dummy – its Breastfeeding Care Pathway says 'Avoid teats and dummies as they interfere with breastfeeding'. If sucking is indeed protective, then the breastfeeding baby who is bedsharing with her mother has ample sucking opportunities all night long.

There's a significant debate about the dummy/SIDS research that we'll cover in Chapter 20. And check out Chapter 12 for more information on dummies.

Swaddling

The AAP states that "there is insufficient evidence to recommend routine swaddling as a strategy for reducing the incidence of SIDS." There are studies on each side of the issue. Some have found swaddling to be protective; others point out that it can be a suffocation and maybe a SIDS risk if a swaddled baby rolls onto his stomach.[52] In the UK there is no official Department of Health advice on swaddling. See Chapter 12 for a further discussion of swaddling.

Obesity

Two studies have looked at the relationship between a mother being significantly overweight and her baby dying unexpectedly. One study found that mothers with a body mass index of 30 or more had babies who were at greater risk, especially during the first month. But many of the newborn deaths were clearly related to health issues surrounding pregnancy and birth. And any unexplained deaths were recorded as SIDS. Suffocation isn't mentioned.[53]

Another study reported increased *suffocation* deaths, *not* SIDS deaths, for the babies of mothers who weighed more than 79.5 kg (12.5 stone) pre-pregnancy, but it lumped together high-risk and low-risk sleep surfaces and didn't include feeding method—two common errors that have biased many studies (see Chapter 20).[54]

So it's hard to know what to do with the information at this point. It's true that serious obesity can make bedsharing more complicated. A soft or narrow surface or very large breast could be a smothering risk, especially in the earliest days, particularly for very small babies who have less motor control. But body shape and size, breast size, muscle mass, bed surface, and other factors play into the equation. So it really comes down to your own best judgment about your body and your own situation. Ensuring that your bed is especially firm and that there's plenty of space can help to keep your baby as safe as possible if you fall asleep together.

Young Mother

Several studies have found a higher risk of SIDS with young mothers, but it's hard to tease out any age-related risk from other risk factors that may vary with age, like smoking, alcohol use, and parenting style.[55]

No Solid Evidence for These

SIDS is so scary that there are bound to be claims out there on how to reduce the risk with this product or that procedure. Here are the main issues we've heard about.

Toxins in Mattresses

You may have heard that toxins in cot and adult mattresses increase the risk of SIDS. Sounds reasonable. They certainly *smell* toxic when they're new, and they give off fumes for more than just a few days. It's been pretty well studied, though.[56] No connection has been found, and no toxin-blocking or low-toxin product has been shown to reduce the risk of SIDS. Still, there's no harm in giving any new mattress a good airing before putting a baby—or an adult—on it for the night.

Other Chemicals and Metals

There have also been studies looking at certain metals, including silver, lead, and mercury, and nitrates in drinking water. While those substances can all be toxic, they don't seem to be linked to an increase in SIDS.[57]

Bedsharing

There's no solid evidence to connect bedsharing with SIDS. Take a look at Chapter 20, and you'll see why.

All This Information and No Known Cause for SIDS?

There's a difference between a *risk* factor and a *cause*. We know that smoking is a *risk* factor for dying early. If a man who smokes dies of a heart attack at 55, did smoking *cause* his death? We can never say for sure. We do know that it put him at higher *risk*. With SIDS, we know some of the *risk* factors. And we know that every "SIDS" case actually has a cause that we just can't find. The more we learn, the lower the SIDS rate will get, because only the unsolved mysteries will remain.

Sudden Unexpected Infant Death

There's no standard way to investigate a sudden infant death. Even when everything is carefully recorded and researched, it's sometimes impossible to separate out a baby who *stopped* breathing from a baby who *couldn't* breathe. So the line between the two can be blurred, even for the most rigorous scientists.

Because they recognized the difficulty in precisely defining these different types of infant deaths, medical groups and researchers began using the term "sudden *unexpected* infant death" (SUID) to record and report on a range of causes of infant death in the mid-1990s, blending SIDS, ASSB, poisoning, heart problems, and more into a single category. The "unknown" category includes deaths for which too little evidence was gathered to make a determination. Deaths from trauma, such as car accidents, are not included.

Lumping so much together may make information easier to record, but it makes it harder for mothers to know what is and isn't risky, which is why Ella, the mother at the chapter's beginning, is *sure* her bed is dangerous for her baby but doesn't know *why*.

This chapter helped you sort out the difference between breathing hazards and SIDS. As you'll see in the next chapter, that puts you well ahead of some of the researchers and campaigns that have made Ella so afraid.

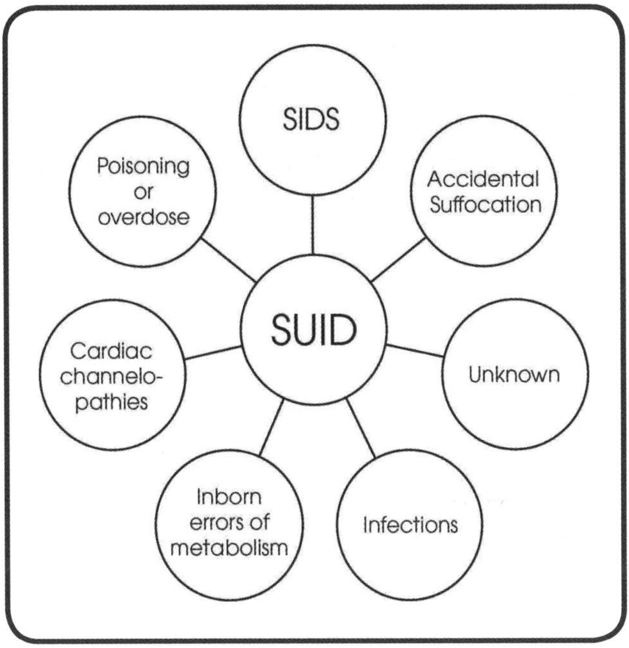

The U.S. Centers for Disease Control and Prevention categories of sudden unexpected infant death (SUID)

Something to Sleep On

At least three-quarters of SIDS deaths involve smoking, leaving the baby to sleep on his stomach to sleep, or formula-feeding.[58] Being left alone is another big one. Deaths due to ASSB (breathing hazards) can usually be avoided with the help of the Safe Surface checklist.

All of that makes the bedsharing risk for the Safe Sleep Seven baby *exceedingly* low. Some respected researchers are convinced that responsible bedsharing with breastfeeding will turn out to be the safest option of all. In part it's because breastfeeding—a life-saver and health promoter throughout their lives—lasts longer when mothers bedshare with their babies,[59] and many other health threats rise with early weaning. There are lots more things humans eventually die of besides SIDS, and early weaning increases the risk for many of those. Bedsharing is the lowest-stress arrangement for the vast majority of babies, and it's been the norm for as long as there have been mothers and babies.

Follow the Safe Sleep Seven and Safe Surface guidelines as much as you can, follow your head, and follow your heart. And the odds are *overwhelmingly* in your favour that the first thing you'll see in the morning is each other's beautiful face.

chapter 20

Bedsharing Controversies and Common Sense

When I brought Preston home from the hospital I was terrified of SIDS. The first few nights I mostly just sat on the sofa staring at him asleep in my arms. Once sleep deprivation kicked in, I tried putting him in a cradle next to my bed, but I couldn't sleep at all. I felt this strong desire to be close to Preston, but I didn't want to risk his life by bringing him into our bed.

So when he was five or six days old I started putting him in his car seat to sleep and I slept next to him on the floor. It just made sense for us to be next to each other.

After about four weeks, I read that keeping Preston in his car seat for an extended period of time could put him at risk for suffocation. There was lots of information telling me what I *shouldn't* do and not much telling me what I *should* do.

—Jillian

Most babies are pretty healthy. Policies designed to protect the health of a *few* babies should not be applied to *all* babies if harm can result. And that's what this whole chapter is about: the flaws in the research and logic surrounding infant sleep, the flawed policies that grew out of them, and the unnecessary fears and damage that have resulted.

> Advice that is given routinely about the care of *healthy* babies must have at least as strong an evidence base as the treatment of those babies who are *ill*, because healthy babies are far more common, and the potential for unsuspected harm is relatively great, a lesson already bitterly learned [when we told mothers to put babies face down] for infant sleeping position.[1]—P. J. Fleming et al. (emphasis added)

The risks of SIDS and overlying are *incredibly low* in Safe Sleep Seven mothers, because of their lifestyle, nighttime behaviours, and the surfaces on which they sleep. But you would never guess that by looking at the bedsharing warnings all around us. One billboard pictured a meat cleaver in bed with a baby, with the caption "Your baby sleeping with you can be just as dangerous."[2] Another showed a double-bed headboard made to look like a tombstone: "This could be your baby's final resting place."[3] A few small groups would even like to make bedsharing illegal so that they can prosecute parents if something happens to the baby.

Incredible.

If all that were supported by science, it might make sense. But it's not. And there are many reasons why bedsharing is important. When a young baby sleeps alone, he's more likely to be given formula,[4] which increases his risk not just of SIDS, but of a long list of other illnesses, both immediately and throughout his life.[5] His mother won't get as much sleep. As you read in Chapter 18, his risk of lifelong stress-related problems may rise. And he misses out on a full one-third of his normal daily contact with her.

Those are pretty compelling reasons to find ways to make bedsharing safe for breastfeeding mothers and babies. Because if you fit the Safe Sleep Seven criteria, *sleeping with your baby may be the healthiest arrangement of all.*

So why have the cautions got so out of hand? It's a combination of research problems and misunderstandings about how to apply the results of the research. Let's start with the research.

The Flawed Science of "Safe Sleep"

Good biological research studies follow certain rules. We'll look at some of the errors that have affected infant sleep research, and how they affect you. Then we'll describe an infant sleep study that avoided each error.

Study Flaw #1: The Wrong "Normal"

The scientific method, which all good biology research follows, uses normal as its starting point. For instance, a new drug or technique or approach has to be shown to be effective and low-risk. Normal doesn't have to be tested.

The Bedsharing Connection

Breastfeeding mothers and babies sharing sleep is a biologically normal behaviour. (Just watch other mammal mothers with their babies.) Formula-feeding and separate sleep are the *departures* from normal that need to be shown to be effective and safe, not the other way around.

In its report on SIDS and other sleep-related deaths, the American Academy of Pediatrics wrote, *"It is statistically much more difficult to demonstrate safety (i.e., no risk) in small subgroups. Breastfeeding mothers who do not smoke and have not consumed alcohol or arousal-altering medications or drugs are one such subgroup. . . . The task force, therefore, believes that there is insufficient evidence to recommend any bedsharing situation in the hospital or at home as safe."*[6]

> A 2012 study found that *"breastfeeding has been linked to impaired sleep consolidation"*.[7] Well, no. Breastfeeding is normal. Longer sleep at an early age is not normal.[8] Flawed view of normal→flawed conclusion.

But the "subgroup" they described—non-smoking, sober,

breast-feeding mothers—is normal! *It's supposed to be the starting point,* not the group that gets ignored. A report's *first* step in looking at infant deaths in adult beds should have been to figure out what's wrong with the beds, not what's wrong with the mothers.

Studies That Start with Normal

Dr. Kathleen Kendall-Tackett is among the researchers who are investigating what mothers actually do. Her studies support what anthropologists have always observed: around the world, mothers and babies tend to sleep together.

Study Flaw #2: Murky Definitions

Everything in a research study should be very clearly defined, and important categories should be kept very clear and very separate. Murky definitions lead to murky conclusions.

For instance, suppose we blurred the line between car crash deaths and poisoning. We'd be able to say things like "Of course, there are fewer poisonings in Newtown, but that's because they're more likely to wear their seat belts."

The Bedsharing Connection

Does the Newtown logic sound illogical? Here's a comment from a 2012 study: *"Bed-sharing has been suggested in the literature to increase the infant risk for SIDS due to the risks of overlaying or entrapment, wedging, falling or strangulation."*[9]

Not a single one of those risks has anything to do with SIDS (which is death from no known cause). They're all breathing hazards and are easily avoided in Safe Sleep Seven beds. SIDS is not the result of a breathing hazard, and deaths caused by breathing hazards are not SIDS deaths. Pretty basic stuff, but a *huge* number of studies and guidelines mix up the two and reach faulty conclusions. And the all-inclusive category of sudden unexpected infant death (SUID), described in the last chapter, not only combines SIDS and suffocation but throws in poisonings, infanticide, and more. Newtown logic for sure!

Here's a list of some "modifiable SIDS risk factors" from a U.S.

Researchers mixing up definitions in a study is like cooks mixing up eggs and chickens in a recipe. They could end up with an omelette or a chicken salad. Here's a sampling of the mixed-up definitions in published research studies:

• *Solitary sleep:* A baby alone in another room, *or* a baby in the same room but not in the same bed.

• *Co-sleeping:* A baby in the same room as another person, *or* a baby in a bed with someone, *or* a baby asleep with someone on a sofa or bed or beanbag chair or other risky shared sleep surface, *and* the person could be awake or asleep, drunk or sober, mother, other adult, or child.

• *Bedsharing:* A baby sharing a bed with his mother, *or* with someone else, *or* with a bunch of people, *or* a baby sharing a sofa or reclining chair or beanbag or anything else, with his mother, *or* with somebody else, *and* that person or people could be awake or asleep, drunk or sober, adult or child.

Please pass the omelette. But be sure to pluck it first. (For a list of Sweet Sleep definitions, see Chapter 2.)

Centers for Disease Control and Prevention manual for health care workers:

- Soft sleep surfaces
- Loose bedding
- Inappropriate sleep surfaces (such as a sofa or waterbed)
- Sharing the same sleep surface (such as a bed) with an individual other than a parent or sharing the same sleep surface with an individual who is overly tired or under the influence of alcohol or drugs.[10]

Once again, they've confused ASSB and SIDS risks. Adult use of alcohol or drugs can be a SIDS risk, probably from inattention. But when it involves a sleep surface, they're talking suffocation, not

When an infant death on a sofa is called a "bedsharing death", bedsharing gets a bad press. When an infant death in a reclining chair is called a "co-sleeping death", bedsharing gets a bad press. If SIDS occurs in an unsafe shared sleep setting, it's likely to be called a co-sleeping or bedsharing death anyway—yet another check mark in the baby-died-in-adult-bed column. When researchers include *all* kinds of people and *all* kinds of surfaces in their studies, and then tell *mothers* not to *bedshare*, they can send responsible mothers from low-risk beds to riskier places where there's a definite suffocation risk.[13] Once researchers and health professionals slide away from crisp, clear definitions in their warnings, the warnings themselves can be dangerous.

SIDS. Are you starting to see a pattern?

And this is from a study with "bedsharing" in the title: *"Any piece of furniture (bed, couch, sofa, or other) on which the parent and infant were sleeping was considered to be a bed for this analysis,"*[11] even though sofas aren't beds and half of all parents aren't mothers. And from a widely cited 2006 study,[12] *"Bed sharing was defined as a shared sleep surface consisting of either a bed or sofa."* In that study, ASSB deaths involving pillows, blankets, and other soft surfaces were also included in the SIDS figures. It's well known that sofas can be a major suffocation risk, but the words "smothering" and "suffocation" don't appear anywhere in the study.

The American Academy of Pediatrics offers this in its safe sleep recommendations: *"Cosleeping arrangements can include bed-sharing or sleeping in the same room in close proximity. Bed-sharing refers to a specific type of cosleeping when the infant is sleeping on the same surface with another person. Because the term cosleeping can be misconstrued and does not precisely describe sleep arrangements, the AAP recommends use of the terms 'room-sharing' and 'bed-sharing'."*[14] The trouble is, they've defined "room-sharing" but they still haven't defined bedsharing. So mothers are still likely to choose a risky surface because they're still afraid to bedshare.

We're now more than 40 years into researching SIDS, there's still no universally recognized definition for responsible bedsharing, and the number of inaccurate check marks in the bedsharing column keeps growing.

Studies That Use Clear Definitions

Four researchers who tend to use very clear definitions in their studies are Drs. Helen Ball in the United Kingdom, Nils Bergman in South Africa, and Kathleen Kendall-Tackett and James McKenna in the United States. Interestingly, their conclusions support the safety and normality of bedsharing.

Study Flaw #3: Missing Variables

The Furniture Factor

The American Academy of Pediatrics acknowledges that "*there are some cultures for which bed-sharing is the norm and SIDS rates are low, but there are other cultures for which bedsharing is the norm and SIDS rates are high. In general, the bed-sharing practiced in cultures with low SIDS rates is often different from that in the United States and other Western countries (e.g., with firm mats on the floor, separate mat for the infant, and/or absence of soft bedding).*"[15]

But these are differences in furniture, not differences in biology. Which means the issue is breathing hazards, not SIDS. There are guidelines for safe *baby* furniture. Why not for safe baby-*sharing* furniture? That's what our Safe Surface checklist in Chapter 2 is all about. The furniture factor is fixable. And it has nothing to do with SIDS.

A variable is any factor that could affect the results of a study. If you're looking at breast cancer rates, obviously you would consider gender an important variable. Studies that don't take every likely variable into account may miss important connections.

That's one of the reasons scientists like to see lots of different studies done by lots of different people using lots of different approaches and getting similar results. It's an indication that nothing important got overlooked. Because once an error like that gets into the research literature, it can echo for years.

The Bedsharing Connection

In 2010, a Fox News station in Milwaukee, Wisconsin, reported on the confusing definitions and missing variables in Milwaukee County's recent publicity campaign against all bedsharing (sidebar below). The reporter learned that *all* the past year's Milwaukee "bedsharing deaths" involved adult alcohol use, a baby on a pillow, chaotic and substandard living conditions, and/or smoking. And every one of the deaths involved a formula-fed baby.

> **You Have To See This Video**
>
> The video at goo.gl/9arQAT covers the whole bedsharing controversy in a nutshell, and includes an interview with Dr. James McKenna.

A Study That Sorted Out Known Variables

A 2009 study by public health officials in Alaska did its best to tease apart known risk factors and look at each of them separately.[16] These authors studied five well-documented risks in 126 infants who died while bedsharing:

1. Face down position
2. Sleeping with someone other than the mother
3. Maternal tobacco use
4. Impaired bed partner
5. Sofa or waterbed

They found that 99 per cent of the bedsharing babies who died had at least one risk factor. It wasn't the bedsharing. It was the condition of the adult and the safety of the surface.

Study Flaw #4: Inconsistent Data Collection

A good study relies on accurate and consistent data collection. Easy enough when you're counting website hits, but much harder when people's behaviours are involved.

Consider three possible witness accounts of the same crime: "I was in the store. I saw him pull out a gun and point it at her." "I didn't see a gun. I think he was pulling out his wallet to pay her." "I don't think it was him at all. He's too tall." Taking careful note of a situation takes skill, practice, training, and objectivity.

When a study involves real situations, it can be hard to measure all the important variables at all the right times. Is information being recorded consistently? Does it include all the known variables? How accurate are participants' responses?

The Bedsharing Connection

Gathering information at a death scene is always complicated, and research conclusions are only as good as the data collected. In the United States, some states require that the person who investigates an infant death be a doctor with specialized training. Some just require that it be a doctor. Other states don't require any special degree or training at all. The U.S. Centers for Disease Control and Prevention has a death scene report form, but its use isn't required everywhere, and bedsharing isn't clearly defined.[17]

Adult alcohol consumption is a known risk factor for sleep-related infant death.[18] Yet an often-cited 2005 study explained, *"We did not collect data on alcohol consumption as our previous experience had demonstrated the difficulty of obtaining accurate information."*[19] They ignored a key variable for both SIDS and suffocation data, and drew questionable conclusions as a result.

Some examiners record how the baby was fed and whether a dummy was used, while others don't. Some examiners ask about household smoking, and some don't. Many investigators record sofa deaths and pillow deaths as bedsharing deaths. Sometimes information given by the adults involved isn't accurate. In one case, the investigator was urged to run a toxicology screen on the baby—something he didn't do routinely—and found evidence of a drug overdose.[20] In the end, death scene investigators with a huge range of approaches, definitions, levels of accuracy and detail, and training provide the data for the "never bedshare" studies.

A Study with Consistent Data Collection

Instead of relying on information from families that had lost a baby or investigators' reports of those deaths, researchers in a 2012 study interviewed ordinary families in two very different populations in the same city—white British families, and South Asian families with a SIDS rate that was only one-quarter as high. The investigators asked about the families' accustomed infant sleep positions and locations (distinguishing clearly between bedsharing and sofa-sharing), household smoking and alcohol use, feeding method (including formula and solid foods), dummy use, and swaddling.[21]

They found that *"South Asian infant care practices were more likely to protect infants from the most important SIDS risks such as smoking, alcohol consumption, sofa-sharing and solitary sleep. These differences may explain the lower rate of SIDS in this population."* The South Asian population, with its much lower SIDS risk, was somewhat more likely to breastfeed than the white British population . . . and was more than three and a half times as likely to bedshare regularly.

Study Flaw #5: Personal Opinions and Assumptions

Researchers have to work hard to keep biases and assumptions out of their conclusions. It's not always easy to do. One witness in the store sees a gun, another witness sees a wallet, and a third sees something completely different. It's not just how well trained they are in observing a scene. Part of it is the experiences, beliefs, and biases they bring to the scene in the first place.

The Bedsharing Connection

Researchers can be so sure of the reason for an outcome that they go looking for data that support it—an approach sometimes called "ideology in search of data". That may be what happened in this 2005 study: *"Of 46 SIDS infants who bedshared during their last sleep, 40 (87 percent) were found in the parents' bed, two in a cot, three in a baby basket, and one not known."*[22] In other words, some of the babies in the bedsharing column actually died in a cot or basket or even in a place that wasn't recorded. The study assumed that *having been* in a parent's bed at any time that night (or the preceding 24 hours; it's hard to tell) makes it more likely that a baby will die *later,* wherever he is. That's sort of like calling it a changing table death if the baby had a nappy change before being put in a cot.

Death scene investigators, rescue teams, health service staff, parents—they all bring their personal background to an infant death. Sometimes they overlook things that they believe couldn't be relevant, or that they may have done as parents themselves. Sometimes they assume that the baby's death was caused by a parent sleeping with the baby and don't question further: "Bed, sofa, what does it matter? It's sleeping with the baby that did it."

Death in a cot is often assumed to be SIDS at first, unless there's some other obvious explanation, and death when a baby is in contact with another human is often assumed to be a bedsharing or overlying death until proven otherwise. Both assumptions have distorted what many believe about bedsharing, SIDS, and suffocation.

Studies That Avoid Personal Biases

One way around the problem of personal bias is to work with populations rather than individual death scenes. The study of South Asian and white British families that was described above collected data on behaviour patterns and previously established SIDS rates. The *typical* settings and parenting behaviours of each population were investigated. It's harder for personal biases to creep in when the study doesn't involve questioning the parents of each baby who died.

Study Flaw #6: Financial Influence

Would you trust the results of a lung cancer study that received money from the tobacco industry? Money talks.[23] Friendships talk.[24] Industries and other special interest groups all know this. Research shows that even the smallest gift—a pen or a pizza—can make a difference.[25] Marketing to health care providers is a *multibillion-dollar* industry, because it works.[26] Researchers, consumer groups, policy makers, and even research journals can all be influenced. For a fascinating (and alarming) look at how advertising spend can influence health care, see nofreelunch.org.

The Bedsharing Connection

Research funds are hard to come by, and many institutions and individuals are grateful for commercial support. But even doctors and researchers who are *sure* they're not being influenced by their funding sources and relationships . . . are. One example is the tobacco-SIDS connection. An American tobacco company funded a review of the SIDS literature, with a focus on smoking.[27] The researchers found that second-hand smoke was a significant risk factor. But after discussion with the company, they downgraded the strength of their findings. Within five years, the compromised study was cited at least 19 times in the medical literature.[28] In one Safe Sleep brochure, smoking—one of the biggest risk factors for SIDS—is listed under "other important tips."[29] This is despite other studies showing that even secondhand smoke increases the risk of SIDS.[30]

Some Safe Sleep organizations have formula companies and baby equipment manufacturers listed among their contributors. One Safe Sleep brochure suggests, *"If possible, give your baby only breast milk for at least the first six months"*.[31] No other risk-reducing measure, even avoiding tobacco, begins with the weakening phrase "if possible". Breastfeeding is at the end of the brochure, along with those "other important tips", and there's no mention of formula-feeding as a risk.

And here's one that blew us away: at the time of this writing, the website[32] for the American Academy of Pediatrics' 2011 report on SIDS and other sleep-related infant deaths[33] displays, as one of a rotating series of banner ads, an ad for *formula,* which is a major SIDS risk factor! The report itself *does* recommend breastfeeding as a way to reduce SIDS,[34] *but nowhere does it name artificial feeding as a risk.* But then, calling formula-feeding a SIDS risk would have looked pretty awkward under a formula ad. In fact, we didn't find *any* AAP literature that links formula-feeding to health risk problems.

And here's a question. Which is more likely to raise research funding: studying something that affects a very small group of babies or studying something that's presented as a big risk to all babies?

Studies Without Financial Bias

This one's tough. We live in a world with limited money for research and publication. And it's a world with plenty of commercial interests that want to have a hand in shaping the studies that shape the policies, and in which commercial involvement can be difficult to trace.

Study Flaw #7: Generalizing

A solid study limits its findings and recommendations to the group it was researching; it doesn't apply the results of one study to a different group. "Standing here on my farm, I see that one in four vehicles going by is a pickup truck. That must mean that a quarter of all vehicles are pickup trucks." The problem with that mini-study? The researcher's data from country roads may not apply in an urban setting. It's a mistake to generalize beyond what's actually investigated.

The Bedsharing Connection

A dummy is a substitute for sucking at the breast. The American Academy of Pediatrics suggests that all parents have their babies sleep separately and consider using a dummy at sleep times because "several studies have found a protective effect of dummies on the incidence of SIDS".[35]

Here's what the studies actually found: some babies who *routinely* use dummies and sleep separately seem to be at a greater risk of dying on a night when there's no dummy available and they're sleeping separately.[36] This could make some sense. For a vulnerable baby who is used to soothing and stimulating himself by sucking, being without a dummy might be stressful and even interfere with arousal. But it doesn't make sense to apply the results of these dummy studies to babies who *don't* use them, or who breastfeed off and on throughout the night while bedsharing.

And here's the surprising result: one study found that the average time a dummy stays in a baby's mouth at night is only half an hour.[37] Another found it to be a mere 11 minutes, with three-quarters of the dummy episodes lasting less than 15 minutes and only 3 per cent lasting for more than an hour.[38] Yet the AAP doesn't suggest putting the dummy back in the baby's mouth when it falls out. Why would a baby's last bedtime feed need immediate follow-up sucking? How would having a dummy for a brief time at bedtime protect against SIDS at four in the morning?

Babies who use dummies are less likely to use their own fingers for comfort,[39] so the baby who needs sucking but loses the dummy is left with nothing at all. It's been proposed that sucking helps regulate breathing or arousal.[40] Could it be that those few babies who keep a dummy in their mouth throughout the night are the only ones who are at risk without it?

Dummies have been linked to breastfeeding problems, including premature weaning (see Chapter 12), though the reason for the connection isn't clear. But solid research has to show that the presumed benefit outweighs the known risk, and it hasn't done that. At the time of writing, no research has shown that offering a dummy to *all* babies is safe and effective just because *some* babies who sleep alone may be helped by them.

Study Results That Don't Exceed the Data

A good example of a study that does not overgeneralize is one in which researchers observed sleeping breastfed babies in a lab with infrared cameras. They studied the babies for two nights in a row once a month, for their first five months. On one night in the lab, the babies were in a room alone; on the other night they bedshared. On separate-sleep nights they spent more time in the deeper sleep stages that may be harder to rouse from, with longer periods of sleep apnoea (not breathing) than bedsharers had.[41] No policy implications, no attempt to generalize to other situations, just a tight study with clear parameters on which future studies can build. It counted pickup trucks and reported the numbers. It's simply a building block, and it's simply based on normal.

Study Flaw #8: The Wrong Kind of Study

Two common types of scientific studies could be called "looking-back" (*retrospective*) studies and "looking-forward" (*prospective*) studies.

Retrospective studies are observations or descriptions of what has already happened: "Hmmm. I see that the children in pink jackets tend to have longer hair. I wonder if wearing a pink jacket results in longer hair." A retrospective study can help determine what *questions* a study might ask.

Prospective studies can *test* those questions: "Hmmm. I gave some children pink jackets and I gave some blue jackets. There's been no increase in hair length after a year *just because* a child was wearing a pink jacket. I'll have to rethink my original hunch."

Both types of studies are valuable. But a study that gathers data in order to *identify* a question can't also *answer* that question. In the pink jacket example, the observer's hunch fitted the data collected . . . but the conclusion was wrong.

The Bedsharing Connection

If a condition is as rare as SIDS, it's really hard and really expensive to do good prospective (answer-the-question) research. The fewer people there are in a study, the less reliable the results are. If we followed 10,000 babies for a year, we could expect to see and be able to study four or five SIDS deaths. Each death is hugely tragic for that baby's family, but those numbers are far too small for drawing any conclusions.

As a result, most safe-sleep studies are retrospective and look at deaths that have already occurred. They're the kind of study that comes up with good questions, not good answers. Researchers have received some good information from them. But they've also made some errors.

A meta-analysis combines the results from a number of smaller studies into one larger study, in order to have bigger numbers to work from. The trouble is, a meta-analysis is only as good as the studies it combines. A flawed 2013 meta-analysis of five studies found bedsharing to be risky,[42] but one of the five studies was the study discussed above that didn't look at alcohol and included some cot and Moses basket deaths in the bedsharing column.[43] (See goo.gl/nP2c4f for more of the concerns.) Flawed conclusions can echo for years this way. When we're stuck having to sort good conclusions from flawed ones, and clear definitions from murky ones, one of the best lights along our path is just plain common sense.

Study Flaw #9: Lack of Plausibility

Research needs to make logical sense. If an outcome just doesn't sound logical, the first step is to see if there's an error in the study itself.

The Bedsharing Connection

No one has ever offered a reason why a mother's body being a few inches from her baby could cause a baby to die of SIDS. Rolling over on a baby is *suffocation,* not SIDS. And suffocation and other breathing hazards are extremely unlikely when the Safe Sleep Seven are in place. The conclusion that bedsharing is dangerous for *all* mothers and babies just doesn't make any logical or biological sense.

Some More Plausible Research Conclusions

Studies like Ball's, Bergman's, Kendall-Tackett's, and McKenna's that have looked at sleep and behaviour patterns in breastfeeding mothers and babies (see Chapter 4) are among the best on maternal-infant sleep behaviours. Their studies, from 1990 to the present, have found universal patterns of behaviour and universal physiological responses in normal breastfeeding mothers and their normal babies, and they have found no evidence that normal is risky.

Policy Problems

The second part of the bedsharing controversy comes from public policies. They're supposed to be based on research, of course, and we've already seen some of the research flaws. But policy making has its own potential for problems. Here are some of them.

Policy Problem #1: Using the Wrong Kind of Study

As we saw above, retrospective observations are a good starting point for research. But they're not a basis for responsible policies.[44] Policies that rest on hunches rather than solid evidence can steer people dangerously wrong. The confident "always put babies on their stomachs" recommendation from the past is a good example.

A Change for the Better: Start with Clear, Solid Evidence

Cautious suggestions are often made before there's strong research support. But an emphatic "always/never" approach to infant sleep isn't appropriate without really strong data. Campaigns that encourage parents to put separate-sleeping babies on their backs have a strong evidence base at this point. The no-bedsharing campaigns don't.

Policy Problem #2: Using Emotion Instead of Research

Everyone likes stories. They draw us in and we remember them. We process stories more easily than we process facts and figures.[45] But emotion can keep us from thinking rationally.

On September 11, 2001, nearly 3,000 people died in the United States as a result of four terrorist-caused plane crashes. In the months following 9/11, travel fatalities *rose*![46] The reason? It seems that many people were afraid to fly and so they drove instead. But cars are not as safe as planes, even though plane crashes—especially the ones of 9/11—are much more dramatic and newsworthy, and create powerful, emotional stories.

"My baby died in the . . . It was right after we . . . She was the centre of our lives. We even . . ." Stories also seem to offer an automatic solution: just don't do what that person did, and all will be well. Every SIDS and ASSB story describes a terrible tragedy, but the power of stories doesn't change the reality of the statistics.[47] *SIDS is extremely rare in Safe Sleep Seven families, and ASSB risks can be virtually eliminated with a responsibly prepared bed.* Powerful stories shouldn't be used to sell a weak public policy. (And we just have to say: That US public health campaign showing the baby in bed with the butcher knife? The fluffy bedding would be a much bigger problem than the mother. And the baby himself was at an age where SIDS and bedsharing was not an issue anyway. Emotion over facts!)

A Change for the Better: Stick to the Facts

Policy makers need to pay attention to all three of the circles in the previous chapter's diagrams, do the maths, and listen to the numbers, not the stories. Exaggerated threat messages—meat cleavers in the bed, headboards as tombstones—can backfire in unexpected and negative ways. *Bedsharing without other risks is not a risk factor for SIDS.* It doesn't have to be a risk factor for breathing hazards either.

Policy Problem #3: Making Unrealistic Recommendations

A responsible public policy has to be *doable.*[48] It has to fit human nature, or it won't work. Most breastfeeding mothers sleep with their babies at least some of the time.[49] They always have. It just makes nights easier. There's little chance of changing their behaviour with an unrealistic, no-exceptions recommendation. And sure enough, campaigns to stop it haven't been very effective.[50] In fact, the number of bedsharing women is climbing, in spite of the no-bedsharing campaigns.[51]

A few pamphlets speak to the realities of breastfeeding mothers and babies. They describe the all-important cuddle curl position and give information on making the bed safe, while warning against smoking, awareness-altering substances, and unsafe shared sleep surfaces. The Uppity Science Chick handout (goo.gl/P5TKhf) is an example of well-thought-out guidelines for bedsharing by breastfeeding mothers.

A Change for the Better: Don't Recommend What You Can't Get

According to Dr. Helen Ball, when mothers become too overwhelmed or exhausted by getting out of bed to breastfeed, they *"generally pursue one of three options: (1) feed the baby formula (or formula plus some 'heavy' indigestible substance, such as cereal or baby rice) so that he or she does not require frequent (or any) night feeding; (2) undertake an 'infant-training' program . . . ; or (3) sleep next to the baby, allowing easy access to breasts, and eliminating the need for either mother or baby to wake fully for breastfeeds."*[52]

For all kinds of excellent, research-based reasons, health authorities around the world say that breastfeeding needs to be promoted, protected, and supported. Since breastfeeding mothers tend to bedshare, and bedsharing mothers tend to breastfeed,[53] one of the best ways to promote breastfeeding is just to help mothers do what they naturally do . . . safely.

Policy Problem #4: Lumping

Public policy can change a simple practice fairly easily. Putting a baby to sleep on her back takes a single, stress-free moment to do, and it has clearly saved lives, though we still don't know if it's important for babies outside the diagram's "vulnerable baby" circle or for bedsharing babies. "Back to Sleep", "Back Is Best", "This Side Up"—they've all been *dramatically* successful.

But creating a simple message like that for a specific high-risk population and then saying that it applies to everyone is a mistake. For example, we know that some drivers don't wear a seat belt. Some drink and drive. Some speed. Some won't put the baby in a car seat. Now imagine this public policy campaign: "*Because of the potential harm to babies from unsafe drivers,* no one *is allowed to drive with a baby in the car.*"

Most parents would still drive with the baby in the car sometimes, even though they'd feel guilty about it. But safe car seats wouldn't be manufactured because babies weren't supposed to be in cars. So now, because safe and unsafe drivers were lumped together in a single policy, most babies would be at even greater risk than before.

When it comes to bedsharing policies, policy makers settled on a simple, clear statement: "All *mothers should stay away from their babies during sleep. In your room, but not on your bed.*" The trouble is, all mothers are not alike, just as all drivers are not alike. Simple statements can cast such a broad net that it catches the majority for whom bedsharing may be *lower*-risk than separate sleep because it stimulates the baby, protects breastfeeding, and keeps mothers from falling asleep in truly risky places.

A Change for the Better: Tailor the Message to the Mother

As one research study points out, "*Bed-sharing subjects who breastfed had a risk profile distinct from those who were not breastfed cases. Risk and situational profiles can be used to identify families in greater need of early guidance and to prepare educational content to promote safe sleep.*"[54]

Policy Problem #5: Financial Persuasion and Personal Bias

SIDS committees and support organizations sometimes receive support from formula companies and other industries with an interest in policy making. Just as with researchers, conclusions can be distorted when commercial interests weigh in.

Parents of SIDS victims are part of the committees and organizations as well. It can be almost impossible to see SIDS risk as "vanishingly small" for some babies when the risk was 100 per cent for your own. Many excellent public safety campaigns—Mothers Against Drunk Driving, for example—have been initiated or promoted by grieving families. But it's important to keep private emotions separate from public policy.

A Change for the Better

It gets back to "stick to the facts". That can be tough to do when your funding sources or your committee members have a commercial or emotional interest in the campaign. It's tough to do when your own child died and you desperately want to protect other babies. A Safe Sleep campaign needs to be vigilant in keeping bias from affecting its recommendations.

Policy Problem #6: TLI (Too Little Information)

One Safe Sleep brochure from a U.S. government source says, *"Your baby should not sleep in an adult bed, on a couch, or on a chair alone, with you, or with anyone else. Room sharing—keeping baby's sleep area in the same room where you sleep—reduces the risk of SIDS and other sleep-related causes of infant death."*[55] It's like going to a completely grass-covered park where the signs say *"Keep off the grass. Walk somewhere else instead."* Where, exactly, *are* tired mothers supposed to go to breastfeed at night when they're likely to fall asleep breastfeeding? The Safe Sleep campaigns don't say, and you can see how Jillian, at this chapter's beginning, increased her own anxiety and her baby's risk just trying to do the right thing. We take much better care of ourselves and do it with more confidence when we have more information about our options.

A Change for the Better: Explain the Issues and Options

As one research study author points out, *"Risk-free and single-risk SIDS cases are rare, and most contain multiple risks. Parent education should be comprehensive and address compensatory strategies for non-modifiable risks [risks that can't be changed]."*[56]

Mothers need to have a clear explanation of SIDS and ASSB (breathing hazard) risks. They need different recommendations based on their different lives. They need and deserve an explanation and education campaign—full information about their options—not alarmist threat messages.

The Academy of Breastfeeding Medicine is an international group of doctors who are "dedicated to the promotion, protection, and support of breastfeeding and human lactation". Its Clinical Protocol #6: Guideline on Co-Sleeping and Breastfeeding (bfmed.org/Media/Files/Protocols/Protocol_6.pdf) could be a model for policy makers. One of the important statements in the protocol is simply, *"Parents should be educated about risks and benefits of co-sleeping and unsafe co-sleeping practices and should be allowed to make their own informed decision."*[57]

Parents are empowered, not frightened, when they're given clear information about their choices. Campaigns based on full information can open doors for communication. Policies based on prohibitions close them.

Policy Problem #7: Not Balancing Value and Risk

In the United States, more than 30,000 people are killed on the roads every year.[58] That's more than ten times the number of SIDS deaths each year. An entire small city's worth of people are killed in car accidents each year.

We know how to eliminate every one of those road deaths: just eliminate cars. Too drastic? Well, suppose we dropped the national speed limit to 20 miles per hour, and drivers and passengers wore helmets and used harnesses like the ones racing car drivers have? Still too drastic? One study found that even a return to the 55 mph speed limit of the 1970s would save more than 1,000 lives a year.[59] But our culture believes that the benefits of convenience and speed are worth 30,000 lives every year. So we let it go at that.

Roller coasters? Now that's another story. Nobody *needs* to ride a roller coaster. So we believe that *no one* should ever have to die on one. A single roller coaster fatality makes the news (the power of stories again), the ride is closed, and the improvements are made before anyone else can use it. It's very simple to make a strict, no-exceptions policy about something that doesn't really matter and isn't going to change anyone's daily life—how tall you have to be to ride the roller coaster, for instance. Anyone who objects can always ride on the merry-go-round.

It's quite another story to try to alter a behaviour that's really valuable to a whole lot of people. Big picture policies need to make sense, be clearly defined, and be doable if they're going to work.

A Change for the Better: Write the Policy and Recommendations as if Breastfeeding Is Really Important—Because It Is

The Academy of Breastfeeding Medicine's Clinical Protocol #6: Guideline on Co-Sleeping and Breastfeeding says, "*Because breastfeeding is the best form of nutrient for infants, any recommendations for infant care that impede its initiation or duration need to be carefully weighed against the many known benefits to infants, their mothers, and society. . . . There is currently not enough evidence to support routine recommendations against co-sleeping.*"[60]

To change from bedsharing to putting a baby in a cot is truly life-altering for a Safe Sleep Seven mother and baby, and is not a change for the better.

Bedsharing Research Video Clips You Might Enjoy

A 2008 lecture by Dr. Helen Ball at the National Childbirth Trust Conference: goo.gl/f4vePY

A 2013 interview with Dr. James McKenna on "Cosleeping: Public Policy, Science and Parents Civil Rights": goo.gl/Ma2a6j

A 2012 interview with Dr. Mayim Bialik on "Myths and Truths about Co-Sleeping": goo.gl/hrBo0H

Putting It All Together

Good research starts with normal and uses clear, consistent definitions and procedures to study what isn't normal. Its data collectors are uniformly trained. The research tries to take account of any variables that might affect the outcome. Those who conduct and publish the studies avoid personal and funding-related biases. Policy makers use the results without relying on exaggeration, generalization, or scare tactics to get the point across. They lay out the consequences of each option so that people can make informed decisions about what will work in their own situation.

None of this has happened so far in the more prominent Safe Sleep campaigns.

Something to Sleep On

We hope this chapter reassures you that the "never-bedshare" warnings are based largely on inadequate and inconsistent research, translated into emotion-rich, information-poor public policy. We hope it can encourage some policy makers to take another look at the *quality* of the research behind their statements.

Whether or not you decide to bedshare, once or always, is up to you. But if you are a Safe Sleep Seven mother, you should have the full support of your community, as if breastfeeding really matters. Because it does.

> We . . . believe that we are justified in urging professionals to be cautious about issuing warnings to parents regarding bedsharing. There is at present no evidence linking this practice, when engaged in responsibly, with any sort of problematic outcome. We question the assumption that solitary sleep is safer and more beneficial to children's well-being. Rather than issuing warnings to parents about bedsharing practices, our empirical evidence and review suggest that a conversation with parents about the meanings and contexts of bedsharing—its advantages and disadvantages as parents see them—would be far more helpful.[61]
> —Paul Okami, PhD, Thomas Weisner, PhD, and Richard Omstead, PhD

LA LECHE LEAGUE
WOMANLY ART

part six

Help

chapter 21

Defusing Criticism

> As an American mother living in Russia, my child-rearing abilities were constantly under surveillance by the "grandmother police". Perfect strangers would walk up and describe everything I was doing wrong. Clearly, they thought I was incompetent. By the time my second child was born, I learned to say the following phrase in Russian: "I'm a bad mother, there's nothing you can do about it." This stopped them in their tracks and ended these unwelcome lectures from complete strangers.
>
> —Theresa

Overheard at a La Leche League meeting: *"I'm here because we're going to my parents' for the weekend. I need some reinforcement from other breastfeeding mothers."*

In a different culture or a different time in history, nobody would think twice about you breastfeeding and having your baby in your bed, because that's what most mothers would have done. Today, you may be totally confident about the breastfeeding part—after all, it has official support now. But if you use a bedside cot or even just have your baby in your room, you're probably going against what your mother did. And if you bedshare, you may be going against public policy as well.

All Kinds of Criticisms, All Kinds of Critics

Every mother everywhere has always had *someone* who doesn't like *something* she's doing. Mothers and mothers-in-law, sisters and friends, doctors, midwives and even strangers have probably been giving you advice or questioning your choices from the moment your pregnancy test strip turned blue. But most people are just trying to help. Here are some comments you might hear and ideas about how to respond.

They're Just Making Conversation

Maybe the person you're talking to is just asking an innocent question. After all, it's hard to know what to ask about a new baby, especially if you've never had one before. "Has he read any good books lately?" doesn't work. When you get simple and straightforward questions, all you need to give are simple and straightforward answers. Or no answers at all, and maybe a dash of humour. We tend to get defensive and overdo it when we're braced for disapproval.

They Feel Rejected

All parents want to feel they did a good job, and they want their children to think so too. When you do something differently, they may feel that you're saying they did it wrong. Nobody likes that feeling.

We all do the best we can with the information that we have at the time. Maybe you can acknowledge how you appreciate the way they parented and still respond to their concerns: "I'm glad you brought me up to be open to new ideas. That's how I learned about ways to make bedsharing safe, and it's certainly working out well for us. Thanks for being such a good mum—and such a wonderful grandma."

They're Worried About the Dangers

The "danger of bedsharing" is a pretty widespread message these days, and your friends and families may have heard about it. What they haven't heard about is the Safe Sleep Seven.

First, it helps to acknowledge that you understand what they're saying—bedsharing *can* be dangerous, for certain babies, certain families, and certain beds. But then you can reassure them that you've done your homework and you've learned that the risks are the lowest for families *like yours.* We have several handouts and an infographic in the Tearsheet Toolkit that can help explain the specifics.

They're Worried That Bedsharing Teaches Bad Sleep Habits

When people say sleep *habits,* they're often talking about sleep *physiology.* Sleep physiology is wired in and changes in its own good time. Little ones who share their mother's bed tend not to have the same bedtime "issues" that beleaguer so many families today. They may not want to settle down—what child does?—but they don't fear their sleeping space. The child who feels more secure usually sleeps more soundly. And *that's* a sleep habit worth cultivating!

They Just Don't Approve

Their disapproval is often voiced as "You'll never get him out of your bed." What it actually shows is a lack of understanding of normal child development.

We adults like to sleep near someone else, and of course children do too. One way to respond to this kind of comment is to say, "Sometimes I wish that were true—that he'd stay little forever. But I know that he'll grow up and eventually want his own space."

They're Worried That Bedsharing Will Make Him Spoiled, Clingy, or Neurotic

As you know from earlier chapters, the opposite is true. But how do you convince them of that? A great approach is to share your enthusiasm about the new information. "I thought so too, but there's some really good new research coming out."

If playing the research card doesn't work, you might ask for stories about their own routines with their children . . . or point out that William Shakespeare almost certainly slept with his parents.

They're Worried That Bedsharing Will Make Him Gay

A growing body of research indicates that sexual orientation is built-in from the start and isn't changed by experiences, upbringing, or culture.[1] Sharing sleep won't make a child gay or straight. Or blond or brunette, for that matter. Sharing sleep with a loving parent *can* make a child more self-confident, happier, and better able to make friends.[2]

They're Worried About Incest

Some cultures don't understand the difference between sensual and sexual. Sensual experiences include things like a warm blanket on a cold night, eating chocolate mousse, smelling fresh laundry, and anything else that makes you smile and say, "Mmmm . . ."

A lot of us miss those warm, snuggly, cuddly bodies when they decide to leave for good. But bedsharing doesn't lead to inappropriate or criminal behaviour. Deviant behaviour comes from deviant people, and they don't need a bed to commit a crime.

They're Worried That It Will Harm Your Marriage

Having children can be stressful for any relationship. At least bedsharing can take some of the stress out of the nights.

Having your baby in your bed doesn't have to mean missing out on affection and intimacy. You probably don't want to get into a discussion of your sex life with other people, but you can always try Nakita's response:

> My family tells me that if we don't move him out of our bed, we'll never be able to make another baby. I've just started telling them, "Well, we didn't make our first baby in a bed, so I don't see why we would need to make the other ones there." That usually makes them uncomfortable enough that they stop discussing our sleeping arrangements.
>
> —Nakita

If someone is concerned about your baby being exposed to sex, you can offer reassurance that you and your partner are enjoying discovering all the options outside your bedroom.

> I just got the typical comment, "You should be in bed with your *husband*." To which I replied, "I am!"
>
> —Amy

They Think You Should Sleep-Train Your Baby

They may feel it worked well for them or that it's important to do. They may believe that your child is "too old" to be waking up. Some neutral possibilities: "Thanks for suggesting that. I'll look into it if we decide to make a change" or "I'm glad that worked for you and Jack, but children are all so different. This is working well for us right now."

Criticism Response Techniques

There are some basic "defusing" approaches that may help you respond in a whole range of situations.

The RRID Response

A basic response for defusing any kind of criticism from any kind of person is to get RRID of it:

Respect
Reflect
Inspect
Deflect

Respect

It never hurts to begin a discussion with *an expression of respect*. Even a simple statement like "I know you only want the best for me" is a respectful opening. The problem is that a sentence like that is often followed with "but," as in, "I know you only want the best for me, but I'm still not going to listen to you." That "but" changes the whole meaning. So "watch your buts" in your opening comments.

To your mother-in-law you might say, "I'm so glad that you're here, helping out." To a health professional or doctor you might say, "You're always so flexible. I really appreciate it." If the conversation begins well, it stands a better chance of ending well. (And pointing out positive behaviours can help strengthen or even create them. Everyone likes praise. Praise your mother-in-law for something—anything—good that she does and she's likely to do more of it.)

Reflect

Reflective listening means repeating or summarizing what was said to you, using slightly different words. "I didn't do it that way" could be met with "You're right. I hadn't thought about how upsetting it could feel when I do it differently." If you get the level of intensity or the tone or reason wrong, the other person will correct it: "No, it doesn't upset me at all. I just don't understand why you'd do it that way." Or the other person might respond, "It *does* upset me. I feel as if you think I didn't bring you up well." Now you've homed in on what the person is really saying and feeling, without the distraction of your own opinions or feelings.

In sending back a response that mirrors what you think the other person is saying, and listening to the response, you show that you're both hearing and understanding what's being said. Feeling understood is fundamental to feeling accepted. And feeling accepted makes it easier to accept in return. If other people think you "get" them, they're more likely to want to "get" you too.

Some of the best reflective responses begin with the pronoun "I." Starting a sentence with "You did (that)" is likely to be met immediately with "I did not!" Starting a sentence with "I (feel bothered by/bad when/discouraged if)" focuses on how you feel rather than pointing a finger. (Keep the focus on *your* feelings—saying "I feel upset because you're such an idiot" won't help.)

Inspect

When someone questions your approach to child rearing—or to anything, really—it helps to *inspect* the underlying issues rather than just pushing back. This is the meat of the conversation, still relying on respect and reflective listening. What exactly is the other person's concern? What's his or her information base?

You can be reassuring, serious, humble, flip, or a hundred other combinations that match the personalities and situation. The point is to hear the other person out, and then to make sure that you get heard, so information and concern can flow both ways—respectfully. You may be able to share your perspective less threateningly if it seems like it's something that you're both discovering together. You might say, "I just read that . . . ," as if the information was as new to you as it is to your critic.

If the other person just wants to blow off steam, a simple "Mmmm" may be all you need. Your critic may just need to see that you're mothering responsibly. Mix respect and small bits of information and over time you might even win a supporter.

> I always said, "I imagine a fox in a den, or a cat with a litter of kittens, or a cavewoman with her baby. I imagine the mother creating a separate place for her babies to sleep, away from her, in another room or den or part of the cave, ignoring their cries, getting up to go feed them, and leaving them crying to go back to sleep alone. And then I think, does that make any sense?" This worked with some of my sceptical relatives.
>
> —Catherine

Deflect

There's a fair chance you and your critic may just have to agree to disagree and avoid the subject in the future. Changing someone else's mind is usually slow work, requiring several conversations over a period of time. When you feel you've both talked it through enough, you can end the discussion by *deflecting the conversation,* turning it in a different direction.

For instance, you might ask them what *they* did. People love to talk about their own experiences. Once they've talked themselves out, you can change the subject.

Or you can help them see it from the child's perspective: "Do you ever remember getting into bed with your parents? Aren't those the best memories?"

Or reassure them that if what you're doing now stops working, you'll reconsider.

Or side with them in a vague way: "We're working on it, but we're taking it slowly."

> I think people end up bedsharing when they don't even know that's what they're doing. My in-laws didn't think it was a good idea to bedshare and were concerned about the safety of the baby. As I talked with them, though, I realized that they hadn't slept apart from their own children. My husband and his brother slept in the same room as their parents until they were four and seven! My in-laws are always telling us about how they'd all end up in the same bed. My own boys are now comfortable spending the night at their grandparents' house, where they too often end up sleeping with Grandma and Grandpa in the big king-size bed.
>
> —Lillian

Should you push back against criticism? It depends. In some cultures, pushing back shows backbone and earns respect, but in others it can escalate a discussion into an argument. You know what works best in your family.

And sometimes the best deflection is simply, "So, how about some lunch?"

Teachable Moments

There may be moments when you sense that the door has cracked open briefly and your critic would be willing to listen. It's called a *teachable moment*. Teachable moments don't last long, so go for small bits of clear transmission through the usual static. Be gentle. A few sentences, and then move on. You can't usually change someone's mind in one conversation. But over time, those teachable moments add up. There may not be a *lightbulb moment*. More likely the bulb will light slowly over time.

Our babies slept with us until they were toddlers. Once they were over 12 or 18 months, my mother-in-law wasn't quite comfortable with it. When Teddy was three, we went to visit her over Christmas. Teddy crawled into bed with us instead of going to the cute bed my mother-in-law had made up for him. She kind of scrunched up her nose and asked, "Can't he sleep by himself yet?"

Her daughter, Susie, had a baby a few years later. When Madelyn was about two, my mother-in-law told me excitedly, "I think they're still bedsharing! Madelyn crawled into her mum's bed at bedtime. They looked so cosy!" My mother-in-law had certainly changed her mind about bedsharing!

—Lillian

Your Partner's Family, Your Partner's Turn

It's usually (though not always) best to let your *partner* do the talking if the criticism comes from your *partner's* family, coworkers, and friends. Your relationship with them is still forming and more easily damaged. If each of you tackles your own "inner circle," it can save a lot of hard feelings in the long run.

When my son was a year old, my father-in-law was adamant that our son should sleep in his own bed. I remember standing in his kitchen one evening when my husband explained to him that letting him cry it out is not part of how we parent. His dad got all worked up and said, "Your mother was really upset about letting you cry too, but we knew it was for the best." My husband finally said, "I understand how you feel, Dad, but it's our bed, and it's our son, and we're doing what *we* feel is right." It was never brought up again. Our son is sleeping in our bed behind me as I type.

—Mariah

If Your Partner Isn't on Board

There's nothing more fundamental than the two of you agreeing on who you're sleeping with! Mothers usually warm up to the notion of bedsharing faster than their partners do. Sometimes having the baby close at night feels natural and obvious to a partner right from the start. To others it can sound totally weird. But there's nobody whose support helps more than your partner's.

Most partners are trying to be helpful. So if you're feeling that bedsharing is the best route to go, how can you get your partner on board?

One way is to try to have the discussion when you're both coherent—during the day, not in the middle of the night.

> With the birth of our first child, my wife researched a "strange" style of sleeping where you actually keep the baby in your bed at night. My first reaction was, "How could it be good for the two of us?" But it was. My daughter, my wife, and I all slept better, more soundly, and I (as the father) rested more easily knowing my family was next to me. I believe the mere fact that we slept together brought us closer, somehow overnight, like magic. Friends and family thought we were crazy, but we began to stop caring. We adopted the accepting philosophy that each family does what works for them.
>
> After about two years, my daughter told us she wanted to sleep in her own room. My first reaction was, "What? I'm not ready for that yet!" But *she* was. No, they won't sleep with you forever. I know our time with children in our bed is limited. But for me, bedsharing has become a good thing that I'm still not ready to end.
>
> —Dave

Take a look at your partner's pros and cons, and discuss your own thinking, maybe RRID-style. What will it mean if you and the baby continue to sleep separately? What will you gain and lose with sleeping apart from the baby, and how close is each of you comfortable with? What will the advantages be to your partner (little or no nighttime baby care for the partner, a happier baby and mother, more sleep for everyone)? What's the plan if you get really sleepy?

Share the information in the Tearsheet Toolkit. If your partner's interested in more information, you can point out the sections on normal sleep and sleep science from this book. And you might both have fun deciding on your sleep personalities in Chapter 7.

Ask if he or she would be willing to try bedsharing (or using a bedside cot, or having the baby in the room, or whatever you think would work) for a set period of time—maybe a week or two. The first few nights of a change can be awkward for everyone, so a single weekend isn't usually long enough. But there's almost always room for rearranging and negotiating as you go.

The only constant in parenting is that everything keeps changing, so *whatever* your starting points, you and your partner will most likely end up with something different along the way.

> I'm not exactly sure I needed support for the decision to bedshare. For me, it was what worked for my family and I really didn't care much what others said about it. At times, family or friends would make snide remarks about weaning or bedsharing. It never affected our choices.
>
> My husband's cousin is bedsharing with her now two-year-old, and breastfed him in part because of our example.
>
> —Jolie

When Your Health Care Provider Disagrees

This one's tough. Really tough. Your health care providers should heartily approve of room-sharing because it's what leading medical associations recommend. And using a bedside cot isn't "having your baby in your bed". But bedsharing? There are some strong and stern voices speaking to health care providers: "Dangerous. Don't. End of discussion."

Some doctors and health visitors aren't open to patients offering information. Yours may be. There's a tearsheet in the Tearsheet Toolkit with some talking points. We're all less likely to take in information that doesn't come from our peers or superiors, but maybe you can find enough common ground for the two of you to work from. As one wise doctor said about another controversial health issue, "I'll bring this up at each visit, because it's my job to make sure you have the information. But of course the decision is yours to make."

> My health visitor brought up bedsharing only once, very gently, asking questions rather than immediately jumping down my throat. (I was impressed!) When she learned that I was educated on the matter, had done my research, knew the risks and benefits, and could completely explain my case in a calm and educated way, she said, "Well, I may not agree with you, but I can't say I'm the top parenting expert or anything. You know what you're doing." She and I have a mutual respect for each other since we had that discussion on the topic of bedsharing.
>
> —Meredith

You may decide that your health care provider's approach just doesn't match your needs. That doesn't mean he or she is a poor care provider; it just means the fit is poor. At a La Leche League meeting, one mother complained about her doctor's rigid, dogmatic approach. A second mother said, "That's too bad. My doctor has been especially flexible. He really listens to me." It turned out they were talking about the same doctor. True story. Your friends may have some recommendations, but find the person *you* feel comfortable with. Try to keep in mind that you have every right to change doctors and find one who is more sympathetic.

> My health visitor told me that my most important job as a mother was to teach my child independence before he left for college and at 12 months old I was failing him by not teaching him to sleep alone. She was very insistent. When I replied that since we were only $^{1}/_{18}$th finished we would have plenty of time to catch up, she scoffed and told me that wasn't how it was done. That was the last time we went to her.
>
> —Emily

Questions, Questions

One very useful strategy with health care professionals is to answer a direct question with another question.

> **Health visitor:** Where does your baby sleep?
>
> **Mother:** It depends. Sometimes she sleeps in her car seat when we're driving. She sleeps in my sling when I'm going for a walk. And she falls asleep in my lap while I'm breastfeeding her. Why?
>
> **Health visitor:** I need you to know about safe sleep. Never bed-share with your baby, and . . . *[provides other warnings.]*
>
> **Mother:** Do you have some printed information I can read?
>
> **Health visitor:** Here's a brochure. I want you to promise never to bedshare, and . . . *[repeats other warnings.]*
>
> **Mother:** I appreciate your concern, and really appreciate the printed information you've given me. *[Note that she hasn't promised anything.]*
>
> **Health visitor:** I need your promise that you'll never bedshare.
>
> **Mother:** You haven't asked me to promise anything else, and I haven't had a chance to read what you've given me. Why is *this* issue so important to you?
>
> **Health visitor:** Because . . . *[explains.]*
>
> **Mother:** Oh, I see. And again, I appreciate your concern and the printed information you've given me. *[Mother then changes the subject.]*

If you ask for printed information and listen attentively to the health visitor's advice, she can check off "Mother was informed about safe sleep" on her checklist.

If You Don't Want to Discuss It

Many mothers decide not to tell their health visitor that they're bedsharing. But it will add to your health visitor's overall experience if you "come clean" at *some* point, even a few years from now when she is impressed with what a terrific child you're raising. Explain what your family did, and why, and what you thought of the experience. If they don't hear stories like yours, they'll never learn how common those stories are.

> It's hard being a new mother. It's a lot harder if you feel that you have to fit in with other people's notions. Many of these notions, such as leaving babies to cry, can actually undermine breastfeeding. Fortunately, they're on the wane, but there seems to be a stubborn streak in our society that keeps them alive. At La Leche League, I found a ready supply of information and encouragement to help me find what felt best for me, my babies, and my family.
>
> —Barbara

Something to Sleep On

Having to defend yourself and your decisions isn't fun. So spend some time with "yea-sayers"—people who *get* what you're doing because they're doing it too. It's amazing what a few real, live people who "walk your walk" can do for your whole mothering experience, day and night.

Most critics don't keep criticizing if you're calm and confident about your choices. The proof is in the pudding. As your critics watch how well your child is turning out, you may even earn their respect. In fact, your own discoveries and self-assurance may help other mothers.

Mothers have protected their babies by sleeping near or next to them since time began, and most breastfeeding mothers today do it at least some of the time. You have the company of billions of mothers all over the world. Picture all those women, all those babies, all those beds. They're cuddling, snuggling, touching, breastfeeding, and snoozing *together* at this very moment. It's an old image, it's a modern image, and it's rooted deeply in the instincts and biology of mothers and babies.

chapter 22

Your Frequently Asked Questions (FAQs)

When our son Eli was two, a car accident left me with serious back pain. Nights were tough. We'd had the mattress on the floor, but now I couldn't get on and off it. Eli was an "athletic sleeper", and every time he jiggled the mattress, it felt like a knife in my back. I couldn't turn onto my side to breastfeed. Suddenly our family bed didn't work.

We tackled the problems one at a time. Friends set up our standard bed frame for easier on-and-off. We put it against the wall, and it has a footboard, so there was only one side he could fall from. We put our floor mattress on that side, where my partner David slept so he wouldn't disturb me, and it was perfect falling-out-of-bed protection for Eli.

Eli and I practiced "statue breastfeeding," with me lying as still as a statue against my body pillow and him snuggling against me to breastfeed. At night, Eli started out on the floor with David, where he could snuggle, have a story, and get the wiggles out. When he got drowsy, David would lift him up beside me on the bed. If he got too wiggly, he had to leave the "statue bed" and get on the "wiggle bed". My back is almost fine now. We still play "statue breastfeeding" sometimes, but now it's just for fun.

—Holly

Questions about your baby's sleep and bedsharing can come up at any time. If your question isn't answered in this chapter, double-check the index to see if it's addressed somewhere else in the book. Ask the other mums at a local La Leche League group or online forum or at a similar mother-to-mother gathering. Or ask your breastfeeding helpers and friends for ideas. Real live mothers are always full of real-life ideas. With some fresh perspectives, most sleep questions can be put to bed.

> If the problem you're experiencing is more about breastfeeding than sleeping, check *The Womanly Art of Breastfeeding*, eighth edition. It's a great go-to resource for any breastfeeding question.

Nipple Clinging

Q: *How can I keep my baby from wanting to sleep with my nipple in her mouth?*

A: Maybe she's one of those babies who needs the stimulation or reassurance that lots of nighttime sucking provides. But by around four to six months, there's probably some room to compromise. Two approaches from some formerly frazzled mothers:

- Put a finger lightly under your baby's chin, slide your nipple out, then immediately use your finger to push up gently under her chin to close her mouth. Keeping it closed causes her tongue to fill more of her mouth, taking up the space where your breast was. Keep your finger there until she goes into a deeper sleep and slowly relax it away.
- Slip your finger into her mouth alongside your nipple, then slowly draw out your nipple and leave your finger in her mouth for a while. She might start sucking vigorously when you do this, so wait until she settles again. For some reason, it's usually easier to sneak your finger out of her mouth than your nipple. Once your nipple is out of her mouth, try to back up a bit so that the breast is not right

there when she partially wakes up. Sometimes it helps to put a hand on the baby's chest or abdomen to help her stay calm and go into a deeper sleep.

Bottom line: Wait for deeper sleep and move slowly. Keeping her mouth closed and her body calm and stable may help.

Babysitters

Q: ***We're ready to start leaving the baby. What do we need to know about babysitters and sleep?***

A: The hardest time of the day to have a babysitter is often bedtime. Some babies and toddlers are happier just staying up, taking walks (especially outside), or falling asleep in the babysitter's arms. Go over where and how to put the baby down for sleep (tummy-up on a safe surface). And of course the baby under six months is better off sleeping in the same room as the babysitter.

Maybe you don't even need a babysitter. Many breastfeeding babies go easily to restaurants, cinemas, parties, even bowling. (See Chapter 5 for hints on breastfeeding in public.) People are often surprised at how calm a baby in a babycarrier can be, and you can always leave if you need to. As for the ones who aren't so calm when you go out? They're often the very ones who may need to be older before they can cope with being with a babysitter. Give yourselves some time.

Bottom line: No need to go out without your baby or child until both of you are ready for it. If you do get a babysitter, make sure to go over baby-on-back, safe surface, and your favourite comforting techniques.

Leaving a Baby Overnight

Q: ***I have to go away overnight for a business trip. Can my three-month-old baby bedshare with my husband?***

A: Risk rises with a baby younger than about four months, of course, because your husband isn't a breastfeeding mother. But you know your husband and baby. Is he a regular part of your bedsharing nights? Is he used to sleeping with your baby? Is his sleep personality a good fit (see Chapter 7)? If you're concerned, a bedside cot or Moses basket at the bedside might be a good alternative.

Is there any way to bring your baby with you? Some mothers have arranged for someone to come with them and take care of the baby during the day. Others have brought the baby along "on the job". It all depends on your baby and your circumstances.

Bottom line: You might be able to bring your baby along. If he stays behind, trust your judgment about the best people and places for nights.

Overnights with Grandma

Q: ***My toddler is spending the night with his grandparents and they want to bedshare. Is that safe?***

A: Not just safe, but often a lot of fun, so long as no one smokes. And oh, the pleasure of a little one in their bed after so many years without!

Have a talk with your child and his grandparents about what the plan is if he changes his mind at 2.00 a.m. Sleep time at Grandma's house won't be "just like home". Part of the fun is trying new things and finding special favourites that don't happen at home. Grace's three-year-old son was so excited when he slept at his grandmother's with his older cousins in neighbouring beds that he sang "Happy Birthday" over and over until his cousin Abbie told him to zip it.

Bottom line: Feel free to let your child bedshare with his favourite adults once he's old enough to look forward to it.

Bedsharing with an Older Child

Q: *Our six-year-old wants to sleep with her four-month-old brother. Is that okay?*

A: Consider waiting until the baby's closer to a year, then take their sizes and abilities into account. Once they're closer in size and strength, it's a common and often very happy arrangement.

Bottom line: It's risky putting a young baby and older child in bed together.

Overnight Custody Visits

Q: *My baby's father and I don't live together. He wants an overnight custody visit. How does that work for sleep?*

A: Bedsharing with anyone but you isn't a good idea for at least the first four months. After that, use your judgment about the safety of *this* baby with *this* adult.

Wise custody arrangements don't require that babies under two years spend more than a few hours at a time away from the person they're most closely attached to. Young breastfed babies have a particularly strong—and totally normal and appropriate—emotional and physical need for their mothers, which means that they're not that easy for someone else to take care of for long stretches. Maybe you could propose more *daytime* contact until your child is comfortable with an overnight stay. If you can't avoid overnight visits for your infant:

- Go over the tearsheet for childcare providers ("Childcare Naps, Breastfed Babies, Bedsharing Families") with the other parent for information on sleeping away from you.
- For both their sakes, share your best soothing and calming techniques and bedtime routines, but expect that a different household will follow somewhat different patterns.

- For an older child, an overnight stay may be smoother if someone familiar in the other household can share the room, or lie with your child until he falls asleep and be willing to return if he wakes up.
- Having a security blanket or toy can provide some night-time (and daytime) stability to a child who has two homes.

Bottom line: Avoid other-parent bedsharing with a baby under four months, and work together on ways to make a rough situation go more smoothly for the child you both love.

Time Changes

Q: ***We just turned our clocks forward and now my baby wakes up with the sun, which is much earlier than I want to get up. Is there anything I can do?***

A: Ah, the agony of time changes! No matter where babies sleep or how they're fed, most of them don't honour the new time any more than cockerels do. Some babies don't seem to notice, but then if you have one of those, you're not reading this part, are you? Trips with time zone changes are a similar challenge: easier to deal with because everything's different, harder to deal with because you're all a little more tired. Here are some ideas mothers have shared with us:

- We have heavy blackout curtains that block most of the light. It takes Oliver maybe 15 minutes a day to adjust on his own.
- My partner's work schedule has to shift immediately, but I shift my own clock—and the children's—slowly over the first week.
- Depending on which way the clock is changing, I try to snuggle her longer than usual in the morning and keep her up later at night, or I wake her early and go some-

where stimulating, then I plan drowsy activities—maybe going for a car ride in the dark and coming home to a dimly lit house and the bedtime routine—and hope for an earlier-to-bed night or two while she adjusts.

- We always have a couple of rough days and nights, and then somehow it just smooths out on its own.
- Our baby was really resistant, so *we* changed. We go to bed about nine o'clock now, and get up about five. We've been surprised; we actually like the new routine and the way our day plays out . . . at least when we're not having or being company. [Note: They've hit on the "front-loading" concept from Chapter 10!]

Bottom line: Babies adjust on their own, but you may be able to help your baby make the switch faster with a little ingenuity.

Tooth Decay and Night Breastfeeding

Q: ***My 18-month-old baby needs a filling! The dentist told me we have to stop breastfeeding at night. Is that true?***

A: There's no evidence that nighttime breastfeeding itself causes tooth decay.[1] Dr. Brian Palmer studied children's skulls that were thousands of years old—way older than toothpaste or sealants—and he found almost no tooth decay.[2] Makes sense. Nearly all mammals nurse at night. Most of them have teeth right from birth and never get tooth decay. Night-weaning your baby is almost certainly not necessary and can lead to early weaning, with everything that means to your and your baby's health and relationship.

How your baby gets your milk matters, though. Breastfeeding doesn't allow milk to pool around the teeth; the milk is pulled right to the back of the throat and swallowed. Expressed milk given by bottle can pool around the teeth and expose them to milk sugars for longer than normal.

The type of milk matters. Formula lacks the lactoferrin, sIgA (secretory immunoglobulin A), IgG (immunoglobulin G), and the high pH level of human milk that help inhibit cavity formation.[3] It has only 1/100th the cavity-inhibiting lysozyme of human milk![4] And unlike your milk, it doesn't deposit tooth-strengthening calcium and phosphorus.[5]

Anatomy matters. If your child has a tight, thick attachment of the skin that stretches between his upper lip and gum (the kind that can cause a space between the front teeth later on), it may cause milk to get trapped and grow bacteria.[6]

The main problem is our modern diet, not our milk.[7] The prehistoric children whose teeth Palmer examined had a diet that was low in sugar. Today's dried fruits and sweets can trap sugar against tiny teeth. And processed foods like crackers and cereals may not start out as sugar, but adding saliva changes some of their starches to sugar.

There can be other reasons for modern tooth decay, even in children whose diets include no problem foods. Smoking and diet during pregnancy, and certain illnesses in pregnancy can make a baby's first teeth more prone to tooth decay.[8] (In those rare cases, their permanent teeth are almost always fine.) *Streptococcus mutans,* a particularly nasty mouth bacterium that some parents and children have, interacts with sugars and is especially hard on tooth enamel. Babies can pick up this bacterium from adult carriers who share food, utensils, or mouth kisses with them.

The best way to avoid tooth decay is to wipe or brush your child's teeth thoroughly at least twice a day and limit sugars and sticky foods. Swishing or sipping water after eating also helps. It makes sense not to offer anything other than water or your milk after bedtime teeth cleaning. And ask your dentist about using xylitol to help fight harmful mouth bacteria.

In extreme cases, some dentists recommend wiping a child's teeth after each feed, including during the night (which, as you can imagine, neither mother nor baby enjoys). We haven't found any studies, but some mothers who have done it think it made a difference.

Bottom line: Under normal circumstances, night breastfeeding does not cause tooth decay unless another type of

carbohydrate is present. Good oral hygiene can reduce the mouth bacteria that can cause tooth decay.

Ill Mother and Bedsharing

Q: *I think I'm getting ill. Is it still safe to sleep with my baby?*

A: Almost always, unless you start a medication with drowsiness as a side effect. You and your baby have been a unit ever since she was conceived. More and more health facilities treat the "breastfeeding couple" as a single unit because your baby is both nourished by your milk and strengthened by your immune system. By the time you know you're ill, you've already given your baby your germs too (next to impossible to avoid, no matter what you do). And since you've also started giving her your antibodies through your milk, there's no need to disrupt your usual night routine. That's especially good news if your illness is really getting you down. Go to bed with a jug of water and your baby, and fight the bug for both of you.

Your milk protects your baby against more than just your shared germs. If your baby picks up an illness that *you* haven't been exposed to, she passes those germs to you through breastfeeding, and you quickly begin making targeted antibodies to pass right back.[9] The biggest problem is those times when you're more ill than your baby, who wonders why Mum has suddenly become so boring.

See the "Medications and Breastfeeding" section below for guidelines and information sources about any medications you're taking. Note that anything that makes you drowsy removes one of the Safe Sleep Seven criteria, so it would be safer for your baby to have a close but separate sleeping surface.

There are *very, very few* illnesses that require any kind of mother-baby or baby-milk separation. The NHS (nhs.uk), the Breastfeeding Network (breastfeedingnetwork.org.uk), the Centers for Disease Control and Prevention (cdc.gov) and the World Health Organization (who.int/eng) all have information on breastfeeding during specific maternal diseases and after vaccinations.

Ill Baby and Bedsharing

Q: ***My baby is ill. Is it still safe to sleep with him?***

A: This one's a judgment call. How ill is he? Is he familiar with bedsharing? Common or garden-variety illnesses and a bedsharing baby go together well. An extremely sick baby can benefit from Kangaroo Care. Take your comfort level and your baby's needs into account, and by all means keep up the breastfeeding. You're his best line of defence.

Breastfeeding provides fluids and nutrition when he refuses other food sources. It's soothing for both of you, and research says what we mothers already know: it's also a first-class pain reliever.[10]

If the problem is gastrointestinal, there's no need to stop breastfeeding. Your milk is healing and the calories are important.[11] But you may find yourself breastfeeding more often and for shorter times. Small meals are perfect for an unhappy tummy, and even if most of it comes back up, it digests so quickly that you know some of it is staying down. With a vomiting child, you even have an emptier breast that can offer comfort with a lower, slower flow. Breathing problems? There's a section on humidifiers in Chapter 12. The most effective (though least convenient) is a steamy bathroom where you can sit and hold him or make a nest on the floor for both of you.

Even after he seems well, your child might breastfeed more than usual for a while to make up for any shortfall in calories. Remember that illness was a trauma that he needs to recover from. It'll pass. And in the midst of it all? It can be a surprisingly sweet time, mothering a baby who just wants to be held. Even if extra washing is involved.

Bottom line: Whatever arrangements you're comfortable with, give him lots of body contact and lots of breastfeeding.

Medications and Bedsharing

Q: ***My doctor has prescribed a medication for me. Is it safe to take it and sleep with my baby?***

A: It depends. Medications that affect your responsiveness—that make you groggy—are not safe to take while bedsharing. If you have to take that kind of medication, find out how long the half-life is by consulting one of the resources listed below. A medication's "half-life" is how long it takes for half of the drug to leave your bloodstream. Multiply the half-life by five. That's how long you need to wait for the medication to be virtually out of your system. Just like alcohol, medications that pass into your milk also pass out of it, so there's no need to "pump and dump", except for comfort and to keep up your milk production.

Here are some reliable resources for information about medications use by breastfeeding mothers:

- National Health Service's *Quick Reference Guide for Drugs in Breast Milk* (ukmicentral.nhs.uk/drugpreg/guide.htm)
- Breastfeeding Network (breastfeedingnetwork.org.uk)
- LactMed, the U.S. National Institutes of Health's Drugs and Lactation Database (lactmed.nlm.nih.gov)
- Dr. Thomas Hale's Infant Risk Center (infantrisk.com)

Bottom line: If a medication makes you sleepy or impaired, you can usually bedshare after five half-lives have passed.

Jeremy developed asthma when he was under six months old. At our first appointment, the specialist said he wanted to send Jeremy to the hospital for five to seven days so he could try out different medications and treatments. I told him that I was breastfeeding, and he said, "Well, you'll have to wean him from breastfeeding, of course." I said that I was *not* going to wean him and asked what he was planning to do that I couldn't do at home. If he just wanted to try out medications, we could do that, and I could report on how Jeremy responded. The specialist was *very* taken aback. He told me that most of the mothers he dealt with appreciated having a break!

I didn't wean, and we soon found a medication that helped. When Jeremy was about two, the specialist commented on how well

Jeremy was doing. He said it was unusual for a child who developed asthma so young to be as healthy as Jeremy, and he admitted to me, "You're the only mother I've had who continued to breastfeed, and he's done so much better than the other babies I've seen."

—Judith

Reflux and Sleep

Q: *My baby has reflux and his nights are miserable. What can we do?*

A: Gastro-oesophageal reflux (GORD, GER or GERD) occurs when the valve between the stomach and oesophagus (food pathway) opens, or doesn't close completely, and stomach contents and acids rise into the oesophagus. We normally have reflux many times a day and don't notice, but when it's severe, it can be really painful. Symptoms include arching during breastfeeding, pulling on and off the breast as if he wants to feed but it hurts, frequent swallowing between feeds, fussing in a car seat or whenever he's bent in the middle or lying flat, and salivating or having near-constant congestion or rumbly breathing. See llli.org/faq/ger.html for more information.

First, though, you need to figure out if reflux is actually the problem. Infant reflux is easily confused with milk oversupply and allergy, either of which an experienced breastfeeding helper can help you with.

If it's truly reflux, your GP can suggest some treatment options. Thickened feeds and simethicone drops have *not* been found to be effective,[12] but there may be other treatments that may help. You may hear that a baby with reflux should sleep on his stomach to avoid inhaling regurgitated milk. A baby on his stomach may be *more* likely to choke—and of course it's riskier for a baby to sleep on his stomach *alone*—unless he's on a sloping adult chest.

Breastfeeds are naturally smaller and more frequent than formula-feedings, which is good. But nighttimes can still be hard because there's no gravity to keep stomach fluids down when your baby's lying flat. Here are some ideas that might make sleeping easier for your baby:

- Breastfeed your baby while he lies on his *left* side. The opening from the stomach to the oesophagus is usually on our right side, so "right side up" may keep his stomach contents down better and may hurt less. (If you have heartburn yourself, see if lying on your left side helps. Some of us get instant relief.) During the day, the Magic Baby Hold (Chapter 14) also keeps his right side higher.
- Consider a wedge under the cot mattress to keep his head higher than his feet. The newer adult mattresses don't bend, and a wedge on top of your mattress is a suffocation risk, but the next few options may work for you.
- Depending on your body configuration and the size of your baby, you may be able to cuddle your baby with his shoulders on your arm, even when you breastfeed, to keep his head higher than his feet.
- Prop yourself up on pillows and let your baby sleep on your chest.
- Put a towel or disposable bed pads (available online or in the adult incontinence section at your local pharmacy) over or under your bottom sheet, to protect against regurgitated milk.
- Read *Colic Solved* by Dr. Bryan Vartabedian for in-depth information on treating babies with reflux.
- Use a mechanical bed that raises the entire head of the bed—granted, an expensive option.

Because feeds can be uncomfortable for them, babies with reflux may occasionally "go on strike". Breastfeeding strikes are covered in *The Womanly Art of Breastfeeding* and on the LLLI website at llli.org/faq/strike.html. Many babies do at least a little breastfeeding at night, even while they're "on strike". Breastfeeding strikes usually end well, especially if you stay in touch with a skilled breastfeeding helper—don't hesitate to call one.

Reflux isn't fun for either of you, but breastfeeding does help, and your baby will be comforted by your presence if nighttimes are tough.

Bottom line: First make sure it's not oversupply or allergies, then try left side down, head higher than feet, small and frequent feeds. Consult your doctor or a specialist for expert help.

Baby's in the Hospital and Sleep

Q: ***My breastfed baby has to go into hospital, but we've always slept together. How do we handle sleep in the hospital?***

A: The first step is to be with your baby as much as you can. Remind the hospital that your baby needs to feed directly from your breast, so that you can pick up the hospital's germs and make antibodies for him.

Hospitals have many different rules about where babies have to sleep . . . or they may *think* they do. Some put any child from an infant to a three-year-old in a metal cot. Others go to great lengths to keep breastfeeding mothers and babies together, day and night.

How you approach your baby's time in the hospital will go a long way towards determining how helpful the members of the staff will be. *Expect* that your baby won't leave your arms unless he absolutely has to. Bring a notebook (preferably a bright colour) in which you record times, procedures, and medications. It's a good record for you and an important signal to the staff. Be good-natured and confident about the importance of your presence to your baby's health. Ask if the sleeping arrangements can be adapted so that you and your baby can stay together. All they can say is no, and even a no may be negotiable. Change doesn't happen if people don't ask for it.

Some hospitals have double-size hospital beds for mothers to bedshare with their babies. If there's just a standard hospital bed, you might be able to pull up the side rails and lay a sheet sideways across the mattress and up over the rail on one side, tucking the sheet end under the mattress to make a smooth and fall-proof wall on the baby's side of the bed—an old maternity hospital technique.

If you can't get around the metal cot, request a room that also has a standard hospital bed for you. If that's not possible, a reclining sleep chair is better than an ordinary chair. When he's awake, hold him as much as possible. Mothers have even shared an oxygen tent with their babies. Linda threaded her son's oxygen tube through her bra so that it blew on to his face while she held him. At night, you may be able to bring the cot right up against your bed or sleep chair so your hand and your smell can reassure and comfort him.

These are all ideas that have worked in some places. If you just can't be close to your baby at night, see if you can put something small with your scent on it in the cot. Being present when you can and continuing to breastfeed when you can will go a long way towards making your baby feel more secure.

Bottom line: Look for creative ways to bedshare or at least spend as much time as you can, as close to him as you can, to reassure and comfort you both. *Expect* the hospital's help with this and you may be more likely to get it.

Bedsharing While *You're* Hospitalized

Q: *I'm having an operation next week. How can we make our baby's nights as normal as possible while I'm in the hospital?*

A: Some people assume that a baby should be kept away from a hospitalized mother so she can rest and recuperate. But you'll recover faster and your baby will cope better if you stay together as much as possible. Ask if you can have your baby with you during your hospital stay as much as possible during the daytime, along with a person who will be responsible for the baby's care. The hospital may be able to arrange a seperate room for you if you ask in advance.

Most medications, including anaesthesia for surgery, are compatible with breastfeeding. There's no need to "pump and dump", except for your own comfort. But if you're taking pain relief or medication that makes you groggy or drowsy, or if you're impaired in any way, arrange to have an awake and aware adult present whenever you're asleep with your baby. Read the section on "Medications and Bedsharing" for more information.

Your partner or a family member or friend can stay in the room to take her from you when you need sleep or be an extra pair of hands for nappy changes and other baby care. Don't expect the hospital staff to help; it's really not their job.

Try to stabilize your baby's life at home as much as possible by having a consistent "nighttime roommate" for her. Carmela found some interesting wiggle room for actual bedsharing (see below). With an older baby, having a bedsharer "spoon" with the baby's back against the adult's front may be more reassuring than being face-to-unfamiliar-face.

Bottom line: Keep your baby with you as much as possible, arrange for consistent care when he can't be with you, and know that this too shall pass.

> Fifteen days after my Paco was born, I needed urgent surgery. The hospital was baby-friendly, so I had him with me at all times. But I had not counted on having so much pain after the surgery. I felt so horrible that I had to tell my husband to take Paco away. I just physically could not do it. One of my sisters went to my parents' house (near the hospital) and slept there with her little nursling and mine, bedsharing and breastfeeding them both that whole night. And the next morning I had my baby back and everything went well from then on.
>
> —Carmela

Pets in the Bed

Q: *We've always had the dog on our bed. What happens when we add a baby?*

A: Isn't it interesting that so many people sleep with their pets on the bed but are shocked about sleeping with a child? Of course, no matter how much we love our pets, our baby is more important. We know of no research on pets and bedsharing, so we're back, once again, to common sense. What size and temperament is your pet? Where on the bed does your pet normally sleep?

A medium to small dog who is low energy and sleeps at the foot of the bed may not be a problem, but a large dog that likes to sleep with his head on your pillow may be. Even a small dog that moves around on the bed a lot may not be safe for bedsharing.

You'll have to let your dog know that the bedtime rules have changed. With a firm command, point to the new sleeping place off the bed. You may have to do this repeatedly. If you're not sure your dog will stay off the bed after you fall asleep, you may need to shut him out of the room or put him in a crate (which most dogs actually like). For great ideas about how to get dogs to do what you want, see Cesar Millan's website at cesarsway.com. You might consider starting the process before your baby's born.

Cats are a different story. They don't generally care about commands, and size isn't as much of an issue. What really matters is where she likes to sleep. If your cat sleeps anywhere but at the foot of the bed, it probably isn't a good idea to have her on the bed with your baby. If she hops on when you're asleep, you might need to shut her out of the bedroom (move the litter box too). Cats generally respond best to positive reinforcement, so a treat outside the bedroom might convince her it's a better place to be. Cat behaviourist Jackson Galaxy has tips that might help at jacksongalaxy.com.

Both dogs and cats may see the baby as someone to mother or as a threat to their own place in the family. The more you include your pet in your time with the baby (in a safe way), letting your pet know that the baby is higher in the pecking order, the quicker he or she will be likely to accept the new member of the family and the new sleeping arrangements.

If your pet is neither a dog nor a cat, it's probably not an animal that would be appropriate for bedsharing with a baby, but then again, you probably don't sleep with the family iguana either!

Bottom line: Most pets aren't good bedmates for very young babies. With time, you'll learn how your baby and your pet interact.

Abrupt End to Breastfeeding and Bedsharing

Q: *Something's happened and I have to stop breastfeeding my baby. Can we still sleep together?*

A: First of all, make sure that stopping breastfeeding is necessary. Check out the "Medications and Bedsharing" section above. Even major breast surgery doesn't require weaning on the other side, and often breastfeeding can continue on the surgical side as well. A non-medical event? Brainstorm with a breastfeeding helper. There may be a creative way around it.

If weaning is unavoidable and the two of you already have a well-accustomed and smoothly running breastfeeding and bedsharing relationship, you may find yourself continuing to sleep in a cuddle curl even after weaning. By the time your baby is about four months old, the cuddle-curl isn't necessary.

See Chapter 23 and the Helpful Websites Tearsheet for sources of help, including breastfeeding helpers and hotlines to help you figure out medication issues and brainstorm with you. Weaning is a very big, life-altering step, and you and your baby deserve every chance to find a way around it.

Bottom line: First, look for a way around premature or abrupt weaning, and get help from a breastfeeding helper, if you can.

Abrupt End to Bedsharing

Q: *Something's happened and I can't be with my baby at night anymore. How can I get him to sleep in a separate bed?*

A: Situations like this are so tough! A common scenario is a partner who no longer wants the baby in your bed. If that's the case, there may be room for negotiation. Does your partner complain about needing more sleep? Many couples arrange for two safe sleep places—one for mother and baby, one for the partner.

Some partners insist that the *baby* has to go somewhere else. Would a bedside cot be acceptable to your partner? Remember that babies are safest within sight and sound of an adult for about the first six months. You can ease your baby into the new arrangement, putting him into the cot at the beginning of the night, bringing him to your bed for breastfeeding, and then returning him to the cot. Just make sure that you don't fall asleep with him somewhere less safe (like a sofa or reclining chair) during feeds.

Routines can help a baby or child learn that a new place is safe. Consider saying the same phrase, poem, story, or singing the same lullaby as you tuck him in each night. Marianne got into the habit of reciting *Goodnight Moon* before bed every night (after reading it for a month every night, she knew it by heart) and it became her son's signal to wind down to sleep.

Will your baby be in another household altogether? That's got to be incredibly tough, and our hearts go out to you. If you can, share all you know about your baby's sleep-time routines and preferences. Send along one of your unwashed T-shirts to help your baby feel connected to you while he learns new routines. Or put a small stuffed toy under your shirt for a night so that it soaks up your smell. You could also send along a recording of your voice singing your bedtime lullaby or saying your bedtime poem or phrase (even if you have to borrow the caregiver's phone to record a quick sentence or two).

All this assumes that the new caregivers want you to maintain a relationship with your baby. If that's not the case, we urge you to talk through your situation with someone knowledgeable about parent/child separations. Even the most complicated, distressing situation may have partial solutions you haven't thought of.

Bottom line: Gentle, consistent transitions with as much of your presence, smell, and voice as possible, can help him get used to sleeping elsewhere.

Something to Sleep On

Our bottom bottom line: Sleep challenges can be hard and there aren't usually one-size-fits-all solutions. Sometimes common sense and ingenuity are your only tools. Other times the right resource or helper can add some tips to make it work. Keep the Safe Sleep Seven in mind, and know that, one way or another, there's almost always a way around whatever's making you lose sleep.

chapter 23

Getting Help, Giving Help

> I was very lucky with my first child. My wonderful independent midwife encouraged me to listen to my instincts and gave me suggestions about breastfeeding, babywearing, and attending LLL meetings before and after the baby was born. She even had "Third Thursday" bring-and-share lunches at her house where new and seasoned families met to mingle and build a support system. It was *so* helpful to talk to other families and see how they dealt with a baby in life's various aspects. It helped both my husband and me get grounded in our own parenting style.
>
> —Nan

Women react differently from men when they're under stress. Instead of the well-known male adrenaline-based "fight-or-flight" response, we're more likely to "tend and befriend."[1] It's the same hormonal response that drives our births and releases our milk. When the going gets tough, oxytocin gets going. It makes us want to reach out to other women, both to get help and to give help. We want to be part of a group. We want to share resources and responsibilities. And we want to do it while nurturing our children. Any stressed new breastfeeding mother (and what new mother today isn't stressed?) is already awash in oxytocin and deserves a place where she can bring her baby, be with other women, and not only *get* support and information but *give* support and information.

Finding Your Friends

When we start a new school or college, most of us feel lost in a sea of new faces at first. With luck, we gradually find a smaller group of like-minded people, and that's the group we turn to first for help with assignments, reassurance after a bad exam result, and just to hang out. Our friends give us companionship and confidence-building that all the research and reading in the world can't provide.

The same thing happens with mothering. Who you put in your circle of friends reinforces how—and how confidently—you mother. If you've decided, based on what you've learned, that you and your breastfed baby sleep better and more safely together, but your usual friends don't approve, you might want to find a different (or just a second) group of friends. *Everything* about mothering is easier when you hang out with mothers who think about babies the way you do. Here are some ways to find those friends (who may just be looking for you as well):

- *Get to know your neighbours.* There may be a kindred spirit right next door. Maybe not *that* next door; maybe the *other* next door. Or maybe the door across the way. Or maybe the woman in the park with her baby in a sling. Think about spending time with the people who make you feel better and avoiding the others for now.
- *Talk to other mums.* In your GP's waiting room, at a mother and baby group, at the swimming pool, or anywhere else you see the mother of a child your child's age in a likely setting, a potential new friend may be hoping *you'll* make the first move.
- *Go to your antenatal class reunion.* See if you click with some of the other couples.
- *Look on notice boards at your local library, local café or*

heath centre. That's where a lot of mothers' groups post meeting notices. Or put up one of your own signs inviting other mothers of young children to meet there on a certain day and time.

- *Visit your local La Leche League or other mother-to-mother group.* It often leads to meeting new friends with similar parenting styles. (More about this below.)
- *Find a mother and baby group with a similar philosophy.* Little questions can loom large when you don't have a sounding board. If you can't find a suitable group, start your own by networking with friends to find mums with children the same age as yours. (And it's okay if your baby is really too young to play.)
- *Join an online group.* It's definitely not the same as getting a hug from a real-life friend, but it can be even better than that friend at three o'clock in the morning!
- *Ask your breastfeeding helper.* Your breastfeeding peer supporter, doula, or health visitor may not be one of your friends, but she might know where mums like you hang out.
- *Put down the books.* If this book serves as a valuable resource, wonderful! But it's not a substitute for a circle of like-minded, real-life friends.

Online Forums for Meeting Other Bedsharing Mothers

forums.llli.org/index.php

mothering.com/community

Facebook Groups:

Co-sleeping and Bedsharing Community—goo.gl/FcyN2p

Bedsharing, Co-Sleeping, Family-Bed—goo.gl/Kcyoyq

Co-Sleeping—goo.gl/5alYGw

Co-sleeping and Breastfeeding—goo.gl/iapra3

La Leche League Friends

Just by reading this book, you've connected with breastfeeding mothers around the world through La Leche League International. Use these connections in whatever way works for you, from finding friends to developing your own style or getting help with a specific problem.

> Sharing my story with other mothers, laughing together, and hearing stories so much like mine were enough to make me feel sane and normal again. In some other gatherings of mothers and babies, I felt that mothers were putting on a front about how terrific motherhood was, how on top of things they were, and how "good" their babies were. It seemed like a recipe for feeling like an inadequate mother, and I was sad for the mothers who felt unable to be truthful with each other. At LLL, I found a positive but honest atmosphere. I learned to accept my babies for who they were, to respond to their needs without thought for whether they "should" have them, and to settle into our own family rhythms, confident that if they worked for us, then they were right for us.
>
> —Barbara

That's *exactly* what La Leche League has always been about. In 1956, seven young mothers realized that breastfeeding their babies in a bottle-feeding culture was much easier if they spent time together. Their not-so-small idea really took off, and today La Leche League International is a not-for-profit, non-sectarian organization with more than 3,000 Groups in 70 countries around the world. La Leche League has helped millions of mothers breastfeed their babies, all through one mother helping a mother and that mother helping another.

Meeting in Person

La Leche League in-person meetings are the heart of our organization. They are free, informal gatherings that may meet in one another's homes or at an easily accessible public location. Some groups meet in a café or restaurant, where mums can drop in and share ideas and help. There's always a La Leche League Leader on hand as a resource.

Almost anywhere you go in the world, La Leche League meetings give you a safe place to complain without being urged to stop breastfeeding. You can ask questions and get practical answers from women who understand. No matter what you ask, there are usually several mothers who can offer insights or suggestions from their own experience—or at least who have the same questions, which is also reassuring. Sleep comes up at nearly every meeting: where, how, and how long. Many bedshare and others talk about the ways they keep their babies close. Even if you don't come away with an answer to your question, you'll come away knowing that you're among friends who understand. You can come late, leave early, take a fussy baby for a walk, change a nappy, and compare notes with other mothers who quickly come to feel like old friends.

It really helps if you can connect with a group while you're pregnant, but definitely try to do it while you're still floundering in the choppy seas of early motherhood. You can find the La Leche League group closest to you by entering your UK postcode or town at laleche.org.uk/find-lll-group or use the interactive interactive map on the home page of the LLLI website at llli.org. Don't like the style of the first group? Try another (even online)! At every meeting, you'll hear a lot of different perspectives and see a lot of different styles. Just take what feels right to you, and leave the rest.

If there's one message that all the different groups have in common, it's this: it's okay to love your baby—to hold and snuggle and breastfeed without *anyone else's* permission or approval. If someone's advice makes you uncomfortable, trust your instincts and trust your baby. Because there never was and never will be another baby—another relationship—just like yours.

Meeting Online

You can meet other breastfeeding mothers and LLLI Leaders online through the LLLI forums (forums.llli.org), Facebook page, Pinterest board, and Twitter. You'll also find information in several languages and LLL contacts throughout the world on the LLLI (llli.org) and LLLGB (laleche.org.uk) websites.

- facebook.com/breastfeedinglllgb
- #LaLecheLeague1 or @lllgb
- lalecheleague

Personal Help

If you want information tailored to *your* situation, you can always contact an LLL Leader and talk it through. Don't worry that you're bothering her, or that she won't want to help, or that your question is silly. The whole point of being an LLL Leader is to help other breastfeeding mothers. She had those same "silly" questions herself. And, if she can't help you, she's likely to know about other resources. Some of those resources are in the sidebar and on the Helpful Websites tearsheet.

Of course, if you think there may be a medical problem affecting your or your baby's sleep, check with your doctor. Even though some doctors won't support bedsharing or know much about breastfeeding, they can help you determine if there's a medical issue.

Breastfeeding Help that Really Helps

Mother-to-Mother Help

La Leche League GB: laleche.org.uk

La Leche League International: llli.org

Australian Breastfeeding Association: breastfeeding .asn.au

Professional Help

Lactation Consultants of Great Britain: lcgb.org

Our Sister Book

This is a book about sleep. But there's a very blurry line between sleep and waking, and between both of those and breastfeeding. Strategies that help with calming also help with sleeping. Smoothly running breastfeeding makes both days and nights easier. That means there are ideas for daytime parenting that can help you with nighttime parenting. *The Womanly Art of Breastfeeding* (8th edition or newer) has ideas on smoother days that can also make for smoother nights.

Giving Back

Not having any problems? You're needed at La Leche League meetings! Diane remembers the meeting when she realized that she was giving at least as much as she was getting. She went home amazed and proud. In fact, she'd been an expert from before her very first meeting, and you're already an expert yourself. After just a few nights with your baby, you had a lot of wisdom to share with a woman who hadn't had her baby yet, because no expert remembered *her* stage better than *you* did. At the same time, you were looking to the mothers of two-week-olds for some perspective, because they'd so recently been where you were.

Feel free to answer a Facebook post asking for sleep tips or to strike up a conversation with the tired mother of a younger baby while in a queue at the checkout. Be the reassuring voice that supports the new mother whose family wants her baby to cry it out. Now that you've read this book, you know the research behind your reassurances. Or show a friend how to breastfeed lying down and how to switch sides. *That* isn't in the research; you learned it from experience.

What you say can make all the difference to another mother. And when she helps another mother, you become the starting point of an ever-widening circle of mother wisdom. In fact, you'll help mothers whom you never even notice. They'll be noticing *you*—how you handle your baby, what comments you make, how comfortably you breastfeed your baby, how confidently you talk about your parenting and your nights. That's the power of mothers helping mothers. You're already one of the ripples in the pool of bedsharing and breastfeeding knowledge. Enjoy watching your ripples spread. And sleep sweetly.

appendix

Tearsheet Toolkit

Sometimes you don't want a whole book. And sometimes you want to be able to tear something out of a book! Here's your chance. Each page in this section is complete on its own two sides, ready to be torn out. You can put these sheets on your refrigerator or by your computer, or hand them to your in-laws or childcare provider—whatever you need. Online copies are available at llli.org/sweetsleepbook.

- Bedsharing Quick Start
- The Safe Sleep Seven Bedsharing Song
- Safe Sleep Seven Infographic
- Should Baby Sleep in Mum's Bed?
- The Safe Sleep Seven
- The Safe Surface Checklist
- Infant Sleep Research Websites
- Helpful Websites
- Bedsharing Talking Points
- Talking with Your Doctor About Bedsharing
- Breast or Bottle for Better Sleep?
- Childcare Naps, Breastfed Babies, Bedsharing Families
- Baby Sleep Stealers
- Baby Soothers

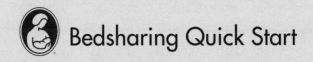

Bedsharing Quick Start

From *Sweet Sleep: Nighttime and Naptime Strategies for the Breastfeeding Family*

Desperate for sleep? Tired of getting up? Your baby can't sleep alone? If you can check off each item under the "Safe Sleep Seven" below, then you can *make your bed as SIDS-safe as a cot and greatly reduce other risks in just a few steps*. Follow these steps for "emergency bedsharing" and sleep better tonight (unless you want to do it again tomorrow).

The Safe Sleep Seven

You need to be

- ☐ 1. A non-smoker
- ☐ 2. Sober (no drugs, alcohol, or medications that make you drowsy)
- ☐ 3. Breastfeeding

Your baby needs to be

- ☐ 4. Full-term and healthy
- ☐ 5. Kept on his back when he's not breastfeeding
- ☐ 6. Unswaddled, in a sleepsuit or light pyjamas

And you both need to be

- ☐ 7. On a safe surface

Here's how to make your bed a safe surface:

1. Have your partner, other children, and pets sleep somewhere else. Or you and the baby do. *Just for tonight.*
2. Strip the bed. Take everything off except a thin mattress pad (if you use one) and bottom sheet. Everything.
3. Put back your own pillow(s), top sheet, and lightweight blanket or duvet. No heavy covers or quilts.
4. Put your baby on his back in the middle of the bed. Lie down next to him, on your side and facing him, with his face at about the level of your breast. If your bed is near a wall, put yourself between him and the wall.
5. Breastfeed your baby and get some sleep.

There. A simple, quick, and research-supported bedsharing arrangement. Just for tonight. You'll find the details and research in Chapter 2 of *Sweet Sleep*.

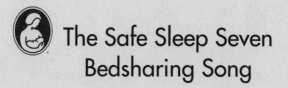

The Safe Sleep Seven Bedsharing Song

(to the tune of "Row, Row, Row Your Boat")

No smoke, sober mum
Baby at your breast
Healthy baby on his back
Keep him lightly dressed.

Not too soft a bed
Watch the cords and gaps
Keep the covers off his head
For your nights and naps.

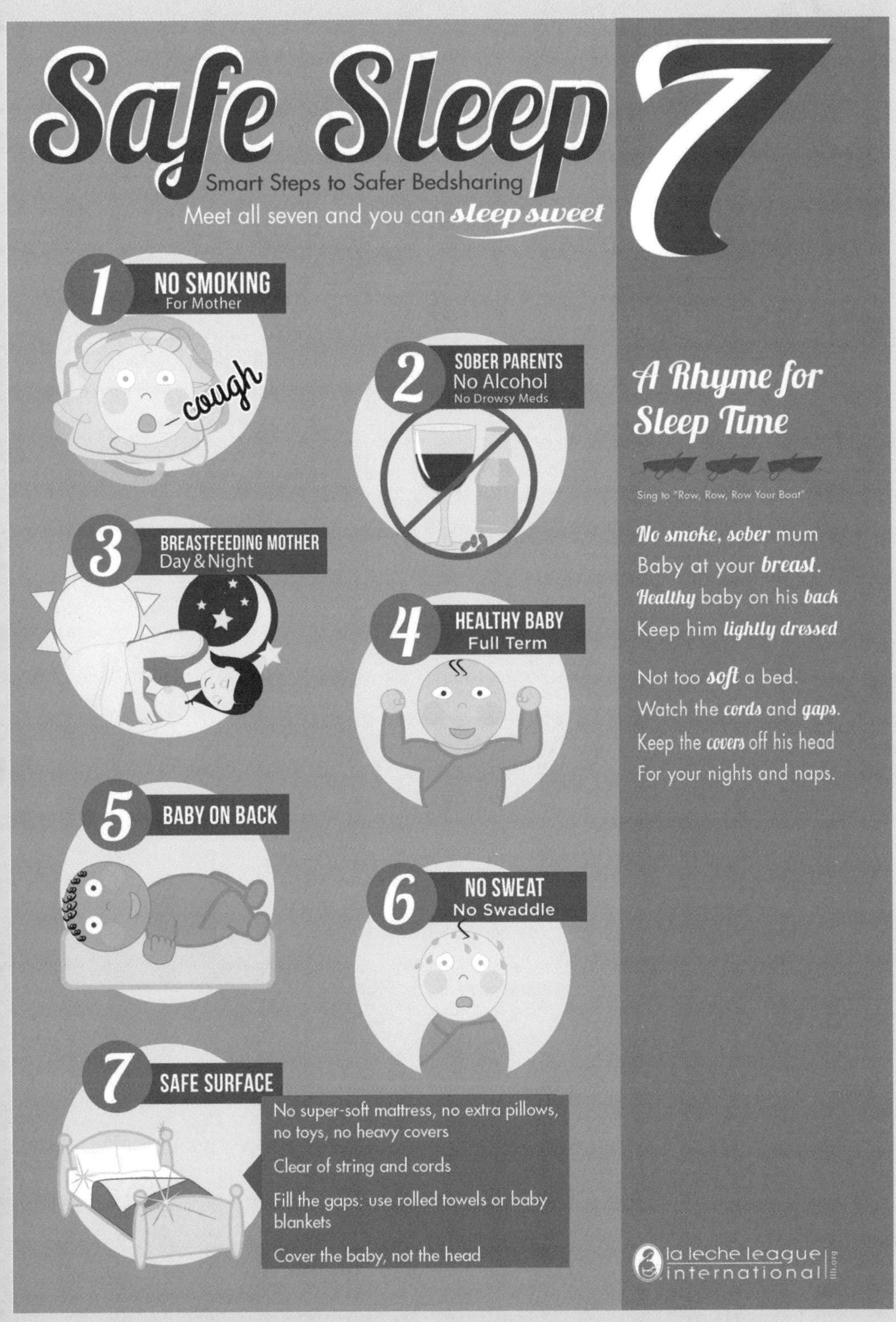

Safe Sleep 7
Smart Steps to Safer Bedsharing
Meet all seven and you can sleep sweet
1 NO SMOKING
For Mother
cough
2 SOBER PARENTS
No Alcohol
No Drowsy Meds
3 BREASTFEEDING MOTHER
Day & Night
4 HEALTHY BABY
Full Term
5 BABY ON BACK
6 NO SWEAT
No Swaddle
7 SAFE SURFACE
No super-soft mattress, no extra pillows, no toys, no heavy covers
Clear of string and cords
Fill the gaps: use rolled towels or baby blankets
Cover the baby, not the head
A Rhyme for Sleep Time
Sing to "Row, Row, Row Your Boat"
No smoke, sober mum
Baby at your breast.
Healthy baby on his back
Keep him lightly dressed.
Not too soft a bed.
Watch the cords and gaps.
Keep the covers off his head
For your nights and naps.
la leche league international
llli.org

Should Baby Sleep in Mum's Bed?

From *Sweet Sleep: Nighttime and Naptime Strategies for the Breastfeeding Family*

You might have been surprised to learn that the new baby doesn't sleep in a cot or Moses basket, but snuggles in every night next to his or her mother. And maybe you have some questions. . . .

Is it dangerous?

Research has found that having a baby in a separate room for the first half year or so is dangerous. Babies can't protect themselves when they're alone, they can sleep dangerously deeply when they're alone, and it's important that their mothers can hear them and they can hear their mothers.

You may have heard some of the public health campaigns warning parents not to bring the baby into their bed. Some are pretty scary. But the campaigns are aimed at people for whom bedsharing really is unsafe. Research actually shows that when all the following factors are in place, sleeping with baby in the bed is as safe as having the baby in a cot:

1. Non-smoker
2. Sober and unimpaired mother
3. Breastfeeding mother
4. Healthy baby
5. Baby on back for sleep
6. Baby lightly dressed and unswaddled
7. Safe surface, free of suffocation and injury risks

Won't this make the mother even more tired?

All new mothers are tired and need all the sleep they can get. Research shows that breastfeeding mothers who sleep with their babies actually get the *most* sleep. They don't have to get up, they don't have to warm a bottle—many of them don't even have to wake up!

Doesn't this teach the baby bad sleep habits? How will the baby ever learn to sleep on his or her own?

Babies get teeth, walk, and talk just as soon as they can. You can push them, but it won't really change who they are and it will only frustrate both of you. Sleep training belongs in that category. Hunger and crying and separation aren't good for the baby. She may stop crying, but research finds that her stress level stays too high to be healthy. Sleep problems in children are rare. Research shows that nighttime waking is very normal, right into toddlerhood. Babies and small children have needs at night, just as they have needs during the day. In their own time—as fast as they can—they'll grow out of them. Just as surely as they'll get their teeth.

Isn't this bad for a marriage?

A new baby can be stressful for any couple. (You may remember that time yourself!) But bedsharing can actually help a relationship. Everyone is more rested, and snuggling together as a family is something that parents and children remember fondly. Couples do sometimes have to get creative about intimate times together, but lots of bedsharing families have more than one child, so *something* must be working!

The Safe Sleep Seven

From *Sweet Sleep: Nighttime and Naptime Strategies for the Breastfeeding Family*

If you are:

- ☐ 1. A non-smoker
- ☐ 2. Sober and unimpaired
- ☐ 3. A breastfeeding mother

and your baby is:

- ☐ 4. Healthy and full-term
- ☐ 5. On his back
- ☐ 6. Lightly dressed

and you both are:

- ☐ 7. On a safe surface

then solid research indicates that your baby's SIDS risk is no greater in your bed than in a cot. And your automatic behaviours and responsiveness as a breastfeeding mother make it practically impossible to roll over on him. Other smothering risks are simple to deal with. They're covered in the Safe Surface checklist on the other side of this page. By about four months, research indicates that bedsharing with a healthy baby is equally safe with any responsible non-smoking adult on a safe surface.

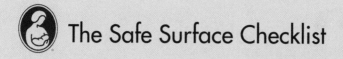

The Safe Surface Checklist

From *Sweet Sleep: Nighttime and Naptime Strategies for the Breastfeeding Family*

Avoid these possible smothering risks:

- ☐ Sofas and reclining chairs
- ☐ Softness or sagging that keeps a baby from lifting his head free
- ☐ Spaces between mattress and headboard, side rails, and wall where a baby could get stuck
- ☐ A bed partner who thrashes or sleeps exceptionally soundly
- ☐ Other children
- ☐ Pets that could interfere

Clear your bed of:

- ☐ Unused pillows
- ☐ Stuffed toys
- ☐ Heavy covers and blankets
- ☐ Anything nearby that dangles or tangles (such as cords, strings, scarves, ribbons, elastics)

Check your bed for possible hazards:

- ☐ Distance to floor
- ☐ Landing surface
- ☐ Sharp, poking, or pinching places

If you can meet the Safe Sleep Seven criteria on the other side of this page, then solid research indicates that your baby's SIDS risk is no greater in your bed than in a cot. And your automatic behaviours and responsiveness as a breastfeeding mother make it practically impossible for you to roll over on him. By about four months, research indicates that bedsharing with a healthy baby by a responsible adult on a safe surface is as safe as any other sleep arrangement.

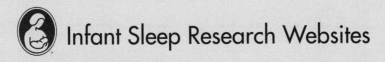

Infant Sleep Research Websites

From *Sweet Sleep: Nighttime and Naptime Strategies for the Breastfeeding Family*

Dr. Nils Bergman: kangaroomothercare.com

The Centre for Attachment (Lauren Lindsey Porter and Kate Dent Rennie): centreforattachment.com

Infant Sleep Information Source (Dr. Helen Ball and the Durham University Parent-Infant Sleep Lab): isisonline.org.uk

Harvard Center on the Developing Child: developingchild.harvard.edu/topics/science_of_early_childhood

Dr. Kathleen Kendall-Tackett: uppitysciencechick.com and praeclaruspress.com/Sleep-resources.html

Dr. James McKenna: cosleeping.nd.edu

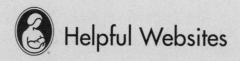

Helpful Websites

From *Sweet Sleep: Nighttime and Naptime Strategies for the Breastfeeding Family*

Mother-to-Mother Help

La Leche League GB: laleche.org.uk
Natural Mamas: naturalmamas.co.uk
Australian Breastfeeding Association: breastfeeding.asn.au

Professional Help

Lactation Consultants of Great Britain: lcgb.org

Doulas

Doula UK: doula.org.uk
Australian Doulas: australiandoulas.com.au
Doula NZ: doula.org.nz
WOMBS: wombs.org.za

Medication Information

Lactmed: toxnet.nlm.nih.gov
Breastfeeding Network: breastfeedingnetwork.org.uk

Bedsharing

Dr. Helen Ball: dur.ac.uk/sleep.lab
Dr. Jim McKenna: cosleeping.nd.edu
Infant Sleep Information Source: isisonline.org.uk
Kangaroo Mother Care: kangaroomothercare.com
The Home for Natural Family Living: mothering.com/sleep

beofen-tv.co.il/cgi-bin/chiq.pl (Hebrew)
htdormirsinllorar.com (Spanish)

General Help

Attachment Parenting International: attachmentparenting.org
Breastfeeding Made Simple: breastfeedingmadesimple.com
Dr. William Sears: askdrsears.com
Dr. Jay Gordon: drjaygordon.com
Kellymom: kellymom.com

Videos

Dr. Helen Ball lecture: goo.gl/f4vePY
Dr. James McKenna interview and newscast: goo.gl/9arQAT

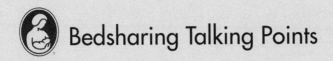

Bedsharing Talking Points

From *Sweet Sleep: Nighttime and Naptime Strategies for the Breastfeeding Family*

- Bedsharing definition: Baby and mother share the same safe sleep surface all or part of the night. Sharing sleep on sofas and reclining chairs is not bedsharing. Failing to distinguish between safe and unsafe surfaces is a common research error.
- SIDS is not suffocation and breathing hazards are not SIDS. Failing to distinguish between SIDS and suffocation is a common research error.
- No physiological explanation has ever been proposed for a baby dying of SIDS simply because he's near his mother.
- Breastfeeding mothers instinctively protect their infants in their sleep.[1] They adopt a cuddle curl position, and they touch and kiss their babies and adjust the baby's environment, often without waking.[2] Breastfed babies instinctively stay in that protected cove.[3]
- The bedsharing, breastfeeding mother's sleep-wake cycles synchronize with her baby's, allowing for low-stress, low-level arousals for each.[4]
- Most infants have bedshared with their mothers throughout history and worldwide.[5]
- Sixty to 75 percent of U.S. and British breastfeeding mothers bedshare at some point.[6]
- Babies' cardiac, respiratory, and other physiological systems are partly regulated by maternal skin-to-skin contact and shared sleep.[7]
- All mothers in the early postnatal period have fragmented sleep and most take several naps during the daytime.[8]
- Babies take between six weeks and four months to *begin* sleeping longer stretches.[9]
- Most breastfed babies breastfeed several times at night during the first six months.[10]
- By about six weeks, breastfeeding mothers tend to stop returning the baby to the cot after feeds[11] and adopt other strategies to maximize their sleep. These include supplementing with formula and moving to a less safe surface to share sleep.[12] One study found that more than 40 per cent of breastfeeding mothers fell asleep at some point sitting up in a sofa, reclining chair, or armchair.[13]
- The American Academy of Pediatrics, summarizing four studies, states that bedsharing does not put babies at higher risk of death after three months. Findings in the studies themselves ranged from 8 weeks to 14 weeks.[14]
- Excellent resources are the Academy of Breastfeeding Medicine's Clinical Protocol #6: Guideline on Co-Sleeping and Breastfeeding (bfmed.org/Media/Files/Protocols/Protocol_6.pdf), Dr. Helen Ball's website (isisonline.org.uk), and Dr. James McKenna's website (cosleeping.nd.edu).
- Breastfeeding mothers *will* bedshare.[15] Failure to provide safe bedsharing information may result in more harm than good.[16]
- Exclusive breastfeeding for the first six months is recommended by virtually every health authority in the world.[17]
- Exclusively breastfeeding families have the lowest rates of infant mortality in the world and in the United States, including SIDS and suffocation deaths.[18]
- Babies do not have the ability to self-soothe[19] or use adult strategies such as reading or counting sheep to put themselves to sleep.
- When mothers fully adopt the Safe Sleep Seven (llli.org/sweetsleepbook), the published risk of SIDS or suffocation for their babies is minute. All seven practices must be fully adopted.

References: Bedsharing Talking Points

1. Ball, H. L. Breastfeeding, bedsharing, and infant sleep. *Birth* 30 (2003): 181–188.

2. Mosko, S., Richard, C., McKenna, J. Maternal sleep and arousals during bedsharing with infants. *Sleep* 20, no. 2 (1997): 142–150.

3. Richard, C., Mosko, S., McKenna, J., et al. Sleeping position, orientation, and proximity in bedsharing infants and mothers. *Sleep* 19, no. 9 (1996): 685–690. Baddock, S. A., Galland, B. C., Bolton, D. P. G., et al. Differences in infant and parent behaviors during routine bed sharing compared with cot sleeping in the home setting. *Pediatrics* 117, no. 5 (2006): 1599–1607.

4. Mosko, S., Richard, C., McKenna, J. Maternal sleep and arousals during bedsharing with infants. *Sleep* 20, no. 2 (1997): 142–150.

5. McKenna, J. J., Ball, H. L., Gettler, L. T. Mother-infant cosleeping, breastfeeding and sudden infant death syndrome: what biological anthropology has discovered about normal infant sleep and pediatric sleep medicine. *American Journal of Physical Anthropology* 134, suppl. 45 (2007): 133–161.

6. Ball, H. L. Breastfeeding, bed-sharing, and infant sleep. Birth 30, no. 3 (2003): 181–188. Ball, H. L. Bed-sharing practices of initially breastfed infants in the first 6 months of life. *Infant and Child Development* 16, no. 4 (2007): 387–401. Ball, H. L. Reasons to bed-share: why parents sleep with their infants. *Journal of Reproductive and Infant Psychology* 20, no. 4 (2002): 207–221. Kendall-Tackett, K., Cong, Z., Hale, T. W. Mother-infant sleep locations and nighttime feeding behavior. *Clinical Lactation* 1, no. 1 (2010): 27–30. Lahr, M. B., Rosenberg, K. D. Maternal-infant bedsharing: risk factors for bedsharing in a population-based survey of new mothers and implications for SIDS risk reduction. *Maternal and Child Health Journal* 11, no. 3 (2007): 277–286. Blair, P. S., Ball, H. L. The prevalence and characteristics associated with parent-infant bed-sharing in England. *Archives of Disease in Childhood* 89, no. 12 (2004): 1106–1110.

7. Moore, E. R., Anderson, G. C., Bergman, N., et al. Early skin-to-skin contact for mothers and their healthy newborn infants. *Cochrane Database of Systematic Reviews* 5 (2012), CD003519.

8. Montgomery-Downs, H. E., et al. Normative longitudinal maternal sleep: the first 4 postpartum months. *American Journal of Obstetrics and Gynecology* 203, no. 5 (2010): 465e1–7.

9. Parmelee, A. H. Jr., Wenner, W. H., Schulz, H. R. Infant sleep patterns: from birth to 16 weeks of age. *Journal of Pediatrics* 65 (1964): 576–582.

10. Kent, J. C., Mitoulas, L. R., Cregan, M. D., et al. Volume and frequency of breastfeedings and fat content of breast milk throughout the day. *Pediatrics* 117, no. 3 (2006): e387–e395.

11. Ball, H. L. Breastfeeding, bed-sharing, and infant sleep. *Birth* 30, no. 3 (2003): 181–188.

12. Volpe, L. E., Ball, H. L., McKenna, J. J. Nighttime parenting strategies and sleep-related risks to infants. *Social Science and Medicine* 79 (2012): 92–100.

13. Kendall-Tackett, K., Cong, Z., Hale, T. W. Mother-infant sleep locations and nighttime feeding behavior. *Clinical Lactation* 1, no. 1 (2010): 27–30.

14. Blair, P. S., Fleming, P. J., Smith, I. J., et al. Babies sleeping with parents: case-control study of factors influencing the risk of the sudden infant death syndrome. CESDI SUDI Research Group. *BMJ* 319, no. 7223 (1999): 1457–1461. Carpenter, R. G., Irgens, L. M., Blair, P. S., et al. Sudden unexplained infant death in 20 regions in Europe: case control study. *Lancet* 363, no. 9404 (2004): 185–191. Tappin, D., Ecob, R., Brooke, H. Bedsharing, roomsharing, and sudden infant death syndrome in Scotland: a case-control study. *Journal of Pediatrics* 147, no. 1 (2005): 32–37. Vennemann, M. M., Bajanowski, T., Brinkmann, B., et al. Sleep environment risk factors for sudden infant death syndrome: the German Sudden Infant Death Syndrome Study. *Pediatrics* 123, no. 4 (2009): 1162–1170. Ruys, J. H., De Jonge, G. A., Brand, R., et al. Bed sharing in the first four months of life: a risk factor for sudden infant death. *Acta Paediatrica* 96, no. 10 (2007): 1399–1403.

15. Ball, H. L. Breastfeeding, bed-sharing, and infant sleep. Birth 30, no. 3 (2003): 181–188. Ball, H. L. Bed-sharing practices of initially breastfed infants in the first 6 months of life. *Infant and Child Development* 16, no. 4 (2007): 387–401. Ball, H. L. Reasons to bed-share: why parents sleep with their infants. *Journal of Reproductive and Infant Psychology* 20, no. 4 (2002): 207–221. Kendall-Tackett, K., Cong, Z., Hale, T. W. Mother-infant sleep locations and nighttime feeding behavior. *Clinical Lactation* 1, no. 1 (2010): 27–30. Lahr, M. B., Rosenberg, K. D., Lapidus, J. A. Maternal-infant bedsharing: risk factors for bedsharing in a population-based survey of new mothers and implications for SIDS risk reduction. *Maternal and Child Health Journal* 11, no. 3 (2007): 277–286. Blair, P. S. The prevalence and characteristics associated with parent-infant bed-sharing in England. *Archives of Disease in Childhood* 89, no. 12 (2004): 1106–1110.

16. Blair, P. S., Sidebotham, P., Evason-Coombe, C., Edmonds, M., Heckstall-Smith, E., and Fleming, P. Hazardous cosleeping environments and risk factors amenable to change: case-control study of SIDS in south west England. *BMJ* 339 (2009):b3666. doi:10.1136/bmj.b3666.

17. World Health Organization, United Nations Children's Fund. *Global Strategy for Infant and Young Child Feeding*. Geneva: World Health Organization, 2003; 30. American Academy of Pediatrics, Breastfeeding and the use of human milk. *Pediatrics* 129, no. 3 (2012): e827–e841.

18. Hauck, F. R., Thompson, J. M., Tanabe, K. O., et al. Breastfeeding and reduced risk of sudden infant death syndrome: a meta-analysis. *Pediatrics* 128, no. 1 (2011): 103–110.

19. Emde, R. N. Early emotional development: new modes of thinking for research and intervention. *Pediatrics* 102, no. 5, suppl. E (1998): 1236–1243.

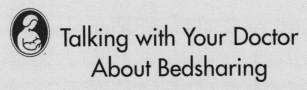

Talking with Your Doctor About Bedsharing

From *Sweet Sleep: Nighttime and Naptime Strategies for the Breastfeeding Family*

Some parents choose not to discuss their sleeping arrangements with medical caregivers, even if asked. If you do choose to, here are some points you may find helpful:

- I really do appreciate your willingness to listen. It's one of the reasons we come to you.
- Although the public health campaigns suggest that all bedsharing with babies is dangerous, the research shows that the issue is complex, and not a one-size-fits-all.
- Most of the research mixes up SIDS and suffocation. There are ways to make bedsharing safety comparable to a cot's.
- SIDS is linked to smoking, formula-feeding, alcohol, a baby sleeping on his stomach, an overheated baby, a preemie or a baby with significant health issues, and a baby left alone. That's not us.
- Suffocation and other breathing risks are linked to an impaired adult or a soft or cluttered or otherwise hazardous surface. That's not us.
- Like other breastfeeding mothers, I sleep with my baby in a specific, protective position, away from pillows, and he stays there to be near my breast. A bottle-feeding mother doesn't sleep in that position and her baby is less likely to stay put.
- I make sure my baby sleeps next to me and not next to someone else.
- No studies have found an increased risk for babies when all those other risks are accounted for. The 2013 Carpenter meta-analysis that says otherwise is based on studies with poor definitions and missing data.
- Research studies have found no increased risk with bedsharing after about four months.
- Like other breastfeeding mothers, I wake up frequently to tend him and feed him, and often don't even know I'm doing it. If he were across the room, he wouldn't be tended nearly so carefully.
- He doesn't need a dummy. I'm right there to breastfeed him.
- If a mother doesn't bedshare, she's less likely to breastfeed as long as medical organizations recommend, with big health consequences.
- The brochures say my baby shouldn't sleep on a chair or a reclining chair or a sofa or a bed to breastfeed at night. He sleeps when we breastfeed. Where, exactly, am I supposed to go at 3 a.m. if I'm really tired?
- Sleep training isn't something we're comfortable with. The research that promotes it doesn't look at the internal changes or the long-term outcomes. Sleep training raises his cortisol level and keeps it high even after he stops crying. And it's not good for breastfeeding.

You might want to share the tearsheets on Bedsharing Talking Points and the Safe Sleep and Safe Surface checklists. The talking points sheet has references on the other side that support the statements above.

Breast or Bottle for Better Sleep?

From *Sweet Sleep: Nighttime and Naptime Strategies for the Breastfeeding Family*

Nights may be difficult at first.
But oh, how much better it gets when you're breastfeeding and bedsharing!

Night Breastfeeding with Bedsharing	Night Bottle-feeding with a Cot
Means staying in bed	Means getting out of bed
Usually means lying down	Means sitting up
Means warm feet	Can mean cold feet
Can make night feeds simple and even pleasurable	Requires preparation and cleanup
Usually means no tears	Often means a crying baby
Usually means back to sleep faster	Often means a longer time up
Can put you back to sleep	Won't help you fall asleep
Can sometimes happen in your sleep	Never happens in your sleep
Means no more babies for a bit	Means you're fertile sooner
Keeps your stress low	Increases your stress
Keeps your baby's stress low	Increases your baby's stress
Is on tap 24/7	Means purchase, preparation, and cleanup
Means snuggling together back to sleep	Means going back to separate beds
Saves money for the family	Makes money for the pharmaceutical industry
Actually gives you the most sleep of all new mothers	Actually reduces your sleep

Your Milk	Formula
Has hundreds of goodies including: • Interferon and white blood cells • Antibacterial and antiviral agents • Intestinal soothers and growth hormones	Has a label's worth, including: • Tropical oils and corn syrup • Cow's milk or soya beans • Intestinal irritants
Everything a baby is known to need	Known and unknown deficiencies
Changes with every meal and every day	Is the same old same old
Promotes normal health	Means more visits to the doctor, now and in the future
Is nearly free	Costs about $100–300 a month for basic types
Promotes normal brain development	Is linked to lower IQ
Is always clean, straight from the source	Is easily and frequently contaminated
Promotes normal health in infancy and beyond	Has been linked to increases in many infant illnesses, including SIDS, ear infections, urinary tract infections, respiratory infections, allergies, and to many long-term problems including malocclusion, breast cancer, childhood lymphoma, vision deficits, obesity, and diabetes
Is worth working through any early problems	Doesn't have to be your first choice

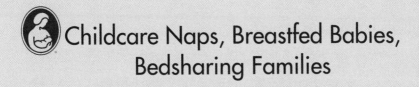

Childcare Naps, Breastfed Babies, Bedsharing Families

From *Sweet Sleep: Nighttime and Naptime Strategies for the Breastfeeding Family*

Many breastfeeding families also bedshare. This sheet may help you understand the breastfed, bedsharing baby's sleep patterns. Breastfed babies typically breastfeed to sleep with body contact during feeding and often during sleep as well. They are less likely to have a special blanket or toy. Many do not use a dummy. The following feeding and naptime suggestions may be helpful:

- Fussing and crying should not be ignored. Ignoring cries will make subsequent sleep more difficult.
- Offering a bottle of expressed milk may help these babies to fall asleep.
- Hold the baby snugly and fairly upright while giving a bottle.
- Keep the bottle fairly horizontal, which allows for a slower milk flow and more relaxed feeding.
- A full feeding usually takes about 20 minutes.
- Offering "snack" bottles as the baby wants will give him more adult contact and more opportunities to nap.
- The baby may be allowed to fall asleep during the feed.
- Unused milk can be refrigerated for the next feed. Encouraging the baby to finish a bottle may cause overfeeding that can interfere with sleep. Feeding length should be determined by the baby's behaviour, not by the amount taken.
- Only milk provided by the mother may be used. Formula and solids are not to be introduced without the mother's written permission.
- Additional information: ______________________________

____
____
____
____

More information on the reverse side.

Suggested calming techniques:

- Use a sling or other carrier provided by the mother. Babies often nap in a carrier. Check with the mother on moving the sleeping baby to a cot.
- Provide an article of the mother's clothing with her scent on it, to be kept in the cot.
- Offer a dummy to promote sleep, with the mother's approval. Remove it if the baby is awake and happy.
- Additional information: ______________________________

____

____

Napping/feeding behaviour:

- Some breastfed babies prefer lengthy naps at nursery or the childminder's with very few feeds. This is normal.
- Some breastfed babies prefer many shorter naps and a larger number of feeds. This too is normal.
- Avoid feeding the baby within _____ minutes of his mother's return. She may want to breastfeed him before taking him home.
- Additional information: ______________________________

____

____

Basic safety precautions:

- SIDS is most likely during the first four months, especially during the first few weeks of nursery. Extra adult supervision while the baby adjusts can help.
- Baby sleeps on his back, on a firm mattress with no other items in the cot besides the mother's article of clothing and a light blanket. Babies who are able to roll over and back on their own may sleep in any position they choose.
- No swaddling or other wrappings.
- Under about six months, the baby should be kept where an adult is able to see and hear him, not in a separate room, even if a baby monitor is used.
- Additional information: ______________________________

____

____

Your attention to the needs of breastfed babies is appreciated! Guidelines for handling expressed milk are available as a tearsheet in *The Womanly Art of Breastfeeding*, eighth edition (2010) (goo.gl/Zal8Ax).

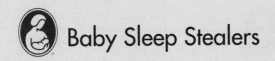

Baby Sleep Stealers

You're awake because your baby's awake. But babies don't fuss or stay awake because they want to. Maybe one of these reasons fits:

- *Your caffeine or chocolate consumption?*
- *Allergy?* Cow's milk, soy, wheat, and laundry detergent are common allergens. Wakefulness despite fatigue can be a sign of allergy.
- *Infection?* Ear infections and urinary tract infections (UTIs) are common culprits.
- *Vaccinations or illnesses?* Any symptoms: vomiting, diarrhoea or constipation, fevers, chills, rashes, sweating?
- *Teething?* Pain from erupting teeth can be more noticeable at night. Teething can start very early and take forever.
- *Medications?* Has anyone—mother or child—taken anything recently, even vitamins or herbs?
- *Family disruptions?* Recent move, other siblings, relatives, too much going on, abuse? Recent yelling or fighting in the household or nearby?
- *Too little holding?* How much holding, carrying, and touching happens in the daytime?
- *Hypersensitive to sound, light, smells, textures?* Scented candles, air fresheners, chemicals, etc.?
- *Headache?* Any falls or accidents? Vision or hearing irregularities?
- *Overstimulation?* Sometimes the brain wants to keep going even when the body is exhausted.
- *Too distracted during the day?* Babies make up for busy days with breastfeeding more at night. Pretty typical around four or five months.
- *Learning exciting new skills?* Did she just learn to roll over? Crawl? Walk? Start solids?
- *Stranger anxiety?* Crops up around nine months.
- *Returning to work or lengthy daytime separation?* Baby can feel more need to reconnect at night, no matter what his age or stage.

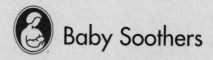

Baby Soothers

From *Sweet Sleep: Nighttime and Naptime Strategies for the Breastfeeding Family*

Your baby is fussing, grumbling, or outright crying, and you just want him to go to sleep! What can you do?

- *Breastfeed.* An almost magical way to help babies unwind and induce sleep.
- *Rule out the common causes.* Take a look at the Baby Sleep Stealers Tear-sheet on the reverse side.
- *Move it, move it.* Moving—walking, dancing, swaying, rocking, *gentle* bouncing, the Magic Baby Hold—may be very soothing to a grumpy baby.
- *Manage the transition.* Often getting the baby to sleep isn't the issue—it's moving the baby from your arms to a new surface. Try waiting until she's so deeply asleep that her arms are limp. You can avoid a drop in temperature if you keep a small blanket against her back as you move her. Or put a hot water bottle or heating pad in the cot and take it out just before you put her down.
- *Change the scenery.* When your baby spends time outdoors during the day, she'll be calmer and sleep better at night. Having a fussy evening? Going outside, even for a minute or two, usually helps. Enjoy seeing the stars—or the streetlights—together. Even a trip into the next room is a change of scenery that might help.
- *Turn up the volume.* Well, not too high. Loud noises can keep babies awake, but so can silence. Babies feel calmest when they hear the reassuring sounds of people around them.
- *Turn off electronics.* TVs, computers, tablets, phones, and other electronic screens emit a type of light that can keep the brain more active.
- *Turn off bright lights.* Lower the lights in the room to candlelight level.
- *Try baby massage or a warm bath.* Maybe get in the bath together. Try putting a warm, wet flannel on her back while she lies on your chest in the bath, and pour warm water over it to keep her warm.
- *Be there.* Even if nothing works, the baby who cries in-arms is less stressed than the baby who cries alone.
- *Sing or read.* A time-honoured way to soothe children to sleep, especially if there's rhythm, as in Dr. Seuss's books or *Goodnight Moon* by Margaret Wise Brown. Dance gently while you read or sing.
- *Try breastfeeding again.* Even if it didn't work before, it might be just what she needs now to send her into dreamland. Needing to breastfeed isn't always the problem. More often than not, though, breastfeeding becomes the answer.

acknowledgements

With Our Thanks

We are tremendously grateful to the expert researchers who so generously offered their wisdom, insights, and feedback to shape this book and give it depth and integrity: Helen Ball, for her many hours of patient guidance, sharing of material, and work on behalf of mothers and babies everywhere—and for being a steady compass on our sometimes rocky canoe; James McKenna, whose studies of mother-baby sleep interactions laid a foundation of normal biology for infant sleep research; and Nils Bergman for providing us with a deeper understanding of the neurobiology of infants and touch, and for offering a burst of clarity at just the right moment.

We could never have written this book without the stories, photographs, support, and insights of all our contributors: Michelle and Andy Adelewitz, Lara Audelo, Carmela Baeza, Sarah Bailey, Barbara Behrmann, Jill Bergman, Jolie Blackbear, Maya Bolman, Hannah Boswell, Jane Bradshaw, Jan Ellen Brown, Dorothy Buel, Vered Bukai, Angela Cahill, Geraldine Cahill, Barbara Cameron, Diana Cassar-Uhl, Maureen Clark, Jean Cotterman, Sara Dale-Bley, Donna Dietz, Sara Dodson, Jill Dye, Sylvia Ellison, Chana Fitton, Kittie Franz, Veronica Garea, Catherine Genna, Lois Gosse, Roberta Graham de Escobedo, Cynthia Gration, Karen Gromada,

Christina Hardyment, Suzanne Haydu, Suzanne Haynes, Donna Henderson, Barbara Higham, Cathy Holland, Sarah Hung, Shanna Jesch, Colleen and David Jones, Kathleen Kendall-Tackett, April Kline, Jessica Kosa, Lindsay Kurz, Melissa Kyle, Heidi Lam, Laura LaRocca, Ali Lee, Nikki Lee, Samantha Leeson, Sagit Lev, Jennifer Lisimachio, Sherrie Littlefield, Eglantina Lucio, Susan Ludington, Lisa Mandell, RuthAnna Mather, Amber McCann, Jeanette McCulloch, Trevor McDonald, Angela McSweeney, Wendy Middlemiss, Beth Myler, Amy Nansteel, Ava Nansteel, Kenneth Nansteel, Breelan and Gradyn Nash, Isabel Nelson, Jack Newman, Micaela Notarangelo, Nicola O'Byrne, Leigh Anne O'Connor, Jeanette Panchula, Nan Perigo, Tricia Phillip, Esmaralda Pitman, Lisa Pitman, Lauren Porter, Barbara Robinson, Lesley Robinson, Nikki Rogers, Lisa Rotondi, Kathleen Salisbury, Alyssa Schnell, Kate Sharp, Mellanie Sheppard, Lillian Shipman, Susanna Short, Christina Smillie, Leslie Stern, Barbara Sturmfels, James Swain, Marija Taraba, Therese Tee, Laurel Tharrington, Josephina Tohman, Laura Ulrich, Annie Urban, Marianne Vakiener, Angeline Wee, Lissa Welles, Amy West, Brad West, Monica Whitmore, Eric and Kasey Wiessinger, Scott and Laura Wiessinger, Wendy Williams, Margaret Wills, Linda Wyatt, and Theresa Yaroshevich.

We thank the LLLI Leader review team, whose careful reading and thoughtful editing suggestions made this an even better book: Kathy Grossman, Barbara Higham, and Laura Maxson. A very special thank-you to Barbara Emanuel and LaJuana Oswalt, who gave *Sweet Sleep* its start and supported our work and concepts so staunchly throughout the writing process. And our heartfelt thanks to Ann Calandro and the co-chairs of the LLLI board of directors, Cindy Garrison and Lydia deRaad, who provided valuable insights and wise guidance.

We also thank the staff of the LLLI office. Josh Dobbelstein worked patiently and skilfully to prepare and create the photos and illustrations. Staff members Susan Comer, Dave Davis, Sandhya Matthews, Jackie Philp, Holly Stevens, and Nicole St. Pierre kept other projects running smoothly while the executive staff was focused on the book.

Our thanks to the publishing professionals who paved the way for this book: Marnie Cochran, our wise and wonderful executive editor at Random House, for believing in a book about bedsharing for breastfeeding families and for her patience in allowing time for the book to grow into what it needed to be; Stephanie Kip Rostan of Levine|Greenberg Literary Agency, for her gracious and expert facilitation of this complex project; and Maura Kye-Casella of Don Congdon Associates, who was always there with great advice, cheering us on every step of the way.

For help with preparing this Pinter & Martin edition, we would like to thank Lois Rowlands, Sue Upstone, Ellen Mateer, Rachel O'Leary at LLLGB, and Helen Bilton and Debbie Kennett.

A big thank-you to our partners, who embraced bedsharing, and our children, who showed us how important it could be. And to La Leche League, which taught us to trust the mothering instinct that brought our babies into our bed. Most of all we thank the many, many mothers who were and are the heart of La Leche League. You remind us, always, to listen to our mother-wisdom. And yours.

notes

Introduction

1. Steube, A. The risks of not breastfeeding for mothers and infants. *Reviews in Obstetrics and Gynecology* 2, no. 4 (2009): 222–231. Smith, J. P., Dunstone, M. D., Elliott-Rudder, M. E. Voldemort and health professional knowledge of breastfeeding: do journal titles and abstracts accurately convey findings on differential health outcomes for formula fed infants. *ACERH Working Paper* no. 4 (2008).

Chapter 2: The Safe Sleep Seven

1. Ball, H. L. Breastfeeding, bed-sharing, and infant sleep. *Birth* 30, no. 3 (2003): 181–188. Ball, H. L., Hooker, E., Kelly, P. J. Where will the baby sleep? Attitudes and practices of new and experienced parents regarding cosleeping with their newborn infants. *American Anthropologist* 101, no. 1 (1999): 143–151.
2. U.S. Department of Health and Human Services. Executive summary: the surgeon general's call to action to support breastfeeding. *Breastfeeding Medicine* 6, no. 1 (2011): 3–5.
3. Imong, S. M., Jackson, D. A., Wongsawasdii, L., et al. Predictors of breast milk intake in rural northern Thailand. *Journal of Pediatric Gastroenterology and Nutrition* 8, no. 3 (1989): 359–370. Kent, J. C. Volume and frequency of breastfeedings and fat content of breast milk throughout the day. *Pediatrics* 117, no. 3 (2006): e387–e395.
4. Howel, D., Ball, H. Association between length of exclusive breastfeeding and subsequent breastfeeding continuation. *Journal of Human Lactation* 29, no. 4 (2013): 579–585.
5. National Institute for Health and Care Excellence, www.nice.org.uk/guidance/CG37/chapter/1-Guidance.
6. Kendall-Tackett, K., Cong, Z., Hale, T. W. Mother-infant sleep locations and nighttime feeding behavior. *Clinical Lactation* 1, no. 1 (2010): 27–30.
7. Colson, E. R., Willinger, M., Rybin, D., et al. Trends and factors associated with infant bed sharing, 1993–2010. The National Infant Sleep Position Study. *JAMA Pediatrics* 167, no. 11 (2013): 1032–1037.
8. Ball, H. L. Breastfeeding, bed-sharing, and infant sleep. *Birth* 30, no. 3 (2003): 181–188. Ball, H. L. Bed-sharing practices of initially breastfed infants in the first 6 months of life. *Infant and Child Development* 16, no. 4 (2007): 387–401. Ball, H. L. Reasons to bed-share: why parents sleep with their infants. *Journal of Reproductive and Infant Psychology* 20, no. 4 (2002): 207–221. Kendall-Tackett, K., Cong, Z., Hale, T. W. Mother-infant sleep locations and nighttime feeding behavior. *Clinical Lactation* 1, no. 1 (2010): 27–30. Lahr, M. B., Rosenberg, K. D., Lapidus, J. A. Maternal-infant bedsharing: risk factors for bedsharing in a population-based survey of new mothers and implications for SIDS risk reduction. *Maternal and Child Health Journal* 11, no. 3 (2007): 277–286. Blair, P. S. The prevalence and characteristics associated with parent-infant bed-sharing in England. *Archives of Disease in Childhood* 89, no. 12 (2004): 1106–1110.
9. Quillin, S. I. M. Interaction between feeding method and co-sleeping on maternal-newborn sleep. *Journal of Obstetric, Gynecologic, and Neonatal Nursing* 33, no. 5 (2004): 580–588.
10. Ball, H. L., Hooker, E., Kelly, P. J. Where will the baby sleep? Attitudes and practices of new and experienced parents regarding cosleeping with their newborn infants. *American Anthropologist* 101, no. 1 (1999): 143–151.
11. Blair, P. S., Fleming, P. J., Smith, I. J., et al. Babies sleeping with parents: case-control study of factors influencing the risk of the sudden infant death syndrome. CESDI SUDI Research Group. *BMJ* 319, no. 7223 (1999): 1457–1461. Carpenter, R. G., Irgens, L. M., Blair, P. S., et al. Sudden unexplained infant death in 20 regions in Europe: case control study. *Lancet* 363, no. 9404 (2004): 185–191. Tappin, D., Ecob, R., Brooke, H. Bedsharing, roomsharing, and sudden infant death syndrome in Scotland: a case-control study. *Journal of Pediatrics* 147, no. 1 (2005): 32–37. Vennemann, M. M., Bajanowski, T., Brinkmann, B., et al. Sleep environment risk factors for sudden infant death syndrome: the German Sudden Infant Death Syndrome Study. *Pediatrics* 123, no. 4 (2009): 1162–1170. Ruys, J. H., De Jonge, G.

A., Brand, R., et al. Bed-sharing in the first four months of life: a risk factor for sudden infant death. *Acta Paediatrica* 96, no. 10 (2007): 1399–1403.
12. Dietz, P. M., England, L. J., Shapiro-Mendoza, C. K., et al. Infant morbidity and mortality attributable to prenatal smoking in the U.S. *American Journal of Preventive Medicine* 39, no. 1 (2010): 45–52.
13. Vennemann, M. M., Hense, H. W., Bajanowski, T., et al. Bed sharing and the risk of sudden infant death syndrome: can we resolve the debate? *Journal of Pediatrics* 160, no. 1 (2012): 44–48.
14. Vennemann, M. M., Hense, H. W., Bajanowski, T., et al. Bed sharing and the risk of sudden infant death syndrome: can we resolve the debate? *Journal of Pediatrics* 160, no. 1 (2012): 44–48. Zhang, K., Wang, X. Maternal smoking and increased risk of sudden infant death syndrome: a meta-analysis. *Legal Medicine (Tokyo)* 15, no. 3 (2013): 115–121. Fleming, P., Blair, P. S. Sudden infant death syndrome and parental smoking. *Early Human Development* 83, no. 11 (2007): 721–725.
15. First Candle, in conjunction with the American Academy of Pediatrics, "Room-Sharing Is Safer than Bed-Sharing,"
firstcandle.org/new- expectant-parents/bedtime-basics-for-babies/room-sharing-is-safer-than-bed-sharing. Public Health Agency of Canada's Joint Statement on Safe Sleep. "Preventing Sudden Infant Deaths in Canada." 2012, phac-aspc.gc.ca/hp-ps/dca-dea/stages-etapes/childhood-enfance_0-2/sids/pdf /jsss-ecss2011-eng.pdf. Tappin, D., Ecob, R., Brooke, H. Bedsharing, roomsharing, and sudden infant death syndrome in Scotland: a case-control study. *Journal of Pediatrics* 147, no. 1 (2009): 32. Carpenter, R. G., Irgens, L. M., Blair, P. S., et al. Sudden unexplained infant death in 20 regions in Europe: case control study. *Lancet* 36, no. 9404 (2004): 185–191. Blair, P. S., Fleming, P. J., Smith, I. J., et al. Babies sleeping with parents: case-control study of factors influencing the risk of the sudden infant death syndrome. CESDI SUDI Research Group. *BMJ* 319, no. 7223 (1999): 1457–1461.
16. Ip, S., Chung, M., Raman, G., et al. *Breastfeeding and Maternal and Infant Health Outcomes in Developed Countries.* Rockville, MD: Agency for Healthcare Research and Quality, 2007. McVea, K. L., Turner, P. D., Peppler, D. K. The role of breastfeeding in sudden infant death syndrome. *Journal of Human Lactation* 16 (2000): 13–20.
17. Hale, T. W. *Medications and Mother's Milk 2012: A Manual of Lactational Pharmacology.* Amarillo, TX: Hale Publishing, 2012.
18. Arnestad, M., Andersen, M., Vege, A., et al. Changes in the epidemiological pattern of sudden infant death syndrome in southeast Norway, 1984–1998: implications for future prevention and research. *Archives of Disease in Childhood* 85, no. 2 (2001): 108–115. Blabey, M. H., Gessner, B. D. Infant bed-sharing practices and associated risk factors among births and infant deaths in Alaska. *Public Health Reports* 124, no. 4 (2009): 527–534.
19. Hauck, F. R., Herman, S. M., Donovan, M., et al. Sleep environment and the risk of sudden infant death syndrome in an urban population: the Chicago Infant Mortality Study. *Pediatrics* 111 (2003): 1207–1214.
20. Ho, E., Collantes, A., Kapur, B. M., et al. Alcohol and breast feeding: calculation of time to zero level in milk. *Biology of the Neonate* 80, no. 3 (2001): 219–222.
21. Hale, T. W. *Medications and Mother's Milk 2012: A Manual of Lactational Pharmacology.* Amarillo, TX: Hale Publishing, 2012.
22. Mennella, J. Alcohol's effect on lactation. *Alcohol Research and Health* 25 no. 3 (2001): 230–234.
23. Mennella, J. A., Gerrish, C. J. Effects of exposure to alcohol in mother's milk on infant sleep. *Pediatrics* 101.5 (1998): e2–e2.
24. Mennella, J. A., Pepino, M. Y., Teff, K. L. Acute alcohol consumption disrupts the hormonal milieu of lactating women. *Journal of Clinical Endocrinology and Metabolism* 90 no. 4 (2005): 1979–1985.
25. Mennella, J. A. Regulation of milk intake after exposure to alcohol in mothers' milk. *Alcoholism: Clinical and Experimental Research* 25, no. 4 (2001): 590–593.
26. Maruff, P., Falleti, M. G., Collie, A., et al. Fatigue-related impairment in the speed, accuracy and variability of psychomotor performance: comparison with blood alcohol levels. *J Sleep Res* 14, no. 1 (2005): 21–27.
27. Ball, H. Parent-infant bed-sharing behavior. *Human Nature* 17, no. 3 (2006): 301–318. Ball, H. L., Klingaman, K. Breastfeeding and mother-infant sleep proximity. *In* Trevathan, W. R., Smith, E. O., McKenna, J. J. (eds.), *Evolutionary Medicine.* New York: Oxford University Press, 1999.
28. Richard, C., Mosko, S., McKenna, J., et al. Sleeping position, orientation, and proximity in bedsharing infants and mothers. *Sleep* 19, no. 9 (1996): 685–690. Baddock, S. A., Galland, B. C., Bolton, D. P. G., et al. Differences in infant and parent behaviors during routine bed sharing compared with cot sleeping in the home setting. *Pediatrics* 117, no. 5 (2006): 1599–1607.
29. Ball, H. Parent-infant bed-sharing behavior. *Human Nature* 17, no. 3 (2006): 301–318. Ball, H. L., Klingaman, K. Breastfeeding and mother-infant sleep proximity. In Trevathan, W., Smith, E. O., McKenna, J. J. (eds.), *Evolutionary Medicine and Health: New Perspectives.* Oxford: Oxford University Press, 2008.

30. Ball, H. Parent-infant bed-sharing behavior. *Human Nature* 17, no. 3 (2006): 301–318. McKenna, J. J., Ball, H. L., Gettler, L. T. Mother-infant cosleeping, breastfeeding and sudden infant death syndrome: what biological anthropology has discovered about normal infant sleep and pediatric sleep medicine. *American Journal of Physical Anthropology* 134, suppl. 45 (2007): 133–161.

31. Volpe, L. E., Ball, H. L., McKenna, J. J. Nighttime parenting strategies and sleep-related risks to infants. *Social Science and Medicine* no. 79 (2013): 92–100.

32. Blair, P. S., Fleming, P. J., Smith, I. J., et al. Babies sleeping with parents: case-control study of factors influencing the risk of the sudden infant death syndrome. CESDI SUDI Research Group. *BMJ* 319, no. 7223 (1999): 1457–1461. Carpenter, R. G., Irgens, L. M., Blair, P. S., et al. Sudden unexplained infant death in 20 regions in Europe: case control study. *Lancet* 363, no. 9404 (2004): 185–191. Tappin, D., Ecob, R., Brooke, H. Bedsharing, roomsharing, and sudden infant death syndrome in Scotland: a case-control study. *Journal of Pediatrics* 147, no. 1 (2005): 32–37. Vennemann, M. M., Bajanowski, T., Brinkmann, B., et al. Sleep environment risk factors for sudden infant death syndrome: the German Sudden Infant Death Syndrome Study. *Pediatrics* 123, no. 4 (2009): 1162–1170. Ruys, J. H., De Jonge, G. A., Brand, R., et al. Bed sharing in the first four months of life: a risk factor for sudden infant death. *Acta Paediatrica* 96, no. 10 (2007): 1399–1403. Moon, R. Y., et al. SIDS and other sleep-related infant deaths: expansion of recommendations for a safe infant sleeping environment. *Pediatrics* 128, no. 5 (2011): e1341–e1367.

33. Malloy, M. H. Prematurity and sudden infant death syndrome: United States 2005–2007. *Journal of Perinatology* 33, no. 6 (2013): 470–475. Randall, B. B., Paterson, D. S., Haas, E. A., et al. Potential asphixia and brainstem abnormalities in sudden and unexpected death in infants. *Pediatrics* 132, no. 6 (2013): e1616–e1625. Kinney, H. C., Thach, B. T. The sudden infant death syndrome. *New England Journal of Medicine* 361, no. 8 (2009): 795–805. Moon, R. Y., Fu, L. Sudden Infant Death Syndrome: an update. *Pediatrics in Review* 33, no. 7 (2012): 314–320.

34. Horne, R. S., Parslow, P. M., Ferens, D., et al. Arousal responses and risk factors for sudden infant death syndrome. *Sleep Medicine* 3 (2002): S61–S65.

35. Mitchell, E. A., Blair, P. S. SIDS prevention: 3000 lives saved but we can do better. *New Zealand Medical Journal* 125, no. 1359 (2012): 50.

36. Gessner, B. D., Ives, G. C., Perham-Hester, K. A. Association between sudden infant death syndrome and prone sleep position, bed sharing, and sleeping outside an infant crib in Alaska. *Pediatrics* 108, no. 4 (2001): 923–927.

37. Bergman, N. J., Linley, L. L., Fawcus, S. R. Randomized controlled trial of skin-to-skin contact from birth versus conventional incubator for physiological stabilization in 1200- to 2199-gram newborns. *Acta Paediatrica* 93, no. 6 (2004): 779–785.

38. Bergman, N. J., Jürisoo, L. A. The "kangaroo-method" for treating low birth weight babies in a developing country. *Tropical Doctor* 24, no. 2 (1994): 57–60.

39. Vennemann, M. M., Findeisen, M., Butterfaß-Bahloul, T., et al. Modifiable risk factors for SIDS in Germany: results of GeSID. *Acta Paediatrica* 94, no. 6 (2005): 655–660.

40. Moon, R. Y., et al. SIDS and other sleep-related infant deaths: expansion of recommendations for a safe infant sleeping environment. *Pediatrics* 128, no. 5 (2011): e1341–e1367.

41. Kleemann, W. J., Schlaud, M., Poets, C. F., et al. Hyperthermia in sudden infant death. *International Journal of Legal Medicine* 109, no. 3 (1996): 139–142. Ponsonby, A. L., Dwyer, T., Kasl, S. V., et al. The Tasmanian SIDS Case-Control Study: univariable and multivariable risk factor analysis. *Paediatric and Perinatal Epidemiology* 9, no. 3 (1995): 256–272.

42. Ball, H. Airway covering during bed-sharing. *Child: Care, Health, and Development* 35, no. 5 (2009): 728–737.

43. Somers, R. L. Assessment of infant mattress firmness: a do-it-yourself safety test to reduce the risk of asphyxiation. *Australian and New Zealand Journal of Public Health* 36, no. 5 (2012): 490–491.

44. McKenna, J. J., Ball, H. L., Gettler, L. T. Mother-infant cosleeping, breastfeeding and sudden infant death syndrome: what biological anthropology has discovered about normal infant sleep and pediatric sleep medicine. *American Journal of Physical Anthropology* 134, suppl. 45 (2007): 133–161.

Chapter 3: Attached and Attuned

1. McKenna, J. In defense of Maya's mother. *Contemporary Pediatrics* 17, no. 6 (2000): 116–117.

2. Trevathan, W. R., Smith, E. O., McKenna, J. J. *Evolutionary Medicine.* New York: Oxford University Press, 1999.

3. Gallagher, W. Motherless child. *Sciences* 32 (1992): 12–15.

4. Bergman, N. J., Linley, L. L., Fawcus, S. R. Randomized controlled trial of skin-to-skin contact from birth versus conventional incubator for physiological stabilization in 1200- to 2199-gram newborns. *Acta Paediatrica* 93, no. 6 (2004): 779–785.

5. Winnicott, D. *Babies and Their Mothers.* New York: Perseus Publishing, 1987.

6. Lawrence, R. A., Lawrence, R. M. (eds.). *Breastfeeding: A Guide for the Medical Profession,* 7th ed. St. Louis: Elsevier Mosby, 2011.

7. Uvnäs-Moberg, K. *The Oxytocin Factor.* Cambridge, MA: Da Capo Press, 2003.

8. Huang, Y., Hauck, F. R., Signore, C., et al. Influence of bedsharing activity on breastfeeding duration among US mothers. *JAMA Pediatrics* 167, no. 11 (2013): 1038–1044. Perrine, C. G., Scanlon, K. S., Li, R., et al. Baby-friendly hospital practices and meeting exclusive breastfeeding intention. *Pediatrics* 130, no. 1 (2012): 54–60.

9. Hunziker, U. A., Barr, R. G. Increased carrying reduces infant crying: a randomized controlled trial. *Pediatrics* 77, no. 5 (1986): 641–648.

10. Chiron, C., Jambaque, I., Nabbout, R., et al. The right brain hemisphere is dominant in human infants. *Brain* 120 (1997): 1057–1065. Schore, A. N. Effects of a secure attachment relationship on right brain development, affect regulation, and infant mental health. *Infant Mental Health Journal* 22, no. 1–2 (2001): 7–66.

11. Bowlby, J. *A Secure Base: Clinical Applications of Attachment Theory,* vol. 393. Boca Raton, FL: Taylor and Francis, 2005.

12. Brendtro, L. K. The vision of Urie Bronfenbrenner: adults who are crazy about kids. *Reclaiming Children and Youth* 15, no. 3 (2006): 162–166.

13. Schore, A. N. Back to basics attachment, affect regulation, and the developing right brain: linking developmental neuroscience to pediatrics. *Pediatrics in Review* 26, no. 6 (2005): 204–217.

14. Schore, J. R., Schore, A. N. Modern attachment theory: the central role of affect regulation in development and treatment. *Clinical Social Work Journal* 36, no. 1 (2008): 9–20.

15. Schore, A. N. Effects of a secure attachment relationship on right brain development, affect regulation, and infant mental health. *Infant Mental Health Journal* 22, no. 1–2 (2001): 7–66.

16. Schore, A. N. The effects of early relational trauma on right brain development, affect regulation and infant mental health. *Infant Mental Health Journal* 22, no. 1–2 (2001): 201–269. Schore, A. N. Effects of a secure attachment relationship on right brain development, affect regulation, and infant mental health. *Infant Mental Health Journal* 22, no. 1–2 (2001): 7–66. Lipari, J. First impressions count with your newborn: early months time for emotional, cognitive development. *Boston Herald,* Aug. 27, 2000. Tarullo, A. R., Gunnar, M. R. Child maltreatment and the developing HPA axis. *Hormones and Behavior* 50, no. 4 (2006): 632–639. Cicchetti, D., Tucker, D. Development and self-regulatory structures of the mind. *Development and Psychopathology* 6 (1994): 533–549.

17. Schore, A. N. Effects of a secure attachment relationship on right brain development, affect regulation, and infant mental health. *Infant Mental Health Journal* 22, no. 1–2 (2001): 7–66.

18. Middlemiss, W., Granger, D. A., Goldberg, W. A., et al. Asynchrony of mother-infant hypothalamic-pituitary-adrenal axis activity following extinction of infant crying responses induced during the transition to sleep. *Early Human Development* 88, no. 4 (2012): 227–232.

19. "Dangers of Cosleeping." 2010. [News broadcast.] Fox News, Milwaukee, Wisconsin. McKenna, J. J., Mosko, S. S., Richard, C. A. Bedsharing promotes breastfeeding. *Pediatrics* 100, no. 2 (1997): 214–219.

20. McKenna, J. J., Volpe, L. E. Sleeping with baby: an Internet-based sampling of parental experiences, choices, perceptions, and interpretations in a Western industrialized context. *Infant and Child Development* 16, no. 4 (2007): 359–385.

21. Morelli, G. A., Rogoff, B., Oppenheim, D., et al. Cultural variation in infants' sleeping arrangements: questions of independence. *Developmental Psychology* 28, no. 4 (1992): 604.

22. McKenna, J. J. Cultural influences on infant sleep. *Sleep and Breathing in Children: A Developmental Approach.* New York: Marcel Dekker, 2000; 199–230. Lozoff, B., Askew, G. L., Wolf, A. W. Cosleeping and early childhood sleep problems: effects of ethnicity and socioeconomic status. *Journal of Developmental and Behavioral Pediatrics* 17, no. 1 (1996): 9–15. Abbott, S. Holding on and pushing away: comparative perspectives on an eastern Kentucky child-rearing practice. *Ethos* 20, no. 1 (1992): 33–65. Keller, M. A., Goldberg, W. A. Co-sleeping: help or hindrance for young children's independence? *Infant and Child Development* 13, no. 5 (2004): 369–388.

23. Mosko, S., Richard, C., McKenna, J. Infant arousals during mother-infant bed sharing: implications for infant sleep and sudden infant death syndrome research. *Pediatrics* 100, no. 5 (1997): 841–849. Bergman, N. J., Linley, L. L., Fawcus, S. R. Randomized controlled trial of skin-to-skin contact from birth versus conventional incubator for physiological stabilization in 1200- to 2199-gram newborns. *Acta Paediatrica* 93, no. 6 (2004): 779–785. Morgan, B. E., Horn, A. R., Bergman, N. J. Should neonates sleep alone? *Biological Psychiatry* 70, no. 9 (2011): 817–825.

24. Heron, P. Nonreactive co-sleeping and child behavior: getting a good night's sleep all night every night. Master's thesis, University of Bristol, Bristol, United Kingdom, 1994. McKenna, J. J. Cultural influences

on infant sleep. *Sleep and Breathing in Children: A Developmental Approach.* New York: Marcel Dekker, 2000; 199–230.

25. Beijers, R., Riksen-Walraven, J. M., de Weerth, C. Cortisol regulation in 12-month-old human infants: associations with the infants' early history of breastfeeding and co-sleeping. *Stress* 16, no. 3 (2013): 267–277.

26. Keller, M. A., Goldberg, W. A. Co-sleeping: help or hindrance for young children's independence? *Infant and Child Development* 13, no. 5 (2004): 369–388.

27. Heron, P. Nonreactive co-sleeping and child behavior: getting a good night's sleep all night every night. Master's thesis, University of Bristol, Bristol, United Kingdom, 1994. McKenna, J. J. Cultural influences on infant sleep. *Sleep and Breathing in Children: A Developmental Approach.* New York: Marcel Dekker, 2000; 199–230.

28. Lewis, R. J., Janda, L. H. The relationship between adult sexual adjustment and childhood experience regarding exposure to nudity, sleeping in the parental bed, and parental attitudes toward sexuality. *Archives of Sexual Behavior* 17 (1998): 349–363.

29. Crawford, M. Parenting practices in the Basque country: implications of infant and childhood sleeping location for personality development. *Ethos* 22 (1994): 42–82.

30. Okami, P., Weisner, T., Olmstead, R. Outcome correlates of parent-child bedsharing: an eighteen-year longitudinal study. *Journal of Developmental and Behavioral Pediatrics* 23, no. 4 (2002): 244–253.

31. Forbes, F., Weiss, D. S., Folen, R. A. The cosleeping habits of military children. *Military Medicine* 157 (1992): 196–200.

32. Tollenaar, M. S., Beijers, R., Jansen, J., et al. Solitary sleeping in young infants is associated with heightened cortisol reactivity to a bathing session but not to a vaccination. *Psychoneuroendocrinology* 37, no. 2 (2012): 167–177.

33. Maselko, J., Kubzansky, L., Lipsitt, L., et al. Mother's affection at 8 months predicts emotional distress in adulthood. *Journal of Epidemiology and Community Health* 65, no. 7 (2011): 621–625.

34. McEwen, B. S. Physiology and neurobiology of stress and adaptation: central role of the brain. *Physiological Reviews* 87, no. 3 (2007): 873–904.

Chapter 4: Normal Sleep

1. Hale, T. W., Hartmann, P. *Textbook of Human Lactation.* Amarillo, TX: Hale Publishing, 2007; ch. 14.

2. Byars, K. C., Yolton, K., Rausch, J., et al. Prevalence, patterns, and persistence of sleep problems in the first 3 years of life. *Pediatrics* 129, no. 2 (2012): e276–e284.

3. Lyamin, O., Pryaslova, J., Lance, V., et al. Animal behaviour: continuous activity in cetaceans after birth. *Nature* 435, no. 7046 (2005): 1177.

4. Stickgold, R. Sleep-dependent memory consolidation. *Nature* 437, no. 7063 (2005): 1272–1278.

5. Gumustekin, K., Seven, B., Karabulut, N., et al. Effects of sleep deprivation, nicotine, and selenium on wound healing in rats. *International Journal of Neuroscience* 114, no. 11 (2004): 1433–1442.

6. Zager, A., Andersen, M. L., Ruiz, F. S., et al. Effects of acute and chronic sleep loss on immune modulation of rats. *Regulatory, Integrative and Comparative Physiology* 293 (2007): R504–R509.

7. Morrissey, M., Duntley, S., Anch, A., et al. Active sleep and its role in the prevention of apoptosis in the developing brain. *Medical Hypotheses* 62, no. 6 (2004): 876–879.

8. Thase, M. Depression and sleep: pathophysiology and treatment. *Dialogues in Clinical Neuroscience* 8, no. 2 (2006): 217–226.

9. Turner, T. H., Drummond, S. P. A., Salamat, J. S., et al. Effects of 42 hr sleep deprivation on component processes of verbal working memory. *Neuropsychology* 21, no. 6 (2007): 787–795.

10. Hasler, G., Buysse, D. J., Klaghofer, R., et al. The association between short sleep duration and obesity in young adults: a 13-year prospective study. *Sleep* 27, no. 4 (2004): 661–666. webmd.com/heart-disease /news/20030127/sleep-less-more-linked-to-heart-disease.

11. Adan, A., Archer, S. N., Hidalgo, M. P., et al. Circadian typology: a comprehensive review. *Chronobiology International* 29, no. 9 (2012): 1153–1175.

12. Cohen Engler, A., Hadash, A., Shehadeh, N., et al. Breastfeeding may improve nocturnal sleep and reduce infantile colic: potential role of breast milk melatonin. *European Journal of Pediatrics* 171, no. 4 (2012): 729–732.

13. Ekirch, A. R. *At Day's Close: Night in Times Past.* New York: W. W. Norton, 2006. Koslofsky, C. *Evenings' Empire: A History of the Night in Early Modern Europe.* Cambridge: Cambridge University Press, 2011; 6. Wehr, T. A. In short photoperiods, human sleep is biphasic. *Journal of Sleep Research* 1, no. 2 (1992): 103–107. Brown, W. A. Acknowledging preindustrial patterns of sleep may revolutionize approach to sleep dysfunction. *Applied Neurology* 2006.

14. Wehr, T. A., Schwartz, P. J., Turner, E. H., et al. Bimodal patterns of human melatonin secretion consistent with a two-oscillator model of regulation. *Neuroscience Letters* 194, no. 1 (1995): 105–108.

15. Randall, D. K. Rethinking sleep. *New York Times,* Sept. 23, 2012.
16. Blyton, D. M., Sullivan, C. E., Edwards, N. Lactation is associated with an increase in slow-wave sleep in women. *Journal of Sleep Research* 11, no. 4 (2002): 297–303.
17. Quillin, S. I., Glenn, L. L. Interaction between feeding method and co-sleeping on maternal-newborn sleep. *Journal of Obstetric, Gynecologic, and Neonatal Nursing* 33, no. 5 (2004): 580–588. Kendall-Tackett, K. A., Cong, Z., Hale, T. W. The effect of feeding method on sleep duration, maternal well-being, and postpartum depression. *Clinical Lactation* 2, no. 2 (2011): 22–26.
18. Mirmiran, M., Maas, Y. G., Ariagno, R. L. Development of fetal and neonatal sleep and circadian rhythms. *Sleep Medicine Reviews* 7, no. 4 (2003): 321–334. Mirmiran, M., Lunshof, S. Perinatal development of human circadian rhythms. *Progress in Brain Research* 111 (1996): 217–226. Van den Bergh, B. R., Mulder, E. J. Fetal sleep organization: a biological precursor of self-regulation in childhood and adolescence? *Biological Psychology* 89, no. 3 (2012): 584–590.
19. Mosko, S., Richard, C., McKenna, J. Maternal sleep and arousals during bedsharing with infants. *Sleep* 20, no. 2 (1997): 142–150. Mosko, S., Richard, C., McKenna, J. Infant arousals during mother-infant bed sharing: implications for infant sleep and sudden infant death syndrome research. *Pediatrics* 100, no. 5 (1997): 841–849.
20. World Health Organization, United Nations Children's Fund. *Global Strategy for Infant and Young Child Feeding.* Geneva: World Health Organization, 2003.
21. Morgan, B. E., Horn, A. R., Bergman, N. J. Should neonates sleep alone? *Biological Psychiatry* 70, no. 9 (2011): 817–825.
22. Ludington-Hoe, S. M., Johnson, M. W., Morgan, K., et al. Neurophysiologic assessment of neonatal sleep organization: preliminary results of a randomized, controlled trial of skin contact with preterm infants. *Pediatrics* 117, no. 5 (2006): e909–e923.
23. First Candle, in conjunction with the American Academy of Pediatrics. "Room-Sharing Is Safer than Bed-Sharing." firstcandle.org/new-expectant-parents/bedtime-basics-for-babies/room-sharing-is-safer-than-bed-sharing. Public Health Agency of Canada's Joint Statement on Safe Sleep. "Preventing Sudden Infant Deaths in Canada." 2012. phac-aspc.gc.ca/hp-ps/dca-dea/stages-etapes/childhood-enfance_0-2/sids/pdf/jsss-ecss2011-eng.pdf. Tappin, D., Ecob, R., Brooke, H. Bedsharing, roomsharing, and sudden infant death syndrome in Scotland: a case-control study. *Journal of Pediatrics* 147, no. 1 (2009): 32. Carpenter, R. G., Irgens, L. M., Blair, P. S., et al. Sudden unexplained infant death in 20 regions in Europe: case control study. *Lancet* 36, no. 9404 (2004): 185–191. Blair, P. S., Fleming, P. J., Smith, I. J., et al. Babies sleeping with parents: case-control study of factors influencing the risk of the sudden infant death syndrome. CESDI SUDI Research Group. *BMJ* 319, no. 7223 (1999): 1457–1461.
24. Hofer, M. A. Hidden regulators in attachment, separation, and loss. *Monographs of the Society for Research in Child Development* 59, no. 2–3 (1994): 192–207.
25. Mosko, S., Richard, C., McKenna, J., et al. Maternal proximity and infant CO_2 environment during bedsharing and possible implications for SIDS research. *American Journal of Physical Anthropology* 103, no. 3 (1997): 315–328.
26. McKenna, J. J., Mosko, S. S. Sleep and arousal, synchrony and independence, among mothers and infants sleeping apart and together (same bed): an experiment in evolutionary medicine. *Acta Paediatrica* 83, no. S397 (1994): 94–102.
27. Mosko, S., Richard, C., McKenna, J. Maternal sleep and arousals during bedsharing with infants. *Sleep* 20, no. 2 (1997): 142–150. Mosko, S., Richard, C., McKenna, J. Infant arousals during mother-infant bed sharing: implications for infant sleep and sudden infant death syndrome research. *Pediatrics* 100, no. 5 (1997): 841–849.
28. Quillin, S. I. Infant and mother sleep patterns during 4th postpartum week. *Issues in Comprehensive Pediatric Nursing* 20 (1997): 115e23.
29. Gettler, L. T., McKenna, J. J. Evolutionary perspectives on mother-infant sleep proximity and breastfeeding in a laboratory setting. *American Journal of Physical Anthropology* 144, no. 3 (2011): 454–462. Quillin, S. I., Glenn, L. L. Interaction between feeding method and co-sleeping on maternal-newborn sleep. *Journal of Obstetric, Gynecologic, and Neonatal Nursing* 33, no. 5 (2004): 580–588.
30. Ball, H. L. Breastfeeding, bed sharing, and infant sleep. *Birth* 30, no. 3 (2003): 181–188. Huang, Y., Hauck, F. R., Signore, C., et al. Influence of bedsharing activity on breastfeeding duration among US mothers. *JAMA Pediatrics* 167, no. 11 (2013): 1038–1044. Doan, T., Gardiner, A., Gay, C. L., et al. Breast-feeding increases sleep duration of new parents. *Journal of Perinatal and Neonatal Nursing* 21, no. 3 (2007): 200–206.
31. Annagur, A., Annagur, B. B., Sahin, A., et al. Is maternal depressive symptomatology effective on success of exclusive breastfeeding during postpartum 6 weeks? *Breastfeeding Medicine* 8 (2013): 53–57.
32. McKenna, J. J., Mosko, S., Dungy, C., McAninch, J. Sleep and arousal patterns of co-sleeping human mother/infant pairs: a preliminary physiological study with implications for the study of Sudden Infant

Death Syndrome (SIDS). *American Journal of Physical Anthropology* 83 (1990): 331–347; McKenna, J. J., Mosko, S. S., Richard, C. A. Bedsharing promotes breastfeeding. *Pediatrics* 100, no. 2 (1997): 214–219; Mosko, S., Richard, C., McKenna, J. J. Maternal sleep and arousals during bedsharing with infants. *Sleep* 20, no. 2 (1997): 142–150.

33. Randall, B. B., Paterson, D. S., Haas, E. A., et al. Potential asphyxia and brainstem abnormalities in sudden and unexpected death in infants. *Pediatrics* 132, no. 6 (2013): e1616–e1625. Paterson, D. S., Trachtenberg, F. L., Thompson, E. G., et al. Multiple serotonergic brainstem abnormalities in sudden infant death syndrome. *Journal of the American Medical Association* 296, no. 17 (2006): 2124–2132. Kato, I., Franco, P., Groswasser, J., et al. Incomplete arousal processes in infants who were victims of sudden death. *American Journal of Respiratory and Critical Care Medicine* 168, no. 11 (2003): 1298–1303.

34. Peirano, P., Algarin, C., Uauy, R. Sleep-wake states and their regulatory mechanisms throughout early human development. *Journal of Pediatrics* 143, no. 4 (2003): 70–79.

35. Kent, J. C., Mitoulas, L. R., Cregan, M. D., et al. Volume and frequency of breastfeedings and fat content of breast milk throughout the day. Pediatrics 117, no. 3 (2006): e387–e395.

36. Coons, S., Guilleminault, C. Development of sleep-wake patterns and non-rapid eye movement sleep stages during the first six months of life in normal infants. *Pediatrics* 69, no. 6 (1982): 793–798. Galbally, M., Lewis, A. J., McEgan, K., et al. Breastfeeding and infant sleep patterns: an Australian population study. *Journal of Paediatrics and Child Health* 49, no. 2 (2013): e147–e152.

37. Gertner, S., Greenbaum, C. W., Sadeh, A., et al. Sleep-wake patterns in preterm infants and 6 month's home environment: implications for early cognitive development. *Early Human Development* 68, no. 2 (2002): 93–102. Heraghty, J. L., Hilliard, T. N., Henderson, A. J., et al. The physiology of sleep in infants. *Archives of Disease in Childhood* 93, no. 11 (2008): 982–985. Lodemore, M. R., Petersen, S. A., Wailoo, M. P. Factors affecting the development of night time temperature rhythms. *Archives of Disease in Childhood* 67, no. 10 (1992): 1259–1261.

38. Fifer, W. P., Byrd, D. L., Kaku, M., et al. Newborn infants learn during sleep. *Proceedings of the National Academy of Sciences of the United States of America* 107, no. 22 (2010): 10320–10323. Ludington-Hoe, S. M., Johnson, M. W., Morgan, K., et al. Neurophysiologic assessment of neonatal sleep organization: preliminary results of a randomized, controlled trial of skin contact with preterm infants. *Pediatrics* 117, no. 5 (2006): e909–e923.

39. Parmelee, A. H. Jr., Wenner, W. H., Schulz, H. R. Infant sleep patterns: from birth to 16 weeks of age. *Journal of Pediatrics* 65 (1964): 576–582. Rivkees, S. A. Developing circadian rhythmicity in infants. *Pediatrics* 112, no. 2 (2003): 373–381. Coons, S., Guilleminault, C. Development of sleep-wake patterns and non-rapid eye movement sleep stages during the first six months of life in normal infants. *Pediatrics* 69, no. 6 (1982): 793–798. Peirano, P., Algarín, C., Uauy, R. Sleep-wake states and their regulatory mechanisms throughout early human development. *Journal of Pediatrics* 143, no. 4 (2003): 70–79.

40. McGraw, K., Hoffmann, R., Harker, C., et al. The development of circadian rhythms in a human infant. *Sleep* 22, no. 3 (1999): 303. Guilleminault, C., Leger, D., Pelayo, R., et al. Development of circadian rhythmicity of temperature in full-term normal infants. *Neurophysiologie Clinique/Clinical Neurophysiology* 26, no. 1 (1996): 21–29.

41. Moore, T., Ucko, L. E. Night waking in early infancy: part I. *Archives of Disease in Childhood* 32, no. 164 (1957): 333–342.

42. Acebo, C., Sadeh, A., Seifer, R. Sleep/wake patterns derived from activity monitoring and maternal report for healthy 1- to 5-year-old children. *Sleep* 28, no. 12 (2005): 1568. Scher, A. A longitudinal study of night waking in the first year. *Child: Care, Health and Development* 17, no. 5 (1991): 295–302.

43. Adams, S. M., Jones, D. R., Esmail, A., et al. What affects the age of first sleeping through the night? *Journal of Paediatrics and Child Health* 40, no. 3 (2004): 96–101.

44. Jenni, O. G., Fuhrer, H. Z., Iglowstein, I., et al. A longitudinal study of bed sharing and sleep problems among Swiss children in the first 10 years of life. *Pediatrics* 115, suppl. 1 (2005): 233–240.

Chapter 5: Naps

1. http://www.schoolofbabywearing.com/Images/TICKS.pdf.

2. Esposito, G., Yoshida, S., Ohnishi, R., et al. Infant calming responses during maternal carrying in humans and mice. *Current Biology* 23, no. 9 (2013): 739–745.

3. Karen, R. *Becoming Attached: First Relationships and How They Shape Our Capacity to Love.* New York: Warner Books, 1994.

4. First Candle, in conjunction with the American Academy of Pediatrics. "Room-Sharing Is Safer than Bed-Sharing." firstcandle.org/new-expectant-parents/bedtime-basics-for-babies/room-sharing-is-safer-than-bed-sharing. Public Health Agency of Canada's Joint Statement on Safe Sleep. "Preventing Sudden Infant Deaths in Canada." 2012. phac-aspc.gc.ca/hp-ps/dca-dea/stages-etapes/childhood-enfance_0-2/sids/pdf/jsss-ecss2011-eng.pdf. Tappin, D., Ecob, R., Brooke, H. Bedsharing,

roomsharing, and sudden infant death syndrome in Scotland: a case-control study. *Journal of Pediatrics* 147, no. 1 (2009): 32. Carpenter, R. G., Irgens, L. M., Blair, P. S., et al. Sudden unexplained infant death in 20 regions in Europe: case control study. *Lancet* 36, no. 9404 (2004): 185–191. Blair, P. S., Fleming, P. J., Smith, I. J., et al. Babies sleeping with parents: case-control study of factors influencing the risk of the sudden infant death syndrome. CESDI SUDI Research Group. *BMJ* 319, no. 7223 (1999): 1457–1461.

5. St. James-Roberts, I., Alvarez, M., Csipke, E., et al. Infant crying and sleeping in London, Copenhagen and when parents adopt a proximal form of care. *Pediatrics* 117, no. 6 (2006): e1146–e1155.

Chapter 6: Nights

1. Kent, J. C., Mitoulas, L. R., Cregan, M. D., et al. Volume and frequency of breastfeedings and fat content of breast milk throughout the day. *Pediatrics* 117, no. 3 (2006): e387–e395.
2. First Candle, in conjunction with the American Academy of Pediatrics. "Room-Sharing Is Safer than Bed-Sharing." firstcandle.org/new-expectant-parents/bedtime-basics-for-babies/room-sharing-is-safer-than-bed-sharing. Public Health Agency of Canada's Joint Statement on Safe Sleep. "Preventing Sudden Infant Deaths in Canada." 2012. phac-aspc.gc.ca/hp-ps/dca-dea/stages-etapes/childhood-enfance_0-2/sids/pdf/jsss-ecss2011-eng.pdf. Tappin, D., Ecob, R., Brooke, H. Bedsharing, roomsharing, and sudden infant death syndrome in Scotland: a case-control study. *Journal of Pediatrics* 147, no. 1 (2009): 32. Carpenter, R. G., Irgens, L. M., Blair, P. S., et al. Sudden unexplained infant death in 20 regions in Europe: case control study. *Lancet* 36, no. 9404 (2004): 185–191. Blair, P. S., Fleming, P. J., Smith, I. J., et al. Babies sleeping with parents: case-control study of factors influencing the risk of the sudden infant death syndrome. CESDI SUDI Research Group. *BMJ* 319, no. 7223 (1999): 1457–1461.
3. Eunice Kennedy Shriver National Institute of Child Health and Human Development. Safe sleep for your baby. NIH pub. 12-5759. 2013. nichd.nih.gov/publications/pubs/Documents/Safe_Sleep_Environment_English_2013.pdf.
4. Kendall-Tackett, K., Cong, Z., Hale, T. W. Mother-infant sleep locations and nighttime feeding behavior. *Clinical Lactation* 1, no. 1 (2010): 27–30.
5. Canadian Paediatric Society. Consumer information bulletin—safe sleep practices for infants. hc-sc.gc.ca/cps-spc/pubs/cons/sleep-sommeil-eng.php. Moon, R. Y., et al. SIDS and other sleep-related infant deaths: expansion of recommendations for a safe infant sleeping environment. *Pediatrics* 128, no. 5 (2011): e1341–e1367.
6. Richardson, H. L., Walker, A. M., Horne, R. S. Minimizing the risks of sudden infant death syndrome: to swaddle or not to swaddle? *Journal of Pediatrics* 155, no. 4 (2009): 475–481. Richardson, H. L., Walker, A. M., Horne, R. S. Influence of swaddling experience on spontaneous arousal patterns and autonomic control in sleeping infants. *Journal of Pediatrics* 157, no. 1 (2010): 85–91.

Chapter 7: Sleep Personalities and Places

1. Chess, S., Thomas, A., Birch, H. G. *Your Child Is a Person: A Psychological Approach to Childhood Without Guilt*. New York: Viking Press, 1965.
2. Chess, S., Thomas, A. *Temperament: Theory and Practice*. New York: Brunner/Mazel, 1996.
3. Sears, W., Sears, M. *The Fussy Baby Book: Parenting Your High-Need Child from Birth to Five*. London: Harper Thorsons, 2009.
4. Price, A. M. H., Wake, M., Ukoumunne, O. C., et al. Five-year follow-up of harms and benefits of behavioral infant sleep intervention: randomized trial. *Pediatrics* 130, no. 4 (2012): 643–651.
5. Hayes, M. J., Parker, K. G., Salliven, B., et al. Bedsharing, temperament and sleep disturbances in early childhood. *Sleep* 24, no. 6 (2001).
6. Richard, C., Mosko, S., McKenna, J., et al. Sleeping position, orientation, and proximity in bedsharing infants and mothers. *Sleep* 19, no. 9 (1996): 685–690.

Chapter 8: Working

1. Doan, T., Gardiner, A., Gay, C. L., et al. Breast-feeding increases sleep duration of new parents. *Journal of Perinatal Neonatal Nursing* 21, no. 3 (2007): 200–206.
2. Moon, R. Y., Sprague, B. M., Patel, K. M. Stable Prevalence but Changing Risk Factors for Sudden Infant Death Syndrome in Child Care Settings in 2001. *Pediatrics* 116, no. 4 (October 1, 2005): 972–77.
3. Watamura, S. E., Donzella, B., Alwin, J., & Gunnar, M. R. Morning-to-afternoon increases in cortisol concentrations for infants and toddlers at child care: Age differences and behavioral correlates. *Child Development* 74, no. 4 (2003): 1006–1020. Dettling, A. C., Parker, S. W., Lane, S., Sebanc, A., Gunnar, M. R. Quality of care and temperament determine changes in cortisol concentrations over the day for young children in childcare. *Psychoneuroendocrinology* 25, no. 8 (2000): 819–836.

Chapter 9: Alternate Routes

1. Slutzah, M., Codipilly, C. N., Potak, D., et al. Refrigerator storage of expressed human milk in the neonatal intensive care unit. *Journal of Pediatrics* 156, no. 1 (2010): 26–28.
2. cdc.gov/breastfeeding/recommendations/handling_breastmilk.htm.
3. Cohen Engler, A., Hadash, A., Shehadeh, N., et al. Breastfeeding may improve nocturnal sleep and reduce infantile colic: potential role of breast milk melatonin. *European Journal of Pediatrics* 171, no. 4 (2012): 729–732.
4. Malloy, M. H. Prematurity and sudden infant death syndrome: United States 2005–2007. *Journal of Perinatology* 33, no. 6 (2013): 470–475.
5. Blair, P., Ward Platt, M. P., Smith, I. J., et al. Sudden infant death syndrome and sleeping position in pre-term and low birthweight infants: an opportunity for targeted intervention. *Archives of Disease in Childhood* 91, no. 2 (2006): 101–106.
6. Feldman, R., Eidelman, A. I., Sirota, L., et al. Comparison of skin-to-skin (kangaroo) and traditional care: parenting outcomes and preterm infant development. *Pediatrics* 110, no. 1, pt. 1 (2002): 16–26.
7. Bergman, N. J., Linley, L. L., Fawcus, S. R. Randomized controlled trial of skin-to-skin contact from birth versus conventional incubator for physiological stabilization in 1200- to 2199-gram newborns. *Acta Paediatrica* 93, no. 6 (2004): 779–785. Ludington-Hoe, S. M., Lewis, T., Morgan, K., et al. Breast and infant temperatures with twins during shared kangaroo care. *Journal of Obstetric, Gynecologic, and Neonatal Nursing* 35, no. 2 (2006): 223–231.
8. kangaroomothercare.com.
9. Byers, J. F. Components of developmental care and the evidence for their use in the NICU. *MCN: The American Journal of Maternal Child Nursing* 28, no. 3 (2003): 174–180.
10. Sheehan, N. Sisters kept close. *Worcester Sunday Telegram,* Nov. 19, 1995. Sheehan, N. A sister's helping hand. *Reader's Digest* 148 (1996): 155.
11. Colson, E. R., Bergman, D. M., Shapiro, E., et al. Position for newborn sleep: associations with parents' perceptions of their nursery experience. *Birth* 28, no. 4 (2001): 249–253. Polizzi, J., Byers, J. F., Kiehl, E. Co-bedding versus traditional bedding of multiple-gestation infants in the NICU. *Journal for Healthcare Quality* 25, no. 1 (2003): 5–11, 60. Stainton, C., Jozsa, E., Fethney, J. Responses to co-bedding of low birth weight twins in neonatal intensive care. *Neonatal, Paediatric and Child Health Nursing* 8, no. 2 (2005): 4–12.
12. Lai, N. M., Foong, S. C., Foong, W. C., et al. Co-bedding in neonatal nursery for promoting growth and neurodevelopment in stable preterm twins. *Cochrane Database of Systematic Reviews* 12 (2012), CD008313.
13. Tomashek, K. M., Wallman, C., American Academy of Pediatrics, Committee on Fetus and Newborn. Cobedding twins and higher order multiples in a hospital setting. *Pediatrics* 120, no. 6 (2007): 1359–1366. [Published correction appears in *Pediatrics* 12, no. 1 (2008): 227.]
14. Ball, H. L. Together or apart? A behavioural and physiological investigation of sleeping arrangements for twin babies. *Midwifery* 23, no. 4 (2007): 404–412.
15. Damato, E. G., Brubaker, J. A., Burant, C. Sleeping arrangements in families with twins. *Newborn and Infant Nursing Reviews* 12, no. 3 (2012): 171–178.
16. Gribble, K. D. A model for caregiving of adopted children after institutionalization. *Journal of Child and Adolescent Psychiatric Nursing* 20, no. 1 (2007): 14–26.

Chapter 10: Your Own Sleep Needs

1. secretsofbabybehavior.com/2011/09/weighing-pros-and-cons-of-napping-for.html.
2. toxnet.nlm.nih.gov/cgi-bin/sis/search/f?./temp/~R53OFz:1.
3. Shochat, T., Flint-Bretler, O., Tzischinsky, O. Sleep patterns, electronic media exposure and daytime sleep-related behaviours among Israeli adolescents. *Acta Paediatrica* 99, no. 9 (2010): 1396–1400. Cain, N., Gradisar, M. Electronic media use and sleep in school-aged children and adolescents: a review. *Sleep Medicine* 11, no. 8 (2010): 735–742. Vollmer, C., Michel, U., Randler, C. Outdoor light at night (LAN) is correlated with eveningness in adolescents. *Chronobiology International* 29, no. 4 (2012): 502–508.
4. Sanchez-Barcelo, E. J., Mediavilla, M. D., Reiter, R. J. Clinical uses of melatonin in pediatrics. *International Journal of Pediatrics* 892624 (2011); Arslanoglu, S., Bertino, E., Nicocia, M., et al. Potential chronobiotic role of human milk in sleep regulation. *Journal of Perinatal Medicine* 40 (2012): 1–8.
5. Vollmer, C., Michel, U., Randler, C. Outdoor light at night (LAN) is correlated with eveningness in adolescents. *Chronobiology International* 29, no. 4 (2012): 502–508. Santos, R. V., Viana, V. A., Boscolo, R. A., et al. Moderate exercise training modulates cytokayine profile and sleep in elderly people. *Cytokayine* 60, no. 3 (2012): 731–735.
6. Kline, C. E., Ewing, G. B., Burch, J. B., et al. Exercise training improves selected aspects of daytime

functioning in adults with obstructive sleep apnea. *Journal of Clinical Sleep Medicine* 8, no. 4 (2012): 357–365.
7. Brzezinski, A., Vangel, M. G., Wurtman, R. J., et al. Effects of exogenous melatonin on sleep: a meta-analysis. *Sleep Medicine Reviews* 9 (2005): 41–50.
8. Gitto, E., Aversa, S., Reiter, R. J., et al. Update on the use of melatonin in pediatrics. *Journal of Pineal Research* 50 (2011): 21–28.
9. Gitto, E., Aversa, S., Reiter, R. J., et al. Update on the use of melatonin in pediatrics. *Journal of Pineal Research* 50 (2011): 21–28.
10. Hale, T. W. *Medications and Mother's Milk 2012: A Manual of Lactational Pharmacology.* Amarillo, TX: Hale Publishing, 2012.
11. Bent, S., Padula, A., Moore, D., et al. Valerian for sleep: a systematic review and meta-analysis. *American Journal of Medicine* 119, no. 12 (2006): 1005–1012.
12. Hale, T. W. *Medications and Mother's Milk 2012: A Manual of Lactational Pharmacology.* Amarillo, TX: Hale Publishing, 2012.
13. Hale, T. W. *Medications and Mother's Milk 2012: A Manual of Lactational Pharmacology.* Amarillo, TX: Hale Publishing, 2012.
14. Hale, T. W. *Medications and Mother's Milk 2012: A Manual of Lactational Pharmacology.* Amarillo, TX: Hale Publishing, 2012.
15. Sachs, H., Committee on Drugs. The transfer of drugs and therapeutics into human breast milk: an update on selected topics. *Pediatrics* 132, no. 3 (2013): 796–809.
16. Kendall-Tackett, K. A. Trauma associated with perinatal events: birth experience, prematurity, and childbearing loss. *Handbook of Women, Stress, and Trauma.* New York: Brunner-Routledge, 2005; 53–74. Beck, C. T., Watson, S. Impact of Birth Trauma on Breast-Feeding: A Tale of Two Pathways. *Nursing Research* 57, no. 4 (2008): 228–236.
17. Kendall-Tackett, K. A. Violence against women in the perinatal period: the influence of lifetime violence and abuse on pregnancy and postpartum. *Trauma Psychology* 3, no. 1 (2008): 8–11.
18. Goyal, D., Gay, C., Lee. K. Fragmented maternal sleep is more strongly correlated with depressive symptoms than infant temperament at three months postpartum. *Archives of Women's Mental Health* 12, no. 4 (2009): 229–237.
19. Dennis, C. L., McQueen, K. The relationship between infant-feeding outcomes and postpartum depression: a qualitative systematic review. *Pediatrics* 123, no. 4 (2009): e736–e751.
20. Sachs, H., Committee on Drugs. The transfer of drugs and therapeutics into human breast milk: an update on selected topics. *Pediatrics* 132, no. 3 (2013): 796–809.
21. Kendall-Tackett, K. A. (ed.). *Psychoneuroimmunology of Chronic Disease.* Washington, DC: American Psychological Association, 2010.
22. Su, K. P. Biological mechanism of antidepressant effect of omega-3 fatty acids: how does fish oil act as a "mind-body interface"? *Neurosignals* 17 (2009): 144–152. Kendall-Tackett, K. A new paradigm for depression in new mothers: the central role of inflammation and how breastfeeding and anti-inflammatory treatments protect maternal mental health. *International Breastfeeding Journal* 2 (2007): 6. Kiecolt-Glaser, J. K., Belury, M. A., Porter, K., et al. Depressive symptoms, omega-6:omega-3 fatty acids, and inflammation in older adults. *Psychosomatic Medicine* 69 (2007): 217–224. Robles, T. F., Glaser, R., Kiecolt-Glaser, J. K. Out of balance: a new look at chronic stress, depression, and immunity. *Current Directions in Psychological Science* 14 (2005): 111–115.
23. Peet, M., Stokayes, C. Omega-3 fatty acids in the treatment of psychiatric disorders. *Drugs* 65 (2005): 1051–1059. Lin, P. Y., Su, K. P. A meta-analytic review of double-blind, placebo-controlled trials of antidepressant efficacy of omega-3 fatty acids. *Journal of Clinical Psychiatry* 68 (2007): 1056–1061. Lucas, M., Asselin, G., Mérette, C., et al. Ethyl-eicosapentaenoic acid for the treatment of psychological distress and depressive symptoms in middle-aged women: a double-blind, placebo-controlled, randomized clinical trial. *American Journal of Clinical Nutrition* 89 (2009): 641–651.
24. Kendall-Tackett, K. A. Long-chain omega-3 fatty acids and women's mental health in the perinatal period. *Journal of Midwifery and Women's Health* 55, no. 6 (2010): 561–567.
25. McNamara, R. K. Evaluation of docosahexaenoic acid deficiency as a preventable risk factor for recurrent affective disorders: current status, future directions, and dietary recommendations. *Prostaglandins, Leukotrienes, and Essential Fatty Acids* 81 (2009): 223–231. Llorente, A. M., Jensen, C. L., Voigt, R. G., et al. Effect of maternal docosahexaenoic acid supplementation on postpartum depression and information processing. *American Journal of Obstetrics and Gynecology* 188 (2003): 1348–1353.
26. Kendall-Tackett, K. A. Long-chain omega-3 fatty acids and women's mental health in the perinatal period. *Journal of Midwifery and Women's Health* 55, no. 6 (2010): 561–567.
27. Maruff, P., Falleti, M. G., Collie, A., et al. Fatigue-related impairment in the speed, accuracy and variability of psychomotor performance: comparison with blood alcohol levels. *Journal of Sleep Research*

14, no. 1 (2005): 21–27. Falleti, M. G., Maruff, P., Collie, A., et al. Qualitative similarities in cognitive impairment associated with 24 h of sustained wakefulness and a blood alcohol concentration of 0.05%. *Journal of Sleep Research* 12, no. 4 (2003): 265–274.

28. Connor, J., Norton, R., Ameratunga, S., et al. Driver sleepiness and risk of serious injury to car occupants: population based case control study. *BMJ* 324 (2002): 1125. Ahlstrom, C., Kircher, K., Fors, C., et al. Measuring driver impairments: sleepiness, distraction, and workload. *IEEE Pulse* 3, no. 2 (2012): 22–30. Robb, G., Sultana, S., Ameratunga, S., et al. A systematic review of epidemiological studies investigating risk factors for work-related road traffic crashes and injuries. *Injury Prevention* 14, no. 1 (2008): 51–58. Ftouni, S., Sletten, T. L., Howard, M., et al. Objective and subjective measures of sleepiness, and their associations with on-road driving events in shift workers. *Journal of Sleep Research* 22, no. 1 (2013): 58–69.

Chapter 11: Gentle Sleep Nudging Methods

1. Weinraub, M., Bender, R. H., Friedman, S. L., et al. Patterns of developmental change in infants' nighttime sleep awakenings from 6 through 36 months of age. *Developmental Psychology* 48, no. 6 (2012): 1511.

2. Mindell, J. A., Kuhn, B., Lewin, D. S., et al. Behavioral treatment of bedtime problems and night wakings in infants and young children. *Sleep* 29, no. 10 (2006): 1263–1276.

3. Rivkees, S. A. Developing circadian rhythmicity in infants. *Pediatrics* 112, no. 2 (2003): 373–381. Parmelee, A. H. Jr., Wenner, W. H., Schulz, H. R. Infant sleep patterns: from birth to 16 weeks of age. *Journal of Pediatrics* 65 (1964): 576–582. Coons, S., Guilleminault, C. Development of sleep-wake patterns and non-rapid eye movement sleep stages during the first six months of life in normal infants. *Pediatrics* 69, no. 6 (1982): 793–798. Peirano, P., Algarín, C., Uauy, R. Sleep-wake states and their regulatory mechanisms throughout early human development. *Journal of Pediatrics* 143, no. 4 (2003): 70–79.

4. Quillin, S. I. Infant and mother sleep patterns during 4th postpartum week. *Issues in Comprehensive Pediatric Nursing* 20 (1997): 115e23.

5. Esposito, G., Yoshida, S., Ohnishi, R., et al. Infant calming responses during maternal carrying in humans and mice. *Current Biology* 23, no. 9 (2013): 739–745.

6. Galbally, M., Lewis, A. J., McEgan, K., et al. Breastfeeding and infant sleep patterns: an Australian population study. *Journal of Paediatrics and Child Health* 49, no. 2 (2013): e147–e152.

7. Ip, S., Chung, M., Raman, G., et al. *Breastfeeding and Maternal and Infant Health Outcomes in Developed Countries.* Rockville, MD: Agency for Healthcare Research and Quality, 2007.

8. Penders, J., Thijs, C., Vink, C., et al. Factors influencing the composition of the intestinal microbiota in early infancy. *Pediatrics* 118 (2006): 511–521.

9. Stuebe, A. The risks of not breastfeeding for mothers and infants. *Reviews in Obstetrics and Gynecology* 2, no. 4 (2009): 222. Horta, B. L., Bahl, R., Martinés, J. C., et al. *Evidence on the Long-Term Effects of Breastfeeding: Systematic Review and Meta-analyses.* Geneva: World Health Organization, 2007.

10. Howel, D., Ball, H. Association between length of exclusive breastfeeding and subsequent breastfeeding continuation. *Journal of Human Lactation* 29, no. 4 (2013): 579–585.

11. Doan, T., Gardiner, A., Gay, C. L., et al. Breast-feeding increases sleep duration of new parents. *Journal of Perinatal Neonatal Nursing* 21, no. 3 (2007): 200–206.

12. Macknin, M. L., Medendorp, S. V., Maier, M. C. Infant sleep and bedtime cereal. *American Journal of Diseases of Children* 143, no. 9 (1989): 1066–1068. Keane, V., et al. Do solids help baby sleep through the night? *American Journal of Diseases of Children* 142 (1988): 404–405.

13. Huh, S. Y., Rifas-Shiman, S. L., Taveras, E. M., et al. Timing of solid food introduction and risk of obesity in preschool-aged children. *Pediatrics* 127, no. 3 (2011): e544–e551.

14. McEwen, B. S. Physiology and neurobiology of stress and adaptation: central role of the brain. *Physiological Reviews* 87, no. 3 (2007): 873–904.

15. Harrison, Y. The relationship between daytime exposure to light and night-time sleep in 6–12-week-old infants. *Journal of Sleep Research* 13, no. 4 (2004): 345–352.

16. Taylor, A. F., Kuo, F. E., Sullivan, W. C. Coping with ADD: the surprising connection to green play settings. *Environment and Behavior* 33, no. 1 (2001): 54–77.

17. Teti, D. M., Kim, B. R., Mayer, G., et al. Maternal emotional availability at bedtime predicts infant sleep quality. *Journal of Family Psychology* 24, no. 3 (2010): 307–315.

18. Mao, A., et al. A comparison of the sleep-wake patterns of cosleeping and solitary-sleeping infants. *Child Psychiatry and Human Development* 35, no. 2 (2004): 95–105.

19. Scher, A. A longitudinal study of night waking in the first year. *Child: Care, Health and Development* 17, no. 5 (1991): 295–302.

20. Jenni, O. G., Fuhrer, H. Z., Iglowstein, I., et al. A longitudinal study of bed sharing and sleep problems among Swiss children in the first 10 years of life. *Pediatrics* 115, suppl. 1 (2005): 233–240.

Chapter 12: Sleep Gadgets

1. Karp, H. *The Happiest Baby on the Block*. New York: Bantam, 2008. McRury, J. M., Zolotor, A. J. A randomized, controlled trial of a behavioral intervention to reduce crying among infants. *Journal of the American Board of Family Medicine* 23, no. 3 (2010): 315–322.

2. Moore, E. R., Anderson, G. C., Bergman, N. Early skin-to-skin contact for mothers and their healthy newborn infants. *Cochrane Database of Systematic Reviews* 3 (2007). Ransjo-Arvidson, A., Matthiesen, A., Lilja, G., et al. Maternal analgesia during labor disturbs newborn behavior. *Birth* 28 (2001): 5–12.

3. Van Sleuwen, B. E., Engelberts, A. C., Boere-Boonekamp, et al. Swaddling: a systematic review. *Pediatrics* 120, no. 4 (2007): e1097–e1106.

4. Mahan, S. T., Kasser, J. R. Does swaddling influence developmental dysplasia of the hip? *Pediatrics* 121, no. 1 (2008): 177–178. Mahan, S. T., Kasser, J. R. Safe swaddling and healthy hips: don't toss the baby out with the bathwater: in reply. *Pediatrics* 121, no. 5 (2008): 1077a. Yurdakok, K., Yavuz, T., Taylor, C. E. Swaddling and acute respiratory infections. *American Journal of Public Health* 80, no. 7 (1990): 873–875. Van Gestel, J. P. J., L'Hoir, M. P., ten Berge, M., Jansen, N. J. G., Plötz, F. B. Risks of ancient practices in modern times. *Pediatrics* 110, no. 6 (2002): e78–e7.

5. Feldman, R., Weller, A., Leckman, J. F., Kuint, J., Eidelman, A. I. The nature of the mother's tie to her infant: Maternal bonding under conditions of proximity, separation, and potential loss, *Journal of Child Psychology and Psychiatry* 40, no. 6 (1999): 929–939.

6. Matthiesen, A. S., Ransjo-Arvidson, A. B., Nissen, E., et al. Postpartum maternal oxytocin release by newborns: effects of infant hand massage and sucking. *Birth* 28, no. 1 (2001): 13–19. Genna, C. W., Barak, D. Facilitating autonomous infant hand use during breastfeeding. *Clinical Lactation* no. 1 (2010): 15–20.

7. Moon, R. Y., et al. SIDS and other sleep-related infant deaths: expansion of recommendations for a safe infant sleeping environment. *Pediatrics* 128, no. 5 (2011): e1341–e1367.

8. Howard, C. R., Howard, F. M., Lanphear, B., et al. The effects of early pacifier use on breastfeeding duration. *Pediatrics* 103, no. 3 (1999): e33. Vogel, A. M., Hutchison, B. L., Mitchell, E. A. The impact of pacifier use on breastfeeding: a prospective cohort study. *Journal of Paediatrics and Child Health* 37, no. 1 (2001): 58–63.

9. Howard, C. R., Howard, F. M., Lanphear, B., et al. Randomized clinical trial of pacifier use and bottle-feeding or cupfeeding and their effect on breastfeeding. *Pediatrics* 111, no. 3 (2003): 511–518.

10. Wolf, A. W., Lozoff, B. Object attachment, thumbsucking, and the passage to sleep. *Journal of the American Academy of Child and Adolescent Psychiatry* 28, no. 2 (1989): 287–292.

11. Jenni, O. G., Fuhrer, H. Z., Iglowstein, I., et al. A longitudinal study of bed sharing and sleep problems among Swiss children in the first 10 years of life. *Pediatrics* 115, suppl. 1 (2005): 233–240.

12. Henley, D. V., Lipson, N., Korach, K. S., et al. Prepubertal gynecomastia linked to lavender and tea tree oils. *New England Journal of Medicine* 356, no. 5 (2007): 479–485.

13. Kemper, K. J., Romm, A. J., Gardiner, P. Prepubertal gynecomastia linked to lavender and tea tree oils. *New England Journal of Medicine* 356, no. 24 (2007): 2541–2542.

14. Hirokawa, K., Nishimoto, T., Taniguchi, T. Effects of lavender aroma on sleep quality in healthy Japanese students. *Perceptual and Motor Skills* 114, no. 1 (2012): 111–122.

15. Field, T., Field, T., Cullen, C., et al. Lavender bath oil reduces stress and crying and enhances sleep in very young infants. *Early Human Development* 84, no. 6 (2008): 399–401.

16. Day, L. M., Ozanne-Smith, J., Parsons, B. J., et al. Eucalyptus oil poisoning among young children: mechanisms of access and the potential for prevention. *Australian and New Zealand Journal of Public Health* 21, no. 3 (1997): 297–302. Tibballs, J. Clinical effects and management of eucalyptus oil ingestion in infants and young children. *Medical Journal of Australia* 163, no. 4 (1995): 177–180. Webb, N. J., Pitt, W. R. Eucalyptus oil poisoning in childhood: 41 cases in south-east Queensland. *Journal of Paediatrics and Child Health* 29, no. 5 (1993): 368–371.

17. Hugh, S. C., Wolter, N. E., Propst, E. J., Gordon, K. A., Cushing, S. L., Papsin, B. C. Infant sleep machines and hazardous sound pressure levels. *Pediatrics* 133 (2014): 1–5.

18. Mitchell, E. A. SIDS: past, present and future. *Acta Paediatrica* 98, no. 11 (2009): 1712–1719.

19. Fu, L. Y., Moon, R. Y. Apparent life-threatening events (ALTEs) and the role of home monitors. *Pediatrics in Review* 28, no. 6 (2007): 203–208.

20. McKenna, J. J., McDade, T. Why babies should never sleep alone: a review of the co-sleeping controversy in relation to SIDS, bedsharing and breast feeding. *Paediatric Respiratory Reviews* 6, no. 2 (2005): 134–152. McKenna, J. J., Volpe, L. E. Sleeping with baby: an Internet-based sampling of parental experiences, choices, perceptions, and interpretations in a Western industrialized context. *Infant and Child Development* 16, no. 4 (2007): 359–385.

21. Esposito, G., Yoshida, S., Ohnishi, R., et al. Infant calming responses during maternal carrying in humans and mice. *Current Biology* 23, no. 9 (2013): 739–745.

22. Zeedyk, S. *What's Life in a Baby Buggy Like? The Impact of Buggy Orientation on Parent-Infant Interaction and Infant Stress.* London: National Literacy Trust, 2008.
23. fda.gov/ForConsumers/ConsumerUpdates/ucm227575.htm. fda.gov/MedicalDevices/Safety/AlertsandNotices/ucm227301.htm.
24. Moon R. Y., et al. SIDS and other sleep-related infant deaths: expansion of recommendations for a safe infant sleeping environment. *Pediatrics* 128, no. 5 (2011): 1030–1039.
25. Rossato, N. E. [Newborn sleep positioners and sudden infant death syndrome risk]. *Archivos Argentinos de Pediatría* 111, no. 1 (2013): 62–68.
26. cpsc.gov/en/Newsroom/News-Releases/2012/CPSC-Adopts-New-Federal-Standard-for-Portable-Bed-Rails.
27. Yeh, E. S., Rochette, L. M., McKenzie, L. B., et al. Injuries associated with cribs, playpens, and bassinets among young children in the US, 1990–2008. *Pediatrics* 127, no. 3 (2011): 479–486.
28. Hugh, S. C., Wolter, N. E., Propst, E. J., Gordon, K. A., Cushing, S. L., Papsin, B. C. Infant sleep machines and hazardous sound pressure levels. *Pediatrics* 133 no. 4 (2014): 677–681.

Chapter 13: The First Few Days

1. DiGirolamo, A. M., Grummer-Strawn, L. M., Fein, S. B. Effect of maternity-care practices on breastfeeding. *Pediatrics* 122, suppl. 2 (2008): S43–S49.
2. Sachs, H. C., Committee on Drugs. The transfer of drugs and therapeutics into human breast milk: an update on selected topics. *Pediatrics*, Aug. 26, 2013.
3. Keefe, MR. The impact of infant rooming-in on maternal sleep at night. *Journal of Obstetric, Gynecologic, and Neonatal Nursing* 17, no. 2 (1988): 122–126.
4. Ball, H. L., Ward-Platt, M. P., Heslop, E., et al. Randomised trial of infant sleep location on the postnatal ward. *Archives of Disease in Childhood* 91, no. 12 (2006): 1005–1010.
5. Kendall-Tackett, K., Cong, Z., Hale, T. W. Mother-infant sleep locations and nighttime feeding behavior. *Clinical Lactation* 1, no. 1 (2010): 27–30.
6. Crenshaw, J. Care practice #6: no separation of mother and baby, with unlimited opportunities for breastfeeding. *Journal of Perinatal Education* 16, no. 3 (2007): 39–43.
7. Ball, H. L., Ward-Platt, M. P., Heslop, E., et al. Randomised trial of infant sleep location on the postnatal ward. *Archives of Disease in Childhood* 91, no. 12 (2006): 1005–1010.
8. Ball, H. L., Ward-Platt, M. P., Howel, D., et al. Randomised trial of sidecar crib use on breastfeeding duration (NECOT). *Archives of Disease in Childhood* 96, no. 7 (2011): 630–634.
9. Tully, K. P., Ball, H. L. Postnatal unit bassinet types when rooming-in after cesarean birth implications for breastfeeding and infant safety. *Journal of Human Lactation* 28, no. 4 (2012): 495–505.
10. Moore, E. R., Anderson, G. C., Bergman, N. Early skin-to-skin contact for mothers and their healthy newborn infants. *Cochrane Database of Systemic Reviews* 3 (2007).
11. Morrison, B., Ludington-Hoe, S. Interruptions to breastfeeding dyads in a DRP unit. *MCN: The American Journal of Maternal Child Nursing* 37, no. 1 (2012): 36–41.
12. Noel-Weiss, J., Woodend, A. K., Peterson, W., et al. An observational study of associations among maternal fluids during parturition, neonatal output, and breastfed newborn weight loss. *International Breastfeeding Journal* 6, no. 9 (2011).
13. Bergman, N. J. Neonatal stomach volume and physiology suggest feeding at 1-h intervals. *Acta Paediatrica* 102, no. 8 (2013): 773–777.
14. Kent, J. C., Mitoulas, L. R., Cregan, M. D., et al. Volume and frequency of breastfeedings and fat content of breast milk throughout the day. *Pediatrics* 117, no. 3 (2006): e387–e395.

Chapter 14: The First Two Weeks

1. Smith, L. J., Kroeger, M. *Impact of Birthing Practices on Breastfeeding.* Boston: Jones Bartlett Publishers, 2010.
2. Gray, L., Miller, L. W., Philipp, B. L., et al. Breastfeeding is analgesic in healthy newborns. *Pediatrics* 109, no. 4 (2002): 590–593.
3. Tsai, S. Y., Thomas, K. A., Lentz, M. J., et al. Light is beneficial for infant circadian entrainment: an actigraphic study. *Journal of Advanced Nursing* 68, no. 8 (2012): 1738–1747.
4. Parker, L. A., Sullivan, S., Krueger, C., et al. Effect of early breast milk expression on milk volume and timing of lactogenesis stage II among mothers of very low birth weight infants: a pilot study. *Journal of Perinatology* 32, no. 3 (2012): 205–209.
5. Heraghty, J. L., Hilliard, T. N., Henderson, A. J., et al. The physiology of sleep in infants. *Archives of Disease in Childhood* 93, no. 11 (2008): 982–985.
6. Stern, G., Kruckman, L. Multi-disciplinary perspectives on post-partum depression: an anthropological critique. *Social Science and Medicine* 17, no. 15 (1983): 1027–1041. Arms, S. How other cultures prevent

postpartum depression social structures that protect new mothers' mental health. uppitysciencechick.com/how_other_cultures.pdf.

7. Carek, P. J., Laibstain, S. E., Carek, S. M. Exercise for the treatment of depression and anxiety. *International Journal of Psychiatry in Medicine* 41, no. 1 (2011): 15–28. Golden, R. N., Gaynes, B. N., Ekstrom, R. D., et al. The efficacy of light therapy in the treatment of mood disorders: a review and meta-analysis of the evidence. *American Journal of Psychiatry* 162, no. 4 (2005): 656–662.

Chapter 15: Two Weeks to Four Months

1. Mosko, S., Richard, C., McKenna, J. Infant arousals during mother-infant bed sharing: implications for infant sleep and sudden infant death syndrome research. *Pediatrics* 100, no. 5 (1997): 841–849.

2. Esposito, G., Yoshida, S., Ohnishi, R., et al. Infant calming responses during maternal carrying in humans and mice. *Current Biology* 23, no. 9 (2013): 739–745.

3. Adapted from Danner, S. C., Cerutti, E. R. *Nursing Your Baby Beyond the First Days*. Rochester, NY: Childbirth Graphics, 1989.

Chapter 16: Four Months to Toddlerhood

1. U.S. Department of Health and Human Services, *The Surgeon General's Call to Action to Support Breastfeeding*. Rockville, MD: Office of the Surgeon General, 2011. World Health Organization. "The Optimal Duration of Exclusive Breastfeeding." Press release, 2001.

2. Upadhyay, A., Aggarwal, R., Narayan, S., et al. Analgesic effect of expressed breast milk in procedural pain in term neonates: a randomized, placebo-controlled, double-blind trial. *Acta Paediatrica* 93, no. 4 (2004): 518–522. Shah, P. S., Herbozo, C., Aliwalas, L. L., Shah, V. S. Breastfeeding or breast milk for procedural pain in neonates. *Cochrane Database Systematic Review,* 12 (2012).

3. Van der Wijden, C., Kleijnen, J., Van den Berk, T. Lactational amenorrhea for family planning. *Cochrane Database of Systematic Reviews* 4 (2003).

4. Peterson, A. E., Pérez-Escamilla, R., Labbok, M. H., et al. Multicenter study of the lactational amenorrhea method (LAM) III: effectiveness, duration, and satisfaction with reduced client-provider contact. *Contraception* 62, no. 5 (2000): 221–230.

5. Scher, A., Ratson, M. Motor development and sleep problems among 9-month-olds. *Perceptual and Motor Skills* 87, no. 3 (1998): 1218. Scher, A. A longitudinal study of night waking in the first year. *Child: Care, Health and Development* 17, no. 5 (1991): 295–302.

6. Scher, A. Attachment and sleep: a study of night waking in 12-month-old infants. *Developmental Psychobiology* 38, no. 4 (2001): 274–285.

7. Goodlin-Jones, B. L., Burnham, M. M., Gaylor, E. E., et al. Night waking, sleep-wake organization, and self-soothing in the first year of life. *Journal of Developmental and Behavioral Pediatrics* 22, no. 4 (2001): 226.

8. Jenni, O. G., Fuhrer, H. Z., Iglowstein, I., et al. A longitudinal study of bed sharing and sleep problems among Swiss children in the first 10 years of life. *Pediatrics* 115, suppl. 1 (2005): 233–240.

Chapter 17: Toddlerhood and Beyond

1. Mahendran, R., Vaingankar, J. A., Mythily, S., et al. Co-sleeping and clinical correlates in children seen at a child guidance clinic. *Singapore Medical Journal* 47, no. 11 (2006): 957.

2. Bharti, B., Malhi, P., Kashyap, S. Patterns and problems of sleep in school going children. *Indian Journal of Pediatrics* 43 (2006): 35–38.

3. Latz, S., Wolf, A. W., Lozoff, B. Cosleeping in context: sleep practices and problems in young children in Japan and the United States. *Archives of Pediatrics and Adolescent Medicine* 153, no. 4 (1999): 339.

4. Jenni, O. G., Fuhrer, H. Z., Iglowstein, I., et al. A longitudinal study of bed sharing and sleep problems among Swiss children in the first 10 years of life. *Pediatrics* 115, suppl. 1 (2005): 233–240.

5. Schachter, F. F., Fuchs, M. L., Bijur, P. E., et al. Cosleeping and sleep problems in Hispanic-American urban young children. *Pediatrics* 84, no. 3 (1989): 522–530.

6. Elias, M. F., Nicolson, N. A., Bora, C., et al. Sleep/wake patterns of breast-fed infants in the first 2 years of life. *Pediatrics* 77, no. 3 (1986): 322–329.

7. Okami, P., Weisner, T., Olmstead, R. Outcome correlates of parent-child bedsharing: an eighteen-year longitudinal study. *Journal of Developmental and Behavioral Pediatrics* 23, no. 4 (2002): 244–253.

8. Mindell, J. A., Telofski, L. S., Wiegand, B., et al. A nightly bedtime routine: impact on sleep in young children and maternal mood. *Sleep* 32, no. 5 (2009): 599–606.

9. Morelli, G. A., Rogoff, B., Oppenheim, D., et al. Cultural variation in infants' sleeping arrangements: questions of independence. *Developmental Psychology* 28, no. 4 (1992): 604.

10. Brown, M. L., Pope, A. W., Brown, E. J. Treatment of primary nocturnal enuresis in children: a review. *Child: Care, Health and Development* 37, no. 2 (2011): 153–160.

11. Brown, M. L., Pope, A. W., Brown, E. J. Treatment of primary nocturnal enuresis in children: a review.

Child: Care, Health and Development 37, no. 2 (2011): 153–160. Cohen-Zrubavel, V., Kushnir, B., Kushnir, J., et al. Sleep and sleepiness in children with nocturnal enuresis. *Sleep* 34, no. 2 (2011): 191–194.

Chapter 18: Sleep-Training Concerns

1. Miller, P. M., Commons, M. L. Why not crying it out, part 1: the science that tells us that responsiveness is key. *Clinical Lactation* 4, no. 2 (2013): 57–61. Miller, P. M., Commons, M. L. Why not crying it out, part 2: can certain infant care practices cause excessive stress? *Clinical Lactation* 4, no. 2 (2013): 62–65.

2. Underwood, M. *A treatise on the diseases of children, with directions for the management of infants from the birth.* London: J. Matthews, 1799.

3. Buchan, W. *Advice to mothers, on the subject of their own health, and on the means of promoting the health, strength, and beauty of their offspring.* London: T. Cadell and W. Davies, 1811.

4. Smiles, S. *Physical education; or, the nurture and management of children, founded on the study of their nature and constitution.* London: Oliver & Boyd, Tweeddale Court, and Simpkin, Marshall & Co., 1838.

5. Cadogan, W. An essay upon nursing: and the management of children, from their birth to three years of age. *By William Cadogan . . . In a Letter to One of the Governors of the Foundling Hospital.* London: J. Roberts, 1750.

6. Parkes, Mrs. W. *Domestic Duties, or, Instructions to Young Married Ladies, on the Management of Their Households, and the Regulations of Their Conduct in the Various Relations and Duties of Married Life.* New York: J. J. Harper, 1829.

7. Child, L. *The Mother's Book.* Boston: Carter, Hendee and Babcock, 1831.

8. Sigourney, L. H. *Letters to Mothers.* New York: Harper Brothers, 1854.

9. Chavasse, P. H. *Advice to a mother on the management of her children and on the treatment on the moment of some of their more pressing illnesses and accidents.* Philadelphia: JB Lippincott & Company, 1868.

10. Harland, M. *Common Sense in the Nursery.* New York: C. Scribner, 1885.

11. Ip, S., Chung, M., Raman, G., et al. *Breastfeeding and Maternal and Infant Health Outcomes in Developed Countries.* Rockville, MD: Agency for Healthcare Research and Quality, 2007.

12. Langstein, R. *Atlas der Hygiene des Sauglings und Kleinkindes.* Berlin: Springer-Verlag, 1918. Cited in Lawrence, R. A., Lawrence, R. M. (eds.), *Breastfeeding: A Guide for the Medical Profession,* 7th ed. St. Louis: Elsevier Mosby, 2011. Horta, B. L., Bahl, R., Martinés, J. C., et al. *Evidence on the Long-Term Effects of Breastfeeding: Systematic Review and Meta-analyses.* Geneva: World Health Organization, 2007.

13. Blunden, S. L., Thompson, K. R., Dawson, D. Behavioural sleep treatments and nighttime crying in infants: challenging the status quo. *Sleep Medicine Reviews* 15, no. 5 (2011): 327–334.

14. Truby King, F. *Feeding and care of baby.* London: Society for the Health of Women and Children, 1913.

15. Spock, B. *Baby and Child Care.* New York: Pocket Books, 1946.

16. Bowlby, J. *Maternal care and mental health: A report prepared on behalf of the World Health Organization as a contribution to the United Nations programme for the welfare of homeless children.* World Health Organization, 1952.

17. Ginott, H. *Between Parent and Child.* New York: Three Rivers Press, 1965.

18. Bell, S. M., Ainsworth, M. D. Infant crying and maternal responsiveness. *Child Development* 43, no. 4 (1972): 1171–1190.

19. Bowlby, J. *A Secure Base: Parent-Child Attachment and Healthy Human Development.* New York: Basic Books, 1990.

20. Mindell, J. A., Kuhn, B., Lewin, D. S., et al. Behavioral treatment of bedtime problems and night wakings in infants and young children. *Sleep* 29, no. 10 (2006): 1263–1276.

21. Mindell, J. A. Empirically supported treatments in pediatric psychology: bedtime refusal and night wakings in young children. *Journal of Pediatric Psychology* 24, no. 6 (1999): 465–481.

22. Cherney, E. New advice on getting babies to sleep. *Wall Street Journal,* Nov. 15, 2005.

23. Douglas, P. S., Hill, P. S. Behavioral sleep interventions in the first six months of life do not improve outcomes for mothers or infants: a systematic review. *Journal of Developmental and Behavioral Pediatrics* 34, no. 7 (2013): 497–507.

24. Mindell, J. A. Empirically supported treatments in pediatric psychology: bedtime refusal and night wakings in young children. *Journal of Pediatric Psychology* 24, no. 6 (1999): 465–481.

25. Hofer, M. A. Psychobiological roots of early attachment. *Current Directions in Psychological Science* 15, no. 2 (2006): 84–88.

26. Bugental, D. B., Martorell, G. A., Barraza, V. The hormonal costs of subtle forms of infant maltreatment. *Hormones and Behavior* 43, no. 1 (2003): 237–244. Grant, K. A., McMahon, C., Austin, M.

P., et al. Maternal prenatal anxiety, postnatal caregiving and infants' cortisol responses to the still-face procedure. *Developmental Psychobiology* 51, no. 8 (2009): 625–637.
27. Ludington-Hoe, S. M., Cong, X., Hashemi, F. Infant crying: nature, physiologic consequences, and select interventions. *Neonatal Network* 21, no. 2 (2002): 29–36.
28. Labott, S. M., Ahleman, S., Wolever, M. E., et al. The physiological and psychological effects of the expression and inhibition of emotion. *Behavioral Medicine* 16, no. 4 (1990): 182–189. Brazy, J. E. Effects of crying on cerebral blood volume and cytochrome aa3. *Journal of Pediatrics* 112, no. 3 (1988): 457–461. Gunnar, M. R., Donzella, B. Social regulation of the cortisol levels in early human development. *Psychoneuroendocrinology* 27, no. 1–2 (2002): 199–220.
29. Rowe, J. W., Shelton, R. L., Helderman, J. H., et al. Influence of the emetic reflex on vasopressin release in man. *Kidney International* 16, no. 6 (1979): 729–735. Beebe, B. Coconstructing mother-infant distress: the microsynchrony of maternal impingement and infant avoidance in the face-to-face encounter. *Psychoanalytic Inquiry* 20, no. 3 (2000): 421–440.
30. Panksepp, J. Neuroscience: feeling the pain of social loss. *Science* 302, no. 5643 (2003): 237–239. Eisenberger, N. I., Lieberman, M. D., Williams, K. D. Does rejection hurt? An fMRI study of social exclusion. *Science* 302, no. 5643 (2003): 290–292. Eisenberger, N. I., Lieberman, M. D. Why rejection hurts: a common neural alarm system for physical and social pain. *Trends in Cognitive Science* 8, no. 7 (2004): 294–300.
31. Miller, P. M., Commons, M. L. Why not crying it out, part 1: the science that tells us that responsiveness is key. *Clinical Lactation* 4, no. 2 (2013): 57–61. Miller, P. M., Commons, M. L. Why not crying it out, part 2: can certain infant care practices cause excessive stress? *Clinical Lactation* 4, no. 2 (2013): 62–65. Belsky, J. Variation in susceptibility to environmental influence: an evolutionary argument. *Psychological Inquiry* 8, no. 3 (1997): 182–186. Pluess, M., Belsky, J. Differential susceptibility to parenting and quality child care. *Developmental Psychology* 46, no. 2 (2010): 379.
32. Ludington-Hoe, S. M., Cong, X., Hashemi, F. Infant crying: nature, physiologic consequences, and select interventions. *Neonatal Network* 21, no. 2 (2002): 29–36.
33. Christensson, K., Cabrera, T., Christensson, E., et al. Separation distress call in the human neonate in the absence of maternal body contact. *Acta Paediatrica* 84, no. 5 (1995): 468–473.
34. Bergman, N. Breastfeeding and perinatal neuroscience. In Genna, C. W. (ed.), *Supporting Sucking Skills in Breastfeeding Infants*. Sudbury, MA: Jones and Bartlett, 2012. Despopoulos, A., Silbernagl, S. *Color Atlas of Physiology*, 3rd ed. Stuttgart: Georg Thieme Verlag, 1986.
35. Blunden, S. L., Thompson, K. R., Dawson, D. Behavioural sleep treatments and night time crying in infants: challenging the status quo. *Sleep Medicine Reviews* 15, no. 5 (2011): 327–334. Chess, S., Thomas, A. *Origins and Evolution of Behaviour Disorders*. New York: Brunner/Mazel, 1984. McKenna, J. Cultural influences on infant and childhood sleep biology and the science that studies it. In Loughlin, G., Carroll, J. L., Marcus, C. L. (eds.). *Toward a More Inclusive Paradigm in Sleep and Breathing in Children: A Developmental Approach*. New York: Marcel Dekker, 2000; 199–230.
36. Waynforth, D. The influence of parent-infant cosleeping, nursing, and child care on cortisol and SIgA immunity in a sample of British children. *Developmental Psychobiology* 49, no. 6 (2007): 640–648. Middlemiss, W., Granger, D. A., Goldberg, W. A., et al. Asynchrony of mother-infant hypothalamic-pituitary-adrenal axis activity following extinction of infant crying responses induced during the transition to sleep. *Early Human Development* 88, no. 4 (2012): 227–232.
37. Swain, J. E., Kim, P., Ho, S. S. Neuroendocrinology of parental response to baby-cry. *Journal of Neuroendocrinology* 23, no. 11 (2011): 1036–1041. Swain, J. E., Konrath, S., Dayton, C. J., et al. Toward a neuroscience of interactive parent-infant dyad empathy. *Behavioral and Brain Sciences* 36, no. 4 (2013): 438–439.
38. Ainsworth, M., Blehar, M. C., Waters, E., et al. *Patterns of Attachment*. Hillsdale, NJ: Erlbaum, 1978. Musser, E. D., Kaiser-Laurent, H., Ablow, J. C. The neural correlates of maternal sensitivity: an fMRI study. *Developmental Cognitive Neuroscience* 2, no. 4 (2012): 428–436. Swain, J. E. Baby stimuli and the parent brain: functional neuroimaging of the neural substrates of parent-infant attachment. *Psychiatry (Edgmont)* 5, no. 8 (2008): 28–36. Laurent, H. K., Stevens, A., Ablow, J. C. Neural correlates of hypothalamic-pituitary-adrenal regulation of mothers with their infants. *Biological Psychiatry* 70, no. 9 (2011): 826–832. Pinyerd, B. J. Infant colic and maternal mental health: nursing research and practice concerns. *Issues in Comprehensive Pediatric Nursing* 15, no. 3 (1992): 155–167. Mindell, J., Kuhn, B., Lewin, D., et al. Behavioral treatment of bedtime problems and night wakings in infants and young children. *Sleep* 29 (2006): 1263–1276.
39. Kim, P., Feldman, R., Mayes, L. C., et al. Breastfeeding, brain activation to own infant cry, and maternal sensitivity. *Journal of Child Psychology and Psychiatry* 52, no. 8 (2011): 907–915.
40. Swain, J. E., Kim, P., Ho, S. S. Neuroendocrinology of parental response to baby-cry. *Journal of Neuroendocrinology* 23, no. 11 (2011): 1036–1041.

41. Wood, R., Gustafson, G. Infant crying and adults' anticipated caregiving responses: acoustic and contextual influences. *Child Development* 72 (2001): 1287–1300.
42. Blunden, S. L., Thompson, K. R., Dawson, D. Behavioural sleep treatments and night time crying in infants: challenging the status quo. *Sleep Medicine Reviews* 15, no. 5 (2011): 327–334. Christensson, K., Cabrera, T. Christensson, E., et al. Separation distress call in the human neonate in the absence of maternal body contact. *Acta Paediatrica* 84, no. 5 (1995): 468–473.
43. Stallings, J., et al. The effects of infant cries and odors on sympathy, cortisol, and autonomic responses in new mothers and nonpostpartum women. *Parenting* 1, no. 1–2 (2001): 71–100.
44. Panksepp, J. Neuroscience. Feeling the pain of social loss. *Science* 302, no. 5643 (2003): 237–239. Eisenberger, N. I., Lieberman, M. D., Williams, K. D. Does rejection hurt? An fMRI study of social exclusion. *Science* 302, no. 5643 (2003): 290–292. Eisenberger, N. I., Lieberman, M. D. Why rejection hurts: a common neural alarm system for physical and social pain. *Trends in Cognitive Science* 8, no. 7 (2004): 294–300.
45. Hardyment, C. *Dream Babies: Child Care from Locke to Spock.* London: J. Cape, 1983.
46. Porter, L. L. The science of attachment: the biological roots of love. *Mothering* 119 (2003): 60–70.
47. Swain, J. E., Kim, P., Ho, S. S. Neuroendocrinology of parental response to baby-cry. *Neuroendocrinology* 23, no. 11 (2011): 1036–1041.
48. Feldman, R., Singer, M., Zagoory, O. Touch attenuates infants' physiological reactivity to stress. *Developmental Science* 1, no. 2 (2010): 271–278.
49. Ball, H. L., Ward-Platt, M. P., Heslop, E., et al. Randomised trial of infant sleep location on the postnatal ward. *Archives of Disease in Childhood* 91, no. 12 (2006): 1005–1010.
50. McKenna, J. J., Volpe, L. E. Sleeping with baby: an Internet-based sampling of parental experiences, choices, perceptions, and interpretations in a Western industrialized context. *Infant and Child Development* 16, no. 4 (2007): 359–385. McKenna, J. J., Mosko, S. S., Richard, C. A. Bedsharing promotes breastfeeding. *Pediatrics* 100, no. 2 (1997): 214–219.
51. Daly, S. E. J., Hartmann, P. E. Infant demand and milk supply. Part 1: infant demand and milk production in lactating women. *Journal of Human Lactation* 11, no. 1 (1995): 21–25.
52. McKenna, J. J., Volpe, L. E. Sleeping with baby: an Internet-based sampling of parental experiences, choices, perceptions, and interpretations in a Western industrialized context. *Infant and Child Development* 16, no. 4 (2007): 359–385. Huang, Y., Hauck, F. R., Signore, C., et al. Influence of bedsharing activity on breastfeeding duration among US mothers. *JAMA Pediatrics* 167, no. 11 (2013): 1038–1044. Ball, H. L. Bed-sharing practices of initially breastfed infants in the first 6 months of life. *Infant and Child Development* 16, no. 4 (2007): 387–401.
53. Ramos, K. D., Youngclarke, D. M. Parenting advice books about child sleep: cosleeping and crying it out. *Sleep* 29, no. 12 (2006): 1616–1623.
54. Blunden, S. L., Thompson, K. R., Dawson, D. Behavioural sleep treatments and night time crying in infants: challenging the status quo. *Sleep Medicine Reviews* 15, no. 5 (2011): 327–334.
55. Mindell, J. A., Kuhn, B., Lewin, D. S., et al. Behavioral treatment of bedtime problems and night wakings in infants and young children. *Sleep* 29, no. 10 (2006): 1263.
56. Benhamou, I. Sleep disorders of early childhood: a review. *Israel Journal of Psychiatry and Related Sciences* 37, no. 3 (2000): 190.
57. Porges, S. W., Furman, S. A. The early development of the autonomic nervous system provides a neural platform for social behavior: a polyvagal perspective. *Infant Child Development* 20, no. 1 (Feb. 2011): 106–118. Emde, R. N. Early emotional development: new modes of thinking for research and intervention. *Pediatrics* 102, no. 5, suppl. E (1998): 1236–1243.
58. Bell, S. M., Ainsworth, M. D. S. Infant crying and maternal responsiveness. *Child Development* 43 (1972): 1171–1190. Cassidy, J. Emotion regulation: influences of attachment relationships. *Monographs of the Society for Research in Child Development* 59 (1994): 228–283.
59. Bowlby, J. *A Secure Base: Parent-Child Attachment and Healthy Human Development.* New York: Basic Books, 1990. Sunderland, M. *The Science of Parenting.* New York: DK Publishing, 2006. Miller, A. *For Your Own Good: Hidden Cruelty in Child-Rearing and the Roots of Violence.* New York: Farrar, Straus, Giroux, 1984.
60. O'Mara, P. *The Way Back Home.* Santa Fe, NM: Mothering Publications, 1991.
61. Mandler, J. Perceptual and conceptual processes in infancy. *Journal of Cognition and Development* 1, no. 1 (2000): 3–36.
62. naturalchild.org/guest/lauren_lindsey_porter.html.
63. Miller, A. *Thou Shalt Not Be Aware: Society's Betrayal of the Child.* New York: Meridian Books, 1984.
64. Lin, H. C., McFatter, R. Empathy and distress: two distinct but related emotions in response to infant crying. *Infant Behavior and Development* 35, no. 4 (2012): 887–897. Swain, J. E., Konrath, S., Dayton, C.

J., et al. Toward a neuroscience of interactive parent-infant dyad empathy. *Behavioral and Brain Sciences* 36, no. 4 (2013): 438–439.

65. Millard, A. V. The place of the clock in pediatric advice: rationales, cultural themes, and impediments to breastfeeding. *Social Science and Medicine* 31, no. 2 (1990): 211–221.

66. Weinraub, M., Bender, R. H., Friedman, S. L., et al. Patterns of developmental change in infants' nighttime sleep awakenings from 6 through 36 months of age. *Developmental Psychology* 48 (2012): 1501–1528.

67. Bell, S. M., Ainsworth, M. D. S. Infant crying and maternal responsiveness. *Child Development* 43 (1972): 1171–1190.

68. Bretherton, I. The origins of attachment theory: John Bowlby and Mary Ainsworth. *Developmental Psychology* 28 (1992): 28, 759–775. van Ijzendoorn, M. H., Hubbard, F. O. Are infant crying and maternal responsiveness during the first year related to infant-mother attachment at 15 months? *Attachment and Human Development* 2, no. 3 (2000): 371–391.

69. Blunden, S. L., Thompson, K. R., Dawson, D. Behavioural sleep treatments and nighttime crying in infants: challenging the status quo. *Sleep Medicine Reviews* 15, no. 5 (2011): 327–334.

70. Middlemiss, W., Granger, D. A., Goldberg, W. A., et al. Asynchrony of mother-infant hypothalamic-pituitary-adrenal axis activity following extinction of infant crying responses induced during the transition to sleep. *Early Human Development* 88, no. 4 (2012): 227–232.

71. Blunden, S. L., Thompson, K. R., Dawson, D. Behavioural sleep treatments and nighttime crying in infants: challenging the status quo. *Sleep Medicine Reviews* 15, no. 5 (2011): 327–334.

72. Karr-Morse, R., Wiley, M. S. *Ghosts from the Nursery.* New York: Atlantic Monthly Press, 1997. Magid, K., McKelvey, C. *High Risk.* New York: Bantam Books, 1988.

73. Karr-Morse, R., Wiley, M. S. *Ghosts from the Nursery.* New York: Atlantic Monthly Press, 1997. Lipari, J. First impressions count with your newborn: early months time for emotional, cognitive development. *Boston Herald,* Aug. 27, 2000. Tarullo, A. R., Gunnar, M. R. Child maltreatment and the developing HPA axis. *Hormones and Behavior* 50, no. 4 (2006): 632–639. Cicchetti, D., Tucker, D. Development and self-regulatory structures of the mind. *Development and Psychopathology* 6 (1994): 533–549.

74. Shatz, C. J. The developing brain. *Scientific American* 267, 3 (1992): 60–67.

75. Edmiston, E., Wang, F., Mazure, C., et al. Corticostriatal-limbic gray matter morphology in adolescents with self-reported exposure to childhood maltreatment. *Archives of Pediatric and Adolescent Medicine* 165, no. 12 (2011): 1069–1077. Frodl, T., Reinhold, E., Koutsouleris, N., et al. Interaction of childhood stress with hippocampus and prefrontal cortex volume reduction in major depression. *Journal of Psychiatric Research* 44, no. 13 (2010): 799–807. Maheu, F. S., Dozier, M., Guyer, A. E., et al. A preliminary study of medial temporal lobe function in youths with a history of caregiver deprivation and emotional neglect. *Cognitive Affective and Behavioral Neuroscience* 10, 1 (2010): 34–49. Mueller, S., Maheu, F., Dozier, M., et al. Early-life stress is associated with impairment in cognitive control in adolescence: an fMRI study. *Neuropsychologia* 48, no. 10 (2010): 3037–3044.

76. Massie, H., Szajnberg, N. The relationship between mothering in infancy, childhood experience and adult mental health: results of the Brody prospective longitudinal study from birth to age 30. *International Journal of Psycho-analysis* 83, pt. 1 (2002): 35–55. Gunnar, M. R., et al. Stress reactivity and attachment security. *Developmental Psychobiology* 29, no. 3 (1996): 191–204.

77. Dekel, S., Farber, B. A. Models of intimacy of securely and avoidantly attached young adults: a narrative approach. *Journal of Nervous and Mental Disease* 200, no. 2 (2012): 156–162.

78. Gordon, M. Roots of empathy: responsive parenting, caring societies. *Keio Journal of Medicine* 52, no. 4 (2003): 236–243.

79. Kim, P., Leckman, J. F., Mayes, L. C., et al. Perceived quality of maternal care in childhood and structure and function of mothers' brain. *Developmental Science* 13, no. 4 (2010): 662–673. Carlson, V., Cicchetti, D., Barnett, D., et al. Disorganized/disoriented attachment relationships in maltreated infants. *Developmental Psychology* 25, no. 4 (1989): 525–531.

80. Maselko, J., Kubzansky, L., Lipsitt, L., et al. Mother's affection at 8 months predicts emotional distress in adulthood. *Journal of Epidemiology and Community Health* 65, no. 7 (2011): 621–625.

81. Middlemiss, W., Granger, D. A., Goldberg, W. A., et al. Asynchrony of mother-infant hypothalamic-pituitary-adrenal axis activity following extinction of infant crying responses induced during the transition to sleep. *Early Human Development* 88, no. 4 (2012): 227–232.

82. Teicher, M., Anderson, S., Polcari, A. Developmental neurobiology of childhood stress and trauma. *Psychiatric Clinics of North America* (2002): 297–426.

83. Morgan, B. E., Horn, A. R., Bergman, N. J. Should neonates sleep alone? *Biological Psychiatry* 70, no. 9 (2011): 817–825. Mosko, S., Richard, C., McKenna, J. Infant arousals during mother-infant bed sharing: implications for infant sleep and sudden infant death syndrome research. *Pediatrics* 100, no. 5 (1997): 841–849.

84. Baumgartner, T., Heinrichs, M., Vonlanthen, A., et al. Oxytocin shapes the neural circuitry of trust and trust adaptation in humans. *Neuron* 58, no. 4 (2008): 639–650.

85. McEwen, B. S. Physiology and neurobiology of stress and adaptation: central role of the brain. *Physiological Reviews* 87, no. 3 (2007): 873–904. McEwen, B. S. Protective and damaging effects of stress mediators: the good and bad sides of the response to stress. *Metabolism* 51, no. 6, suppl. 1 (2002): 2–4.

Chapter 19: Suffocation and SIDS: Reality and Risks

1. Shapiro-Mendoza, C. K., Tomashek, K. M., Anderson, R. N., et al. Recent national trends in sudden, unexpected infant deaths: more evidence supporting a change in classification or reporting. *American Journal of Epidemiology* 163, 8 (2006): 762–769.

2. Adapted from Moon, R. Y., et al. SIDS and other sleep-related infant deaths: expansion of recommendations for a safe infant sleeping environment. *Pediatrics* 1285 (2011): e1341–e1367.

3. Filiano, J. J., Kinney, H. C. A perspective on neuropathologic findings in victims of the sudden infant death syndrome: the triple-risk model. *Neonatology* 65, no. 3–4 (1994): 194–197.

4. Filiano, J. J., Kinney, H. C. A perspective on neuropathologic findings in victims of the sudden infant death syndrome: the triple-risk model. *Neonatology* 65, no. 3–4 (1994): 194–197. S. Karger AG, Basel. DOI:10.1159/000244052.

5. Blair, P. S., Fleming, P. J., Smith, I. J., et al. Babies sleeping with parents: case-control study of factors influencing the risk of the sudden infant death syndrome. CESDI SUDI Research Group. *BMJ* 319, no. 7223 (1999): 1457–1461. Carpenter, R. G., Irgens, L. M., Blair, P. S., et al. Sudden unexplained infant death in 20 regions in Europe: case control study. *Lancet* 363, no. 9404 (2004): 185–191. Tappin, D., Ecob, R., Brooke, H. Bedsharing, roomsharing, and sudden infant death syndrome in Scotland: a case-control study. *Journal of Pediatrics* 147, no. 1 (2005): 32–37. Vennemann, M. M., Bajanowski, T., Brinkmann, B., et al. Sleep environment risk factors for sudden infant death syndrome: the German Sudden Infant Death Syndrome Study. *Pediatrics* 123, no. 4 (2009): 1162–1170. Ruys, J. H., De Jonge, G. A., Brand, R., et al. Bed sharing in the first four months of life: a risk factor for sudden infant death. *Acta Paediatrica* 96, no. 10 (2007): 1399–1403.

6. Liamputtong, P. *Childrearing and Infant Care Issues: A Cross-Cultural Perspective.* Hauppauge, NY: Nova, 2007.

7. Ball, H. L., Moya, E., Fairley, L., et al. Infant care practices related to sudden infant death syndrome in South Asian and white British families in the UK. *Paediatric and Perinatal Epidemiology* 26, no. 1 (2012): 3–12.

8. Moon, R. Y., et al. SIDS and other sleep-related infant deaths: expansion of recommendations for a safe infant sleeping environment. *Pediatrics* 128, no. 5 (2011): 1030–1039.

9. Moon, R. Y., et al. SIDS and other sleep-related infant deaths: expansion of recommendations for a safe infant sleeping environment. *Pediatrics* 128, no. 5 (2011): 1030–1039.

10. Hauck, F. R., Tanabe, K. O. International trends in sudden infant death syndrome: stabilization of rates requires further action. *Pediatrics* 122 (2008): 660–666.

11. Zhang, K., Wang, X. Maternal smoking and increased risk of sudden infant death syndrome: a meta-analysis. *Legal Medicine (Tokyo)* 15, no. 3 (2013): 115–121. Fleming, P., Blair, P. S. Sudden infant death syndrome and parental smoking. *Early Human Development* 83, no. 11 (2007): 721–725.

12. Mitchell, E. A., Taylor, B. J., Ford, R. P. K., et al. Four modifiable and other major risk factors for cot death: the New Zealand study. *Journal of Paediatrics and Child Health* 28, no. 1 (1992): S3–S8.

13. Carpenter, R. G., Irgens, L. M., Blair, P. S., et al. Sudden unexplained infant death in 20 regions in Europe: case control study. *Lancet* 36, no. 9404 (2004): 185–191.

14. Hauck, F. R., Thompson, J. M., Tanabe, K. O., et al. Breastfeeding and reduced risk of sudden infant death syndrome: a meta-analysis. *Pediatrics* 128, no. 1 (2011): 103–110.

15. Mitchell, E. A., Scragg, R., Stewart, A. W., et al. Results from the first year of the New Zealand cot death study. *New Zealand Medical Journal* 104, no. 906 (1991): 71–76. Schoendorf, K. C., Kiely, J. L. Relationship of sudden infant death syndrome to maternal smoking during and after pregnancy. *Pediatrics* 90, no. 6 (1992): 905–908. Fleming, P., Blair, P. S. Sudden infant death syndrome and parental smoking. *Early Human Development* 83, no. 11 (2007): 721–725. Vennemann, M. M., Hense, H. W., Bajanowski, T., et al. Bed sharing and the risk of sudden infant death syndrome: can we resolve the debate? *Journal of Pediatrics* 160, no. 1 (2012): 44–48. Zhang, K., Wang, X. Maternal smoking and increased risk of sudden infant death syndrome: a meta-analysis. *Legal Medicine* (Tokyo) 15, no. 3 (2013): 115–121.

16. Byard, R. W., Beal, S. M. Gastric aspiration and sleeping position in infancy and early childhood. *Journal of Paediatrics and Child Health* 36, no. 4 (2000): 403–405.

17. Mitchell, E. A., Scragg, R., Stewart, A. W., et al. Results from the first year of the New Zealand cot death study. *New Zealand Medical Journal* 104, no. 906 (1991): 71–76. Mitchell, E. A., Taylor, B. J., Ford,

R. P., et al. Four modifiable and other major risk factors for cot death: the New Zealand study. *Journal of Paediatrics and Child Health* 28, suppl. 2 (1992): S3–S8.

18. Li, D. K., Petitti, D. B., Willinger, M., et al. Infant sleeping position and the risk of sudden infant death syndrome in California, 1997–2000. *American Journal of Epidemiology* 157, no. 5 (2003): 446–455.

19. Dwyer, T., Ponsonby, A. L. Sudden infant death syndrome and prone sleeping position. *Annals of Epidemiology* 19, no. 4 (2009): 245–249. Wong, F. Y., Witcombe, N. B., Yiallourou, S. R., et al. Cerebral oxygenation is depressed during sleep in healthy term infants when they sleep prone. *Pediatrics* 127, no. 3 (2011): e558–e565.

20. Siren, P. M., Siren, M. J. Critical diaphragm failure in sudden infant death syndrome. *Upsala Journal of Medical Sciences* 116, no. 2 (2011): 115–123.

21. Bergman, N. J., Jürisoo, L. A. The "kangaroo-method" for treating low birth weight babies in a developing country. *Tropical Doctor* 24, no. 2 (1994): 57–60. Widstrom, A. M., Lilja, G., Aaltomaa-Michalias, P., et al. Newborn behaviour to locate the breast when skin-to-skin: a possible method for enabling early self-regulation. *Acta Paediatrica* 100, no. 1 (2011): 79–85. Bergman, N. J., Linley, L. L., Fawcus, S. R. Randomized controlled trial of skin-to-skin contact from birth versus conventional incubator for physiological stabilization in 1200- to 2199-gram newborns. *Acta Paediatrica* 93, no. 6 (2004): 779–785.

22. Dumas, L., Lepage, M., Bystrova, K., et al. Influence of skin-to-skin contact and rooming-in on early mother-infant interaction: a randomized controlled trial. *Clinical Nursing Research* 22, no. 3 (2013): 310–336. Widstrom, A. M., Lilja, G., Aaltomaa-Michalias, P., et al. Newborn behaviour to locate the breast when skin-to-skin: a possible method for enabling early self-regulation. *Acta Paediatrica* 100, no. 1 (2011): 79–85.

23. Moore, E., Anderson, G., Bergman, N. Early skin-to-skin contact for mothers and their healthy newborn infants. *Cochrane Database of Systematic Reviews* 3 (2007), CD003519.

24. Herlenius, E., Kuhn, P. Sudden unexpected postnatal collapse of newborn infants: a review of cases, definitions, risks, and preventive measures. *Translational Stroke Research* 4, no. 2 (2013): 236–247.

25. Blair, P. S., Fleming, P. J., Smith, I. J., et al. Babies sleeping with parents: case-control study of factors influencing the risk of the sudden infant death syndrome. CESDI SUDI Research Group. *BMJ* 319, no. 7223 (1999): 1457–1461. Carpenter, R. G., Irgens, L. M., Blair, P. S., et al. Sudden unexplained infant death in 20 regions in Europe: case control study. *Lancet* 363, no. 9404 (2004): 185–191.

26. McKenna, J. J., Ball, H. L., Gettler, L. T. Mother-infant cosleeping, breastfeeding and sudden infant death syndrome: what biological anthropology has discovered about normal infant sleep and pediatric sleep medicine. *American Journal of Physical Anthropology* suppl. 45 (2007): 133–161. First Candle, in conjunction with the American Academy of Pediatrics. "Room-Sharing Is Safer than Bed-Sharing." firstcandle.org/new-expectant-parents/bedtime-basics-for-babies/room-sharing-is-safer-than-bed-sharing. Public Health Agency of Canada's Joint Statement on Safe Sleep. "Preventing Sudden Infant Deaths in Canada." 2012. phac-aspc.gc.ca/hp-ps/dca-dea/stages-etapes/childhood-enfance_0-2/sids/pdf /jsss-ecss2011-eng.pdf. Tappin, D., Ecob, R., Brooke, H. Bedsharing, roomsharing, and sudden infant death syndrome in Scotland: a case-control study. *Journal of Pediatrics* 147, no. 1 (2009): 32. Carpenter, R. G., Irgens, L. M., Blair, P. S., et al. Sudden unexplained infant death in 20 regions in Europe: case control study. *Lancet* 36, no. 9404 (2004): 185–191. Blair, P. S., Fleming, P. J., Smith, I. J., et al. Babies sleeping with parents: case-control study of factors influencing the risk of the sudden infant death syndrome. CESDI SUDI Research Group. *BMJ* 319, no. 7223 (1999): 1457–1461.

27. Moon, R. Y., et al. SIDS and other sleep-related infant deaths: expansion of recommendations for a safe infant sleeping environment. *Pediatrics* 128, no. 5 (2011): e1341–e1367.

28. U.S. Department of Health and Human Services. *The Surgeon General's Call to Action to Support Breastfeeding*. Washington, DC: U.S. Department of Health and Human Services, Office of the Surgeon General, 2011. surgeongeneral.gov/topics/breastfeeding/index.html.

29. Ip, S., Chung, M., Raman, G., et al. *Breastfeeding and Maternal and Infant Health Outcomes in Developed Countries*. Rockville, MD: Agency for Healthcare Research and Quality, 2007. McVea, K. L., Turner, P. D., Peppler, D. K. The role of breastfeeding in sudden infant death syndrome. *Journal of Human Lactation* 16 (2000): 13–20.

30. Hauck, F. R., Thompson, J. M., Tanabe, K. O., et al. Breastfeeding and reduced risk of sudden infant death syndrome: a meta-analysis. *Pediatrics* 128, no. 1 (2011): 103–110.

31. Heron, M. Deaths: leading causes for 2008. *National Vital Statistics Reports* 60, no. 6 (2012): 1–94. Mitchell, E. A., Stewart, A. W. Gender and the sudden infant death syndrome. New Zealand Cot Death Study Group. *Acta Paediatrica* 86, no. 8 (1997): 854–856.

32. Blair, P. S., Platt, M. W., Smith, I. J., et al. Sudden infant death syndrome and the time of death: factors associated with night-time and day-time deaths. *International Journal of Epidemiology* 35, no. 6 (2006): 1563–1569.

33. Blair, P. S., Platt, M. W., Smith, I. J., et al. Sudden infant death syndrome and the time of death: factors associated with night-time and daytime deaths. *International Journal of Epidemiology* 35, no. 6 (2006): 1563–1569.

34. National Center for Health Statistics. Mortality Data from the National Vital Statistics System. Available at cdc.gov/nchs/nvss.htm.

35. Phillips, D. P., Brewer, K. M., Wadensweiler, P. Alcohol as a risk factor for sudden infant death syndrome (SIDS). *Addiction* 106, no. 3 (2011): 516–525.

36. Blair, P. S., Platt, M. W., Smith, I. J., et al. Sudden infant death syndrome and the time of death: factors associated with night-time and day-time deaths. *International Journal of Epidemiology* 35, no. 6 (2006): 1563–1569.

37. Randall, B. B., Paterson, D. S., Haas, E. A., et al. Potential asphyxia and brainstem abnormalities in sudden and unexpected death in infants. *Pediatrics* 132, no. 6 (2013): e1616–e1625. Paterson, D. S., Trachtenberg, F. L., Thompson, E. G., et al. Multiple serotonergic brainstem abnormalities in sudden infant death syndrome. *Journal of the American Medical Association* 296, no. 17 (2006): 2124–2132. Kato, I., Franco, P., Groswasser, J., et al. Incomplete arousal processes in infants who were victims of sudden death. *American Journal of Respiratory and Critical Care Medicine* 168, no. 11 (2003): 1298–1303. Machaalani, R., Say, M., Waters, K. A. Serotoninergic receptor 1A in the sudden infant death syndrome brainstem medulla and associations with clinical risk factors. *Acta Neuropathologica* 117, no. 3 (2009): 257–265. Ozawa, Y., Takashima, S. Developmental neurotransmitter pathology in the brainstem of sudden infant death syndrome: a review and sleep position. *Forensic Science International* 130 (2002): 53–59.

38. Horne, R. S., Ferens, D., Watts, A. M., et al. Effects of maternal tobacco smoking, sleeping position, and sleep state on arousal in healthy term infants. *Archives of Disease in Childhood Fetal and Neonatal Edition* 87, no. 2 (2002): 100–105.

39. Strandberg-Larsen, K., Grønboek, M., Andersen, A. M. N., et al. Alcohol drinking pattern during pregnancy and risk of infant mortality. *Epidemiology* 20, no. 6 (2009): 884–891. Iyasu, S., Randall, L. L., Welty, T. K., et al. Risk factors for sudden infant death syndrome among northern Plains Indians. *JAMA* 288, no. 21 (2002): 2717–2723.

40. Malloy, M. H., Hoffman, H. J. Prematurity, sudden infant death syndrome, and age of death. *Pediatrics* 96, no. 3, pt. 1 (1995): 464–471.

41. Ip, S., Chung, M., Raman, G., et al. *Breastfeeding and Maternal and Infant Health Outcomes in Developed Countries.* Rockville, MD: Agency for Healthcare Research and Quality, 2007.

42. Malloy, M. H., Hoffman, H. J. Prematurity, sudden infant death syndrome, and age of death. *Pediatrics* 96, no. 3, pt. 1 (1995): 464–471.

43. Parmelee, A. H. Jr., Wenner, W. H., Schulz, H. R. Infant sleep patterns: from birth to 16 weeks of age. *Journal of Pediatrics* 65 (1964): 576–582. Rivkees, S. A. Developing circadian rhythmicity in infants. *Pediatrics* 112, no. 2 (2003): 373–381. Coons, S., Guilleminault, C. Development of sleep-wake patterns and non-rapid eye movement sleep stages during the first six months of life in normal infants. *Pediatrics* 69, no. 6 (1982): 793–798. Peirano, P., Algarín, C., Uauy, R. Sleep-wake states and their regulatory mechanisms throughout early human development. *Journal of Pediatrics* 143, no. 4 (2003): 70–79.

44. Ford, R. P. K., Hassall, I. B., Mitchell, E. A., et al. Life events, social support and the risk of sudden infant death syndrome. *Journal of Child Psychology and Psychiatry* 37 (1996): 835–840.

45. Ponsonby, A. L., Dwyer, T., Gibbons, L. E., et al. Thermal environment and sudden infant death syndrome: case-control study. *BMJ* 304, no. 6822 (1992): 277. Guntheroth, W. G., Spiers, P. S. Thermal stress in sudden infant death: is there an ambiguity with the rebreathing hypothesis? *Pediatrics* 107, no. 4 (2001): 693–698.

46. Moon, R. Y., Sprague, B. M., Patel, K. M. Stable prevalence but changing risk factors for sudden infant death syndrome in child care settings in 2001. *Pediatrics* 116, no. 4 (2005): 972–977.

47. Fleming, P. J., Blair, P. S., Platt, M. W., et al. The UK accelerated immunisation programme and sudden unexpected death in infancy: case-control study. *BMJ* 322, no. 7290 (2001): 822. Jonville-Bera, A. P., Autret-Leca, E., Barbeillon, F., et al. Sudden unexpected death in infants under 3 months of age and vaccination status—a case-control study. *British Journal of Clinical Pharmacology* 51, no. 3 (2001): 271–276. CDC. "Sudden infant death syndrome (SIDS) and vaccines." 2010. cdc.gov/vaccinesafety/Concerns/sids_faq.html.

48. Haglund, B., Cnattingius, S. Cigarette smoking as a risk factor for sudden infant death syndrome: a population-based study. *American Journal of Public Health* 80, no. 1 (1990): 29–32.

49. Paris, C. A., Remler, R., Daling, J. R. Risk factors for sudden infant death syndrome: changes associated with sleep position recommendations. *Journal of Pediatrics* 139, no. 6 (2001): 771–777.

50. Strandberg-Larsen, K., Grønboek, M., Andersen, A. M. N., et al. Alcohol drinking pattern during pregnancy and risk of infant mortality. *Epidemiology* 20, no. 6 (2009): 884–891. Iyasu, S., Randall, L. L., Welty, T. K., et al. Risk factors for sudden infant death syndrome among northern Plains Indians. *Journal*

of the American Medical Association 288, no. 21 (2002): 2717–2723. Fifer, W. P., Fingers, S. T., Youngman, M., et al. Effects of alcohol and smoking during pregnancy on infant autonomic control. *Developmental Psychobiology* 51, no. 3 (2009): 234–242.
51. Weiss, P. P., Kerbl, R. The relatively short duration that a child retains a pacifier in the mouth during sleep: implications for sudden infant death syndrome. *European Journal of Pediatrics* 160, no. 1 (2001): 60.
52. Van Sleuwen, B. E., Engelberts, A. C., Boere-Boonekamp, M. M., et al. Swaddling: a systematic review. *Pediatrics* 120, no. 4 (2007): e1097–e1106.
53. Chen, A., Feresu, S. A., Fernandez, C., et al. Maternal obesity and the risk of infant death in the United States. *Epidemiology* 20, no. 1 (2009): 74.
54. Carroll-Pankhurst, C., Mortimer, E. A. Sudden infant death syndrome, bedsharing, parental weight, and age at death. *Pediatrics* 107, no. 3 (2001): 530–536.
55. Wisborg, K., Kesmodel, U., Henriksen, T. B., et al. A prospective study of smoking during pregnancy and SIDS. *Archives of Disease in Childhood* 83, no. 3 (2000): 203–206.
56. Richardson, B. A. Sudden infant death syndrome: a possible primary cause. *Journal: Forensic Science Society* 34, no. 3 (1994): 199–204. Sprott, T. J. Cot death: cause and prevention—experiences in New Zealand 1995–2004. *Journal of Nutritional and Environmental Medicine* 14, no. 3 (2004): 221–232. Department of Health. Expert group to investigate cot death theories. London: HMSO, 1998. Available at sids-network.org/experts/expert_group_to_investigate_cot_.htm. Blair, P., Fleming, P., Bensley, D., et al. Plastic mattresses and sudden infant death syndrome. *Lancet* 345, no. 8951 (1995): 720. Wilson, C. A., Taylor, B. J., Laing, R. M., et al. Clothing and bedding and its relevance to sudden infant death syndrome: further results from the New Zealand Cot Death Study. *Journal of Paediatrics and Child Health* 30, no. 6 (1994): 506–512. Patriarca, M., Lyon, T. D., Delves, H. T., et al. Determination of low concentrations of potentially toxic elements in human liver from newborns and infants. *Analyst* 124, no. 9 (1999): 1337–1343.
57. Kleemann, W. J., Weller, J. P., Wolf, M., et al. Heavy metals, chlorinated pesticides and polychlorinated biphenyls in sudden infant death syndrome (SIDS). *International Journal of Legal Medicine* 104, no. 2 (1991): 71–75. Erickson, M. M., Poklis, A., Gantner, G. E., et al. Tissue mineral levels in victims of sudden infant death syndrome. I. Toxic metals: lead and cadmium. *Pediatric Research* 17, no. 10 (1983): 779–784.
58. CDC. Infant death scene investigation. 2012. cdc.gov/sids/SceneInvestigation.htm.
59. Santos, I. S., Mota, D. M., Matijasevich, A., et al. Bed-sharing at 3 months and breast-feeding at 1 year in southern Brazil. *Journal of Pediatrics* 155, no. 4 (2009): 505–509.

Chapter 20: Bedsharing Controversies and Common Sense

1. Fleming, P. J., Blair, P. S., Pollard, K., et al. Pacifier use and sudden infant death syndrome: results from the CESDI/SUDI case control study. *Archives of Disease in Childhood* 81, no. 2 (1999): 112–116.
2. Dangers of Cosleeping. 2010. [News broadcast.] Fox News, Milwaukee, Wisconsin.
3. Dangers of Cosleeping. 2010. [News broadcast.] Fox News, Milwaukee, Wisconsin.
4. McKenna, J. J., Mosko, S. S., Richard, C. A. Bedsharing promotes breastfeeding. *Pediatrics* 100, no. 2 (1997): 214–219. Santos, I. S., Mota, D. M., Matijasevich, A., et al. Bed-sharing at 3 months and breast-feeding at 1 year in southern Brazil. *Journal of Pediatrics* 155, no. 4 (2009): 505–509.
5. U.S. Department of Health and Human Services. *The Surgeon General's Call to Action to Support Breastfeeding*. Stuebe, A. The risks of not breastfeeding for mothers and infants. *Reviews in Obstetrics and Gynecology* 2, no. 4 (2009): 222–231.
6. Moon, R. Y., et al. SIDS and other sleep-related infant deaths: expansion of recommendations for a safe infant sleeping environment. *Pediatrics* 128, no. 5 (2011): e1341–e1367.
7. Galland, B. C., et al. Normal sleep patterns in infants and children: a systematic review of observational studies. *Sleep Medicine Reviews* 16, no. 3 (2012): 213–222.
8. Galbally, M., Lewis, A. J., McEgan, K., et al. Breastfeeding and infant sleep patterns: an Australian population study. *Journal of Paediatrics and Child Health* 49, no. 2 (2013): e147–e152.
9. Krouse, A., Craig, J., Watson, U., et al. Bed-sharing influences, attitudes, and practices: implications for promoting safe infant sleep. *Journal of Child Health Care* 16, no. 3 (2012): 274–283.
10. Shapiro-Mendoza, C. *Sudden, Unexplained Infant Death Investigation Curriculum Guide,* Chapter 1. 2007. DHHS, Mat Inf Health Branch, CDC. cdc.gov/sids/PDF/SUIDManual/Chapter1_tag508.pdf.
11. Carroll-Pankhurst, C., Mortimer, E. A. Sudden infant death syndrome, bedsharing, parental weight, and age at death. *Pediatrics* 107, no. 3 (2001): 530–536.
12. Ostfeld, B. M., Perl, H., Esposito, L., et al. Sleep environment, positional, lifestyle, and demographic characteristics associated with bed sharing in sudden infant death syndrome cases: a population-based study. *Pediatrics* 118, no. 5 (2006): 2051–2059.

13. Kendall-Tackett, K., Cong, Z., Hale, T. W. Mother-infant sleep locations and nighttime feeding behavior. *Clinical Lactation* 1, no. 1 (2010): 27–30.
14. Moon, R. Y., et al. SIDS and other sleep-related infant deaths: expansion of recommendations for a safe infant sleeping environment. *Pediatrics* 128, no. 5 (2011): e1341–e1367.
15. Hauck, F. R., Kemp, J. S., Kattwinkel, J., et al. Bedsharing promotes breastfeeding and AAP Task Force on Infant Positioning and SIDS. *Pediatrics* 102, no. 3 (1998): 662–664.
16. Blabey, M. H., Gessner, B. D. Infant bed-sharing practices and associated risk factors among births and infant deaths in Alaska. *Public Health Reports* 124, no. 4 (2009): 527–534.
17. CDC. Infant death scene investigation. 2012. cdc.gov/sids/SceneInvestigation.htm.
18. Blair, P. S., Sidebotham, P., Evason-Coombe, C., et al. Hazardous cosleeping environments and risk factors amenable to change: case-control study of SIDS in southwest England. *BMJ* 339 (2009): b3666. Strandberg-Larsen, K., Grønbœk, M., Andersen, A. M. N., et al. Alcohol drinking pattern during pregnancy and risk of infant mortality. *Epidemiology* 20, no. 6 (2009): 884.
19. Tappin, D., Ecob, R., Brooke, H. Bedsharing, roomsharing, and sudden infant death syndrome in Scotland: a case-control study. *Journal of Pediatrics* 147, no. 1 (2009): 32.
20. Pers. comm., L. J. Smith, Montgomery County Health Commissioner, 2003 [toxicology screens of babies who died of SIDS in Dayton, OH].
21. Ball, H. L., Moya, E., Fairley, L., et al. Infant care practices related to sudden infant death syndrome in South Asian and white British families in the UK. *Paediatrica and Perinatal Epidemiology* 26, no. 1 (2012): 3–12.
22. Tappin, D., Ecob, R., Brooke, H. Bedsharing, roomsharing, and sudden infant death syndrome in Scotland: a case-control study. *Journal of Pediatrics* 147, no. 1 (2005): 32.
23. Kjaergard, L. L., Als-Nielsen, B. Association between competing interests and authors' conclusions: epidemiological study of randomised clinical trials published in the *BMJ*. *BMJ* 325, no. 7358 (2002): 249.
24. Caudill, T. S., Johnson, M. S., Rich, E. C., et al. Physicians, pharmaceutical sales representatives, and the cost of prescribing. *Archives of Family Medicine* 5, no. 4 (1996): 201–206.
25. Katz, D., Caplan, A. L., Merz, J. F. All gifts large and small: toward an understanding of the ethics of pharmaceutical industry gift-giving. *American Journal of Bioethics* 3, no. 3 (2003): 39–46.
26. Choudhry, N. K., Stelfox, H. T., Detsky, A. S. Relationships between authors of clinical practice guidelines and the pharmaceutical industry. *Journal of the American Medical Association* 287, no. 5 (2002): 612–617. Kjaergard, L. L., Als-Nielsen, B. Association between competing interests and authors' conclusions: epidemiological study of randomised clinical trials published in the *BMJ*. *BMJ* 325, no. 7358 (2002): 249.
27. Sullivan, F. M., Barlow, S. M. Review of risk factors for sudden infant death syndrome. *Paediatric and Perinatal Epidemiology* 15 (2001): 144–200.
28. Tong, E. K., England, L., Glantz, S. A. Changing conclusions on secondhand smoke in a sudden infant death syndrome review funded by the tobacco industry. *Pediatrics* 115, no. 3 (2005): e356–e366. Sullivan, F. M., Barlow, S. M. Review of risk factors for sudden infant death syndrome. *Paediatric and Perinatal Epidemiology* 15 (2001): 144–200.
29. First Candle. Safe sleep saves lives! firstcandle.org/cms/wp-content/uploads/2009/12/SafeSleepSavesLives.pdf.
30. Zhang, K., Wang, X. Maternal smoking and increased risk of sudden infant death syndrome: a meta-analysis. *Legal Medicine (Tokyo)* 15, no. 3 (2013): 115–121. Fleming, P., Blair, P. S. Sudden infant death syndrome and parental smoking. *Early Human Development* 83, no. 11 (2007): 721–725.
31. First Candle. Safe sleep saves lives! firstcandle.org/cms/wp-content/uploads/2009/12/SafeSleepSavesLives.pdf.
32. American Academy of Pediatrics, SIDS and other sleep-related infant deaths: expansion of recommendations for a safe infant sleeping environment. 2011. pediatrics.aappublications.org/content/early/2011/10/12/peds.2011-2284.
33. Moon, R. Y., et al. SIDS and other sleep-related infant deaths: expansion of recommendations for a safe infant sleeping environment. *Pediatrics* 128, no. 5 (2011): e1341–e1367.
34. Vennemann, M. M., Bajanowski, T., Brinkmann, B., et al. Does breastfeeding reduce the risk of sudden infant death syndrome? *Pediatrics* 123, no. 3 (2009), e406–e410. Hauck, F. R., Thompson, J. M. D., Tanabe, K. O., et al. Breastfeeding and reduced risk of sudden infant death syndrome: a meta-analysis. *Pediatrics* 128, no. 1 (2011): 103–110.
35. Moon, R. Y., et al. SIDS and other sleep-related infant deaths: expansion of recommendations for a safe infant sleeping environment. *Pediatrics* 128, no. 5 (2011): e1341–e1367.
36. Moon, R. Y., Tanabe, K. O., Yang, D. C., et al. Pacifier use and SIDS: evidence for a consistently reduced risk. *Maternal and Child Health Journal* 16, no. 3 (2012): 609–614. Hauck, F. R., Omojokun, O. O., Siadaty, M. S. Do pacifiers reduce the risk of sudden infant death syndrome? A meta-analysis.

Pediatrics 116, no. 5 (2005): e716–e723. Fleming, P. J., Blair, P. S., Pollard, K., et al. Pacifier use and sudden infant death syndrome: results from the CESDI/SUDI case control study. *Archives of Disease in Childhood* 81, no. 2 (1999): 112–116.

37. Franco, P., Chabanski, S., Scaillet, S., et al. Pacifier use modifies infant's cardiac autonomic controls during sleep. *Early Human Development* 77, no. 1 (2004): 99–108.

38. Weiss, P. P., Kerbl, R. The relatively short duration that a child retains a pacifier in the mouth during sleep: implications for sudden infant death syndrome. *European Journal of Pediatrics* 160, no. 1 (2001): 60.

39. Pollard, K., Fleming, P., Young, J., et al. Night-time non-nutritive sucking in infants aged 1 to 5 months: relationship with infant state, breastfeeding, and bed-sharing versus room-sharing. *Early Human Development* 56, no. 2 (1999): 185–204.

40. Franco, P., Chabanski, S., Scaillet, S., et al. Pacifier use modifies infant's cardiac autonomic controls during sleep. *Early Human Development* 77, no. 1 (2004): 99–108. Moon, R. Y., Fu, L. Sudden infant death syndrome: an update. *Pediatrics in Review* 33, no. 7 (2012): 314–320.

41. Mosko, S., Richard, C., McKenna, J. Infant arousals during mother-infant bed sharing: implications for infant sleep and sudden infant death syndrome research. *Pediatrics* 100, no. 5 (1997): 841–849. Mosko, S., McKenna, J., Dickel, M., et al. Parent-infant cosleeping: the appropriate context for the study of infant sleep and implications for sudden infant death syndrome (SIDS) research. *Journal of Behavioral Medicine* 16, no. 6 (1993): 589–610.

42. Carpenter, R., McGarvey, C., Mitchell, E. A., et al. Bed sharing when parents do not smoke: is there a risk of SIDS? An individual level analysis of five major case-control studies. *BMJ Open* 3, no. 5 (2013).

43. Tappin, D., Ecob, R., Brooke, H. Bedsharing, roomsharing, and sudden infant death syndrome in Scotland: a case-control study. *Journal of Pediatrics* 147, no. 1 (2005): 32.

44. Greenhalgh, T. *How to Read a Paper: The Basics of Evidence-Based Medicine,* 4th ed. Oxford: Wiley-Blackwell.

45. Newman, T. B. The power of stories over statistics. *BMJ* 327, no. 7429 (2003): 1424–1427.

46. Blalock, G., Kadiyali, V., Simon, D. H. Driving fatalities after 9/11: a hidden cost of terrorism. *Applied Economics* 41, no. 14 (2009): 1717–1729.

47. Newman, T. B. The power of stories over statistics. *BMJ* 327, no. 7429 (2003): 1424.

48. Fetherston, C. M., Leach, J. S. Analysis of the ethical issues in the breastfeeding and bedsharing debate. *Breastfeeding Review* 20, no. 3 (2012): 7–17.

49. Ball, H. L. Breastfeeding, bed-sharing, and infant sleep. *Birth* 30, no. 3 (2003): 181–188. Ball, H. L. Bed-sharing practices of initially breastfed infants in the first 6 months of life. *Infant and Child Development* 16, no. 4 (2007): 387–401. Ball, H. L. Reasons to bed-share: why parents sleep with their infants. *Journal of Reproductive and Infant Psychology* 20, no. 4 (2002): 207–221. Kendall-Tackett, K., Cong, Z., Hale, T. W. Mother-infant sleep locations and nighttime feeding behavior. *Clinical Lactation* 1, no. 1 (2010): 27–30. Lahr, M. B., Rosenberg, K. D. Maternal-infant bedsharing: risk factors for bedsharing in a population-based survey of new mothers and implications for SIDS risk reduction. *Maternal and Child Health Journal* 11, no. 3 (2007): 277–286. Blair, P. S., Ball, H. L. The prevalence and characteristics associated with parent-infant bed-sharing in England. *Archives of Disease in Childhood* 89, no. 12 (2004): 1106–1110.

50. Kendall-Tackett, K., Cong, Z., Hale, T. W. Mother-infant sleep locations and nighttime feeding behavior. *Clinical Lactation* 1, no. 1 (2010): 27–30. Chianese, J., Ploof, D., Trovato, C., et al. Inner-city caregivers' perspectives on bed sharing with their infants. *Academic Pediatrics* 9, no. 1 (2009): 26–32.

51. Colson, E. R., Willinger, M., Rybin, D., et al. Trends and factors associated with infant bed sharing, 1993–2010: The National Infant Sleep Position Study. *JAMA Pediatrics* 167, no. 11 (2013): 1032–1037.

52. Ball, H. L. Breastfeeding, bed-sharing, and infant sleep. *Birth* 30, no. 3 (2003): 181–188.

53. McKenna, J. J., Mosko, S. S., Richard, C. A. Bedsharing promotes breastfeeding. *Pediatrics* 100, no. 2 (1997): 214–219.

54. Ostfeld, B. M., Perl, H., Esposito, L., et al. Sleep environment, positional, lifestyle, and demographic characteristics associated with bed sharing in sudden infant death syndrome cases: a population-based study. *Pediatrics* 118, no. 5 (2006): 2051–2059.

55. Eunice Kennedy Shriver National Institute of Child Health and Human Development. What does a safe sleep environment look like? 2013. nichd.nih.gov/publications/pubs/Documents/Safe_Sleep_Environment_English_2013.pdf.

56. Ostfeld, B. M., Esposito, L., Perl, H., et al. Concurrent risks in sudden infant death syndrome. *Pediatrics* 125, no. 3 (2010): 447–453.

57. Academy of Breastfeeding Medicine. ABM clinical protocol #6: guideline on co-sleeping and breastfeeding. Revision, March 2008. *Breastfeeding Medicine* 3, no. 1 (2008): 38–43.

58. CDC. Fast stats: all injuries. 2013. cdc.gov/nchs/fastats/injury.htm.

59. Friedman, L. S., Hedeker, D., Richter, E. D. Long-term effects of repealing the national maximum speed limit in the United States. *American Journal of Public Health* 99, no. 9 (2009): 1626–1631.

60. Academy of Breastfeeding Medicine. ABM clinical protocol #6: guideline on co-sleeping and breastfeeding. Revision, March 2008. *Breastfeeding Medicine* 3, no. 1 (2008): 38–43.
61. Okami, P., Weisner, T., Olmstead, R. Outcome correlates of parent-child bedsharing: an eighteen-year longitudinal study. *Journal of Developmental and Behavioral Pediatrics* 23, no. 4 (2002): 244–253.

Chapter 21: Defusing Criticism

1. Mustanski, B., Chivers, M., Bailey, M. A critical review of recent biological research on human sexual orientation. *Annual Review of Sex Research* 13 (2002): 89–141. Frankowski, B. L. Sexual orientation and adolescents. *Pediatrics* 113, no. 6 (2004): 1827–1832.
2. Massie, H., Szajnberg, N. The relationship between mothering in infancy, childhood experience and adult mental health: results of the Brody prospective longitudinal study from birth to age 30. *International Journal of Psychoanalysis* 83, pt. 1 (2002): 35–55. Gunnar, M. R., et al. Stress reactivity and attachment security. *Developmental Psychobiology* 29, no. 3 (1996): 191–204. Heron, P. Nonreactive co-sleeping and child behavior: getting a good night's sleep all night every night. Master's thesis, University of Bristol, 1994. McKenna, J. J. Cultural influences on infant sleep. *Sleep and Breathing in Children: A Developmental Approach*. New York: Marcel Dekker, 2000; 199–230. Keller, M. A., Goldberg, W. A. Co-sleeping: help or hindrance for young children's independence? *Infant and Child Development* 13, no. 5 (2004): 369–388.

Chapter 22: Your Frequently Asked Questions (FAQs)

1. Iida, H., et al. Association between infant breastfeeding and early childhood caries in the United States. *Pediatrics* 120, no. 4 (2007): e944–e952.
2. Palmer, B. The influence of breastfeeding on the development of the oral cavity: a commentary. *Journal of Human Lactation* 14, no. 2 (1998): 93–98.
3. Erickson, P. R., Mazhari, E. Investigation of the role of human breast milk in caries development. *Pediatric Dentistry* 21, no. 2 (1999): 86–90.
4. Aimutis, W. R. Bioactive properties of milk proteins with particular focus on anticariogenesis. *Journal of Nutrition* 134, no. 4 (2004): 989S–995S.
5. Lawrence, R. A., Lawrence, R. M. (eds.). *Breastfeeding: A Guide for the Medical Profession*, 7th ed. St. Louis: Mosby/Elsevier, 2011.
6. Kotlow, L. A. The influence of the maxillary frenum on the development and pattern of dental caries on anterior teeth in breastfeeding infants: prevention, diagnosis, and treatment. *Journal of Human Lactation* 26, no. 3 (2010): 304–308.
7. Dye, B. A., Shenkin, J. D., Ogden, C. L., et al. The relationship between healthful eating practices and dental caries in children aged 2–5 years in the United States, 1988–1994. *Journal of the American Dental Association* 135, no. 1 (2004): 55–66.
8. Mohebbi, S. Z., et al. Feeding habits as determinants of early childhood caries in a population where prolonged breastfeeding is the norm. *Community Dentistry and Oral Epidemiology* 36, no. 4 (2008): 363–369. Tanaka, K., Miyake, Y., Sasaki, S. The effect of maternal smoking during pregnancy and postnatal household smoking on dental caries in young children. *Journal of Pediatrics* 155, no. 3 (2009): 410–415. Ramos-Gomez, F. J., Weintraub, J. A., Gansky, S. A., et al. Bacterial, behavioral and environmental factors associated with early childhood caries. *Journal of Clinical Pediatric Dentistry* 26, no. 2 (2003): 165–173. Aligne, C. A., Moss, M. E., Auinger, P., et al. Association of pediatric dental caries with passive smoking. *Journal of the American Medical Association* 289, no. 10 (2003): 1258–1264.
9. Labbok, M., Clark, D., Goldman, A. Breastfeeding: maintaining an irreplaceable immunological resource. *Nature Reviews. Immunology* 4 (2004): 565–572.
10. Gray, L., Miller, L. W., Philipp, B. L., et al. Breastfeeding is analgesic in healthy newborns. *Pediatrics* 109, no. 4 (2002): 590–593.
11. World Health Organization. The treatment of diarrhoea: a manual for physicians and other senior health workers. Bulletin WHO/CDD/SER/80.2.
12. Czinn, S. J., Blanchard, S. Gastroesophageal reflux disease in neonates and infants: when and how to treat. *Paediatric Drugs* 15, no. 1 (2013): 19–27.

Chapter 23: Getting Help, Giving Help

1. Taylor, S. E., Klein, L. C., Lewis, B. P., et al. Biobehavioral responses to stress in females: tend-and-befriend, not fight-or-flight. *Psychol Rev* 107, no. 3 (2000): 411–429.

picture credits

ii iStockphoto
ix Studio Moon
xv Fotolia
xix Fotolia
xxiv Shutterstock
3 Ava Nansteel
4 Diane Wiessinger
5 Laura Maxon
13 Diana West
18 Diana West
19 (top) Maureen Clark
19 (bottom) Maureen Clark
28 Shutterstock
31 Shutterstock
41 Foltolia
45 Kenneth Nansteel
47 Josh Dobbelstein
49 (top) Josh Dobbelstein, adapted from Susan Ludington
49 (bottom) Josh Dobbelstein, adapted from Susan Ludington
58 Shutterstock
61 Veer
63 Diane Wiessinger
66 Therese Tee
68 (top) Melissa Kent
68 (bottom) Veer
73 Veer
81 Fotolia
87 Sara Dale-Bley
90 Diane Wiessinger
92 Fotolia
93 Diane Wiessinger
102 iStockphoto
110 iStockphoto
111 iStockphoto
114 Illustrations: Josh Dobbelstein
115 Illustrations: Josh Dobbelstein
116 Illustration: Josh Dobbelstein
120 Veer
131 Getty Images
136 Tricia Phillips
141 Sarah Bailey
152 Shutterstock
154 Diana West
178 iStockphoto

194 Fotolia
206 Maureen Clark
209 Sara Dodson
212 iStockphoto
215 Maggie Muir
219 Helen Ball
222 Therese Tee
225 Fotolia
238 Shutterstock
240 Laura Maxon
251 Diane Wiessinger
259 Shutterstock
270 Josh Dobbelstein, adapted from Sarah Coulter Danner
271 Josh Dobbelstein, adapted from Sarah Coulter Danner
272 Veer
276 Shutterstock
279 iStockphoto
285 Fotolia
291 Shutterstock
296 Marija Taraba
308 Getty Images
311 Shutterstock
315 Truby King, F. *Feeding and Care of Baby.* London: Society for the Health of Women and Children, 1913.
338 Reproduced with permission from *Pediatrics* vol. 28(5), pages e1341–e1367. Copyright © 2011 by the AAP
339 Josh Dobbelstein
341 Adapted from Filiano, J. J., Kinney, H. C. A perspective on neuropathologic findings in victims of the sudden infant death syndrome: the triple-risk model. *Neonatology* 65, no. 3–4 (1994):194–197. S. Kargar AG, Basel. DOI: 10.1159/000244052.
343 Reproduced with permission from *Pediatrics* vol. 28(5), pages e1341–e1367. Copyright © 2011 by the AAP
363 Josh Dobbelstein, adapted from The Centers for Disease Control and Prevention
357 Veer
380 iStockphoto
383 Veer
397 Getty Images
416 Getty Images
417 iStockphoto
424 Veer
425 Shutterstock
429 Josh Dobbelstein
443 Veer
444 Veer

index

about the type

This book was set in Fairfield, the first typeface from the hand of the distinguished American artist and engraver Rudolph Ruzicka (1883–1978). Ruzicka was born in Bohemia (in the present-day Czech Republic) and went to America in 1894. He set up his own shop, devoted to wood engraving and printing, in New York in 1913 after a varied career working as a wood engraver, in photoengraving and banknote printing plants, and as an art director and freelance artist. He designed and illustrated many books, and was the creator of a considerable list of individual prints—wood engravings, line engravings on copper, and aquatints.

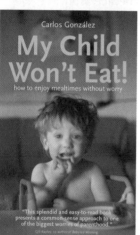

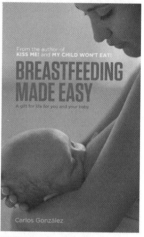

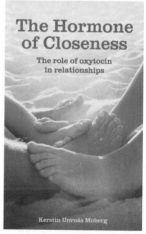